Cultures of Correspondence
in Early Modern Britain

CULTURES
of CORRESPONDENCE
in EARLY
MODERN BRITAIN

Edited by

James Daybell and Andrew Gordon

PENN

UNIVERSITY OF PENNSYLVANIA PRESS

PHILADELPHIA

Published by
University of Pennsylvania Press
Philadelphia, Pennsylvania 19104-4112
www.upenn.edu/pennpress

Printed in the United States of America on acid-free paper
10 9 8 7 6 5 4 3 2 1

A Cataloging-in-Publication record is available from the
Library of Congress
ISBN 978-0-8122-4825-8

Addressed to AGS (Erasmus in NYC) with love

CONTENTS

LIST OF ABBREVIATIONS
AND CONVENTIONS

Original spelling and punctuation have been retained in quotations from manuscripts. Insertions are indicated by upward arrows ^^, and deletions by a strikethrough line. Modern translations of obscure spellings and all expansions have been provided in square brackets. Dates are modernized with the year taken to begin on 1 January, but where the contemporary usage differs in a textual source this is noted. Roman numerals are retained in quotations, but otherwise Arabic numeration is used (bibliographical conventions excepted); monetary sums are given as £ (pounds), s. (shillings), and d. (pence). Place of publication is London unless otherwise stated.

Beinecke	Beinecke Rare Book and Manuscript Library, Yale University
BL	British Library
BL, Add. MS	British Library, Additional Manuscript
BL, Cott. MS	British Library, Cottonian Manuscript
BL, Eg. MS	British Library, Egerton Manuscript
BL, Harl. MS	British Library, Harleian Manuscript
BL, Lansd. MS	British Library, Lansdowne Manuscript
BLJ	*British Library Journal*
Bodl.	Bodleian Library, Oxford
Bodl., Rawl. MS	Bodleian Library, Oxford, Rawlinson Manuscript
CP	Cecil Papers, Hatfield House, Hertfordshire
CUP	Cambridge University Press
EHR	*English Historical Review*
ELH	*English Literary History*
ELR	*English Literary Renaissance*
EMS	*English Manuscript Studies*
fol.	folio

Folger	Folger Shakespeare Library, Washington, D.C.
HJ	*Historical Journal*
HLQ	*Huntington Library Quarterly*
HMC	Historical Manuscripts Commission
JBS	*Journal of British Studies*
LPL	Lambeth Palace Library
OED	*Oxford English Dictionary Online*, OUP
ODNB	*Oxford Dictionary of National Biography,* ed. H. C. G. Matthew and Brian Harrison (Oxford: OUP, 2004); online ed., ed. Lawrence Goldman, January 2005–ongoing
OUP	Oxford University Press
P&P	*Past and Present*
PMLA	*Publications of the Modern Language Association*
RES	*Review of English Studies*
SCJ	*Sixteenth Century Journal*
TNA	The National Archives, Kew
TNA, SP	The National Archives, Kew, State Papers
TRHS	*Transactions of the Royal Historical Society*
UP	University Press
Wing	Wing, Donald, *Short-title Catalogue of Books Printed in England, Scotland, Ireland, Wales, and British America and of English Books Printed in Other Countries: 1641–1700,* 2nd ed., newly revised and enlarged (New York: The Modern Language Association of America, 1982–94)

The Early Modern Letter Opener

JAMES DAYBELL AND ANDREW GORDON

I have accustomed those great persons that know mee, to endure
blotts, blurres, dashes, and botches in my letters.
—Michel de Montaigne, *Essayes*

For those studying historical cultures, letters seem to promise a unique kind
of access to the lives and thoughts of the past. The letter is a powerfully evocative form that has gained in resonance as the practices of personalized correspondence have declined in a digital age.[1] The labors of scholars over the last
two centuries to make available the correspondence of many notable figures
have often been guided by a faith in the value of the letter as a primary textual form. As Pliny the Younger put it, "it is one thing to write a letter, another
thing to write history, one thing to write to a friend, another to write to everyone" (aliud est enim epistulam aliud historiam, aliud amico aliud omnibus
scribere).[2] If Pliny's claim for a distinction between letters and history, between
the private sphere of the personal letter and the public scope of historical writing is recognizable, it is nonetheless deeply disingenuous. Not least
because the source of this apothegm is itself one of the most celebrated of all
letters of antiquity, in which Pliny provides his famous account of the death
of his uncle in the violence of Vesuvius's eruption in 79 A.D. We know of it
precisely because this letter, addressed to the historian Tacitus, was included
in the collection of his correspondence compiled by the author—in a rhetorical trope with which readers of Renaissance prefaces will be familiar, Pliny
tells us that he did so in response to the repeated requests of others.[3] It has

served as both an object of historical study and a model of epistolary style ever
since.[4]

The rhetorical sophistication of Pliny's letter, the specific significance of
its addressee, and its appearance in Pliny's collected correspondence all mark
this out as a highly artificial text, carefully fashioned for consumption. Yet
while these elements suggest some of the complexity of the letter as a literary
construction, they also occlude important aspects of how letters functioned
in the world by offering an image of the letter as a single-authored work and
an exclusively textual form. To recover the cultures of correspondence that
flourished in the early modern period, we need to look further into the engagement of the letter with the world of objects and practices. The materiality
of letter writing and the material practices on which letter writing depended
were typically edited out of collections of correspondence presented as literary works. It is still not uncommon to find editors applying to letters the approach recommended by Michael Hunter for editing seventeenth-century
manuscripts, subordinating "the physical appearance of the document" to a
concern with "the meaning that the author was trying to convey."[5] In following this approach, however, we cut ourselves off from the rich textures of epistolary traffic to which early modern subjects were habituated and which
formed part of the cultural image of the letter. The 400-odd letters that make
up the extant correspondence of Sir Philip Sidney contain barely a word of
comment on his literary activity—a fact that has troubled editors and biographers.[6] Yet his letter work is filled with epistolary negotiations with his
correspondents commenting on the dispatch and receipt of letters and the
routes, bearers, and forms of transport that make up the social networks of
correspondence. As Andrew Zurcher demonstrates in this volume, when we
understand the concerns with correspondence rehearsed in Sidney's letter writing, we are better placed to appreciate the pivotal role played by letters in his
literary works. The man who inherited much of Sidney's mantle as the courtier-
knight and figurehead of the Walsingham-Leicester Protestant grouping,
Robert Devereux, second Earl of Essex, looked to increase his influence in
government by extending his letter-writing activity both at home and abroad.
Confronting the demands of his correspondence commitments, Essex complained of "a world of papers" that demanded his attention.[7] What, we might
ask, did such early modern worlds of letters encompass, and how can we access
them? It is precisely these questions that *Cultures of Correspondence in Early
Modern Britain* looks to address. A strong sense of the complex of practices,
rhetorics, and strategies that make up early modern letter writing is provided

by a letter of 1595 (Figure 0.1) that sheds some light on the particular paper worlds orbiting about the earl. Written by Edward Reynolds, one of the earl's several secretaries, to Anthony Bacon, one of his key advisers, the letter provides a snapshot of an intricate series of letter transactions:

> S^r yo^w shall receave by this bearer a lre to the Deane of Wesminster to receaue Mr Wright into his howse according to her Ma^{ts} pleasure. The other is to Alderman Ratcliffe & Mr Archer for ye apprehending & committing of ye party yt counterfayted his hand, by the best means they may. I do send it open to ye end yow may peruse it. Mr Merrick hath a seale: who will also send some gentleman to delyuer it, if yt please yow. The footeman hath charge to tell yow that yow shall heare from his Lp. this nighte, or to morrow in ye morninge.[8]

In common with many surviving examples of the period, this is a letter about letters. Much correspondence incorporated a phatic component—in a climate of uncertain delivery, confirming receipt of previous letters, advising of letters to be received, and detailing the networks of transmission through which a letter ought to pass, were important features, often vital to the effective tracing of correspondence. Letters are in this sense a highly self-reflexive form in which we find not merely textual instances of the construction of the self, but an acute sensitivity to the cultures and practices of letter writing and a self-conscious creativity in the manipulation of these epistolary tools. In the case of the letter from Reynolds the commentary on letter transactions extends well beyond the page. Enclosing letters whose delivery was to be arranged by the recipient was another common practice: here, the letter for the dean of Westminster, Gabriel Goodman, represents the executive authority of the queen expressed through the earl's hand, and Reynolds sends it on as an instrument to be put into effect by the earl's adviser. The second enclosed letter takes us further behind the scenes, illustrating the labor through which correspondence might be constructed, and just how collaborative this process could prove. Presenting one of the earl's letters to Bacon for review, it shows us how the earl's authority was underwritten not merely by the writing of others but by advice and assistance over epistolary strategies. Nor, as we see, was such assistance merely textual. Reynolds makes clear that the earl's seal, the long-standing device for imprinting the epistolary identity of the author, is at his disposal—yet this detail of letter security sits uneasily alongside the anxiety over forged

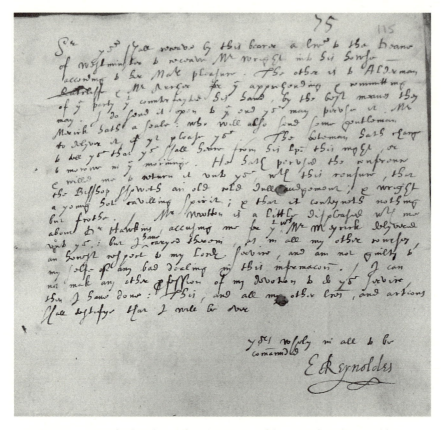

Figure 0.1. Lambeth Palace Library, MS 652, fol. 115ʳ. Edward Reynolds to
Anthony Bacon, 21 October 1595.

letters revealed in the reference to the use of a counterfeit hand. In such epistolary episodes we witness the letter's construction as a combined material and
textual project, negotiating complex and sometimes contradictory demands.
But these features of the letter are themselves supported by a further range of
practices that can all too easily elude our study. This letter speaks to the crucial role of bearers both in conveying the material letter and in supplement-
ing it with information not confided to the text, signaling the performative
and oral aspects of epistolary culture. In the case of the footman, the charge
given for verbal interaction registers in the text, but in doing so it draws our
attention to both the supra-verbal, and the supra-material. In this single ex-

ample, then, we have traveled a long way from the literary letter as constructed since antiquity.

*   *   *

We title this collection the *Cultures of Correspondence in Early Modern Britain* because we seek to open up the study of correspondence to multiple avenues of inquiry, showing how reading the letter against different contexts and expectations of letter writing can force us to rethink the work undertaken and achieved by this most overdetermined of forms. Among those different frameworks is a disciplinary confluence that draws together scholars of rhetoric, literary analysis, linguistics, history, historical geography, material culture, paleography and other fields to address the letter. We do not seek simply to promote the virtues of interdisciplinary study—itself a hackneyed claim among early modern scholars—but rather to demonstrate the many disciplines that find themselves implicated in the folds of the early modern letter and to point out how such diverse perspectives can prompt new and valuable questions about the correspondence cultures that are our focus. One of the tasks of this book then is to reconstruct and decode what might be termed the social materiality of letter writing, in other words, not only the physical features of letters but also the social and cultural practices of manuscript letter writing and the material conditions and contexts in which they were produced, disseminated, and consumed. Use of the plural form "cultures" attests to the range of epistolary literacies during the early modern period, which exhibited a complex series of overlapping and interlocking practices rather than a monolithic culture of correspondence. Indeed, Alan Stewart has persuasively argued for what he described as the "radical unmooredness," "the wonderfully miscellaneous, even chaotic" nature of epistolary practices, and the instability of the letter form.[9] Although rules and structures, hierarchies and conventions were present, for example, in the manner of Renaissance epistolographies and postal routes, at a local level letter writing was in many ways an improvised and remarkably ad hoc affair. The letter was a composite form involving multiple competences that can be located in the individual as well as in the collective and there was considerable overlap between these two categories. While letter-writing skills percolated across social groups over the period, collaborative modes existed alongside personal writing technologies (as indeed they do today), and cultures of correspondence were varied and uneven. An awareness of the collaborative nature of epistolary practices, the multiagent possibilities of letter writing—in addition to "letter writers" (in the sense of the name subscribed to correspondence) and recipients, which could involve secretaries, amanuenses, bearers, clerks, and archivists—erodes notions of letters as private and complicates our understanding of early modern subjectivities. To write an early modern letter demanded mastery of a hierarchy of literacy skills, either by individual letter writers or by secretaries and amanuenses. Letter writing required facility with the materials, tools, and technologies of writing; the ability to cut, maintain, and write with quills; prepare and trim paper to size; make ink and apply sealing wax. It demanded skills of penmanship and orthography, knowledge of rhetorical theory and epistolary rules: how to address, date, and sign letters. Integral also was an understanding of the social meanings of material features: the size and quality of paper used, the type of handwriting, the protocols of layout, blank space and the manuscript page, how to fold and seal a letter.[10] In other words, to be "fully literate" in the epistolary arts demanded a recognition of the rhetorical, semiotic, *and* material aspects of the form. Yet, any working definition of "epistolary literacy"—which Susan Whyman has persuasively argued needs to be incorporated as a new cultural category—must therefore be flexible enough to accommodate diverse engagements with the world of letter writing, sensitive to the nuances of different levels of social interaction with letters and the overlapping of manuscript, print, visual, and oral epistolary modes.[11] At one level, we encounter the partially literate bearer of a letter urgently responding to the visual symbol of a gallows on the address leaf of a letter and the unlettered tenant farmer who pays a scrivener to pen a letter of petition on his behalf. At the other end of the spectrum, we observe writers well versed in the politics of letter writing, with widespread correspondence networks, capable of writing in multiple hands and languages, engaging in clandestine correspondence using ciphers and secret codes, disseminating news, and circulating letters in manuscript and print.

The inquiry prompted by this book raises a series of critical and methodological questions. The first and perhaps most daunting of all is the disarming inquiry: what is a letter?[12] The classical description of the familiar letter, revived by humanist letter writers led by Erasmus, advocated conceiving of the letter as a "conversation between absent friends."[13] Following this Erasmian conceptualization, later epistolographies advocated a style of easy familiarity between friends: William Fulwood's *The Enemie of Idlenesse* (1568) urged use of a "certaine familiar reuerence" in correspondence with equals; while Angel Day's

The English Secretorie (1586) advised letter writers to write "louingly" to friends.[14] This formulation stresses the temporal separation of correspondents as a precondition of the letter, but in true humanist fashion it is a fiction that erases all traces of the material world and of the letter itself as a textual object (relegated in this construction to a poor substitute for the voice and company of the missing party). A more mundane definition might posit the letter as a form of written communication dispatched from one named party to another. Such a communication model definition has the advantage of separating the letter into stages within a temporal process, stages we might distinguish in a sequence as those of production, transmission, and reception. While one might posit further competing conceptualizations of the letter, these two radically contrasting models expose the fundamental weaknesses in theorizations about the letter form that this volume seeks to challenge and replace. In the humanist version, the letter is a-material, in that it actively suppresses the terms of its production, the contingencies of its physical existence, and the nature of its worldly transactions—tropes that Montaigne for one emphatically rejects in his response to the Ciceronian letter used as the epigraph to this Introduction. The communication model on the other hand presents another kind of fiction that both downgrades the creative and literary practices so readily associated with early modern letter writing and constrains the temporality of the letter to a narrow space that denies the rich spectrum of appropriations that characterize the manifold afterlives of correspondence.

Each of these models raises its own methodological considerations. Studying the production of letters asks that we interrogate not only the textual strategies of composition but also the physical process of inscription and the material conditions of writing, along with the many material practices that shaped the meaning of correspondence.[15] How does one define the authorship of a letter sent in the Earl of Essex's name, but written out by his secretary Reynolds, sent for oversight to Anthony Bacon, that is to receive the waxy imprint of authenticity from the earl's steward Merrick, before being conveyed by a bearer expected to negotiate the letter's access and supply additional information? In such a sequence, the social processes of correspondence and the material mediations of a textual object defined by its status as an object of transit become evident. All this the humanist "conversation" elides. By reorienting our approach to consider the *material* as well as textual aspects, letter writing emerges as a collaborative, mediated, and layered form that could involve successive acts of drafting, editing, review, and copying by different parties, which distance it from personal writing technologies associated with

the immediacy of *sprezzatura*. Definitions of what constituted a "letter" and
in fact a "letter writer" are informed by considering them in terms of material
practices. A fundamental aim of the book then is the reconstruction of the
material conditions and practices of the early modern letter.

The term "letter" is rather slippery in its usage, in many ways acting as a
catchall term that belies the rich variety of epistolary forms, both "real" and
"fictional," encompassing various types of epistolary writing, such as the verse
epistle, dedicatory epistle, and epistolary novel, as well as the Latinate and vernacular English prose letter. Some sense of the manifold textual genres of the
letter is therefore also necessary. The letter form embraces a wide range of
models, with their own conventions, as much material as linguistic and rhetorical. Letters can be divided formally by function and subgenre (the love
letter, letter of condolence, petitionary and "familiar" letters, as well as the
vituperative letter, which is explored in this volume by Michelle O'Callaghan),
and Renaissance epistolographies provided clear instructions for the protocols
and conventions (material as well as rhetorical) that related to each category—
although it is uncertain how neatly such rules and templates scripted letter
writing in practice, beyond formal modes of correspondence and opening and
closing forms.[16] Whether it be a petition, a suitor's letter, a letter to a kinsman
or kinswoman, all such works needed to negotiate the relative social degree of
each party, and in doing so they deployed strategies from forms of address
and the nuanced politics of handwriting, through layout on the manuscript
page, and color of sealing wax, to the selection of appropriate agents to convey and present the letter to its intended object. The genres of the letter inevitably overflow the conceptual schema of written communication between
two parties. Species of missive documentation embrace such authoritative
forms as the warrant, the passport, the letter of credit, or the bond and cannot be readily divorced from the letter format. John Browne's *The Marchants
Avizo* (1589) provided template letters and documents connected to trade with
the Iberian Peninsula, including "the Forme of a Spanish accompt," "A forme
for making a bill of lading," and "A Letter to be sent in that ship Where you
haue laden goods for any Marchant."[17] Likewise, many legal documents also
borrow an epistolary form, and numerous manuals and formularies, such as
A Newe Boke of Presidentes (first printed in 1543 with several dozen editions
appearing prior to 1641) provided letter-writing instruction complete with templates.[18] The porous boundaries between these different epistolary forms further challenge our notion of correspondence. Should the many thousands of
chancery bills of complaint addressed to Francis Bacon during his tenure as

lord keeper be considered among his incoming correspondence? Such questions highlight the artificial nature of many of the classificatory boundaries we decide upon. Many correspondence projects have limited their interest to the letters written in the name of an individual, including only selective items of correspondence received, despite the risk of skewing the picture of correspondence practice, ignoring the extent to which letters are not only a social production and a social exchange but also often the deliberate product of cultivation by the correspondent—as Bacon has it "when a man would draw an answer by letter backe againe."[19] Determining what constitutes an individual's corpus of correspondence for the early modern period, therefore, requires a flexible and pluralistic definition of letter-writing activities, and any new edition that seeks fully to locate an individual within the cultures of their correspondence ought to encompass not only those letters that he or she penned (including letters penned in a secretarial capacity), but also those received, read, endorsed, archived, and even carried.[20]

What of the temporal range of the letter? The communication model configures the temporal boundaries narrowly and makes the object singular, restricted to a particular moment of reception by an individual reader. As with composition, the reading of letters was not necessarily a solitary act of perusal. Private reading practices were not uncommon, but letters were read in manifestly diverse ways. They might be sent unsealed to be passed around family and wider social contacts for comment; correspondence was sorted and sifted by secretaries for ease of reading; the delivery of letters to the monarch was carefully orchestrated to achieve maximum royal attention; and newsletters were copied and scribally circulated to a diverse audience. Furthermore, attention to the provenance and archival history of early modern letters foregrounds the subsequent uses that preserved, adapted, or redeployed them in systems of storage, in processes of contract or legal contest, or in historical curation. In these processes the material forms of the letter undergo new translations, acquiring endorsements, annotations, foldings, and markings, or being copied into letter books, commonplace books, or even into print, each modulation reframing the meaning and function of the correspondence in question.

The survival of letters was then often intentional and orchestrated, a function of deliberate archival policies to copy or conserve particular correspondence, as is revealed in the essays by Alan Stewart and James Daybell. Conversely, when we study the early modern letter we need always to bear in mind what is lost and what does not survive. One casualty of seeking to recover the cultures of correspondence from the material evidence is the partiality of preservation. As Arnold Hunt argues in this collection, the destruction of letters was likely a far more common practice—and commitment—than we would imagine, so we can suspect that what comes down to us is the product of some acts of selection along the way—a form of editing the archive resembling the more questionable interventions of published correspondence. Even in the remarkable case of a figure like the polymath royal secretary Constantijn Huygens, where some ten thousand items of correspondence survive, it is naive to call this corpus comprehensive.[21] In most cases we have a small fraction of epistolary output, usually in institutional or family archives, or letter books that recorded outgoing and incoming correspondence. Such archival conditions inflect the nature of letters that are extant, privileging letters that relate to business, law, and politics. Establishing a rounded picture of an individual's letter-writing activities is challenging. None of Spenser's "own" letters survive in manuscript, for example, just those he penned as secretary.[22] Extant correspondence is also often very one-sided, and it is particularly difficult to reconstruct epistolary exchanges or to find runs of correspondence over a significant duration. Instead the letters we have are fractured and fleeting, broken and episodic, materially contingent snapshots in time, which present the letter as fragment, rather than the ideal of an epistolary exchange. In their textual content letters are situational, reflecting particular states or conditions—grief, love, penitence—they are synchronic rather diachronic, representing periods of crisis or flux, rather than what is constant and unchanging. The practice of enclosing separable items and other letters within a framing letter can also skew our ability to assess an individual fragment of this epistolary ensemble. All too often the signs of this larger context are lost, with separates in particular designed not to betray their links back to a specific epistolary exchange.

Beyond the dynamic of what survives and what is lost, letters are subject to forms of diversion and perversion. Letters had (and still have) a tendency to go astray, and we encounter the recoverable traces of what goes wrong on epistolary journeys: letters that failed to reach addressees and were never read or an exchange that crossed paths out of sync. Letters were also practiced upon with malicious intent. Andrew Gordon's essay in this collection highlights the manifold means of infiltrating correspondence and the professionalized practices of the counterfeiter. Andrew Zurcher foregrounds the fundamental insecurities of the letter. The disruption and interception of correspondence; the forgery and concealment of letters, all help to destabilize fixed models of letter writing as a binary textual transaction.

Other features of the letter easily submerged by a textual or even material focus include the relation of the letter to spoken communication. If the "conversation" of humanist authors is an imaginative, textually constructed fiction, Lynne Magnusson argues in the collection for the registering of vocal elements in some styles of epistolary discourse. To these we can add the roles alluded to above of bearer or post in imparting information and negotiating access. But these alone do not circumscribe the verbal spheres of the letter. The social sites of letter construction, involving advisers, secretaries, and scribes, where letters might be dictated can be matched in the social contexts of reception, where letters might be read aloud, in groups or to specific people as a mark of confidence. Formal letters of petition were written to be read aloud, which imparts a performative element to the epistle, blurring the boundaries between the textual and oral. The timing and manner in which letters were presented and by whom were key to the effective passage of correspondence in a patronage society where access was paramount. These contexts reflect a common bias in highlighting the letter writing of social elites and the court, but in considering oral interchanges with the letter, we can include those forms of mediation that permitted nonliterate engagements with the form. Letters of petition often speak collectively in the voice of a specific community as informed by the mediation of a scribe or scrivener; partially literate recipients might seek out learned neighbors to have their letters read to them. Other appropriations of the letter, in verse libels, in mock letters, and onstage might ventriloquize or perform versions of the letter in specific cultural contexts, just as poetic epistles and fictions provided literary communities with epistolary matter for consumption.

Moreover this reinterpretation of cultures of correspondence has a wider significance beyond the field of Renaissance letter writing since it could be argued that the letter form structures and mirrors a much broader range of early modern transactions. In this sense, the ways in which we read and interpret letters necessarily influences and informs how we understand many other textual interactions and social relationships. To take one fundamental example: the way in which the culture, practices, and grammar of the letter instructed early modern discourses of friendship.[23] Nowhere is this link more clearly discerned perhaps than in the letters of John Donne, who frequently employed a troped language of friendship in correspondence, mirroring that formulated by Erasmus. For Donne the writing and reciprocal exchange of letters represented an intimate part of friendship, and he expended considerable rhetorical energies in cloaking his missives in elaborate conceits of friendship. "I send not my letters," he wrote to Sir Henry Goodere,

> as tribute, nor interest, nor recompence, nor for commerce, nor as testimonialls of my love, nor provokers of yours, not to justifie my custome of writing, nor for a vent and utterance of my meditations: For my letters are either above or under all such offices, yet I write very affectionately, and I chide and accuse my selfe of diminishing that affection which sends them, when I aske my selfe why. Only I am sure that I desire that you might have in your hands letters of mine of all kindes, as conveyances and deliverers of mee to you, whether you accept me as a friend, or as a patient, or as a penitent or as a Bedesman, for I decline no jurisdiction, nor refuse any tenure.[24]

Donne's letter writing is saturated with what Alan Stewart would describe as a grammar of the letter, in other words, "a vocabulary and set of images that originate in the material practices of letter-writing culture of early modern England."[25] Displaying a marked awareness of the physical features of the letter (such as handwriting, paper, seals, postscripts)—and the social practices that animate them (the customs of writing and the rites of delivery), Donne underlines the importance of these elements for an understanding not only of Donne's but of all early modern correspondence.

How to Read an Early Modern Letter

With these methodological challenges in mind, we can begin the process of opening the early modern letter. As a first stage in the process we present here a brief rehearsal of the key considerations of how to read an early modern letter. Studying manuscript letters requires expertise and training in bibliographical techniques that have long been the hallmarks of manuscript studies: codicology or the physical description of manuscripts (watermarks, collation, and binding); paleography (the study of handwriting), transcription practices, attribution, and provenance; sigillography (the study of seals); and diplomatics (the study of documents). These modes of material inquiry, which focus on the physical and contextual complexities of letters, sit alongside rhetorical and textual approaches to the genre, and in combination they elucidate much about the nature and nuances of letters and letter writing. Strikingly, the contents of a letter were the last thing that an early modern reader would have encountered. Instead they would have been confronted by a small folded packet of paper, directed to the recipient on the address leaf usually following standard epistolary protocols, with reference to person and place (and sometimes with postal endorsements, which tracked its journey, as well as visual cues such as sketches of gallows that indicated urgency. The paper packet was normally closed with a wax seal (sometimes with floss or string, often a marker of intimacy), which acted both as a device of authentication normally imbued with symbolic significance and to guarantee security. The color of sealing wax was instructive, normally red, but black to signify periods of mourning. While letters might be left at inns (terminal points for carriers) or households to await the return of absent recipients, others were placed in the hands of the intended addressee by bearers (the identity of whom mostly remains unknown or obscured), who conveyed oral report and may in fact have read letters aloud, which signifies the corporeal and oral dimension to epistolary transactions, dimensions that it is often difficult to reconstruct except in general terms. Understanding the postal conditions that structured habits and patterns of correspondence, as Mark Brayshay magisterially demonstrates in this volume, requires a detailed knowledge of social and spatial geography, of post and carrier networks, more informal arrangements for conveyance, as well as correspondence networks and even sometimes the intricate workings of manuscript networks. The rhythms of national carrier networks, for example, structured the weekly transmission of letters: as Alan Stewart has carefully shown, Shakespeare's correspondence between Stratford and London was dependent on the weekly route of the Stratford carrier to the Bell Inn in Carter Lane, his terminus in the capital.[26] Correspondence also often accompanied other texts and other enclosures and material goods, some acting as inventories of items delivered. Donne's letters conveyed books, or presentation copies of his poems and sermons, or more mundanely a letter to his brother-in-law Robert More accompanied parcels and a horse.[27] Letters were important cultural conduits, agents in textual transmission and the movement of material goods. Other letters acted as introductions to individuals and were carried by bearers on their person as a means to gain access for a face-to-face audience. In such cases of metatextuality, letters must not be viewed in isolation, but rather only make sense when set in dialogue with other textual elements that made up

the broader epistolary transaction. Reconstructing these extratextual contexts—
and indeed the reciprocal exchange that they generated—is an important
part of how we read and interpret early modern letters.

Upon receipt, a letter would have normally been opened (either by the
recipient or by a secretary or some other individual authorized to read the
recipient's correspondence), a process that broke the seal, sometimes tearing
away paper on which the main body of the letter was written. As we have
seen, the reading of letters was often far from the solitary act of perusal that
traditional conceptualizations of the epistolary process portray. Marks accompanying reading, such as the highlighting of key passages or marginal annotations evidence an otherwise invisible activity. The absence of a seal might
indicate that a letter had been sent open for reading within a sanctioned group
of family or friends; arrival with the seal broken, that it had been tampered
with during transit. Scribal endorsements that dated a letter, gutting it for
contents and ease of filing, indicate secretarial intervention, while scribally
circulated or printed copies of letters, often reframed as "true copies" betoken
widening readership communities for whom the activity of copying produced vivid forms of engagement.[28] Early modern genre paintings, diaries,
and form letters themselves suggest the range of private and public spaces in
which letters might be perused: the study, closet, bedchamber, parlor, household,
or inn. On turning to the manuscript page—before considering the modes of
address and closing, salutations, and rhetorical structuring of the letter, which
are laid out in letter-writing manuals of the period—there were various physical features of the manuscript that conveyed significant meaning, what might
be termed the material rhetorics of the manuscript page. These included
handwriting, form and placement of signature, dating, layout of the manuscript page, quality and size of paper used, deployment of blank space, margins and postscripts, all of which were imbued with social cues or codes that
communicated on an extratextual level and were widely understood during
the period. The deployment of significant blank space and the placement
of a signature in the bottom right-hand corner of the page (in accordance with
protocols found in early modern epistolographies) were signs of deference and
respect; conversely the use of large bifolium sheets for short missives, rather
than cropping paper to size, and subscribing a letter immediately after the closing salutation were markers of social standing and status. To write with one's
own hand was a sign of intimacy and respect, while it was standard to use a
secretary for letters to social superiors. Thus, in his letters of submission to
Queen Elizabeth the Earl of Essex obsequiously signed his name in the ex-

treme right bottom of the manuscript page as part of a material rhetoric seeking clemency that worked with his high-blown rhetorical maneuverings for forgiveness; his use of his own hand to do so was a sign of intimacy with the monarch, for subjects of lower social standing this would have been a social offense.[29] More broadly, paleographical analysis of handwriting in letters reveals much about the mechanics of composition, whether or not it was a holograph letter (in the hand of the signatory), or a scribally produced collaborative text, which again unsettles the notion of a letter as a single-authored text. Recent studies of the letter-writing activities of secretariats concentrating on scribal traits and analysis have highlighted the complexity of secretarial practices.[30] Although personal secretaries might be conceptualized as singular, it was also common for multiple secretaries to deal with a person's correspondence, in which cases each was assigned particular duties, delegated according to skill and hierarchy. Individuals might be responsible for different elements of the letter (the main body, signature, the superscription and address, and endorsements), depending on daily attendance and availability. The letter is thus broken down further into its constituent parts, letter writing emerging quite clearly as a procedural form, with differentiation of access to each aspect of the correspondence.

Once read, letters enjoyed complex and compelling afterlives. They were generally endorsed with the date and a brief summary of contents and folded (in a different manner from that for posting) for filing and later retrieval, stored in trunks or cabinets, finding their way later into family muniments rooms, the state papers, and other institutional archives. Others, of course, were forgotten about, discarded, or destroyed as a form of bureaucratic policy. The habit of maintaining letter books during the early modern period meant that some letters exist as fair copies or drafts transcribed into manuscript books for safekeeping or as a form of writing the self. Other letters circulated scribally and in printed form, while a number of high-profile collections of letters found their way into print, for example, Donne's *Letters to Severall Persons of Honour* (1651; reissued 1654), printed posthumously by his son John Donne the younger as a highly selective collection of his father's letters concerned above all with his "literary legacy." Reread with reapplications beyond their initial points of authorship and reception, early modern letters survive in an extraordinarily wide range of texts varying in scribal statuses, some of them never in fact reaching the addressee. While Claudio Guillén has distinguished at least seven textual genres of the Renaissance letter, a material taxonomy would delineate an alternative order of the letter by paying attention to the scribal status: the original sent letter, the rough draft, the personal copy, the letter book, the "circular" letter, the "scribally published" letter.[31] It is perfectly possible therefore for a letter (as with other early modern texts) to exist as a series of different manifestations, with textual and contextual variations, which further destabilizes our notion of the early modern letter as a fixed text, capable of interpretation as two-way closed epistolary exchange.

The Directions of the Early Modern Letter

The field of Renaissance letters and letter writing has witnessed a remarkable growth of interest in recent years, stimulated by the appearance of several landmark studies, a number of exemplary editions of correspondence, and the emergence of digital resources that make manuscript letters available in an unprecedented way. Scholarship in this area is at once broad and genuinely interdisciplinary in methodological terms, with approaches ranging from linguistic and rhetorical, material and archival, historical and gender-based studies, to those interested in form (manuscript and print), circulation, and editing.[32] In broad terms, scholarship has tended to privilege individual letter writers, usually those of canonical status or historical renown, such as John Donne, Philip Sidney, or Elizabeth I; or focused on epistolary form and genres (such as the letter of petition, the love letter, or the printed letter). Cumulatively, recent scholarship has redefined the ways in which we conceptualize, situate, and read early modern letters and letter-writing practices. Lynne Magnusson's *Shakespeare and Social Dialogue: Dramatic Language and Elizabethan Letters* (1999) combined models of linguistic analysis rooted in politeness theory with aspects of Pierre Bourdieu's social theory of language to examine how social relations are encoded and manipulated in Shakespeare's dramatic language—a language deeply imbued with letter-writing practices of the early modern period. Alan Stewart's important book *Shakespeare's Letters* (2008) analyzes the representation of epistolary practices in Shakespeare's dramatic works, highlighting the substitution of the Ciceronian familiar letters recommended by contemporary manuals for pragmatic engagements with the material processes of letter writing and their disruption. Roger Chartier has studied the influence of model letters in the ancien régime in France, while Gary Schneider's *The Culture of Epistolarity: Vernacular Letters and Letter Writing in Early Modern England, 1500–1700* (2005) focuses on the sociocultural function and meaning of epistolary writing.[33] Alongside these large-scale studies of the early modern letter, other scholars have taken a linguistic approach. Susan Fitzmaurice's *The Familiar Letter in Early Modern English* (2002) is a sociohistorical linguistic study examining the linguistic form, function, and practice of familiar letters, both real and fictional, in the seventeenth and eighteenth centuries. Other scholars including notably Graham Williams and Melanie Evans in their studies of the Thynne women and Elizabeth I have brought to the study of correspondence methodologies and insights from historical linguistics and pragmatics.[34] Treated as sites of homoerotic desire, letters have also received queer readings by David M. Bergeron and Alan Bray among others.[35] On the whole these studies have tended to focus on vernacular English prose letters, whereas other works have concentrated on the largely male Latinate world of the republic of letters. Lisa Jardine's *Erasmus, Man of Letters: The Construction of Charisma in Print* (1993) demonstrates Erasmus's self-conscious mastery of print media as a means of fashioning himself as a truly Pan-European scholar.[36] Epistolary networks that stretched across early modern Europe have been studied by scholars of the mid- to late seventeenth century interested in the Royal Society and the scientific revolution, and the newsletter and intelligence networks have received considerable attention.[37] Others including James Daybell, Jane Couchman, and Ann Crabb have studied the gendered aspects of letter writing, focusing specifically on early modern women's letters, which is interestingly by far the most industrious area of research on letter writing.[38]

More recently, several scholars influenced by the "material" and "archival turns" have stressed the importance of attending to the physical aspects of letters. Work by Jonathan Gibson, A. R. Braunmuller, and others has emphasized the significance of the physical layout of the manuscript page, while Alan Stewart and Heather Wolfe's *Letterwriting in Renaissance England* (2004), based on the rich holdings of the Folger Shakespeare Library, examines materials associated with the epistolary process, from tools and materials and letter-writing models through secretarial composition and forms of letters to postal conditions, archiving, and afterlives.[39] James Daybell's *The Material Letter* (2012) offers a full-scale study of the social and cultural practices of early modern English manuscript letters, reconstructing the material conditions of the epistolary process from materials and tools to archives and afterlives. There is also an increasing awareness that certain letters enjoyed wider circulation in manuscript (and print) beyond the named addressee of a letter. Notable examples include Philip Sidney's *Letter to Queen Elizabeth*, the Earl of Essex's *Letter of Advice to the Earl of Rutland*, and Lady Rich's *Letter to Queen Elizabeth*.

The "scribal publication" of such letters has been treated in large-scale discussions of manuscript transmission by Harold Love, Henry Woudhuysen, and Arthur Marotti, as well as in seminal work by Peter Beal on Sidney's letter to Elizabeth and Andrew Gordon on the circulation of letters associated with Francis Bacon and the second Earl of Essex, and by James Daybell in his analysis of Lady Rich's *Letter to Queen Elizabeth*.[40] Many printed editions of sixteenth- and seventeenth-century letters have struggled to convey the range of meanings generated by this complex and socially charged genre, but a small number of them have at least sought to represent nontextual features visually, thus providing readers with material texts closer in approximation to the original manuscript.[41] Building on recent material approaches to the early modern letter, this collection assembles a range of scholars from divergent fields, including literary criticism, linguistics, history, and cultural geography, as well as archivists, who together bring a varied form of analysis of the *material text*.

One of the most significant recent developments for the field of early modern letter writing (as in other areas) has been the contribution of scholars in the digital humanities, whose work has the potential to open up new vistas of inquiry at a macro and micro level. Where basic online finding aids such as the British Library manuscript catalog, the National Archives catalog, and A2A archives in the United Kingdom have greatly increased the speed and ease of searching for letters, meta-projects like "Early Modern Letters Online" and its sister project "Women's Early Modern Letters Online" offer a first-line union catalog and finding aid for men's and women's letters for the period 1400–1700.[42] In the United States large-scale digitization programs have been undertaken by major research libraries, such as the Folger Shakespeare Library's Digital Image Collection (Luna) and online finding aids, the Huntington Digital Library, and the Beinecke's Digital Collections, which provide invaluable access to their rich manuscript holdings.[43] Other database projects like State Papers Online and the Cecil Papers provide rich digital images of manuscript letters in collections previously more studied from printed calendars or low-resolution microfilm.[44] Both types of digital resources not only engage in a process of archival recovery but also enable worldwide virtual access to these manuscripts at the click of a button. While these technological advances are in many ways laudable, the seductive appeal of digital images reproduces some of the problems of "substitution" familiar in printed editions. Despite their visual similitude such images are not the same as the physical artifacts themselves, and the ability to use search functions to cherry-pick by key terms can mean that individual letters are read in isolation. At the micro level, digital technologies have led to the development of online editions of letters.[45] The flexibility of digital media platforms enables a richly dynamic form of editing, where text and descriptions of physical features can be read alongside digital images; one can switch between diplomatic and modernized transcriptions; link through to glossaries, historical thesauri, and biographical materials; or produce visualizations of correspondence networks, and chronologies of correspondence. In other words, digital editions harness (for an individual correspondent at least) very powerful analytical tools that assist in the reading and understanding of single letters, bodies of correspondence, or letter writers. At the macro level too, a number of projects, including the University of Oxford's "Cultures of Knowledge" and "Electronic Enlightenment," as well as Stanford's "Mapping the Republic of Letters," are developing sophisticated software programs including visualization tools to look at early modern letter networks.[46] In a world of big data, the ability to process and analyze vast corpora of letters offers the potential to reconstruct circuits of correspondence, to elucidate the nodes of postal activity and uncover previously obscured epistolary relationships. Nevertheless, encoding metadata in a way that is prosopographically rich—beyond the key fields of sender, recipient, date, and place—and therefore meaningful is an extremely time-consuming and laborious task. As with early quantitative work on family reconstitution, perhaps the best results will be achieved on a very small scale.[47] Nevertheless, the dialogue between the digital humanities and the field of early modern letters is an exciting and dynamic one on many levels, and, while it is not without its problems and pitfalls, it has the potential to open up critical and interpretive vistas on a macro as well as micro level.

*   *   *

The study of early modern letters finds itself poised at a crossroads. Hitherto a supplementary cultural form, elevated to study generally only in the case of figures already celebrated for their historical or literary significance, the letter now emerges as the most vital and wide-ranging sociotext of the early modern period and one whose resources remain largely untapped. On the threshold of a massive expansion in the resources available for the study of the early modern letter, we need to engage with early modern society's cultures of correspondence in their diversity and often deceptive familiarity, in order to make sense of what we find. *Cultures of Correspondence in Early Modern Britain* responds directly to this need with twelve essays which address the layered complexity of letters in the early modern period. It is organized into four sections designed not to impose boundaries, disciplinary or categorical, upon the early modern letter, but rather to bring out complementary aspects of the cultures under investigation, releasing the potential of letters to signify in multiple arenas.

We begin in Part I with a pair of essays focused on the material practices behind early modern letter writing. In the first of these, Jonathan Gibson analyzes the cultural politics of script in Tudor letters, placing the prescriptions of Italian writing manuals against the practical evidence of how italic hands were deployed. In the conflict between two mid-sixteenth-century writing masters, Giovambattista Palatino and Giovan Francesco Cresci, Gibson identifies the divergent models that structured the development of early modern English italic as the artificial formality of *Palatinian* that flourished among Tudor aristocrats in the mid-sixteenth century was displaced by *Crescian* italic, a more flexible and quicker alternative that took root from the 1580s. Mapping the interchange of hands and the texts in which they were deployed, Gibson goes beyond the province of paleography to pose questions about the cultural shifts enacted here and the meanings of these contrasted "bibliographical codes." This study of the visible hands of early modern letters is followed by an essay that brings to light the hidden hands that conveyed correspondence in Mark Brayshay's study of letter delivery and the material conditions of the post. Built on a comprehensive mastery of sixteenth- and seventeenth-century postal communications, Brasyhay, a cultural geographer, provides a guide to the diverse ways in which letters were carried, from local posts, private couriers, carriers, messengers, pursuivants, and royal posts through to more ad hoc arrangements in the guise of personal servants and bearers. Spanning a period from the start of the sixteenth century up to the formation of the post office and beyond, his essay brings to light the complex networks that structured the rhythms and patterns of epistolary exchange. Providing an empirically rich excavation of the mechanics of posting, his essay lays the groundwork for theoretical conceptualizations of epistolarity, the material conditions of composition, delivery, and reception, the role of bearers as corporeal extensions of the texts they carried, and the orality of early modern manuscript correspondence.

From the material practices upon which the cultures of correspondence rely, we move in Part II to an examination of the material technologies of the letter and their cultural functions. The three essays grouped together here each examine the question of security in letter writing. The first, by Nadine Akkerman, sheds new light on the functions of cryptography in early modern correspondence. Challenging the conventional picture of a decline in the use of cipher in the early seventeenth century, she demonstrates that the study of this intelligence art was considered an essential tool in early modern statecraft and a valued part of the skill set of contemporary secretaries and counselors. Reestablishing the importance of cipher within seventeenth-century correspondence, Akkerman transforms our understanding of its functions with her investigation of the letters of Elizabeth of Bohemia. For while the exiled monarch was skilled in the science of cryptology, her deployment of codes too basic to have any meaningful intelligence function defies notions of cipher as an epistolary security technology. Akkerman shows how cipher functions instead in the correspondence networks of Elizabeth of Bohemia as a social marker, with the granting of a key to a correspondent the badge of admission to an exclusive grouping that registers the social bonds between correspondents. Akkerman's groundbreaking essay argues that our understanding of cryptography in letters needs to look beyond the codes and their key, to see the rich textures of meaning revealed by reading epistolary cipher within the social fabric of correspondence. Andrew Gordon's essay places the material technologies of letter forgery under the spotlight, locating them within an early modern culture of copying. Pointing to forgery as a metacritical category of textual reflection, he shows how letter forgery affords an insight into the period's imagining of letters and their function. Focusing on the evidence of prosecution, the material practices of forgery that emerge from the investigation of contemporary legal cases foreground correspondence as a social process, in which the devising, producing, and transmitting of counterfeit correspondence involve many hands. Gordon shows how an analytical toolbox for evaluating the material evidence was developed and disseminated through the legal arguments at Star Chamber, yet the existence of such investigative tools only underlines the political expediency that so often shaped legal process in the period. For Gordon the "material fictions" of forged letters encompass not only the material letter and the cultural practices of delivery but also the highly imaginative discursive construction placed upon those operations in the context of early modern treason cases—even when such cases stretched to the breaking point the credibility of the letter as an evidentiary form. In the final essay of Part II Andrew Zurcher shows how the literary imagination of two of the period's greatest writers was informed by correspondence practices. Where the preceding essays challenge understanding of letter technologies, arguing for the richly creative meanings invested within forgery and cryptography, Zurcher's essay demonstrates how the period's fraught concerns over letter security translate into imaginative use of letters by Sidney and Spenser. Both had a grounding in letter intelligence. Sidney, whose father was lord deputy of Ireland, and whose father-in-law, Sir Francis Walsingham, oversaw Elizabeth's intelligence networks, was understandably sensitive to interest in his correspondence, while Spenser, who worked as secretary to Lord Grey in Ireland, had a pivotal role in managing the security of Grey's letters. As Zurcher reminds us, "the whole sprawling narrative of *The Countess of Pembroke's Arcadia* rises here from a short vignette about epistolary security," but his reading goes on to suggest the pivotal role for letters in the author's plan for the incomplete work. In Spenser's *Faerie Queene*, Zurcher points to an epistolary dynamic announced in the "address" to Elizabeth across the two editions and developed particularly in the letters associated with Duessa, which combine elements of counterfeiting and of cipher. This angle of approach leads Zurcher to propose that we rethink Spenser's celebrated allegorical strategies in terms informed by the cultures of correspondence and understand deliberate constraints to have been imposed upon interpretive access to his work so that *The Faerie Queene* "like a ciphered letter, will choose its readers."

In Part III, "Genres and Rhetorics," we turn to the consideration of the linguistic and rhetorical styles of letter writing. The first essay here is from Lynne Magnusson, a pioneer in the rhetorical analysis of early modern letters, whose chapter explores the impact of the sixteenth century's "educational revolution" upon letter writing. In search of evidence for a *translatio epistolarum*, her study of the uses of Ciceronian education in letters and its cultural capital highlights the contrast between the limited English materials and the evidence of humanist educators' success on the Continent. As Magnusson shows, the English context is characterized by the different models of letter writing in circulation, with the Ciceronian familiar letter contending with forms of vernacular correspondence such as those deployed in petitionary and suitors' letters. Combating a tendency to focus on the highest social and scholarly elite, Magnusson's case study of the Herrick correspondence selects a family from a lower social position able to provide more conclusive evidence of the dissemination of Ciceronian approaches to letter writing. The rich hoard of letters preserved by William Herrick enables Magnusson to place the Ciceronian effects of letters from his grammar school–educated nephew Tobias against the epistolary approach of his son John, an ironmonger's apprentice in London, whose letters are more inclusive, revealing the letter as a meeting place of oral and literate communication. Magnusson's study sets up a dialogue of epistolary style within the family that, when mapped onto the social networks of early modern society, helps us to understand why Tobias failed to instrumentalize his Ciceronian education to any remunerative purpose, despite the persistence of his eloquent complaints. A more effective rhetorical branding is the focus of Christopher Burlinson's essay that studies the letter writing of John Stubbs. With his right hand forfeited for its part in authoring the notorious 1579 pamphlet that critiqued the projected marriage plans of Elizabeth, *The Discovery of a Gaping Gulf,* the essay explores the reconstruction of his textual identity and letter-writing practice in the wake of the loss of his right hand. Drawing on the work of Jonathan Goldberg on the inscription of the self through the training of the hand, Burlinson calls for a more responsive interpretation of the material evidence. His reading of Stubbs's letter writing highlights the adoption of the new signature *Scaeva* after his amputation. This epithet drawn from a humanist anecdote in Livy that celebrates devoted and loyal service was added to all his post-1581 letters with the exception of one in French. As Burlinson argues, the new signature is fundamental to the new authorial identity of his left-handed writing through which he both enacted and articulated a rhetoric of submission that is simultaneously material and linguistic. So remarkable did this epistolary identity become that Burlinson finds the signature added to copies of letters that bore no such mark in the original, just as copies of his letter texts seek to incorporate features of his distinct new hand. Ciceronian influences are also discussed in passing in the final essay in Part III, Michelle O'Callaghan's study of vituperative rhetoric in the letters of early modern women. Situating her study in the context of the letter-writing manuals of the period from Angel Day and William Fulwood, she shows how the linguistic strategies of vituperation were built upon the calculation of risks involved. In letters between men, such as Francis Bacon's artful vituperative assault on his enemy Sir Edward Coke, the model strategy is to remain within models of decorum and to pitch vituperation as a form of seemingly friendly censure. As O'Callaghan shows, however, issues of gender inflect the negotiation of models of vituperation in interesting ways. The letters of educated women did not always respect such boundaries or expectations, but rather sought to use the violence of vituperation to greater effect by deploying such particular tactics as the instrumentality of the curse. Female honor codes of the period were constructed around female chastity as well as around social status and reputation, and breaking with social decorum challenged women's actions and words in a more complicated way than merely damning women on gendered grounds. In the case of a particularly splenetic letter from Bridget Willoughby to Clement Fisher occasioned by his act of fomenting discord between her and her father, Lady Bridget was considered to have transgressed the civil boundaries becoming of one of her sex and social standing. Conversely, Christopher Brooke's Juvenalian "ritualized venting of spleen" in a vicious and highly self-conscious literary letter to Lady Eleanor Davies challenged her sexual honor, but moreover attacked her family honor. In concluding, the essay argues for "an uneven relationship between the gendered discourse around anger and the gender of those who used its rhetorical forms in letters, rather than a straightforward equivalence."

Part IV of the collection departs from the material practices and cultural conditions that produced letters, turning to those that determined their survival. Under the rubric of "The Afterlives of Letters," the three essays grouped here investigate what happened next after letters were variously received, read, endorsed, and archived. Broadly the three essays are interested in what might be termed the ordering of knowledge. In an essay that not only challenges the assumed impartiality of the archive but also forces us to rethink the relationship between preservation and destruction, Arnold Hunt excavates the curious but persistent injunction to "burn this letter" found in correspondence of the period. Struggling to make sense of this exhortation, visible to us only by virtue of its countermanding, Hunt's study asks that we pay attention to the genres and subspecies of correspondence already lost to the flames. Reading the conditions of survival in the letters bearing this marker, Hunt elucidates a series of developing tensions that trouble the epistolary transactions of the period, as attitudes that treated letters as either momentary indiscretions or ephemeral effects to be more or less routinely discarded or burned came into conflict with an emergent tendency to value letters as part of a documentary record. Ultimately the essay reinforces our awareness that the early modern archives that come down to us are often the product of a deliberate but invisible process of selection and provides a fitting introduction to the sometimes paradoxical interplay of material and textual rhetorics affecting the survival of early modern letters. The conditions that shaped patterns of survival are also the subject of James Daybell's essay, which examines the gendered archival practices and the future lives of letters. Taking as his starting point, Derrida's suggestive neologism the "matriarchive" (as conceptualized by William H. Sherman), Daybell investigates the survival of early modern women's letters, the ways in which they were archived, valued, and interpreted by future generations. Against the backdrop of principal modes of archival preservation, the essay focuses on the survival of women's letters outside of formal institutional archives through three case studies that examine the status, treatment, and archival afterlife of three distinct groupings of letters within family archives. The first example concerns Lambeth Palace Library's Talbot MS 3205, a volume composed almost entirely of women's letters, which was assembled and bound by the physician-antiquary Dr. Nathaniel Johnston (1629?–1705) and bequeathed to the College of Arms in the late seventeenth century, a collection later transferred to Lambeth Palace Library. The second case study concerns the preservation of Mary Baskerville's letters by her son, the antiquarian Hannibal Baskerville, and the use of correspondence as a material site for family biography. The third relates to a letter book of Margaret Clifford, Countess of Cumberland, assembled by her daughter Anne Clifford, as an act of memorialization of her mother. As such this essay is interested not only in women's direct involvement with early modern archives as repositories of "transgenerational memory," but also in what might be described as the *gendered* politics of archival survival and its impact upon the afterlives of texts produced by early modern female letter writers.

The final essay in the volume by Alan Stewart reexamines the emergence of institutional archives in the Elizabethan and Jacobean era, revealing the place of correspondence within a contemporary competition for archival supremacy. Stewart returns to the source of a potent archival narrative: the formation of the State Paper Office, and finds there a complex, interwoven tale of documentary contestation, in which the authority and jurisdiction of office, officeholder, family, and state are still under construction. Stewart demonstrates the impact of place and location—in the guise of archives, both early modern and modern—on the meaning attached to letters. At a time when digital initiatives such as State Papers Online allow such easy access to images of original documents, a process that separates letters from their material and archival contexts, Stewart asks that we reconsider the nature and formation of early modern archives through a reconstruction of formation of the State Paper Office. Central to his analysis is the status of letters sent to government officials, such as the Cecils, which were at once addressed to private individuals and officeholders. The distinction between private letters and state papers, household repositories and state archives was blurred during the early seventeenth century, and our understanding of the formation of the State Paper Office is contested, capable of multiple and divergent readings dependent on which archive is privileged. Ultimately the essay illustrates the degree to which preservation of letters helped to construct a particular form of narrative about the self and about office. Early modern letters, as this volume shows, were peculiar and complex material texts, rendered all the more complex by the archival conditions and their afterlives.

PART I

Material Practices

CHAPTER I

From Palatino to Cresci

Italian Writing Books and the Italic Scripts of Early Modern English Letters

JONATHAN GIBSON

In this essay, I suggest that the model hands found in certain sixteenth-century Italian writing manuals provide essential information for anyone wanting to understand the varieties of italic script in early modern English letters. In particular, I want to emphasize the importance of a dispute between two mid-century writing masters, Giovambattista Palatino and Giovan Francesco Cresci, who provided strikingly divergent models for the cancellaresca, or Italian chancery hand, the forebear of early modern English italic.[1] The nature of the dispute, the details of Palatino's and Cresci's recommendations, and the importance of this episode for the history of italic in general have all long been known to historians of calligraphy. James Wardrop, Stanley Morison, and A. S. Osley summarized these matters with exemplary clarity in books and articles in the second half of the last century.[2] However, in a striking example of the disabling effect of artificial disciplinary boundaries, the direct relevance of the Cresci-Palatino dispute to early modern English italic practice—to letters and other specific manuscripts—seems to have gone unnoticed. Scholarship on early modern English manuscripts makes little use either of the Italian manuals or of the English-language analysis of them, which in turn does not deal in any detail with the use of italic in early modern English manuscripts.[3] The work of handwriting scholars such as Osley, Wardrop, and Morison belongs to a context alien to many present-day academic specialists in early modern

manuscript culture, as it is closely related to the twentieth-century English revival of italic calligraphy, a movement inspired by William Morris and led by
Edward Johnston and Alfred Fairbank. Unlike much recent manuscript research,
their investigations have a strongly prescriptive undertow, a belief in the aesthetic
and social value for the modern world of the mid-sixteenth-century italic hand.[4]

Attempting to bridge this disciplinary divide, my argument here is that
the shift from one style of italic to another that occurs in the Italian writing-book
tradition—the shift, broadly speaking, from Palatino's recommendations to
Cresci's—is reflected in the italic used in early modern English manuscripts:
mid- to late sixteenth-century manuscripts use Palatinian forms, while the influence of Cresci's models is only visible in the italic written in English closer to
the turn of the century and throughout the early 1600s. An awareness of the
distinction between these two forms of italic is useful, I suggest, both for paleographers seeking to date, identify, and distinguish hands, and for researchers
with a wider interest in the social and cultural roles of handwriting in the period.

The dispute between Palatino and Cresci was, at heart, a very simple one.
Palatino promoted a simple and elegant style of writing cancellaresca that
could produce rather angular and mechanistic results. In reaction, Cresci advocated a much more rounded and cursive (joined-up) style. Difference in
letter shape reflected a difference in materials: while Palatino used an edged
nib (like a modern-day "calligrapher's pen"), Cresci preferred a nib sharpened
more to a point. Though both Palatino's and Cresci's books had a decisive
influence on English manuscript practice, in many cases that influence must
have been indirect, flowing not directly from Palatino's or Cresci's models but
from derivative printed books and manuscript samples.[5] In Italy Palatino's and
Cresci's recommendations appeared within a culture already using cancellaresca widely: in this context, Palatino and Cresci seem to a certain extent to
have been codifying preexistent practice. In England, on the other hand, practice followed in the wake of the writing masters and their manuals (both
Cresci and Palatino themselves and other writing masters influenced by them),
not least because of the comparative rarity of italic handwriting in the earlier
part of the sixteenth century in England.[6]

Palatinian Italic

Cancellaresca is an offshoot of the hands confected by fifteenth-century Flo-
rentine humanists, in particular Poggio Bracciolini and Niccolò Niccoli, who

felt that "gothic" late medieval script was an inappropriate medium in which to copy the classics of Latin literature. The "humanistic" hands these men developed combined Roman capitals with small letters copied (with added serifs to top and tail letters) from Carolingian minuscule, a script of the ninth, tenth, and eleventh centuries wrongly thought by the humanists to represent an ancient Roman style of writing. In its more formal manifestations, humanistic script was the basis for the earliest roman print fonts (featuring, typically, a double-bodied lowercase "a"); in its faster, cursive, form (frequently slanted and typically featuring a single-bodied "*a*"), it was the basis for the earliest italic type.[7]

Cancellaresca derives ultimately from humanistic cursive script and owes its name to its employment from the mid-fifteenth century onward in the papal chancery in Rome, as the swift, practical medium for the production of breves, or briefs, short and straightforward letters in the pope's name. It was described in printed writing books published in Italy from the first quarter of the sixteenth century onward, three of which—texts by Sigismondo Fanti, Ludovico degli Arrighi da Vicenza, and Giovanantonio Tagliente—antedated Palatino's publications.[8] While Fanti's book was—as a result, it seems, of a logistical mix-up—unillustrated, the others used wood blocks to print samples of the hands they were describing. These books promoted cancellaresca as a swift, cursive style of writing suited to everyday use.[9] This script was narrow and ovoid, sloping forward. In late fifteenth-century and early sixteenth-century England, italic or cancellaresca of the sort written by Arrighi was used as a swift business hand in only very limited circumstances: in Latin texts produced at the universities and in diplomatic correspondence.[10] Arrighi, author of the pithiest of the manuals, *La operina*, worked first in the papal chancery, later designing several italic print fonts; he seems not to have survived the sack of Rome in 1527.

As described by Arrighi, cancellaresca was written with a pen with a broad-edged nib cut square across at the end. If such a pen is held with its edge always at an angle of forty-five degrees to the writing line, moving the nib diagonally upward (from bottom left to top right) will produce a diagonal line as thin as the edge of the nib. Moving the nib diagonally downward (from top left to bottom right) will produce a much thicker line, as thick as the nib is wide. Horizontal and vertical lines will be reasonably thick and a curving line will vary in thickness.[11] Figure 1.1 illustrates some of these possibilities. As the variation between thicks and thins in this style of writing is the result of changes in the pen's direction rather than of the pressure of the nib on the paper, it is sometimes referred to as "directional" writing.

Figure 1.1. Writing with an edged pen. Giuliantonio Hercolani, *Lo scrittor vtile et brieue segretario* (1574), plate 4 (Cambridge University Library, shelfmark SSS.28.15), detail. Reproduced by kind permission of the Syndics of Cambridge University Library.

Arrighi's manual claims that each cancellaresca letter begins with one or the other of two contrasting strokes—a horizontal "flat and thick" (*piano & grosso*) line and a right to left, "slanting and thin" (*acuto et sottile*) diagonal.[12] He does not discuss the curves that frequently also appear in his sample scripts, introducing "the essential curved line" "almost surreptitiously."[13] Curved lines are mentioned by Fanti and Tagliente, who were, in terms of historical influence, much less important than Palatino, "a member of academies, a sonneteer, a man of scholarly interests, political sympathies and social connections."[14] The provision in Palatino's 1540 *Libro nuovo* of lucid stroke-by-stroke instructions ultimately had the effect of simplifying and rigidifying cancellaresca, despite the many similarities between his model alphabets and those of Arrighi and Tagliente.[15]

Palatino's great claim was that every letter in cancellaresca could be written with just three types of straight line. The first—the equivalent of Arrighi's thick horizontal stroke—Palatino calls the *testa*, or head.[16] Palatino's second stroke, the *traverso*, is close to being a vertical line. Palatino affects sur-

Figure 1.2. Palatino's three strokes. Giovambattista Palatino, *Libro . . . Nel qual s'insegna à scriuere ogni sorte lettera* (Rome, 1556), sig. A7ᵛ (British Library, shelfmark 819.e.33). © British Library Board.

prise at its omission from other manuals: "I am amazed," he says, "that all previous writers dealing with the methods of handwriting have not mentioned this stroke, which is undoubtedly just as essential as the others" The third stroke, the *taglio*, is the same as Arrighi's thin diagonal stroke.[17] Despite Palatino's blustering, Tagliente had in fact some years earlier written about all three strokes. Although like Palatino he called the thin stroke *taglio* and the vertical stroke *traverso*, he used a different name for the *testa*: *corpo*. or "body."[18] The three strokes can be seen in Figure 1.1 (an image using Tagliente's terms and taken from a manual by a later writing master, Giulantonio Hercolani) and, with Palatino's terminology, in Figure 1.2.

Palatino's stroke-by-stroke instructions for writing *d* are reproduced in Figure 1.3. He starts by drawing the lower part—the bowl—of the letter. First a *testa* is made by pulling the pen from left to right across the paper then pushing it back again to the letter's starting point. A short *traverso* descends to the bottom left corner of the letter and a *taglio* is then drawn to a point at the right of the initial *testa*. Now the stem, or ascender, is constructed out of a *testa* and a *traverso*: the latter drops down to join the lower part of the letter, which is finished off with a little *taglio*, or *taglietto*. The final images in the sequence illustrate Palatino's point that the lower part of the *d* is identical to an *a* ("La .d. nasce da la lettera .a.").[19]

Like Arrighi, Palatino suppresses mention of the curved line—even though his own model alphabets (Figures 1.4 and 1.5) clearly use it. The implication is that cancellaresca consists of a simple succession of straight lines, an approach that, according to modern historians of handwriting, turned out to be a recipe for mechanistic penwork. "All the learner has to do," Wardrop points out, "is to study the model as they set [Palatino's] triad in motion, monotonously back and forth—testa, traverso, taglio—and so on da capo, like the evolutions of a Roman military exercise."[20] Palatino's dissection of cancellaresca

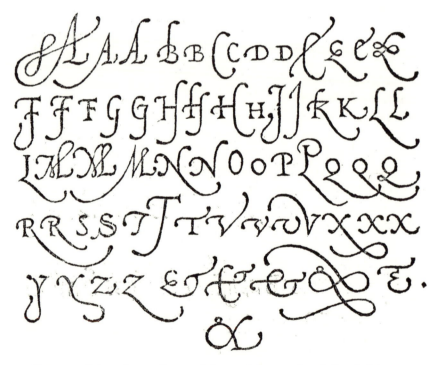

Figure 1.3. How to write the letter *d*. Palatino, *Libro*, sig. B2ᵛ. © British Library Board.

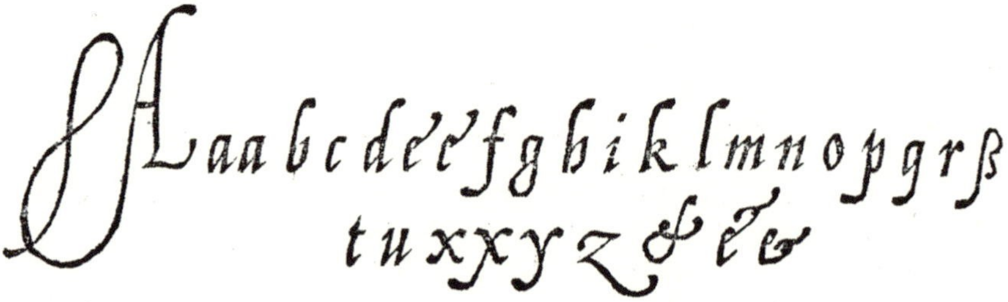

Figure 1.4. Palatino's cancellaresca. Palatino, *Libro*, sig. B8ᵛ. © British Library Board.

Figure 1.5. Palatino's cancellaresca. Palatino, *Libro*, sig. B8ʳ. © British Library Board.

into a succession of different strokes also slowed the script down, in effect inviting the writer to make letters out of distinct strokes separated by pen lifts. Another characteristic of Palatino's lettering is its attenuated proportions: Palatino's letters, with a height-width ratio of 2:1, are taller and narrower than Arrighi's and Tagliente's, which have been estimated at about 3:5. As Osley points out, this leaves less space for diagonal lines, which therefore "have to be made at a sharper angle" and tend to produce "a zig-zag or saw-edge effect."[21] Rather than a nib cut square across, Palatino advised the use for cancellaresca of a nib cut at a slight angle, its right corner slightly lower than its left, thickening the *traverso*.[22]

Under Palatino's example, cancellaresca became stiffer and more formal: in short, less of a practical business hand. This is the form of italic that, as part of humanist pedagogy, was prevalent in the England of the mid-sixteenth century, the neat and swift version of the script advocated by Arrighi and Tagliente having failed to have taken root outside the universities and the diplomatic corps.[23] Manuals by succeeding midcentury writing masters reproduced or slightly adapted Palatino's recommendations: notably, Vespasiano Amphiareo and Augustino da Siena in Italy and Juan de Yciar and Francisco Lucas in Spain produced more rounded scripts.[24] Palatino's *Libro* went through many editions: in James Wardrop's estimation, Palatino "might claim to have influenced, not necessarily for the better, the handwriting of half Europe."[25]

"Palatinian" letterforms, whether derived directly or indirectly from Palatino's manual, can be found in many of the manuscripts of young Tudor aristocrats and royals. Edward VI's indebtedness is unsurprising, as he is known to have owned a copy of the *Libro nuovo*.[26] I have written elsewhere both about the Palatinian script of Edward and his sister Princess Elizabeth (later Elizabeth I).[27] Figures 1.4–1.8 illustrate the constitutive role of Palatino's model alphabets in Elizabeth's famous signature and in her formal italic hand more generally. The Italian manuals did not give step-by-step instructions for the construction of capitals, instead simply providing sample alphabets.[28] In practice, early modern writers of italic used the decorative flourishes in these models as a basis for their own improvisations. Here, the flourish below the *R* at the end of Elizabeth's signature (Figure 1.6) elaborates on one found in Palatino's page of abbreviations (Figure 1.7): although Palatino's *R* here stands for *Reverendissimo* rather than *Regina*. Meanwhile Elizabeth's *Z* (Figure 1.6) is linked to a flourish that appears in the *Libro* one leaf earlier, close to Palatino's own flourished *Z* (Figure 1.8). Elizabeth's letters have more extravagant ascenders and descenders than Edward's; accordingly there is more

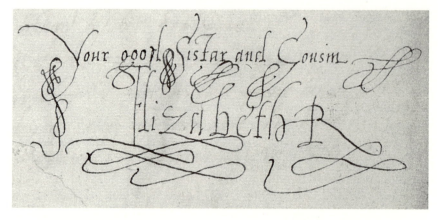

Figure 1.6. Elizabeth I's signature. BL, Cott. MS, Caligula CI, fol. 367ʳ. Elizabeth I to Mary, Queen of Scots, 21 December 1568. © British Library Board.

Figure 1.7. Palatino's abbreviations for *Reverendo* and *Reverendissimo*. Palatino, *Libro*, sig. C1ʳ. © British Library Board.

Figure 1.8. One of Palatino's decorative flourishes. Palatino, *Libro*, sig. B8ʳ. © British Library Board.

interlinear white space. Her Palatinian script is a particularly "pointed" one, with needle-sharp angles between the first *traverso* and *taglio* of her *d*'s, and there is little slope. Lady Jane Grey's Palatino-influenced letters are somewhat shorter and squatter than either Edward's or Elizabeth's. The version written by Barnaby Fitzpatrick, Edward VI's "whipping boy," by contrast, is confident and swift, incorporating more curves than Edward, Elizabeth, or Lady Jane.[29]

In what circumstances was this style of writing used in England, and what were its associations? It was taught to and used by young mid-Tudor aristocrats, as we have seen, and it was important at Oxford and Cambridge (a well-known example being the controlled hand written by Bartholomew Dodington)[30] and in diplomatic correspondence. It was also used for some fair-copy literary manuscripts, for material in Latin or one of the romance languages (whether whole texts or just single words or quotations in manuscripts otherwise written in a different script type), and for other kinds of intratextual emphasis. It also became particularly associated with women's writing.[31] Jonathan Goldberg has written extensively about the high status accorded italic by Renaissance writing masters and their claims that their model alphabets underpinned (and were duplicated in) a high-status calligraphic italic written by aristocrats and royalty. Viewed against the manuscript record these claims seem somewhat hollow.[32] Although they may have learned to write a formal italic hand in their youth, in the mid- to late sixteenth century, when Palatino's influence was at its height in England, adult males of high status did not as a matter of course replicate Palatinian models in their adult writings.[33] Partly, I think, this was due to the slowness and noncursiveness of Palatino's script, which had the effect of distinguishing it sharply from the following three types of cursive hand—swifter, more practical, and, therefore, implicitly more "thoughtful" and prestigious—used in the same period:

1. Secretary hand, the thorny "gothic" script that was the standard medium for everyday correspondence and that was used across all literate parts of society in formal, informal, and semiformal versions.[34]
2. Loose varieties of informal, simplified non-Palatinian italic, written, like informal and semiformal secretary hand, with a rounded or pointed nib rather than an edged one. These were used for informal purposes—personal correspondence, notes, drafts—by middle-class and aristocratic men, particularly men connected with the court.
3. Mixed hand, used for the same purposes and by the same sort of people as loose italic. "Mixed hand" is a term that can be used to describe a variety of different kinds of mixtures of secretary and loose italic letterforms.[35]

In large part because of their greater rapidity, cursive hands of the three types listed above had more worldly, businesslike overtones than Palatinian script, which tended to be used for presentation manuscripts and fair copies. The underlying attitude is not specific to the early modern period, for the assumption that fast, even messy, handwriting has a closer intellectual connection to the meaning of what is written than slow calligraphic neatness is a natural one: many people compose a text in rough longhand before typing out a fair copy, and the first stage usually involves more thought.[36] Such associations had added purchase in early modern England because the production of fair copies was routinely farmed out to subordinates, whether the letter writer's personal secretary or some more casually employed scribe. Writing in one's own hand was considered a sign of intimacy, a means of giving weight to a letter and asserting a strong personal relationship between the correspondents.[37] A hand that was clearly not the hand of a scribe or secretary would thus have made a letter seem more confidential. Here is another reason for the usefulness of the three cursive styles: as their letterforms were less standardized, they could be more easily personalized than formal italic, allowing correspondents to distinguish each other's hands from the hands of scribes with less difficulty.[38]

The use of a scribe was sometimes very convenient: its formal, distancing effect strengthened documents produced under particular circumstances—important set pieces such as crucial petitionary letters to prospective patrons or literary presentation manuscripts, for example. Scribes and secretaries wrote out letters for their masters or mistresses both in fair (or "set") secretary and in fair italic.[39] When working in Ireland between 1580 and 1582 as the personal secretary of Arthur, Lord Grey of Wilton, for example, Edmund Spenser used two formal hands: a secretary hand for everyday business letters and a set italic in the tradition of Palatino for important letters from Grey to the queen.[40] Texts written beautifully in Palatinian italic by scholars,[41] women, or children had in common with scribally produced material a whiff of the schoolroom, a certain artificiality. Thomas Nashe's ironic praise of the formal italic hand of his antagonist, the Cambridge don Gabriel Harvey—it was, he claimed, even better than that of a "magistrall scribe, that holds all his liuing by setting school-boies copies"—is well known.[42] Speed was, perhaps, the root of the matter: women were taught italic, Grace Ioppolo argues, because it was "suitable for the type of occasional writing that women were supposed to do, rather than the daily writing represented by secretary hand."[43] Italic was also, as Nashe's comment reveals, associated with copying rather than original composition. While the ability both of women and of children to write a beautiful italic script was likely to garner praise in itself, the patriarchal culture of the time meant that both were also under less pressure than adult males to produce original content. Women were, as Susan Frye says, "encouraged . . .

to study calligraphy" partly because "it was thought of as copying rather than as any genuine work in the public domain."[44] Letters in formal italic from children to their parents, meanwhile, "highly calligraphic epistles penned as examples of filial deference,"[45] were clearly designed to display calligraphic skill at least as much as intellectual ability. Italic had, also, the reputation of being an easy hand to read and understand; there could be an exciting mystery about the gnarled forms of secretary hand (implicit in its very name), and this was mentioned by more than one early modern English writing master.[46]

Stigma, too (the "stigma of calligraphy"?), seems to have been attached to the semiformal versions of Palatinian script written particularly by women—attempts to write the inherently slow Palatinian hand fast. The deliberation of Palatino's stroke-by-stroke method makes such script look clumsy. A tendency for the horizontal stroke (Palatino's *testa*) to disappear and for the hand to be dominated by the vertical or right-left diagonal line (the *traverso*) and the hairline left-right diagonal (the *taglio*) can be seen in letters written in informal Palatinian italic by Elizabeth, Countess of Shrewsbury (Bess of Hardwick), Mary, Queen of Scots, and Lady Grace Cavendish as well as many others.[47] Meanwhile, the three types of cursive hand listed above, in effect gendered male (italic, secretary, and mixed), tended to blur into one another.[48] Spenser used a mixed hand to annotate documents and occasionally to write Latin text; it seems likely that many of his more "personal" and casual letters (informal letters to friends and family, for example), none of which is known to have survived, would have been written in this hand.[49] The loose adult italic of Robert Devereux, second Earl of Essex, is a very different beast from the Palatinian calligraphy he wrote as a child.[50] Elizabeth I's "scrating hand" is an unusual example of a female rough mixed hand, perhaps deliberately adapted by the queen to avoid the adverse connotations of the semiformal Palatinian italic written by so many other women.[51]

Palatinian italic, however, was used by aristocrats in one very important way, as an important component in the part of every letter most intimately bound up with the writer's identity: the signature. Many middle-class and aristocratic letter writers, like Elizabeth I, worked complicated variations on the ornaments in the writing books to give their signatures a unique flavor and included Palatinian letterforms in their signature even when writing the rest of the letter themselves in a very different script, whether italic, secretary, or mixed. An example is the signature of the dramatist and, perhaps, scrivener Thomas Kyd, which includes a Palatinian *d* quite different from the Crescian letterforms in what seems to be his formal italic.[52] Here, in what looks like an

intriguing paradox, the most apparently artificial and alienating script type—
formal, Palatinian italic—is being used at the point of a letter where maximum
authenticity is required. Perhaps the contrast with the main, meaning-
bearing text of the letter, however, is the explanation, for the significance of a
signature is very different from the complex meaning of an extended passage
of text. The signature simply stands in lieu of its writer's presence: it is more
like an object (a seal, say) than a sentence:[53] the artificiality of Palatinian
italic is thus fully appropriate to its function.[54]

Crescian Italic

The approach to cancellaresca set forth in 1560 in the first writing manual of
Giovan Francesco Cresci, the *Essemplare*, differs drastically from Palatino's.[55]
Cresci's ideas and the letterforms he printed for emulation were just as influential as, perhaps even more influential than, Palatino's. In England, Crescian
elements begin to make themselves fully felt from the 1580s onward, becoming particularly important in the following century. Crucially, in the longer
term, Cresci influenced not just letter shape but also the balance between
script styles, helping to undo the contrast we have just been examining, between
formal Palatinian italic and other scripts (secretary, rough italic, and mixed),
that had previously shaped early modern English correspondents' experience
of letter writing.

Writing twenty years after the appearance of the older man's manual,
Cresci does not name Palatino, but his intention is clear. He claims that most
people now dislike "the old-fashioned, spurious cancellaresca because it is too
lethargic and slow, and most of all because it is unattractive and lacks any
speed." Cresci gives the following explanation: "The reason is it is too pointed
and sharp and, on account of this sharpness, it is difficult to join one letter
with another." Cresci thinks "old-fashioned" cancellaresca does not slope forward enough either. The key problem, he says, though, is the way in which
the nib is cut: "The cause of its being slow to write is that they employ a pen
which is too broad and square at the tip and, when they write, they hold it at
too much to the side." Cresci, then, criticizes the use of the edged pen. He, by
contrast, uses a nib cut to more of a rounded point—not cut cross-wise. In
his handwriting samples, he tells the reader, "you can see how legible the letters are and how readily one is joined to the other, because they are of a somewhat rounded character and the strokes, with which they are made, delight

Figure 1.9. How to write the letter *b*. Giovan Francesco Cresci, *Essemplare di piv sorti di lettere* (1600), plate xxxviii (British Library, shelfmark C.119.c.8). © British Library Board.

the eye; moreover it is possible to write them with dexterity because they have been given their proper slope and because the pen that I use has been cut to a narrower, a little more rounded point than has hitherto been the custom."[56] For Cresci, in an obvious reaction against Palatino's dependence on three types of straight line, the basis of most lowercase letters was what he calls "the round body" of the letter. Again, contrasting with Palatino's parade-ground exercises, he claims that almost all his letters "are made with one stroke or movement of the pen."[57]

In moving away from the edged pen, Cresci is offering scribes more flexibility. Thick parts of letters are now produced not by angling the pen to get the thick part of the nib in the right place but either by using pressure (splaying the nib by pushing hard on the paper makes a thicker line) or by curling the pen round to create circular blobs. This last technique is illustrated by the diagram from Cresci's first book reproduced in Figure 1.9. The wedges at the top of Palatino's ascenders (Figures 1.3 and 1.4) look at first sight a bit like the blobs at the top of Cresci's, but in reality they are constructed very differently. Palatino, like Arrighi before him, started his letters with a double *testa*: he drew the thick part of the nib across the page right to left and then, on top of the first line backward, left to right.[58] As his diagram shows, what Cresci does is create a little filled circle at the top of his ascenders: it becomes a solid circle by turning round on itself and filling itself in before becoming a line that descends to the bottom of the letter, a practice English paleographers call "clubbing."[59] Cresci is also much more permissive than earlier writing masters about joins between letters.

The flexibility that Cresci gave himself led to the assembly of various different model cancellaresca alphabets. Three from his magnum opus of 1571, *Il perfetto scrittore*, are reproduced in Figures 1.10–1.12: they become gradually

Figure 1.10. Cresci's *cancellaresca formatella*. Cresci provides a capitals alphabet for this script that is identical to the one he provides for *cancellaresca alquanto corrente* (reproduced in Figure 1.11). Cresci, *Il perfetto scrittore*, fol. B1ʳ. © British Library Board.

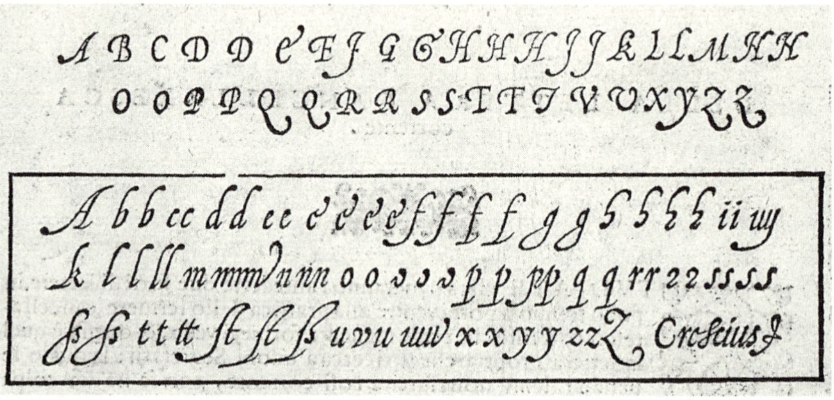

Figure 1.11. Cresci's *cancellaresca alquanto corrente*. The capitals Cresci provides for this script are identical to those in *cancellaresca formatella* (Figure 1.10). Cresci, *Il perfetto scrittore*, fol. B4ʳ. © British Library Board.

looser and curlier, and progressively less like Palatino's models. First comes the stiffest, *cancellaresca formatella* (small letters in Figure 1.10, capitals in Figure 1.11), then a "rather" cursive cancellaresca—*cancellaresca alquanto corrente* (Figure 1.11), then finally the full cursive, *cancellaresca corrente* (Figure 1.12). The differences between Palatino's small letters (Figure 1.4) and the first of these alphabets of Cresci's (Figure 1.10) are comparatively subtle. The difference between the practice of the two writing masters is particularly noticeable in their *o*'s: Cresci's is clearly more circular, while Palatino's resembles a rhombus—a square pulled out of shape. A similar effect is noticeable in the bowls (derived from *o*, of course) of *a*, *c*, *d*, and *p*. Palatino's bowls have clearer "corners" than Cresci's. Similar angularity distinguishes Palatino's *c*'s and *e*'s from Cresci's semicircular forms. The same contrast can be seen at work in the letters based on minims (short vertical lines), *i*, *m*, *n*, and *u*; in these letters, where Cresci curves, Palatino has a straight line. The small letters of Cresci's second alphabet (*alquanto corrente*; Figure 1.11) are taller and thinner and the curves more exaggerated and sinuous. There are a number of new forms: an *f* and a long *s* with descenders that curve first backward (to the left) and then, immediately returning on themselves, forward (to the right); one *h* lacking a left foot but compensating for it with a right foot that curls round and ends in a blob; another *h* whose curling right foot ends with a curl in the opposite direction instead of a blob; an *o* open on its left side with a blob at top right; a *p* with its bowl open at the bottom; a curly *r* in the shape of a top-heavy reversed *s* or a wonky *2*. The third of Cresci's scripts—*cancellaresca corrente*— takes things further still (Figure 1.12): there is now a distinct rightward bulge in many of Cresci's "verticals" and ascenders curl lavishly forward with longer blobs almost touching the tops of succeeding letters and ending with highly exaggerated little curves back to the left. There is one important new letterform in Figure 1.12 (*bottom*): a *d* with an ascender that curves backward (to the left) and whose bowl lacks a *taglietto* at bottom right.

Cresci's scorching critique was rebuffed in print by Palatino, who, nevertheless, rather hypocritically, copied Cresci's script.[60] A later writing master, Marcello Scalzini, did to Cresci what Cresci had done to Palatino, attacking him for producing writing, with too thick a nib, that was too slow and formal. Scalzini's alphabets use forms similar to those in Cresci's *cancellaresca corrente* (Figure 1.12) but are still looser and more extravagant, written with a lightly held quill.[61] A flood of seventeenth-century writing books reproduced hands very similar to Cresci's.[62]

The first English writing book, John de Beau Chesne's *A Booke Containing Divers Sortes of Hands* (1571), included both Palatinian and Crescian alphabets; the seventeenth-century English manuals that followed are heavily Crescian.[63]

From the late sixteenth century onward, Crescian *cancellaresca formatella* tended to be used in England instead of formal Palatinian italic: an example, written by a scribe of the Elizabethan and Jacobean courtier Sir Arthur Gorges, is illustrated in Figure 1.13. Confusingly to modern eyes, this slower and more formal Crescian hand was identified in late sixteenth-century and early seventeenth-century England as "Roman," while the more cursive Crescian

Figure 1.12. Capitals alphabet (*top*) and Sample text (*bottom*) for Cresci's *cancellaresca corrente*. Cresci does not include a minuscules (small letter) alphabet for this script. Cresci, *Il perfetto scrittore*, fols. B8ᵛ, B5ʳ. © British Library Board.

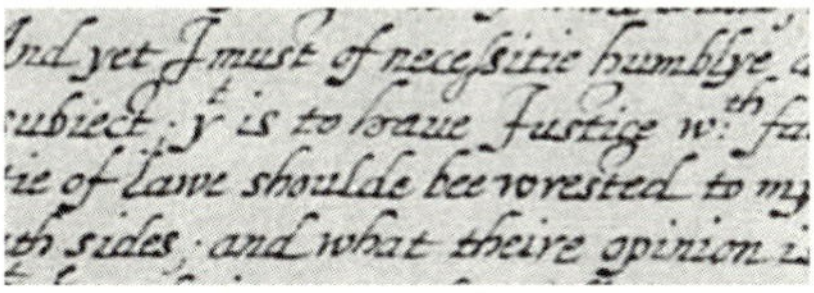
nd yet I must of necessitie humblye a
ubiect, yt is to brave Justice wth fa
ie of lawe shoulde bee wrested to my
th sides, and what theire opinion i

Figure 1.13. The Crescian hand of one of Sir Arthur Gorges's scribes. Hatfield House, Cecil Papers, 75/53: Sir Arthur Gorges to Sir Robert Cecil, December 1599. Reproduced courtesy of the Marquess of Salisbury, Hatfield House.

hands were referred to as "Italian."[64] During this period, Crescian *formatella* performed a very similar cultural function to that performed by its precursor, Palatinian italic: the association with women, children, and scholars remained in place. The "sweet Roman hand" written by Shakespeare's Olivia would have been, I think, either Crescian *cancellaresca formatella* or an older, Palatinian italic.[65] Arthur Gorges uses Crescian *formatella*, in the hand of a scribe, in much the same way as Lord Grey of Wilton used Palatinian italic: to make formal, high-stakes appeals to prestigious addressees.[66] For his more casual and more personal correspondence, Gorges used his own cursive mixed hand;[67] meanwhile, for legal and administrative matters, he used a scribal secretary hand.[68]

Crescian *formatella* differed from Palatinian italic in one important respect: the use of the pointed quill meant that it was much easier to use it as the basis for a more informal script. Cresci's use of a more pointed pen than Palatino—and the examples provided both by Cresci and by the many writing masters he influenced—gave writers much more freedom than had been made possible within Palatino's method. There were now many different ways in which to loop and club one's way from letter to letter. Accordingly, clearly "Crescian" examples of handwriting in English letters vary considerably. Some still have an underlying Palatinian shape: Crescian clubs top angular letterforms, for example, in the formal hand of John Palmer and the informal hand of Lettice Kinnersley.[69] Because Crescian clubs were essentially filled-in loops, a much closer relationship was possible between this formal hand and informal italic, the latter simply tending to open clubs up into loops and to link letters more freely. The two italic hands written by Lady Mary Wroth exemplify this: the hand used for personal letters and literary drafting is a loosened-up, cursive form of the neatly clubbed script used for more formal communications and for literary fair copies.[70] A similar point can be made about the hands of Sir Henry Wotton.[71] Sir John Harington, meanwhile, wrote a neat and businesslike Crescian italic that is easy to confuse with a rather more controlled Crescian script written by a scribe.[72] As Crescian italic was written with a round-nibbed pen, its forms could also easily meld with those of informal secretary hand and informal mixed hand: John Davies, indeed, claims of the "Italian" (or cursive Crescian) hand "who hath this hand at command, may command with facility all other usefull hands."[73] Courtly writers of the late sixteenth century, like John Donne and Sir Walter Ralegh, were, in any case, already writing small and neat variations of loose italic and informal mixed hand—a script style not far removed from Crescian *formatella*,[74] and the process of convergence was facilitated by the gothic origins of some of the letterforms that Cresci introduced to cancellaresca—the *r* like a backward *s* or a *2* (medieval paleographers' "round" *r*); the *d* with a backward-curving ascender ("round or "uncial" *d*)—for these letters were already part of secretary hand.[75] Lewes Bagot is one of many letter writers who produced a neat Crescian hand that nevertheless included a round *d*. In his case, while the ascender of his round *d* is clubbed, many of his other ascenders and descenders (in, for example, *b*, *f*, long *s*, and *t*) open out into loops. The more sloping formal Crescian hand of Bagot's cousin, Jane Skipwith, features more clubbed ascenders, and her clubbed *d* is not a "round" one; the descenders of her *y*'s have closed loops; the loop of her *g* is open.[76]

As I hope these examples have been conveying, the flexibility of Crescian script had a tendency to elide distinctions between formal and informal, male and female, aristocratic and middle-class, secretary and italic, scribe and author. It was able to do precisely the job that had been done by late fifteenth-century and early sixteenth-century cancellaresca script in Italy: true multipurpose business italic could take root in England. The stage was set for the development of later seventeenth-century "round hand" and its transmogrification, in the eighteenth century, into copperplate, the bane of the twentieth-century italic revival.[77] By the time of the Restoration, distinctions between women's and men's hands are hard to formulate: Lucy Hutchinson claimed to have forged her husband's hand in an important letter, a claim that modern scholars have found difficult to pronounce upon, so similar are the script forms used by the two Hutchinsons.[78]

Conclusion

Knowing about the Palatino-Cresci dispute is useful to students of early modern letters in a variety of different ways. The broad and impressionistic contrasts

I have been drawing are, it should be stressed, in need of far more detailed investigation, and my comments on letterforms are cruder than the fine discriminations used by paleographers to identify the hands of specific individuals. I hope, though, that I have demonstrated the value of mapping early modern English italic practice onto the recommendations of the Italian writing masters. As work in this field develops, this process should become a necessary step in deciding which letterforms are unique to a specific hand and which are not. Clearly, as early modern writers did not consistently reproduce the letterforms of the manuals, individual hands will have different relationships with model alphabets (some close, some distant and complex). More generally, future research will surely clarify links between different kinds of Palatinian and Crescian hands and specific writing books, both continental and English. Classifying hands in this way should also help us to begin to excavate more detailed information about the sociocultural provenances of different scripts (including secretary hand, mixed hand, and round hand) and thus to make finer-grained statements about the relationship between different script types and factors such as region, gender, institution, occupation, and family. At the macro level, such work is likely to make considerable use of digital images and pattern recognition software; at the micro level, it will need to draw in material from individual case histories—the detailed contexts, rhetoric, physical structure, and delivery histories of individual letters.[79] Only once such work has been undertaken will we be able to assess properly the cultural meanings or "bibliographical codes" (in Jerome J. McGann's term)[80] of the different varieties of early modern English italic; only then will we able to begin to plumb the full significance of that most obtrusive and most mysterious of the physical features of any early modern letter: the inked letters on the page.

CHAPTER 2

Conveying Correspondence

Early Modern Letter Bearers, Carriers, and Posts

MARK BRAYSHAY

To augment the service provided by royal messengers, from the time of Henry VIII, "standing" posts for the conveyance of official letters by relays of horses and riders were laid along the principal highways of the realm. Until 1635, letter carriage by the state's posts was intended only for authorized government use. By then, however, in part to offset the escalating costs of carrying Crown letters, the services of its posts were offered to the public. Nevertheless, there was no overnight transformation in the ways that personal correspondence was conveyed: England's modern postal service was not suddenly called into existence. A range of other arrangements continued to operate for many decades thereafter, including letter carrying by friends and acquaintances, by private carriers, and by the personal servants and messengers retained by institutions, civic bodies, and wealthy households. Regular services were also offered by common carriers, commercial posts, and couriers employed by corporate organizations.[1] The mode of delivery selected by letter writers depended on the particular circumstances and purposes of their correspondence. Even after 1635, when the state made attempts to impose its monopoly on all letter carrying, the concession accorded to common carriers that allowed them legally to continue to convey private correspondence remained intact. It was not rescinded until 1710. Indeed, due to perceived threats of government interception of private letters and the imperfections and relative costliness of the Inland Letter Office, it still remained difficult to fully eliminate competition to the state's service.[2] Nevertheless, especially after the Restoration, the network of the Inland Letter Office became denser and spatially more extensive. In the 1680s, a Penny Post within London and Westminster, and embracing localities up to ten miles distant, was also formed, and a regularized packet service for England's transatlantic colonies was created.[3]

In the earlier Stuart era, therefore, although its extent was limited and there were uncertainties regarding the safety and reliability of conveyance, the basis of a state letter-carrying service was laid, and it was upon that foundation that the national postal service was thereafter gradually formed. This essay assesses the changing means by which letters—both official and private—were carried in the period between ca. 1500 and ca. 1640 and briefly glances ahead at further developments occurring before the end of seventeenth century. Clearly, an appreciation of the mechanisms, intricacies, and evolving characteristics of postal arrangements open to letter writers is critically important to an understanding of the cultures of correspondence of the early modern period.

Letters Conveyed by Relatives, Acquaintances, Servants, and Local Posts

Letters directed to the nobility and gentry, holders of prestigious offices, and representatives of the judiciary were routinely carried by the personal servants of the senders. Servants were similarly employed when an exchange of letters was undertaken with Privy Counsellors, principal secretaries of state, or other senior courtiers. Offering assured security and displaying appropriate respect, an added advantage was swift delivery and a means to receive replies by return. While bearers' journey costs were often reimbursed by the government for correspondence deemed important to state affairs, if funded by the sender, the expense of dispatching a servant could be heavy. For example, when John Percival, servant of York's "comon clerk" was sent in 1535 to carry "dyvers letters to my lord Chancellor Mr Cromwell" in London, his subsistence cost £2 3s. 4d., and £1 16s. was paid to hire his "ambling horse."[4] In 1550, Canterbury's chamberlain noted 8s. 9d. for George Coster's ride to "London with letters to the Counsell"; whenever possible, however, markedly cheaper foot posts were employed.[5] Travel on horseback often incurred unanticipated expenditure. In 1600, Coventry's mayor sent Francis Naller with letters concerning the enlistment of soldiers to Warwickshire's sheriff. Naller was reimbursed an extra 3d. to reshoe his horse, 6d. for fodder, and 10d. for his unexpected "bayt at

Birmarcham [Birmingham]."[6] The private accounts of the Earl of Bath for 1637–55 provide examples of various means employed by a noble household to carry correspondence. Although the earl's letters were both received and sent "by the post" (by then a publicly available service) and by commercial carriers, payments were recorded not only as rewards to letter bearers of other households but also to meet the expenses of servants such as John Gribble, who was frequently dispatched with letters.[7]

Another common means of sending private letters was by local men offering a commercial postal service.[8] Richard Carew reported the existence of foot posts providing weekly carriage on the main thoroughfares of late Elizabethan Cornwall "whose dispatch is welneere as speedy as the horses."[9] One of those to whom Carew referred was perhaps John May, a foot post for the town of Liskeard, whose will and inventory of 1628 shows that he combined his role as a post with that of husbandman.[10]

Options for the conveyance of letters beyond England and Wales were sometimes limited and, for example, within the realm of Ireland, often hazardous. When a messenger came unprotected from the Earl of Kildare to the English lord deputy in 1580, he was summarily hanged. Indeed, at the height of the Anglo-Irish conflict, those carrying letters for both sides risked attack. While serving as president of Munster, Sir George Carew habitually identified his letter bearers and commented on the dangers they faced; they included relatives, servants, and messengers of both the senders and the recipients.[11] Writing on 7 August 1602, Carew mentioned a "laid post" between Dublin and Cork temporarily erected by Lord Mountjoy; previously, some letters sent by sea had miscarried, others were brought by "foot messengers" described as "slow and negligent."[12]

While it is impossible to gauge the precise quantities of correspondence delivered by relatives, acquaintances, servants, or others acting in impromptu fashion as letter bearers, such carriers were undoubtedly often employed. Indeed, despite being improvised, unsystematic, and, in some instances, potentially dangerous and unreliable, personal letter conveyance of this kind continued to be undertaken throughout the early modern period.

Dedicated Private Courier Systems

A more sophisticated model for carrying letters, which subsequently influenced other systems, was developed by Italian merchants in the late fourteenth century. The operational mechanics may be gleaned from the archives of Francesco Marco Datini, whose mercantile business comprised trading companies in Italy and Spain. Datini's early correspondence was mostly carried overland on foot by couriers (*fanti*) covering about thirty miles per day on well-defined itineraries. Innkeepers (*osti*) managed the *fanti* and guaranteed delivery in return for annual subscription fees retrospectively adjusted to reflect the quantities and weights of letters actually carried. When more urgent correspondence was required, an express courier, a *fante con vantaggio*, could be hired at considerably higher cost.[13] Consortia of Italian merchants collaborated with innkeepers to operate a superior, exclusive letter-carrying service known as the *scarsella*. For example, by 1395, couriers connecting Pisa and Barcelona usually completed the round trip in three weeks, including a six-day rest at the terminus. The cost was eighteen florins but, shared among members of the syndicate according to the weight of each merchant's letters, the expense for individuals was kept low.[14]

In the fifteenth century, to convey correspondence securely between London, Dover, and Calais, foreign merchants based in England devised a service noticeably similar to the *scarsella*. Within a commercial treaty of February 1496 between England and Venice, Florence, the Netherlands, and the Hanseatic League, this so-called Strangers' Post was accorded freedom from state interference.[15] A postmaster managed the dispatch and return of couriers riding either hired hackneys or post-horses to carry the merchants' letters to and from Dover, and in ships crossing the Channel. Christian Shuffling was the Strangers' postmaster in the early years of Elizabeth's reign but, on his death in 1568, he was replaced by Raphael Van Den Putte whose reputation for reliability soon led to warrants for the conveyance of lower-risk English government packets into the Netherlands and France.[16]

The London Company of Merchant Adventurers also employed a postmaster. Thus, in the 1550s, William Paige arranged the conveyance of the merchants' letters between London, Antwerp, and elsewhere.[17] Paige was in turn engaged on an annual fee of 20s. by York's Company of Mercers and Merchant Adventurers to convey their letters to London and the Continent.[18] However, no other special arrangements appear to have existed for carrying the York merchants' letters, which were sent as need arose with packmen and carriers, or with servants, friends, or fellow merchants.[19] Private posts offering carriage to the Continent generally aroused government suspicion, and, in 1591, a prohibition was placed on all letter carriage to and from foreign places except by authorized couriers or the royal messengers.[20] However, even after

1608, when Matthew de Quester was appointed as postmaster for the carriage of all government letters for "foreign parts," informal arrangements for conveying packets across the Channel were still occasionally made. Thus, Edward Quarles, by then the Merchant Adventurers' postmaster, wrote to the Earl of Salisbury on 8 December 1609 enclosing letters and seeking allowance for similar past services.[21]

Letter Conveyance by Carriers

In addition to freight and passengers, both common and private carriers were prominent in the conveyance of letters. Common carriers, some of whom were licensed, regularly plied defined routes both within counties and regions and between London and provincial cities and towns. Letters were collected from inns or other public establishments and delivered to places en route and to the carrier's ultimate destination. Senders took their letters to the inn on the day or days of the carrier being there or simply entrusted them to the innkeeper to be given to the carrier when he came. Incoming letters might await collection at appointed inns but were more often distributed to the homes of recipients either by carriers' men or by local posts. Small payments recorded in surviving household and personal accounts as rewards given to foot posts or carriers' men bringing letters offer glimpses of this end-stage delivery process in operation. Private carriers, providing irregular part-time services, also conveyed letters. While it is not always certain whether the senders or the recipients met the letter-carriage costs, it is clear that for the entire Tudor and Stuart period common carriers offered a relatively inexpensive means for sending private correspondence and packages.[22] Moreover, references to letters and goods brought by carriers point to the existence of a dense network of services across the country. For example, Bryon Patton was a carrier linking York with London in 1562.[23] Canterbury's city chamberlain paid "Robynson the wagoner" in 1586.[24] John Gregorie was a carrier between Plymouth and Exeter for almost twenty years in the late 1500s and early 1600s, while Hugh Helmore operated between London and Exeter.[25] Probate records shed further light. Thus, William Lane was a carrier in Bodmin whose inventory included saddles, saddletrees (for packhorses), weighing scales, quills, and paper.[26] Unfortunately, despite an isolated attempt in 1630 to urge the formation of a national corporation of carriers and others involved in transportation activities, no comprehensive register of operators was established. Even John Taylor's famous 1637 *Carriers Cosmographie* provides a list of only *most* not *all* the "Carriers, Waggons, Foote-posts and Higglers" going into and out of London, and while it makes incidental reference to interconnections between the London carriers and local services beyond the metropolis, it is an imperfect record.

The best known of the Elizabethan and early Stuart carriers were the Hobsons of Cambridge. Thomas Hobson established his enterprise in 1561. His eldest son, also Thomas, inherited the business in 1568 and for the next sixty-two years ran a regular service to London from premises near St. Catharine's College. Hobson's national reputation was underlined when his name was invoked in Gervase Markham's 1617 book title: *Hobson's Horse-Load of Letters*, a tome prescribing letter composition for different categories of recipient.[27] The names of carriers licensed to serve the University of Oxford are known from 1553, when Robert Towe was appointed to provide a connection with London. By 1575, the university's license required *inter alia* that their carrier should depart for London on Wednesdays, returning by Saturday night, and must "provide some honest man to deliver every man's letters by Sunday noon at the latest."[28] In November 1581, Thomas Horn sought to transfer his license as London carrier to another provider while, for himself, he asked to serve as the university's carrier to Devon. Thereafter, sole carriers were engaged to connect with other localities. By 1640 there were nineteen providing links with places spread across England.[29] In 1674 new regulations stipulated ½d. for a single letter from Oxford to London; missives could be left for collection in college butteries.

Other evidence of carriers' rates for private letters is patchy but the university's charge seems remarkably low. The Devon household accounts of the Earl of Bath show that while he was in the city of Bath to take the waters in May 1648 letters brought by the carrier "from Lady Cope & one from Wantage" cost 4d., and another sent away "from Bath by the carrier" to Tawstock cost 3d. Nevertheless, the charge was only half that of sending a letter to the same destination by the state's postal service.[30]

Messengers and Pursuivants

Access to swift secure communications was essential for the exercise and retention of power. In England, messengers of the royal household traditionally composed the Crown's principal agency for the dispatch of letters and other documents.[31] In 1526, Henry VIII's chamber included four ordinary messengers, each in receipt annually of £5 17s. 4d. A fifth served the queen's chamber.[32]

There were, however, additional extraordinary messengers receiving no wages but entitled to their riding costs. By the later sixteenth century, royal messengers could claim a flat-rate daily "riding allowance" of 3s. 4d., but they also accrued additional ad hoc earnings from "rewards" bestowed by recipients of government communications. State expenditure on messengers' riding charges grew inexorably. In 1564, the chamber alone spent £438 4s. 4d. on "messengers, gromes, and others" sent by the council to various parts of the realm. By 1600, the total was £1,506 18s. 6d.[33] On the accession of King James, two more ordinary messengers were engaged for the queen's chamber, an arrangement repeated for Henrietta Maria in the time of Charles I.[34] Moreover, by 1641, the number of ordinary messengers of the king's chamber had increased to forty; another eight "without fee"; and seventy-nine "messengers extraordinary."[35] The fate of chamber messengers during the Commonwealth is not easily established but, in July 1660, forty were appointed for Charles II; among them were sixteen who had previously served his father.[36]

Chamber messengers composed just one group of couriers in royal service. By the 1570s, four ordinary messengers served the Exchequer, and there was one each for the Council of the North, the Counties Palatine of Lancaster and Chester, the Court of First Fruits and Tenths, and the Court of Wards and Liveries. In 1600, another was engaged to serve the lord steward of the household and, by 1602, two more were appointed for the Council of the Marches and Wales.[37] To these must be added not only the large corps of extraordinary messengers but also the couriers accredited to convey letters overseas. For example, in the 1580s, there were at least seven accredited English messengers for France and ten for Flanders.[38]

All Crown messengers were bound by oath and wore livery with a badge or escutcheon bearing the royal coat of arms. They carried their letters, writs, proclamations, warrants, and subpoenas in special boxes.[39] When they delivered documents bearing legal force, took a suspect into custody, collected payments, or conducted inquiries, messengers exercised pursuivant powers. Although along the principal highways where standing posts were engaged, increasing quantities of government letters were conveyed by relays of postboys, messengers continued to be dispatched with high-priority letters, proclamations, and writs. Surviving evidence of their claims for riding charges indicates often lengthy and complicated itineraries undertaken to deliver correspondence directly to single or multiple recipients from whom they were required to obtain certificates of receipt.[40] Notwithstanding some incidents of attack, loss, or accident, an overwhelming majority of messengers completed their commissions within the realm without mishap.

Accredited couriers and the many others who carried letters overseas inevitably faced considerably greater peril, especially during periods of political instability and warfare. For example, in the late 1580s and during the 1590s, some were intercepted in France and their letters were seized. In June 1591, James Painter, one of England's couriers to Paris, was captured by "they of the Somme" and his letters were "cast into the sea."[41] Peter Brown, who served as England's courier to Dieppe, was intercepted in 1593 and imprisoned in Paris; a ransom of three hundred crowns was demanded for his release.[42]

Clearly, letter carrying on behalf of government by accredited state messengers occurred on a considerable scale in the early modern era. However, while messengers offered an exclusive, professional, and privileged means of state communication, their frequent reliance upon the realm's infrastructure of private post-horse providers prompted some government regulation of that network of posts. In turn, it was a logical development to engage the posts on some principal highways to convey a proportion of official correspondence. The requirements of state messengers for post-horses thus in part underpinned the foundation of England's postal service.

Posting and Letters Carried by the State's Posts

The assured availability of post-horses for hire at stages between twelve and twenty miles apart on England's highways was obviously critical in enabling royal messengers and any others charged with the Crown's commissions to travel swiftly in unimpeded fashion. Messengers wearing their badge of office, and others producing an official warrant, were entitled to take up post-horses at purveyance, which was half the prevailing commercial rate. At times when the numbers traveling on official business significantly increased, local officials might be unable to furnish sufficient horses: a failing that exposed a major weakness in the government's communications system. One remedy previously employed for temporary periods was the stationing of either post-horses or a relay of riders on certain routes. For example, in 1506, posts were appointed on wages of 12d. per day for nineteen days in April and twenty-one days in May between London and Exeter.[43] In 1509, and again in 1511, as hostilities worsened on England's border with Scotland, Thomas, Lord Darcy, captain of Berwick, and William Pawne, the town's receiver general, organized a relay of posts to London.[44] These arrangements were not coordinated by any officer at court. However, in 1512, steps were taken in London to establish centralized management by appointing Sir Brian Tuke as England's first "master of the posts" for life. Although payments for posts to Berwick continued to be made by Pawne until March 1513, Tuke ultimately established sole control.[45] Meanwhile, he engaged standing posts on the Dover road and in Calais to provide for the convenient conveyance by postboys of the king's letters. The packet was handed to trusted masters of ships to cross the Channel. Tuke thus formed England's first centrally managed continuous postal relay on the realm's busiest highway. His policy innovation created the foundations of England's postal *system*. He appears to have based the arrangements closely on those developed to serve the Habsburgs in Europe. Francesco Taxis was appointed in 1501 as captain and master of the posts in Brussels where he created links connecting Spain and the Netherlands. By 1505, other Taxis posts provided communications with Vienna, Innsbruck, Antwerp, Calais, and Paris; in 1516 the network was extended to Milan, Rome, and Naples. From their inception, together with government correspondence, the Taxis posts also carried *private* letters, and the diligence of their dispatch was gauged by logging the time of arrival of each postbag at the appointed stages on its route.[46]

As England's master of the posts, Tuke's remit was far wider than merely the management of the still rather confined lines of standing posts. He was appointed to facilitate government communications generally, which also meant assuring the availability of suitable horses to be ridden in post by anyone furnished with a placard or warrant to travel. Tuke gave orders to mayors and other local officials to maintain able and sufficient horses in readiness to serve when needed.[47] In fact, well into the eighteenth century, masters of the posts managed both the nation's postal system for the conveyance of letters *and* the provision of post-horses for the conveyance of travelers.

No regulations or codes of practice survive from Tuke's time as master of the posts (1512–45). It is possible that none were devised. It is therefore not always clear whether a reference to "laid posts" meant the engagement of standing posts or simply instructions to local officials to ensure that enough horses were kept in readiness to serve authorized riders. In most cases, it is likely to have been the latter. Misunderstandings occurred regarding the operation of the new standing post system. For example, Lord Lisle, lord deputy in Calais, erroneously sought reimbursement from Tuke for the riding charges of servants who had carried letters to London. Lisle was informed that such correspondence should have been handed to Thomas Twychet, the post in Calais, to be conveyed by the standing posts.[48] In response to complaints, Tuke wrote at length to Thomas Cromwell on 17 August 1533 and explained that there were no ordinary (that is, standing) posts except those between London and Calais and, only since the previous October, on the route toward Berwick.[49] The London and Calais postmasters received daily wages (12d. and 4d. respectively), but others serving the Dover route at that time were paid "by the packet." All those on the Berwick route received 12d. a day and were required to keep just one horse and rider, which meant delays if there was a simultaneous need to ride both northward and southward. Those sending a letter had been advised to note the day and time of its dispatch as a means of gauging its speed of conveyance, but Tuke reported that few were doing so.[50] In a letter to Lord Lisle in 1535, he noted that "wheresoever the King [is] there be ever posts laid from London to his Grace," but it is not certain that these were standing posts or simply horses held in readiness for royal messengers.[51] From its inception the posting system raised somewhat unrealistic expectations and, perhaps inevitably, a flow of complaints and criticisms arose regarding its shortcomings.

In 1545, Sir William (later, Lord) Paget and John Mason were jointly appointed to succeed Tuke,[52] but it was Mason who played the active role, serving until 1566. In addition to other sporadic evidence, a systematic record of sums advanced to him for the wages of the standing posts survives for 1553–57.[53] More significant, however, are Mason's wages books recording the names of (and monthly amounts paid to) each standing post for 1556–57 and for 1561–62. In the 1550s, all posts received wages; none was remunerated by the packet (Figure 2.1).[54] As well as serving as Southwitham's post on the Berwick highway, Adam Gascoigne was one of the four ordinary chamber messengers and post of the court. He held these court positions until October 1556 when his son, Robert, succeeded him. Twenty years after being named as the Calais post in Tuke's letter to Lord Lisle, Mason's records reveal that Thomas Twychet (or Tychet) remained in service there.

Until he was appointed treasurer of the chamber by Queen Elizabeth, Mason apparently submitted audited accounts of total annual expenditure on the posts to the Exchequer. Beginning in 1559, however, he integrated these records within the chamber accounts and continued to do so until he died in 1566. This evidence reveals the reactive and ephemeral character of England's early standing posts where, apart from the permanent Berwick route, stages on highways to other destinations were engaged and discharged to serve short-term

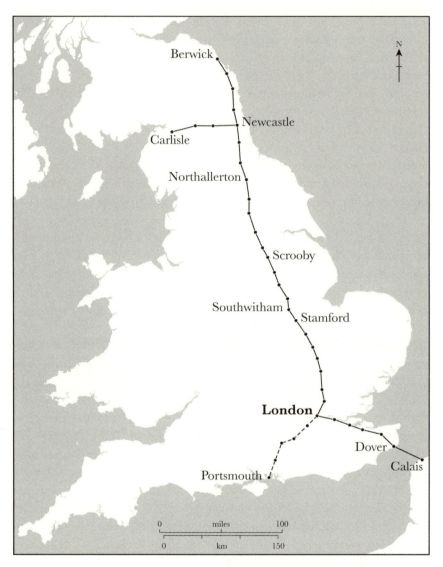

Figure 2.1. Post stages in England where Sir John Mason paid standing posts, 1553–57. Between June and October 1556 standing posts were temporarily engaged toward Portsmouth. Source: The National Archives, E 164/50, Exchequer, account book of John Mason, master of the posts.

needs. Even the arrangements on Dover's road were subject to frequent change. Thus, while daily wages were paid to all for certain periods, there were also times when only William Beswyke in London and John Spritewell in Dover received wages; the other posts were paid only by the packet.[55] A link was established to Redgrave in Suffolk for eighteen days in 1559 during the lord keeper's residence. Similarly, posts were briefly appointed toward Hengrave in 1560 for the Duke of Norfolk. On 1 October 1560, stages to Holyhead were engaged to provide a connection with Ireland and, by 1563, the stages that had operated briefly in 1556 toward Portsmouth were reappointed. For a limited time, a link was also formed to Rye. Extraordinary posts were engaged to serve during the court's summer progresses.[56] However, by 1566—Mason's last year of office—except for those to Berwick (and Carlisle) and Holyhead, all other posts had been discharged and the Dover posts were again on "piece rates." His successor, Thomas Randolph, thus took over standing posts reduced to a number not significantly greater than those engaged by Tuke more than thirty years before, but it is clearly a mistake to suppose that the expansion subsequently occurring in Randolph's time was unprecedented.

In Queen Mary's reign, regulations regarding both post-horse hire and letter carrying toward Dover and Berwick were codified. Although Mason's personal authorship of the codes is not certain, in 1566 his successor referred to "orders appoynted for the better governinge of the Posts" as not being new and that the Privy Council had "seen the lyke setforthe in prynt . . . in Sir Iohn Masons tyme."[57] The orders required the standing posts to keep at least six horses constantly in readiness: four for hire by travelers, and two for carrying the royal packet. Ordinary hire charges for post-horses were set at 2d. per mile and the standing posts were accorded first call on all such business. All those traveling in post were obliged to hire a guide to show the way, blow his horn on arrival at the next stage, and carry the rider's mail (baggage). Ordinarily, hackneymen were barred from hiring out horses to be ridden in post but could furnish "journey" horses at the rate of 1½d. per mile. However, if demand for post-horses exceeded the six belonging to the standing post, he could oblige hackneymen to supply the deficit.[58] In July 1556, the post of the court and the standing posts toward Berwick were also required to keep a register of every letter received for dispatch and the hour that it came into their hands.[59] Although there were successive modifications and elaborations of the rules, key elements of posting in England and Wales were thus devised in Sir John Mason's time.

Thomas Randolph served from 1566 until 1590 but he was frequently engaged in other work that drew him from London and he relied heavily on deputies. Nevertheless, he was by instinct a reformer who gradually refined and strengthened both the codes for the provision of post-horses for hire and the rules for state letter carrying. In May 1574 he produced a comprehensive articulation of posting regulations.[60] Although these orders were thereafter redrafted several times, later versions contained little that was really new.[61] However, in January 1584 a printed schedule of rules directed specifically at the posts on the Berwick route suggests a particular need to strengthen the enforcement of the codes on that highway.[62] The 1574 orders specified those authorized to issue placards for riders to take up post-horses at purveyance. They extended the obligation to all standing posts to record in a ledger the receipt times and the identities of senders and recipients of every letter and packet that came into their hands and added a demand to record the names and arrival times of those riding with placards. The orders confirmed that riders with such commissions could hire post-horses at purveyance rates. Hiring a guide at each stage was obligatory for any person taking up a post-horse. Postboys and guides accompanying riders were to blow their horn at least four times per mile, whenever they passed through a village, and on arrival at a post stage. Each standing post was ordered to "kepe three horses at the leaste continvallie in the stables both winter & somer or have them so neare vnto his howse that on the fvrthest he maie be readie to depart w[i]th the pacqvette w[i]th[i]n one quarter of an houre afte[r] he heareth the boy or man blowe his hornith as bringeth yt." If a standing post's supply ran out, with few exceptions any other men owning horses could be required to supply the want. Penalties were laid down both for instances when an inadequate horse had been provided and for cases where a rider had overexerted, maimed, or killed a post-horse. Those taking up post-horses in the City of London, or "being men of covnten[an]ce," were entitled to have their mounts brought to their homes; otherwise riders were required to take up and return horses at the premises of the standing posts.

Two leather postbags lined with baize or cotton were stipulated for the secure carriage of letters marked for the Crown's special service. Postboys were to ride at least seven miles per hour in summertime, and five miles per hour in the winter, "or more as the waie is good or badd," and if a postboy was reported as "sleeping vpon the waye" 6s. 4d. would be contributed to the "poore mens box at the parishe" where the complainant dwelt. In addition to recording details in their ledgers, a further duty of standing posts was to write the name of the town and the arrival time of all letters and packets on the protective wrapping or parcel within which correspondence was contained. Though few such wrappers survive, individual letters exist upon which the progress of their conveyance was inscribed on the folded, sealed outside of the paper. This evidence is of course far from ideal but nevertheless provides an indication of the speed at which government letters actually traveled.[63]

While aware of the failings of some standing posts serving the queen, and sometimes severe in his criticism, Randolph was also conspicuously protective of them and several times argued in their favor when wages and other emoluments fell into arrears or they faced threats of discharge.[64] As Randolph was not made treasurer of the chamber, after October 1566, the audited accounts of the master of the posts were returned separately to the Exchequer. Like those of Mason, Randolph's accounts chronicle the complex and changeable geography of the standing posts, the temporary engagement of extraordinary posts, and the special roles performed by the post of the court in laying and discharging routes and coordinating the conveyance of letters to and from London and between the various royal palaces and other locations of Privy Council meetings.[65]

Sir John, later Lord, Stanhope, succeeded Randolph in 1590 and his patent accorded more scope to farm the system. Described as "one of those men who thought public office had been created for private gain," Stanhope required postmasters to pay him a fee for admission to their office.[66] He also presided during a period of notable turbulence regarding the engagement and discharge of standing posts. As communications with the south of Ireland became critical in the mid-1590s, new stages were laid toward Bristol and Milford Haven, and to Plymouth, Barnstaple, Padstow, and Penryn. However, notwithstanding the laying, on the orders of the Scottish Privy Council issued after the accession in England of King James, of new posts between Berwick and Edinburgh, several key routes in England and Wales were discharged by the end of March 1605.[67]

Unlike the Taxis network on the Continent, which had been carrying private letters for well over a century, the standing posts in England were still meant only for government correspondence. This exclusivity simply could not last, and, in February 1630, the posts toward Plymouth obtained official permission to offer a weekly service to carry private letters alongside the royal packet, covering the distance to London in three days.[68] They also undertook to deliver letters and dispatches up to twenty miles "out of the road." For those carrying their own letters, horses were offered for hire at 2½d. per mile, plus

4d. per stage for a guide. The direct income for the posts secured by carrying private and business letters was meant to offset the losses they sustained by rendering a service to government for inadequate wages intermittently paid. It is not known whether the private letter post on the Plymouth road was successful. In any case, recognizing the potential to garner the profits of private letter carrying for the Exchequer, a preliminary blueprint, "Orders for a Letter office for missives w[i]th[i]n the Land," was devised.[69] Thomas Witherings, who was appointed postmaster for foreign parts in 1632, was the driving force behind the landmark reforms whereby private correspondence would be carried for the profit of the state. A key proclamation of Charles I, issued in July 1635, thus established the new public "Letter Office" in the realms of England and Scotland. Considerable overlap exists between the ideas laid out in the "Orders for a Letter office" and the text of the proclamation. Carriage charges were codified: single letters carried up to 80 miles were to cost 2d.; between 80 and 140 miles, 4d.; and above 140 miles, 6d.; and 8d. to the borders of (and anywhere within) Scotland. The same scale applied on the route to Chester and Holyhead toward Ireland. The round-trip service to both was to be completed in six days. Pro rata charges applied for packets containing more than one letter. Charges for carriage on the Plymouth road of course already existed, but the proclamation spelled out aspirations for laid posts toward Oxford, Bristol, Colchester, and Norwich. As late as 1639, however, none of these projected routes had been established.[70] Spatial coverage by the state's service was in fact still extremely limited.

More remarkable than the arrival of England's nascent public postal service is the fact that it had taken quite so long to be established. The old means of conveying letters—much cheaper and so well accustomed—were not easily supplanted. In any case, although all other commercial conveyance of letters was banned, common carriers were exempted, and, of course, it remained legal for correspondence to be carried informally by friends, relatives, or servants. Thus, although 1635 represents a turning point, for many decades there was in practice no watertight state monopoly. Matters were made considerably worse by political dislocation and insecurity in the Civil War and the Interregnum. Following a period of contest for the position of master of the posts, parliamentary loyalist Edmund Prideaux was appointed in 1642 and announced his ambition of providing a weekly conveyance of letters to all parts of the kingdom. He did not achieve his extravagant aim. Indeed, some links were periodically disrupted, routes were diverted, and letters stolen. In some cases, staunchly royalist standing posts were replaced by men avowing loyalty to Parliament. For a brief period, Charles I appointed his own posts on routes focused on Oxford. In fiercely contested areas, the dangers for postboys were acute. For example, although the service toward Holyhead and Dublin was after earlier interruptions restored by 1646, Anglesey remained perilous and, between July and November 1648, rather than crossing the Menai Strait the packet was carried from Conway to Porthdinllaen on the Lleyn Peninsula, where the Dublin post barks temporarily docked.[71] By the early 1650s, however, the need for such avoidance maneuvers subsided. Indeed, potential profits from the service were sufficiently attractive in 1653 for Prideaux's successor, Captain John Manley, to accept a two-year contract to farm the posts for an annual payment of £10,000. Detailed guidelines were devised for Manley in September 1654.[72] When his term expired, Cromwell transferred the franchise on the same basis to his principal secretary, John Thurloe.

Partly because of their cumbersome organizational and pricing structures, and partly because of the widespread covert interception of mail, considerable reluctance to entrust letters to public postal services persisted. In England, although in theory arrangements existed for "by-posting" whereby letters could be delivered to intermediate stages on the highway and to locations flanking key routes, cross-posting to avoid London was limited. Indeed, the crude architecture of a system configured to focus on the capital and provide for the specific needs of central government was simply not suited to the geographically complex communication requirements of the wider population. Charging in London for all letter conveyance meant that costs were artificially raised. For example, a letter sent the 108 miles cross-country from Coventry to Bristol ought to have cost 4d., but in fact incurred a charge of 6d. for its journey via the capital. The clandestine interception of letters passing through London further dampened enthusiasm for the public postal service. Occurring across Europe in the early modern period and considered a legitimate means of gathering government intelligence,[73] the secret opening, reading, transcription, and resealing of letters burgeoned in Whitehall during the Commonwealth.[74] The practice was then masterminded by Secretary Thurloe's employee Isaac Dorislaus, but surveillance by these means continued after the Restoration and persisted well into the 1700s.

Notwithstanding its defects and consumer resistance, the political importance and commercial promise of the postal system was acknowledged. In June 1657 an act for "Setling the Postage of England, Scotland and Ireland" created a single General Post Office in London, under the overall control of a postmaster general. Although purporting to serve the communication needs of trade

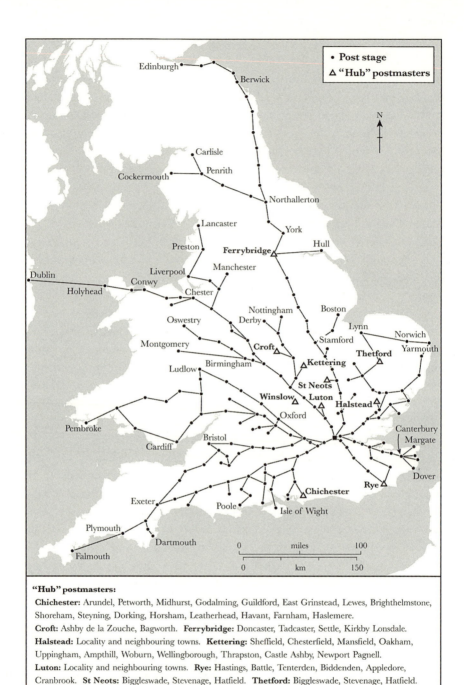

Post stage
△ "Hub" postmasters

N

"Hub" postmasters:

Chichester: Arundel, Petworth, Midhurst, Godalming, Guildford, East Grinstead, Lewes, Brighthelmstone, Shoreham, Steyning, Dorking, Horsham, Leatherhead, Havant, Farnham, Haslemere.
Croft: Ashby de la Zouche, Bagworth. **Ferrybridge:** Doncaster, Tadcaster, Settle, Kirkby Lonsdale.
Halstead: Locality and neighbouring towns. **Kettering:** Sheffield, Chesterfield, Mansfield, Oakham, Uppingham, Ampthill, Woburn, Wellingborough, Thrapston, Castle Ashby, Newport Pagnell.
Luton: Locality and neighbouring towns. **Rye:** Hastings, Battle, Tenterden, Biddenden, Appledore, Cranbrook. **St Neots:** Biggleswade, Stevenage, Hatfield. **Thetford:** Biggleswade, Stevenage, Hatfield.
Winslow: Edgeworth, Stanmore, Watford, Kings Langley, Berkhamstead, Tring.

Figure 2.2. Post stages of England and Wales listed in the accounts of the postmaster general, 1695–97. Principal, but not minor, connections are shown. Source: The National Archives, AO, 154/29, 21 March 1695–25 March 1696; 154/30, 25 March 1696–25 March 1697.

and the wider populace, the act also openly acknowledged the intelligence-gathering mission of the service: "to discover and prevent many dangerous and wicked designes . . . daily contrived against the peace and welfare of this Commonwealth."[75] Though repealed at the Restoration, the 1657 act was replaced by virtually identical legislation in 1660.[76] While neither offered much encouragement to those seeking guaranteed privacy for their correspondence, by the 1660s the rudiments of the national Post Office certainly existed.

The audited accounts of the postmaster general for the final years of the seventeenth century provide intriguing snapshots after almost two centuries of development of the network's organizational structure and spatial pattern in England and Wales (Figure 2.2). The entire system continued to pivot on London, where the Inland Post Office, managed in the mid-1690s by Isaac Manley, comprised twelve letter-receiving offices, staffed by fifteen sorters, three "letter bringers," and three porters; and sixty-four named carriers delivered letters to addresses across the capital. These later developments clearly depended crucially on the foundations laid by royal proclamation in 1635.

In reviewing both the private and official means by which letters were carried in the period between ca. 1500 and ca. 1640, and touching on advances made thereafter, this essay has highlighted the wide range of modes of conveyance that existed. Alongside haphazard and improvised means of delivery undertaken on an unsystematic basis by friends, servants, and other travelers engaged ad hoc to act as bearers, the roles of common carriers in offering regular and geographically comprehensive letter-carrying services have been identified. However, the key advance, in part prompted by the demand by state messengers for assured supplies of post-horses for hire, was the creation of a letter-posting service for official communications. The lucrative business potential of posting private letters was recognized when the state opened its "Letter Office" to the public in 1635 thereby initiating the process that led eventually to the establishment of England's modern comprehensive postal service.

PART II

Technologies and Designs

CHAPTER 3

Enigmatic Cultures of Cryptology

NADINE AKKERMAN

It is not generally known that Elizabeth Stuart (1596–1662), sometime queen of Bohemia, was an ardent cryptologist. This daughter of King James VI and I and Anna of Denmark married the Elector Palatine, Frederick V (1596–1632), in 1613, and moved to Heidelberg, the capital of the Lower Palatinate in Germany. Her husband accepted the Crown of Bohemia, which he was offered in August 1619, and she was crowned queen on 7 November 1619 in Prague. After the battle at White Mountain in 1620, they were forced to flee before the Catholic armies. Through her husband's kin connection with the Prince of Orange they found refuge in The Hague, the Netherlands, where, between 1621 and 1661, the sister of Charles I and aunt of Charles II gradually transformed her ignominious flight into a self-imposed exile. In the process, she created a vibrant, alternative Stuart court on the continent. Her life is generally perceived as highly romantic or tragic, a perception undoubtedly influenced by the mocking epithet—the Winter Queen—given to her by her Catholic enemies. Her voluminous correspondence counters this perception as it was by writing letters that she continued to wield power and remained remarkably politically active. It was through enigmatic cultures of cryptology that she hoped her political movements would remain unchecked by her enemies. Seven cipher keys in particular, recently "decrypted" for the first time, draw attention to a wide intelligence network and illuminate her political role as an intelligencer during the Thirty Years' War: as designer, user, and decoder of cryptography.[1]

The existence of code in her correspondence radically upsets conventional accounts of cryptography in the first half of the seventeenth century. After all, it is commonly assumed that the use of cryptography had disappeared in English manuscript newsletters by 1603, excepting the period 1638 to 1642. It is commonly believed that writers only needed to employ secret modes of writing during times of crisis, and not those of relative peace. As late as 2001 Sabrina A. Baron argued that "manuscript letters [of this period] did not resort to codes, ciphers, or shorthand as letters filled with sensitive information would do during other periods of political stress such as the civil wars."[2] Yet Elizabeth Stuart's correspondence between 1603 and 1638 is saturated with cryptology, belying the earlier supposition that it had disappeared. Her circle used ciphers, codes, and riddles aplenty. What role did cryptology have in these letters then, if it was also used during periods of relative peace, even though it is true that this was not always Elizabeth's personal experience in the 1620s and 1630s? Was cryptology used only for political ends or are there other reasons why Elizabeth's circle employed secret modes of writing? This essay will focus on the enigmatic uses of cryptology by spotlighting Elizabeth's circle, as well as drawing on more familiar examples of secret writing.

Brief Historical Background of Cryptology

From the Middle Ages onward, the language of cryptology was the domain of both the respectable diplomat as well as his shadowy servant, the more infamous spy. Philippe de Commynes (1447–ca. 1511), the medieval writer and diplomat, was the first to suggest that diplomat, messenger, and spy amounted to the same profession.[3] Though this was contested by other contemporary theorists of diplomacy, it became commonplace in later periods to typify the ambassador as an "honourable spy."[4] These seemingly different professional trades belonged to opposite ends of the same spectrum. Ambassador and spy protected the messages in their letters in a similar manner: not just sealed off by a blot of melted wax imprinted with a signet ring but also by means of enciphering. Around 1514 diplomacy and intelligence became inextricably connected, in England too: the rapid development of regular diplomatic institutions was only possible because of organized espionage.[5] In short, encryption was used both in authorized as well as in clandestine business, and those worlds were intricately interwoven.

The art of cryptology became part of royal and aristocratic education and of interest to heads of state in the sixteenth century. The fifteen-year-old Mary Stewart (1542–87) had been instructed in the art of enciphering because she was recognized as the future queen consort of France: in 1557 she was taught to select passages in the letters she sent from France to her mother, Mary of Guise, in Scotland that needed to be rendered in cipher by a secretary.[6] All the leading figures in Queen Elizabeth I's reign employed cryptology. Diplomats, informers, and spies alike sent dispatches protected by cipher keys from foreign locations to their employers. Such keys, which were also needed to unlock the ciphered letters, were well protected by secretaries. Keeping track of and storing cipher keys became an essential function of any smoothly operating secretariat, as some of the contemporary advice manuals and treatises on the office of secretary of state reveal. Nicholas Faunt (1553/54–1608), one of the apprentices of Queen Elizabeth's spymaster Sir Francis Walsingham (ca. 1532–90), describes how a secretary of foreign affairs "may cheifly attend vnto matters of intelligence Cyfers and secrett advertisementes to keep the first in good order to extract the substance of them for present vse, and to see them well digested into small bookes if they bee matteriall, . . . end it wilbee needful yᵗ hee prepare certaine Cabinettes or Coffers fitt to keepe such things."[7] And Robert Beale (1541–1601), one of Faunt's colleagues, wrote about the need for a secretary to "have a speciall Cabinett, whereof he is himselfe to keepe the Keye, for his signetts, Ciphers and secrett Intelligences," further emphasizing that the secretary should do well to protect the cabinet's drawers themselves by a letter code, conjuring up the much more modern image of a Russian Matryoshka doll, codes boxed in codes: "distinguishing the boxes or tills rather by letters than by the names of the Countryes or places, keepinge that only unto himself, for the names may inflame a desire to come by such things."[8] That most early modern secretaries were sedulous in storing cipher keys is evidenced by the fact that the National Archives in Kew alone currently holds over three hundred cipher keys, covering the reigns of Elizabeth I to Charles II.[9]

The need to protect cipher keys was taken all the more seriously because it soon became apparent how useful unriddling cipher keys employed by the enemy could be. In England, cryptanalysts or decipherers, such as Philip van Marnix (1540–98), Baron de Sainte-Aldegonde, and Thomas Phelippes (ca. 1556–1625x27), were first employed to their full potential under Walsingham in the 1570s. Marnix proved skilled in reconstructing Spanish cipher keys, and Phelippes, assisted in his deciphering practices by his wife Mary (d. after 1627), brought down Mary, Queen of Scots.[10] Encryption and decryption was thus essential to statecraft. Cryptology skills spread quickly. Statesmen and intelligencers trained themselves using cryptology manuals such as Giovanni Battista

Porta's *De furtivis literarum notis* (1563).[11] Porta's four books became standard reading, and the practice of encryption and decryption so widespread that it could become the subject of ridicule in Ben Jonson's poem "The New Cry":

> They all get Porta for the sundry ways
> To write in cipher, and the several keys
> To ope the character. . . .
> . . . .
> To break up seals and close 'em.[12]

Jonson mocked the statesmen who advertised self-importance by publicly displaying or pretending to have knowledge of cryptology.

Cryptology Practices in Elizabeth Stuart's Circle

By the first half of the seventeenth century encryption was still practiced widely by ambassadors and their intelligencers. Yet historians do not always appreciate that it also had become a second mode of literacy for royalty and the elite, a way to distinguish themselves from the masses, as Margaret Ferguson and Edith Snook have recently argued.[13] Most of the queen of Bohemia's letters have one clear political purpose: regaining the electoral rights and dignities and being restored to the lost lands in Germany. Hence, at first glance it appears that Elizabeth's circle was not different from any other diplomatic network or spy ring. Cipher and code protected sensitive political content. However, her coded letters also demonstrate how the use of secret writing in diplomatic dispatches does not always have a clear diplomatic or political purpose: instead, on closer inspection, they testify that for a time cryptology could also be used for a wide variety of distinctly elitist social practices.

Not only Elizabeth, but also her most frequent correspondents, diplomats such as Sir Thomas Roe (1581–1644) and Sir Balthazar Gerbier (1591–1667), her agents such as William Curtius (fl. 1630s–1670s), Sir Abraham Williams (fl. 1620s–1640s), Sir Richard Cave (d. 1645), and Johann Joachim von Rusdorf (1589–1640), and her sons Elector Charles Louis (1618–80) and military commander Rupert (1619–82), were keen users of codes. Nearly sixty ciphered letters in her hand survive for the years 1603 to 1642, mainly addressed to Roe, her most loyal correspondent. It is difficult to estimate how many ciphered letters she received during this period, as most of Elizabeth's own archive has never surfaced; her ciphered holograph letters survive in the archives of her correspondents, where most of the return letters can also be found. The latter survive as copies her correspondents kept in letter books for administrative purposes. These secretarial copies can easily deceive the modern eye, however, as encrypted holographs are typically duplicated in plaintext.

In letter books the veil of secrecy is thus often erased. Roe's and Rusdorf's "journals" are prime examples of this practice. They apologize for the use of cipher, but the copies kept in their journals bear no material or textual trace of cryptology. Gerbier's letter books, in contrast, are maintained completely in cipher and code; while the originals have never been retrieved, seventeen letters addressed to Elizabeth survive in his managerial bound books. Tellingly, the handful of holographs of her correspondents that did surface are all in code—twenty of her husband Frederick V's letters deposited in Munich, nineteen of her son Charles Louis's letters in Karlsruhe and the National Art Library of the Victoria and Albert Museum, and four of Roe's in Trinity College Dublin—suggesting that enciphering was the norm for the correspondents who stood closest to her.

She had already decrypted letters in her own hand, letters that her husband sent her from Mannheim and Sedan in the summer months of 1622, when agent William Trumbull (1576x80?–1635) had lent him a cipher key. Her circle would continue to use this same key well into the late 1630s, Charles Louis inheriting it from his father.[14] Like all other keys she would employ, this was a combination of a cipher alphabet, a list of multiple "homophones," or "equivalents used to transform the plaintext into the secret form" (for instance, a = 15 but also 39; b = 16 but also 40), and a nomenclature, "a codelike list of names, words, and syllables" (for instance 179 = Mr. Camerarius; 124 = the King of Sweden).[15] She initiated a coded correspondence with Sir Henry Vane (1589–1655) by sending him two cipher keys in late 1631/early 1632,[16] when he followed her husband to the Swedish army in Germany as special Stuart ambassador, and used cryptography even more frequently, presumably due to her increased political engagement, after she was widowed in November 1632. Gerbier, Rubens's art broker and Stuart resident agent to Brussels, won her trust by sending her several sophisticated cipher keys with hieroglyphic symbols making up the nomenclature. Yet this double spy simultaneously revealed all her secrets by sharing the same keys with her antagonists, Secretary of State Sir John Coke (1563–1644) and Lord Treasurer Richard Weston (bap. 1577, d. 1635).[17]

This faux pas notwithstanding, Elizabeth was well informed about the possibilities and pitfalls of secret writing. Her husband's uncle, Duke August of Brunswick-Lüneburg (1579–1666), was the author of an influential manual on cryptography, *Cryptomenytices*, which he published in 1624, under the pseudonym Gustavus Selenus.[18] In addition, she was a patron of the Dutch poet, diplomat, and polymath Sir Constantijn Huygens (1596–1687), whom she assisted in securing the position of secretary to the Prince of Orange in 1624.[19] Huygens quickly made a name for himself as one of the first cryptanalysts in the Dutch Republic, the new Baron de Sainte-Aldegonde or Thomas Phelippes of the Low Countries: on top of his secretarial salary he received a fee of 100 Dutch guilders per month, the equivalent of £10 sterling, for the decryption of letters.[20] His almanac notes of May 1616 indicate that he had learned the art of decryption at the University of Leiden: in addition to learning the English language, which could function as a secret language in itself within the Dutch Republic because so few spoke it, he regularly took lessons in cryptology.[21] With family members and neighbors as renowned cryptology experts, Elizabeth was certainly knowledgeable about this burgeoning trade.

An auction catalog of 1688 shows that Huygens's library, only one street removed from the queen of Bohemia's court, was well stocked with books on cryptology. Next to several of Porta's works, and Selenus's study, he owned, for instance, Johann Trithemius's *Polygraphie et universelle escriture cabalistique* (1561); Blaise de Vigenère's *Traicté des chiffres, ou Secretes manieres d'escrire* (1587); John Willis's *The Art of Stenographie* (1602–); Daniel Schwenter's *Geheime magische / natürliche Red und Schreibkunst* (ca. 1620); Dominicus de Hottinga's *Polygraphie, ou Methode universelle de l'escriture cachée* (1621); Theophilus Metcalfe's *A Schoolmaster to Radio-Stenography, or Short Writing* (1635), and Pietro Maria Canepari's *De atramentis cujuscunque generis* (1660). In his autobiography, Huygens wrote self-admiringly about his skills as a cryptanalyst: "At every single siege, I proved my skills, anticipating the tricks of the enemy by means of my own knowledge of deceit (in times of war one is allowed to be deceitful). Even if the letters originated in Constantinople or were fantastically shaped, like Griffins or other never before seen fable beasts, I managed to decrypt them."[22] Elizabeth regularly employed Huygens to decrypt letters that her informers had intercepted from the enemy.[23] During the Wars of the Three Kingdoms Sir Edward Hyde (1609–74), Sir Edward Nicholas (1593–1669), and Henry, Lord Jermyn (bap. 1606, d. 1684) would follow her lead in profiting from Huygens's services.[24]

This brings us to a conundrum: if Elizabeth Stuart was so well informed about cryptography, why are her keys not more advanced in hiding the letters' contents? Most of the ciphers are based on a rudimentary substitution system, monoalphabetic and thus fairly easy to break.[25] And why would she use the same keys for years on end—even though she had access to trusted private bearers and alternative, underground postal channels,[26] by which she could easily have replaced the keys more often? Intriguingly, the same questions can be posed in respect of any well-functioning diplomat of the period. A correspondent wrote to Sir Robert Cecil (1563–1612) in 1596, "I send . . . the Alphabet of Mr. Bertons cipher used thes xviii years."[27] Hugo Grotius (1583–1645), Dutch ambassador to Sweden, also used his keys for at least fifteen years on end.[28] There is a tension between, on the one hand, a wide circulation of cipher keys among an ever-expanding group of correspondents and, on the other, the need to keep information secret; there is an inherent paradox in using cipher, thus drawing attention to the fact that you have something to hide, and the desire to communicate secretly. It is precisely such points of friction that can be explained by focusing on the social aspects of cryptography.

Such aspects have for a long time escaped scholarly attention, but in an illuminating essay Hannah J. Crawforth explains how cipher was used in "community-building": "the actual effectiveness . . . of . . . [the] use of cipher as a secret device is less important . . . than the fact it creates a bond between writer and recipient that has the appearance of exclusivity" and is in that respect not different to any other letter-writing convention.[29] This might also explain the simplicity of the cipher keys of playwright and female spy Aphra Behn (1640–89), alias Astraea. As royalist agent 160, she operated on the periphery of Elizabeth's circle. She begged the king's secretary Henry Bennet (1618–85), Baron Arlington, for months for her own key; the straightforwardness of the one she finally received after weeks of pleading seems ridiculous to a modern eye: a = 2, b=3, c = 4, d = 5, and so on.[30] This fact has been used by historians to suggest that she was not a well-trained spy and thus should not be taken too seriously. Yet receiving a cipher key was proof to Behn that she had been admitted to a certain spy ring; the effectiveness of the key itself was beside the point.

Roe, who later became the queen of Bohemia's most loyal servant, initially had to negotiate for three full years before he was allowed to communicate with his mistress in secret mode. On 12/22 July 1623, he wrote from Constantinople "If your Matie will either send or accept a cyphar from mee,

I shall with more boldness Interrupt you with [my] vowes and feruent prayers." Elizabeth, though faithfully answering his letters, did not respond to his suggestion, which he reiterated on 18/28 October 1624, "It is a great want to mee, that I haue no Ciphar from yo[u]r Matie; which makes mee striue to write in Riddles, and to omitt much," on 1/11 April 1625, "if you [but] please to send mee a Ciphar, and hauing read, to burne my letters," and again on 25 May 1625 (Old Style), "a Ciphar w[hi]ch I haue long expected from your Matie, not p[re]suming to send any of myne."[31] The latter comment makes clear that it might be taken as insolence to present a queen with a cipher key. In effect, it would mean submitting to and learning the language of her correspondent, a time-consuming and potentially cumbersome process.

Roe, who felt banished and deserted in Constantinople (and not without cause), sought above all to receive a clear sign of favor in the form of a key Elizabeth had created herself. As Snook also explains, the creator of a cipher key is "at the centre of a circle of knowledge" and "establishes a reading practice in which comprehension of the text depends on being welcomed by the writer into the social relationship that provides access to the code."[32] Elizabeth did not create a key for Roe. Instead, by 9/19 September 1625, she must finally have given him permission to send her a key, or he felt emboldened enough to do so without her explicit authorization, as he writes: "I can safely say nothing of it, but under the cyphar, to which yow wilbe pleased to bee referred."[33] His following letters are written in Greek symbols. By being allowed to communicate in code, Roe had arrived as the queen of Bohemia's loyal servant.

Roe's desire to communicate in code with Elizabeth was not driven by a need to protect information—he was well aware that she read all of the ciphered letters that he addressed to Dudley Carleton (1573–1632), the Stuart resident ambassador in The Hague and future Viscount Dorchester. In fact, he wrote them with that knowledge in mind, as his letter of 15/25 May 1624 typically demonstrates: "Seeing yo[u]r Matie doth take Knowledge, that you read all my discourses to My Lord Ambassador, which are directed to him w[i]th [tha]t intention, . . . I will presume now also to referre yo[u]r Matie to one, [tha]t wayts upon this, enclosed to him."[34] She could have gleaned any Turkish state secrets from those missives. Rather, Roe wanted assurance that he belonged to her innermost circle, enforcing a privileged relationship. By decoding his words, she would effectively duplicate his thoughts and reproduce them on the page. Her handwriting would lend credit to his arguments.

Hence, in addition to simply obscuring information from outsiders, cryptography had a more profound social function as well. Correspondents created their own alternative language in order to bind members of a group or even to form a secret society. In this respect, it is useful to apply literary theories of "scribal publication." Viewing letters in this way can foster awareness that aside from the basic level of obtaining, circulating, and concealing information, the exchange of letters with ciphers had a more meaningful social and political function. Like all other scribal publications, such letters bonded "groups of like-minded individuals into a community, sect or political faction, with the exchange of texts in manuscript serving to nourish a shared set of values and to enrich personal allegiances."[35]

Even though letters were often not copied like other scribal publications such as poems, they nonetheless circulated far beyond their immediate addressee. Recent scholarship has demonstrated that in the early modern period reading was for the most part not a private activity but a social interaction between a speaker, someone who read the text aloud, and one or more listeners.[36] It was common practice for letters to be read and shared in expansive circles. A letter was frequently composed by multiple parties, by the subscriber, the secretary, and letter bearers, but also nearly always intended for multiple audiences. A letter of the young Dudley Carleton (d. 1654), addressed to his uncle and namesake, demonstrates this point:

> I send y[ou]r L[ordshi]p herew[i]th a letter w[hi]ch, I assure y[ou]r
> L[ordshi]p cost Mr Secretary [Sir Edward] Conway no small
> trouble to write; . . . all his men being so busie that he was faine to
> use his owne hand; wh[i]ch he saith will giue y[ou]r L[ordshi]p
> trouble enough to reade, but the Q[ueen] of Bohemia is good at
> finding owt the misterie of such cyfers, and I do presume her Ma^{ty}
> may in the very beginning of Mr Secretaryes letter discouer such
> news as shee will be very willing to hammer out euery word
> thereof, though it cost her Ma^{ty} some paines.[37]

In short, he sent his uncle one of Conway's letters, but instructed him to read it with Elizabeth so that she might decipher the illegible handwriting. The queen of Bohemia's correspondence also reveals that letters were not exclusively meant for the addressee's eyes; on the contrary, an ever-expanding or contracting circle of friends or trusted acquaintances were granted access to a particular epistle and shared its content. Comments such as "as I perceiue by your Majesties letters to your sonne" are also typical.[38] By reading letters collectively, the political consciousness of a group took shape. It is clear from Elizabeth Stuart's epistles that ciphered writings were not only expressions of personal thoughts but also more often the carefully worded consensus of a well-motivated community that formed itself through letter exchange and may also have selected its members by means of the sharing or withholding of cipher keys.

The use of cipher codes could also reestablish intimacy. Elizabeth's letters were constantly intercepted. In 1637, a servant of the imperial party sent Emperor Ferdinand III Elizabeth's and Frederick's letters to Heinrich Matthias von Thurn (1567–1640), which they had written as early as in 1625. The Catholic party intercepted her letters frequently, but even the Swedes, her allies, perused her letters. Although Elizabeth was highly politically active, constantly scheming to abort the peace negotiations of her brother and give effect to her own bellicose plans, the decoded passages often do not seem to hide any particular secret message; on the contrary, they are perhaps gossipy at best. In this respect, these coded letters can perhaps be compared to the eighteenth-century letters exchanged between Madame de Sade and Milli (Mademoiselle) Rousset, which Julie C. Hayes analyzed as follows: "the hidden text reveals no 'secret' in the conventional sense, but instead it should be read as an attempt to seize that which has been appropriated by outsiders, to authenticate the message by reestablishing a personal, privileged relationship. . . . [Their] decisions to encrypt their language, to bury their meaning, however innocent it may be, stem from the desire to preserve a semblance of privacy."[39] One can imagine the need for "the semblance of privacy" to be prevalent if one's letters are constantly intercepted, as was the case with Elizabeth's correspondence. This further corroborates that cryptology was more than a practice to hide facts and plots. It had subtle social functions that the seventeenth-century elite knew all too well.

The Wars of the Three Kingdoms: A Change in Secret Writing

The onset of war changed attitudes toward secret modes of writing considerably, and methods of communication changed as a result. In the pamphlet *The Queen's Maiesties Gracious Answer to the Lord Digbies Letter* (1642; the letter itself is dated 3 February 1641 [Old Style]), Queen Henrietta Maria promised George Digby (1612–77) a cipher ("the time being come that you have a Cypher, which I vouchsafe to confer upon you"), so that his letters from Middelburg would be protected, suddenly as intensely suspect.[40] This might have been a reaction to the ever-increasing practice of women as cryptographers.[41] One could argue that the use of cipher came to be seen as a feminized form of deception during the Wars of the Three Kingdoms, an argument that was later fully exploited in *The King's Cabinet Opened; or, Certain Packets of Secret Letters & Papers* (1645), where the king's use of cipher became yet another piece of evidence to indicate how his power and rhetoric was emasculated by his French wife.[42]

In April 1643, it was a political stratagem of Parliament, which wanted to increase its control over royalist correspondence, to bring the connection of enciphering with spying, rather than a more elite means of communication, again to the fore.[43] It passed an order prohibiting the use of cipher: "That all such should be punished as Spyes and Enemies of the State, who hereafter should send any Letters or Papers written with Cyphers, or any other unknowne Characters."[44] On 21 October 1643, the *Mercurius Aulicus*, a royalist news pamphlet, was quick to point out that Parliament had passed the order purely to taint the royalists. It printed an intercepted, ciphered letter subscribed by a Parliamentarian, a Matthew Durburn—in full but without decipherment—to demonstrate Parliament's hypocrisy, that "themselves [i.e., the Parliamentarians] when they please can practice it [i.e., enciphering], without the least transgression of their order, which it seemes was made only for the punishment of the Kings friends but not for such innocent Rebels as they are."[45] Once cipher codes were officially forbidden, and the Cromwellian secretary of state John Thurloe (bap. 1616, d. 1668) hired mathematician John Wallis (1616–1703) as a cryptanalyst to track down letter writers, correspondents searched for alternative means to maintain their message's secrecy.

One such method was steganography. The science of cryptology dictates that a message can be hidden in two distinctive ways: using methods of cryptography—that is, cipher and codes—or, alternatively, those of steganography. The methods of cryptography make no effort to "conceal the presence of a secret message but renders it unintelligible to outsiders by various transformations of the plaintext."[46] For the interceptor it is immediately evident that the cryptographic letter writer has something to hide; codes and ciphers stare back at you from the very page. That is why as early as October 1642, Roe advised Elizabeth not to use cryptography any longer: "I shall humbly desyre yo[u]r Ma:[ty] to forbeare vsing a Cyphar, for that doth intimate a secret, w[hi]ch would avoyd the light; and if any of yo[u]r letters be taken, they may be opened, and that rayse a iealousye, and bring me to an apologye."[47] Steganography, in contrast, hides "the very existence of the messages."[48]

Lady Brilliana Harley's cutout sheet, a so-called Cardan grille, is a prime example of steganography, undoubtedly utilized to circumvent the prohibition on ciphers, given that she used it in the first months of 1643. She supported the Parliamentarians, but she was the daughter of Edward Conway (ca. 1564–1631), in his own time a zealous supporter of Elizabeth's cause and her frequent correspondent. It is likely that Harley learned secret modes of writing from her father who had after all served as secretary of state between 1623 and 1628. She sent a paper with cutouts to at least two of her addressees through which words that would make up a secretive message could be written. When this cutout sheet was removed the writers were supposed to fill in the gaps, creating meaningless phrases or sentences of disinformation. And, vice versa, when the addressees received Lady Brilliana's letter, they had to pin the cutout sheet on top of the letter to cover the meaningless words. As she explained to her son Edward: "you must pin that end of the paper, that has the cors [sic] made in incke, vpon the little cros on the end of this letter; when you would write to me, make vse of it, and giue the other to your sister Brill."[49] Jacqueline Eales, who has brought this delightful method newly to light, points out that the "vast majority of her [Lady Brilliana's] surviving letters were not, however, written in code."[50] However, steganographic methods are notoriously difficult to detect. Unless Brilliana's correspondence is scoured for small needle marks, one simply cannot be sure. As a material artifact a cutout sheet also had a social function. Like owning a cipher key, it encoded social prestige; key and cutout sheet alike can also be seen as material tokens of intimacy. As Karen Britland observes, "there can never be only *one* cipher key; there must, by necessity be two."[51] The secret possession of such material artifacts nourished friendship pacts, spinning hidden connections between at least two letter writers who were, to use a Donnean phrase, "inter-assured of the mind."[52]

Steganography was increasingly used after 1643, and in some circles, such as that of the queen of Bohemia, replaced cryptography altogether. Like other letter writers, Elizabeth and her circle resorted to methods of steganography when the ban on codes during the Wars of the Three Kingdoms came into effect. One of the chief, technical methods of steganography is the use of invisible ink, or sympathetic ink as it is now more commonly known. Sympathetic ink was not a mystic, magical solution but often simply a colorless liquid such as milk, lemon, apple, orange juice, or, off-putting though it may sound (but most readily available under circumstances such as imprisonment), urine.[53] When heat was applied the hidden text oxidized and thus materialized on the page in a brownish color. On 15 October 1645, Charles I wrote a letter to Elizabeth's son Rupert, using this inventive technique.[54] Also, in the 1650s, Elizabeth appears to have written parts of letters to her master of the household Charles Cotterel (1615–1701) in sympathetic ink.[55]

Nonetheless, that even sympathetic ink might have had a social function becomes apparent in verse written by an alleged spy. Queen Henrietta Maria's cipher-secretary, poet, and suspected royalist spy Abraham Cowley (1618–67) wrote a poem about the magical properties of invisible ink. The speaker compares the warmth of springtime to the heat of the fire, both heat sources bring out "Natures characters," whether those be plants or letters. Addressing the physical paper of the epistle itself, the speaker exclaims

> So, nothing yet in Thee is seen,
> But soon as Genial Heat warms thee within,
> A new-born Wood of various Lines there grows;
> Here buds an A, and there a B,
> Here sprouts a V, and there a T,
> And all the flourishing Letters stand in Rows.
>   ("Written in Juice of Lemmon," stanza 6, lines 31–36)

Anticipating the paper (and of course also the poem's reader) questioning the usefulness of sympathetic ink, the speaker continues:

> Still, seely Paper, thou wilt think
> That all this might as well be writ with [normal] Ink.
> Oh no; there's sense in this, and Mysterie;
> Thou now maist change thy Authors name,
> And to her Hand lay noble claim;
> For as She Reads, she Makes the words in Thee.[56]
>   (Stanza 7, lines 37–42)

In Cowley's poem, the acts of decryption, application of heat, and authorship are conflated, as the words in sympathetic ink will only appear on the page by a joint act of both letter writer and receiver: the words of the letter writer in lemon juice would remain forever transparent if the receiver chose not to inscribe the words anew on the page by holding the letter to a candle. The spy and his or her employer are mutually responsible for authoring the secret message.

The attraction of cryptology surpassed the domain of the diplomat or spy in other respects as well. Most serious cipher manuals have an element of play about them. For instance, John Wilkins (1614–72), who served Elizabeth's son Charles Louis as chaplain from 1644 to 1649, wrote one such manual. His tract, *Mercury, the Secret and Swift Messenger* (1641), includes things "true" but also things "fabulous." For example, he includes formulas for sympathetic ink (pp. 41–42). Those based on lemon juice seem practical enough; the "distiled juyce of Glow-wormes"—not "visible but in the darke"—might have been more difficult to come by. As Ann Geneva also argues, "in examining the welter of secret language devices featured in seventeenth century pamphlets and manuscripts, the obvious pleasure taken in the sheer variety of methods— many quite time-consuming—appears to argue an interest and enjoyment of these devices for their own sake, as well as for their utility."[57] In postscripts to her letters, Lady Brilliana encouraged her son, before pinning on the cutout sheet as a reading lens, to enjoy the nonsensical message she had created as well: "maruell at this nonesence, which I haue written to you to make you merry";[58] "When you have laught at the nonsense, pleas your self with this, that is reson."[59] In the early modern period, it was even thought that the pleasure of solving riddles had a medicinal value, as a treatment against melancholy.[60]

These myriad examples, however different from one another, suggest that cryptography does not exclusively belong to the realm of the diplomat, spy, or head of state. As Crawforth suggests, cryptography is also related to literary traditions such as the emblem, hieroglyphics (used in court masques), anagrams, or acrostics. On the one hand, as Theresa M. Kelley points out, these genres were used by royalists in particular "to broadcast political secrets."[61] On the other hand, they were also seen by a courtly elite as divertissement and entertainment. Marsha S. Collins coined the term "the aesthetics of enigma," explaining that unknown scripts and images were puzzles, brainteasers for the elite, inspiring a sense of curiosity but also of community.[62] The use of cryptology cultivates manuscript coteries.[63] In poetic miscellanies, commonplace books, and loose-sheet libels, author's names were suppressed and replaced by codes and ciphers or thinly disguised anagrams for the delight of coterie dynamics.[64] The challenge to decode mystery demarcates the coterie's boundaries; shared secrets for insiders places the unintelligible, casual reader (or interceptor) outside the circle.

Evidence suggests that by the late 1650s, the ban on secret writing had been lifted again. John White's *A Rich Cabinet with Variety of Inventions* (1653) even promoted the use of cipher when writing love letters, and the appearance of such a publication demonstrates how the market for cryptography manuals expanded histrionically, being aimed at "the upwardly mobile soldier to the pining lover."[65] John Cotgrave's *The Wits Interpreter*, a volume that also published one of Cardinal Richelieu's cipher keys, went through several editions (1655; 1662; 1671), each time revealing more ingredients to concoct secret inks.[66] By the time both methods of cryptology—cryptography and steganography—were discussed by natural philosophers such as Robert Boyle (1627–91) at meetings of the Royal Society, secret characters had become "the conveyors of everyday life and familiar relationships for commoners as well as kings."[67]

Conclusion

The view that "manuscript letters [from 1603 to 1638, or even 1642] did not resort to codes, ciphers, or shorthand as letters filled with sensitive information would do during other periods of political stress such as the civil wars" is mistaken. Such reasoning ignores, first, the fact that the Pan-European Thirty Years' War was taking place, and that Stuart politics was inextricably caught up in it (as one of the main players was a Scottish-born Stuart princess). It overlooks the strong need to safeguard information communicated in writing that existed in the first half of the seventeenth century. Second, and more important, it also disregards the possibility that in addition to concealing information, cryptography might have had a larger and more subtle social function. To look for "secrets" in the strictest sense in ciphered letters is to miss the point; such furtive information is ephemeral, as it is nearly always conveyed by word of mouth.[68] Behn and Roe clearly regarded permission to share a cipher key as an initiation rite, admittance into a secret society, by which they were granted access to a privileged relationship. Exchanging codes created coteries as writing in cipher necessitates joint authorship: the recipient of the message parrots the sender's words through the act of decryption. The time-consuming effort of encryption and decryption signals commitment. Sharing codes, ciphers, recipes for invisible ink created but also maintained coteries, as it could reestablish intimacy: the increase of secret modes of writing during the Wars of the Three Kingdoms, and of methods of steganography in particular, can also be explained by the acute need to reestablish broken bonds, the necessity to restore allegiances during times that seals were broken and letters continually intercepted. Who spoke and enjoyed the same, elite, self-created language in this period? Also, which individuals were grouped together in the cipher keys? Decrypting a key only solves part of the puzzle. Only by analyzing the keys with social networks very much in mind can we truly unlock the mysteries of the cultures of cryptology.

CHAPTER 4

Material Fictions

Counterfeit Correspondence and the Culture of Copying in Early Modern England

ANDREW GORDON

In the third sonnet of *Astrophel and Stella* Philip Sidney famously surveyed contemporary trends in the writing of poetry and had Astrophel hit upon an alternative to imitating current fashions:

> How then? Even thus: in Stella's face I read
> What love and beauty is. And then my deed
> But copying is what in her Nature writes.[1]

Sidney's words send Astrophel back to writing school. The image of Nature as writing master and Stella as copy text follows the methods set out in Peter Bales's *The Writing Schoolemaster* (1590), where the well-known master scrivener prescribed "labour with delight, and diligent heed both of minde, hand, & sight; still uiewing your Coppie, and obseruing euerie grace and comelines therof; by the often use whereof, you shall obtaine to faire writing in short time."[2] Sidney's "but copying" wittily disguises the work of the poet in a *sprezzatura* image of invention naturalized that is itself expressive of another form of mastery; the humanist facility of *copia*.[3] Yet the labors of Astrophel were remembered by the anonymous author of the 1594 sequence *Zepheria*, who adapted Sidney's image to project the hazards of literary representation onto the material act of copying, with all its contingencies.[4]

should it hap . . .
The feature of my pen some grace do win,
Thereof *Zepheria* all the honor hath,
The coppying Scribe may clayme no right therein:
   But if more nice wits censure my lines crooked,
   Thus I excuse, I writ my light remoued.[5]

The extenuation of bad poetry as a failure of copying restores to view the early modern understanding of copying as a material practice subject to error and inaccuracy, where fidelity was always in question. Producing, obtaining, or securing a true copy was far from straightforward, as those involved in the traffic of texts well knew. The author of *Zepheria* can be linked to the Inns of Court, a center for both professional and informal manuscript reproduction.[6] His replacement of the pupil Astrophel with a "coppying Scribe" in Canzon 18 relocates the scene of writing to the world of commercial labor. Sidney's attempts to restrict circulation of *Astrophel and Stella* did not prevent its "being spred abroad in written Coppies" whereby it "gathered much corruption," according to the printer of the posthumous 1591 edition.[7] Meanwhile Sidney himself promoted the dissemination of his letter to Elizabeth, one of the most widely circulating political texts of the period.[8] In different ways each author's output thus evokes the widespread culture of copying that permeated early modern society. The dependence of early modern England upon habits of copying can hardly be overstated: government, commerce, and the law were all built upon manual processes of textual reproduction. For the textual practices of correspondence in particular, the traffic of information, the exercise of authority, the management of patronage relations, and the running of any large household all relied heavily on the activity of copying.[9] The specter that haunts that dependency is forgery.

*   *   *

Forgery is by definition a parasitic practice, appropriating the workings of a host culture. The discourse that surrounds it, the strategies used to address it, and the anxieties that it generates are metacritical; they provide a way in to understanding the self-scrutiny of textual cultures. Anthony Grafton's account of the symbiotic relationship between forgers and critics through the ages has drawn attention to the dual imaginative purpose informing the forger's work: to conceive both "what a text would have looked like when it was written and what it should look like now that he has found it."[10] As a recent analysis of forged manuscripts of the Middle Ages puts it, "a forged document is a manifestation of the *idea* of the document."[11] Studies concentrating on the forgery of historical documents can thus offer particular insight into how historical difference was imagined in a given period, but early modern forgery practice was not confined to faking the past. The letter was a key textual instrument in the period—arguably the most wide-ranging and vital sociotext of its time and one particularly prone to being remade and reimagined through forgery. The present study examines the interventions of forgery as material practice and discursive construction within contemporary cultures of correspondence, drawing in particular on legal engagements with counterfeit letters. Viewed from this angle the study of forgery in letter writing permits us to interrogate the terms upon which contemporary correspondence operated and the criteria by which it was evaluated, so that we can find in forgeries a conception of both how a letter ought to look and how it ought to operate in the world. One purpose behind the current study then is to examine the *idea* of early modern letters as revealed in their forged counterparts, or what I term the "material fictions" of early modern letter forgery, encompassing not only the construction of the counterfeit as material object but also the practices that give it meaning and direction, the framing of correspondence networks, and the manipulation of the social sites of dispatch and receipt. Counterfeit correspondence and the uses to which it is put at the early modern court expose the meanings attributed to letters as a cultural instrument in prosecuting or defending claims of intimacy, confederacy, and hidden malevolence. In the process, correspondence emerges as a place of productive speculation in which material fictions of bad faith are both constructed and contested.

Forgery and the Law

According to Jean Baudrillard, "counterfeit (and fashion at the same time) is born with the Renaissance."[12] The comment occurs in his bold delineation of three historical orders of signification as part of the precession of simulacra in postmodernity. But where his observation may be said to connect particularly with the material and discursive practice of early modern England is in the field of law, for while textual forgery has a long history, it was in the course of the sixteenth century that it took shape as a crime within the compass of English law. Generalized forms of cheating had long been actionable, but the 1541 act "Against them that counterfeit Letters or privy Tokens to receive Money or Goods in other Men's Names," provided individuals with direct forms of redress against the use of forgery in exchange transactions.[13] In 1563 the "Act agaynst the forgyng of Evydences and Wrytinges" instituted penalties for making or publishing "any false and forged Dede Charter Writing Courte Roll or Will."[14] These developments were part of a broader expansion of documentary culture in the period and the increasing importance attached to documentary evidence within legal disputes.[15] In 1607 the jurist John Cowell included "Forger of false deeds" in his legal dictionary, noting that it "commeth of the french *Forger* . . . to beate one an anvile, to fashion, to bring into shape."[16] His description of one who "maketh . . . false writings" evokes the contemporary sense of forgery as a combined art, one where the imaginative work of devising and the physical artifice of creating a forged document parallels the dual concern with imaginative and material operations in literary creation.

Legislation led to advances in the arts of detection applied to forgery. This is particularly evident in the records of Star Chamber where techniques of both philological and material investigation develop a place within legal argument. Anachronism in the handling of verbal conventions confirms one counterfeit in the valediction "*Hic testibus*, a thing not in use since the time of Henry VII., and therefore a badge of forgery and fraud," the discrepancy indicating a forger copying from an outdated example.[17] Investigation of another dubious deed probes the distinction between forging and copying. The two brothers who stood to benefit were in the dock alongside the shadowy figure of one Shute, who had drawn up the document. The deed had already figured in the deliberations of a land commission, and the siblings' defense sought to exploit the gray areas that existed in a culture of copying. Hence Robert Wallis conceded that "Shute did wryte Coppies out of other Coppies but wheather they were forged or noe this depon[t] knoweth not."[18] His defense that the inaccurate deeds were simply bad "copies or transcriptes" rather than deliberate forgeries was undermined by the physical evidence of attempted smoke aging, despite Robert's ingenious denial: "[the documents] were neuer hanged in the smoke but he remembereth that the said Coppis deliu'd unto him [by Shute] he did laye them upon a shelfe wth his Chimbneye in his house."[19]

The cases before Star Chamber involve scrutiny of the historical authenticity of deeds through the early diplomatic strategy of comparing textual formulas as well as examining material means of falsifying a document's appearance. Like other aspects of legal process in the period such cases had a formative effect on the cultural imagination.[20] They testify to the increasing investment of the legal profession in the habits of documentary analysis and demonstrate that the Privy Counsellors who constituted the Star Chamber panel were expected to engage with detailed evaluation of documentary evidence. The same is true of litigants. A landholder such as Henry Fytte could now identify legal grounds for his complaint: "the counterfetting and writing of wch ltres falsely and coruptulie in the name of your said subiecte is against the lawe and statute of this your ma^ties raigne."[21] Within the mediating formulae of legal documents we witness an expanding awareness of the potential for identifying and taking action against textual forgery.

In the investigation of fraudulent letters, cases in Star Chamber reveal the social functions of letters as well as the strategies used to authenticate them. One obvious target for forgery was the letter of credit, which could attract complex strategies for deception. A 1607 case brought by Peter Gleave against two acquaintances of his son Thomas, a scholar short of funds at Cambridge, centers on a forged letter sent in the father's name to Sir Henry Hobart, then a king's attorney in the Court of Wards, requesting that Thomas be furnished with the sum of £45. The counterfeit letter of credit subscribed to "yor very Loueinge Frende" constituted an abuse of the carefully cultivated social relations through which credit operated in the early modern period.[22] The case records are incomplete but the answer and examination of one defendant present a detailed picture of events. Richard Watkinson's evidence makes the son fully complicit in the scheme, alleging that while the other defendant, Isacke Spratt, composed the letter "the said Thomas Gleaue Counterfeyted the compl[ainan]^ts hande, and name thereunto."[23] It was Thomas, too, who delivered the letter and took receipt of the money into his hands. For his own part, Watkinson confessed to having drawn up a counterfeit letter under duress that was promptly burned by Gleave junior when he noticed the former's inclusion of a mocking rhyme subverting the scheme: "Sr Henry Hobart open yr cupbatt [i.e., cupboard] wth owt any gryffe [grief] or ells [will] Tho: Gleive waxe leane for want of relefe."[24] This comic intervention aside, Watkinson's account presents the act of forgery as a collaborative process involving several stages from devising and producing the document to performing the fraudulent transaction via the counterfeit instrument of credit, before spending the ill-procured funds in various dissolute ways. Peter Gleave's prosecution of the case is designed to repair not only his own credit, however, but also that of his son whom he therefore represents as an innocent "corrupted by their wicked Companie" rather than the knowing agent in deception depicted in the other testimony.[25] In rewriting the fraud to secure the textual credit of his name and reassert the integrity of his son's hand, Gleave had the assistance of the creditor, Henry Hobart, now the attorney general, whose signature is appended to the bill of complaint. Hobart's involvement puts added pressure on the veracity of Gleave's account, suggesting that to explain the son's involvement in the material fiction of the counterfeit letter, the client and patron had been pushed to devise a more elaborate fiction of its production.

Defending honor and a good name was central to many cases of counterfeit correspondence. Counterfeit letters might operate effectively as libels, to publish disgrace against a particular party, as with the letter produced and circulated in multiple copies by one Annate that implicated London's comptroller of customs in the production of counterfeit coinage.[26] More significantly the preservation of female virtue was central to the many cases where a disputed contract of marriage depended on the contested authority of courtship letters. The proving of an unwitnessed contract of marriage, whether *de praesanti* or *de futuro* might depend on material evidence of love tokens exchanged between the parties.[27] While rings and other symbolic tokens of betrothal were common, the exchange of letters could offer more substantial evidential commentary on a contested match. In the case of the young William Cavendish, the future Duke of Newcastle, his letters to Margaret Chatterton appear deliberately composed to provide incontrovertible assurance of a marriage contract, explicitly referring to himself as her husband and encouraging her to identify herself as his wife in her reply. Yet this very evidentiary value would form the focus of an aggravated case against Chatterton, prosecuted by Sir Henry Hobart at the urging of William's father, that accused her of engineering forged letters to ensnare him in marriage.[28] The deliberate attempt to discredit the contract of marriage orchestrated by Hobart relied upon evoking a threatening and duplicitous female textual agency. More common are cases that turn on male manipulation of textual tools. A case brought over the abduction and marriage of a thirteen-year-old girl without her parents' consent ignored the daughter's welfare to focus upon entitlement to her inheritance, ruling the marriage contract void as resulting from counterfeit letters.[29] In another case the attempted kidnap of a maidservant, Alice Clemson, exploited the social authority of kinship networks as regulated in letters. The master John Dickens accused George Parker of counterfeiting a letter of recommendation for Parker's marriage suit supposed to be from her benefactor uncle "who yor subject knew was both a louing and a tender uncle to the said Alice Clemson therfore yor subject in kind sort welcomed the said Parker," affording the access to the household that almost resulted in Alice's abduction.[30] The counterfeiting here is not contested, only the object of the deception. The defendants rejected the portrait of the uncle as protector of a vulnerable maid and present their scheme as a deliberate ruse, devised with the knowledge of Alice, to evade a possessive master.

The use of counterfeit letters thus illustrates several of the key social functions of correspondence. Letters appear as both tokens of trust between suitors and forms of social bond that locate unrecognized individuals within networks of kinship and community, vouching for their behavior. The cases also reveal the instrumental authority accorded to species of letters and the gravity with which acts of epistolary impersonation were treated. Court documents demonstrate a keen interest in all aspects of a letter's production and use. Forged letters are quoted extensively where extant, including precise details of dating, valediction, and outer address. Defendants in the Gleave case were asked to detail "who deuised the sayd letter, who first mooued the wrytinge therof, who wrytte the same whether did you Read and Correct alter or amend or haue Redd or cause to be Corrected altred or amended the sayd Letter."[31] Alongside the artifice of producing a counterfeit letter, the cases shed light on a broader spectrum of opportunities for the infiltration of correspondence practices. In the case involving Alice Clemson, upon the delivery of the counterfeit the mistress of the house "went . . . into another rome to reade the Letter," allowing Parker to divulge the plan to Alice while getting hay for his horse.[32] Here the forged letter itself is a form of decoy, providing a pretext in the act of delivery for infiltrating the household and making contact with the maid. Star Chamber cases thus reveal the conceptual shape of correspondence and the constituent elements of a culture that comprises textual rhetorics, material features, and the social rituals attaching to letter-writing, letter-reading, and letter-dissemination practices.

Forgery and Treason

Certain forms of counterfeit correspondence were of particular concern to the Privy Counsellors and judges who made up the Star Chamber council. Forging of the king's seal had been a treasonable offense since at least the twelfth century, but forging the royal sign manual only entered the statute in 1536.[33] Privy Council records from the mid-Tudor period onward show concern at the rising incidence of forged signatures on warrants, passports, licenses, and summonses. At stake was the credibility of the entire medium of missive documentation. In 1598 John Melloes was found to have "counterfeited the hande of . . . The Lo Threasorer and Caused also his Seale of Armes to be made wch he hath also set to diuers lres and warrants."[34] Similar cases show the epistolary marks of executive authority being appropriated to effect false imprisonments or secure others' release. According to a 1597 report, "one Rosse" conducted a campaign of persecution against a Kentish man using "counterfaict warrant in the names of us of her Majesty's Privie Councell" to convey him to London "where he kept him certaine daies, shifting him up and downe from place to place, and tooke from him . . . money."[35] Garrett Swift was imprisoned the following year for "manie lewde practizes comitted by him in counterfaitinge the handes of divers of us of her Majesty's Privie Counsell . . . aswell for the inlargement of some notorious mallefactours as for powder out of her Majesty's store."[36] Members of the Privy Council were so disconcerted by this misappropriation of their identity and authority that in 1596 a "Proclamation for the Punishment of Persons with Forged Credentials" was issued, exhorting "parsons, or vicars of parishes, churchwardens or other her majesty's officers and loving subjects" to close inspection and verification of all licenses, warrants, and summonses.[37] Just as the proceedings of Star Chamber required the impaneled lords and judges to recognize practices for the scrutinizing of textual authority, Elizabeth's government now took the radical step of encouraging documentary skepticism in its officeholders at the most local level.

Tracing examples of forged epistolary authority presents many methodological challenges, but the detection of a forged letter into the Low Countries in the name of Sir Robert Cecil (Figure 4.1) provides an illuminating example. Dated from Greenwich in 1604, the false letter of credit is an artful forgery with a counterfeit seal and a passable but labored imitation of Cecil's signature. Applying modern techniques of forensic analysis to the signature, it is apparent that the line quality, for example in the slanting descender of the *R*, exemplifies the careful slowness of the imitator rather than the swift flourish characteristic of the practiced hand.[38] Alongside seal and signature a forgery needed to conform to material conventions of folding, address, and layout both specific to the genre of letter and particular to the correspondent.[39] In this example the letter seeks to counterfeit authority via a further material mark: a cipher symbol that is to identify future urgent correspondence for dispatch to London. This cunning device delivers a prestigious token of trust that promises to initiate the recipient into an exclusive correspondence network.[40]

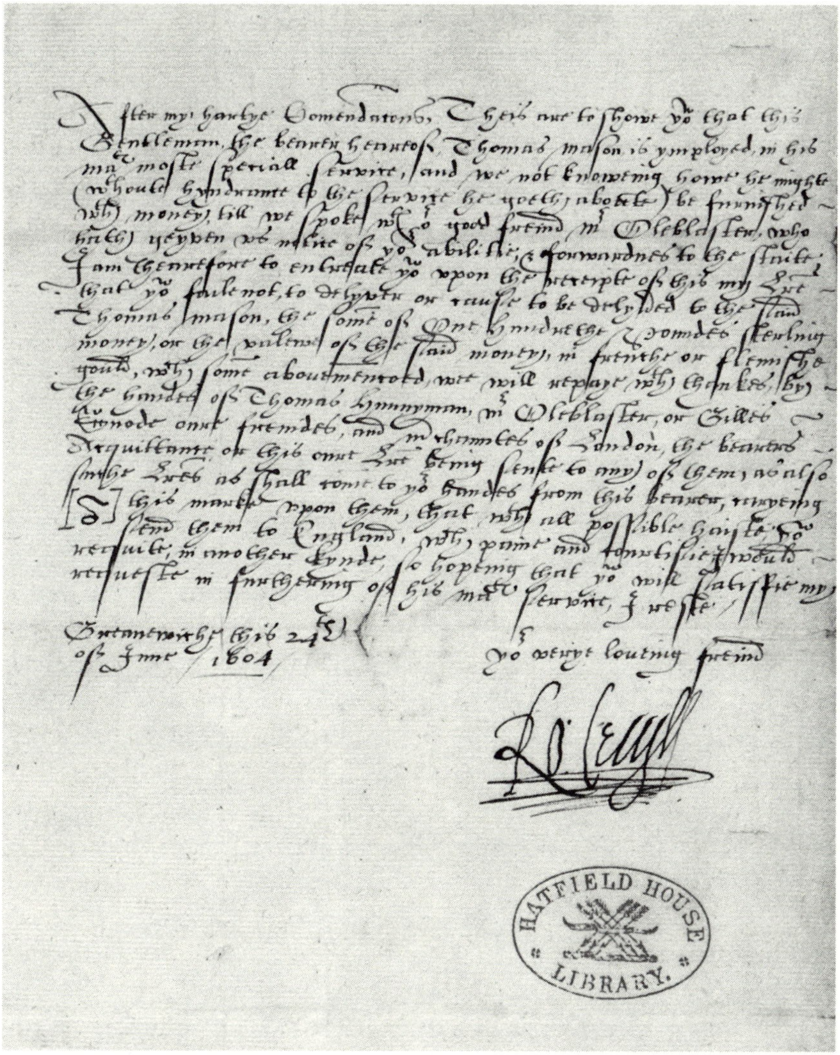

Figure 4.1. Forged letter of credit in Sir Robert Cecil's name, 1604. Hatfield House, Cecil Papers 188/135. Reproduced courtesy of the Marquess of Salisbury, Hatfield House.

As an instrument of credit, the referentiality of the counterfeit Cecil letter encompasses both these material signs of authenticity and the verbal evocation of an international credit network of London merchants. Easily overlooked is the extent to which such an act of counterfeiting depends upon the performance of the bearer, one "Thomas Mason," who must supply the advertised written acquittance and pass himself off as someone employed in Cecil's "most special service." One or more of these multiple aspects of counterfeiting failed to convince the recipients of the letter since it bears the contemporary endorsement "A lre conterfayted in my Lords name and broughte to him from Middleburgh." Sent on to Cecil's secretariat, the rare survival of this discovered counterfeit offers us a glimpse into the levels of artifice involved in appropriating the authority of king or counselor by epistolary means.[41]

It is a characteristic of the early modern period's conflicted investments in the material letter that at the very moment when incidents of forgery were fostering anxiety over the credibility of texts, those pursuing treason prosecutions were placing increasing weight upon textual evidence and in particular, upon letters. The 1534 act (26 Hen. VIII, c. 13) extending the scope of the law to encompass treason by words had transformed the shape of the crime and its evidentiary interests.[42] While witness testimony also grew in importance, the letter took on a particular currency in treason proceedings. Increasingly letters came to be put on trial: their authenticity, challenged; and what they could be made to mean, explored. It was the "exemplary epistolary treason" of Mary, Queen of Scots, that did most to shape the imaginative understanding of letters in treason proceedings.[43] The use of the infamous "casket letters" to implicate Mary in the murder of her husband, Lord Darnley, is now well known, but the foregrounding of textual investigation was integral to the process of incrimination.[44] At the English Conference of 1568 the impaneled lords were required to compare this intimate correspondence—supposedly adulterous letters written from Mary to her adviser, the Earl of Bothwell—with official letters from Mary to Elizabeth, in order to determine their authenticity. Denied access to the originals, Mary protested that "if any such writings there be, they are false and feigned, forged and invented."[45] The construction of textual authenticity was also to the forefront in the print campaign that followed when Elizabeth's secretary of state, Sir William Cecil and the Scottish humanist reformer George Buchanan sought to reproduce the claims of documentary evidence in print, affirming that the letters had been "auowed in presence of persones of most honorable state and authoritie to haie ben written & subscribed as is there alleged, & so deliuered without rasure, diminution, addition, falsifieing or alteration in any point."[46] Twenty years later, Mary's trial at Fotheringhay Castle would build on this groundwork. The careful work of the team assembled by Sir Francis Walsingham, Elizabeth's head of intelligence operations, was able to implicate Mary in the Babington conspiracy, producing damning confessions from her secretaries by the subtle manipulation of a reconstructed cipher correspondence with the confederates.[47] Meanwhile Mary's rhetorical counterstrategy, demanding holograph evidence of her hand in the proceedings, yielded diminishing returns in part because expanding reliance upon secretaries had come to incorporate a form of authorized counterfeiting.[48] Mary's story would cast a long shadow over the prosecution of treason in the period. The rehearsal of arguments for the authenticity of the casket letters and the Babington correspondence promoted the discourse of evidential validity even as the integrity of the material proof was opened to question. The wide dissemination of the details helped to popularize both the narrative model of hidden treasons discovered and the performative uses of material evidence.

The Elizabethan court's appetite for epistolary treason and the vulnerability of prominent figures to such accusations is exemplified by the case of Sir John Perrot. Despite a long record of loyal service to the Crown, Perrot's confrontational style had earned him enemies, and, after the death of his patron Walsingham in 1590, several rivals gained in influence at court. It was in this context that an accusation of treason made by his successor as lord deputy of Ireland, William Fitzwilliam, began to gather momentum.[49] The principal evidence was supplied by an ex-priest, Sir Denis O'Roughan, in the form of a treasonous correspondence between Perrot and the king of Spain. Neither the documents nor their supplier had much credibility, and Perrot clearly thought he was on firm ground. O'Roughan had actually been imprisoned for counterfeiting warrants in Sir John's name during Perrot's tenure as lord deputy: "the same being such as might in some times bring me in question in the hiest degree," as he wrote prophetically to Walsingham in 1585.[50] Learning of the treason charges, Perrot wrote repeated letters to William Cecil (now Lord Burghley) and others over the investigation, advising "Yf y^t lre . . . weare showde to one Foxe nowe aboute ye Courte . . . and to Harry Byrde they will goe neare to proue whether Sr Denyse or what other wrote [it]," and supplied extensive directions for the priest's interrogation.[51] Multiple depositions survive supporting Perrot's account. Sir Henry Wallop attested that he was himself present in Dublin Castle when they "dyd exhibite in the Castle chamber matter of forgerie against the said Bird and Sr Dennyse," and urged consultation of the court records.[52] Others, such as James Meagher wrote offering to confirm the identity of those who had counterfeited the letter.[53]

Perrot's papers preserve his meticulous itemizing of the faults in the counterfeit letter: "written in English but of Irish orthography a very foolish style, the hand not good, the counterfeit of my hand as ill, the paper worse and neither my private or ordinary seal of arms thereunto."[54] The original at the center of this investigation does not survive, but we do have the certified copy of the letter that Fitzwilliam sent to Lord Burghley in London (Figure 4.2.). While our ability to reconstruct the material artifice of forgery from the copy is limited, Fitzwilliam's accompanying letter does acknowledge that the letter is "wrytten in a bastard roman hand," yet supports the attribution by affirming that it is "subscrybyed by Sr John Perrot as to me aperyth."[55] In the copy (written in the same mixed cursive hand as Fitzwilliam's autograph letter) the distinctive orthography survives perhaps in the opening address to the "Most grasius & Sufferant Kynge."[56] Most striking, however, is the guileless touting of treason that has Perrot openly profess: "I wyll undertacke to get y^{or} hyghnes thes 2 lands of england and Iland" in return for written guarantees "under yor hand and seall" that he will be granted "ye holl land of walles" in perpetuity. Perrot pointed out the lack of any seal, to which we can add the absence of any marker of secrecy or even concern for security in this correspondence: no form of encryption or cipher is suggested, nor is there any commentary on delivery or transmission, so often a fundamental object of treason investigations, and a virtually ubiquitous "phatic" feature of most early modern correspondence. Indeed there is not even any response content here to the two earlier letters allegedly delivered from Spain. As Perrot objected: "it were strange that I would forget to write in the supposed letter to the king an answer."[57] From the copy and the commentary on the original, then, it is clear that the counterfeit conformed to few of the observable conventions of either the treasonous letter or epistolary practice more broadly, contrasting sharply with the cunning artifice of the Cecil counterfeit discussed above. That the charge was pursued any further is testament to the political forces grouping against him and Burghley's manipulation of the episode to suit his patronage interests.[58] Nevertheless the prosecutors broadened their case. By the time of the trial, they no longer depended solely upon the counterfeit letter but placed the correspondence within a context of disobedience, using witness testimony of various exasperated exclamations from the hotheaded Sir John (many of them reactions to the receipt of Elizabeth's letters), with one of the impaneled peers Lord Buckhurst reportedly pronouncing that "these speeches did shew

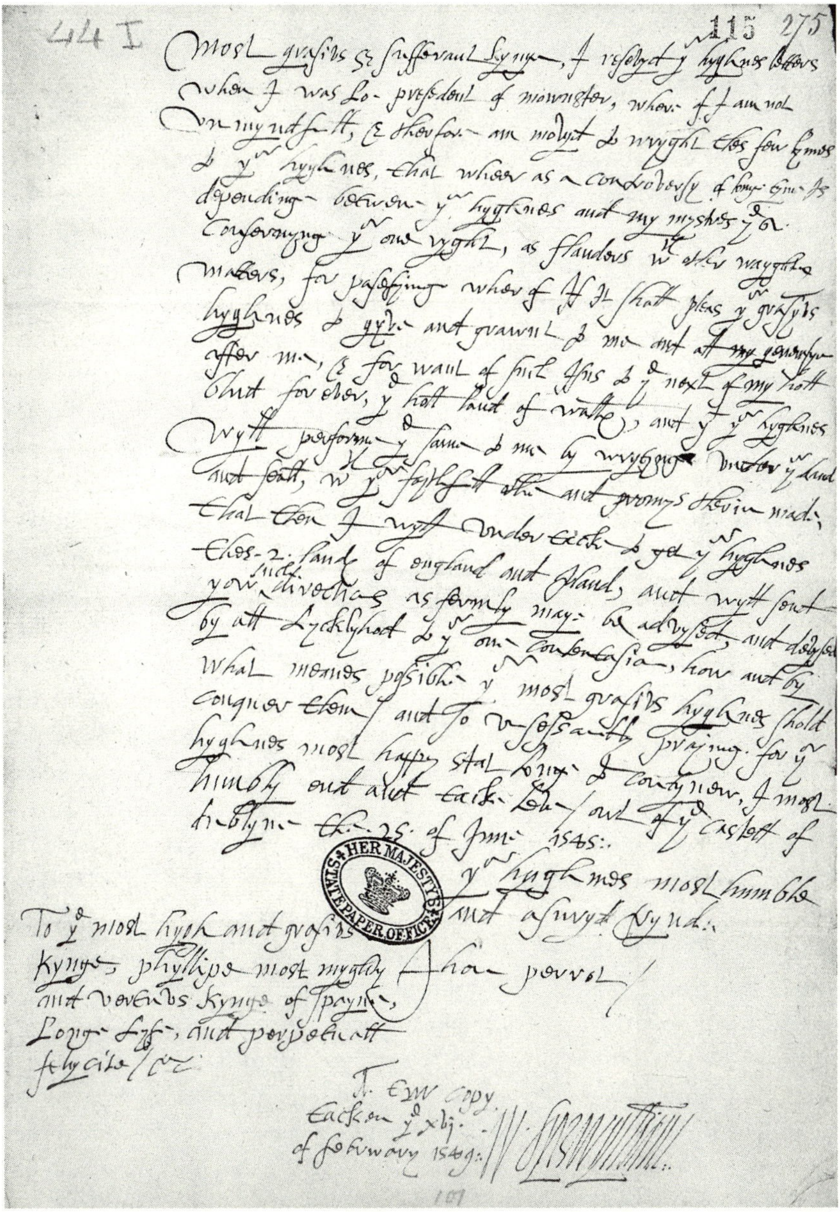

Figure 4.2. "Trew copy" endorsed by William Fitzwilliam of the forged letter supposedly sent by Sir John Perrot to the king of Spain. The National Archives, SP 63/150, fol. 115.

a disloyall mind."[59] Despite special dispensation to have his papers with him in court, Perrot was unable to counter the inference of treason in his words or to discredit O'Roughan conclusively and would die in prison as a convicted traitor.

Perrot's case shows how a counterfeit letter—even a manifest material fiction, unable to withstand any critical scrutiny—might be used to ensnare an exposed individual when the momentum of a treason prosecution coincided with the political interests of a figure as powerful as Burghley. We see here the extent to which treason prosecution in the early modern period was a specu-lative business. Attempts to traffic in treason were hazardous, however, and a number of examples see the tables turned on counterfeiters or those pursuing a case who failed to attract support for their projection of treason. In 1574 the authority of the archbishop of Canterbury Matthew Parker was weakened when he gave credence to accusations of treason implicating leading Puritan reformers and had several preachers imprisoned, all on the basis of a series of counterfeit letters. An alarmed Parker drew Burghley's attention to "[t]his deep, devilish, traitorous dissimulation, this horrible conspiracy," which he confessed "hath so astonied me, that my wit, my memory, be quite gone."[60] But what looked like conspiracy turned out to be a material fiction cultivated by one Humphrey Needham.[61] Needham had produced over forty forged letters in various names, to the amazement of Parker who marveled that "so many [let-ters], should be counterfeited ev^r wth one hand."[62] The damage to Parker's cred-ibility was extensive, undermining at a stroke his anti-Puritan influence.[63] Robert Beale, the clerk of the Privy Council and an active Puritan, criticized the investigation as deliberate persecution of the reformers. Despite Parker's extensive patronage of textual scholarship, Beale pointed out the poor stan-dards of evidentiary analysis on which the case rested: "The Lres Counterfeyc-ted in other mans names and written by com[m]on Scholeboyes, were so grosse, the false ortography and maner of wrytinges and matter so apparent as no wise man woulde euer haue geuen credit unto them."[64] The sudden unraveling of the conspiracy plot illustrates the risks of investing in a treason narrative as one of its principal promoters. The debacle over Needham may have informed the slow pace and deliberate stealth with which Burghley pro-ceeded in gathering evidence against Mary, Queen of Scots. Certainly the cau-tion of the Crown in building a case for treason on epistolary materials is noticeable from the examination of one Murfin about a sensational conspir-acy to bring forces over from Ireland with the intent to mount a rebellion and "deliuer ye Scottish Queene."[65] Murfin implicated Sir George Hastings and the earls of Westmoreland and Desmond as his confederates, along with many others, and to substantiate his claims provided a series of letters, warrants, and covenant deeds—another conventional feature of treason conspiracies. The undated examination by Richard Topcliffe and Thomas Norton likely took place around 1583–84, at a time when material for use against Mary was being compiled.[66] The notes reveal the interrogators' skeptical evaluation of the evidence on a range of forensic documentary criteria. They challenged the supposed sequence of events in Murfin's narrative, carefully reconstructing the forgery process from the material evidence. Assessing the paper stock used, they were able to link several items back to a single sheet and so refute Murfin's dating of the copy of a prophecy supposed to have influenced the conspirators at the outset. They deduced that Murfin "was constrained to make shift to write p[ar]cell of it in margins and corners of the paper, bycause the ded of gyft" (another of the key documents) "being first written had left him no more roome."[67] Another letter was dismissed because "Norton toke exception to the freshnese of ink, and cleanesse of paper as a thing not written thre dayes before."[68] Through comparison of inks, papers, and hands, Topcliffe and Norton refute the existence of any coconspirators and conclude that Murfin had fabricated the fiction alone—a conclusion borne out by a thorough search of his rooms that revealed "the originalles . . . deuised and penned by Murfin him selfe in scribled papers."[69] The detailed report demonstrates that the authentication of letters through critical evaluation of the material evidence and a precise analysis of epistolary practice was a recognized investigative approach. The deployment of these techniques to investigate Murfin's tale of conspiracy where they would be either ignored or suppressed in the case against Perrot provides further evidence of the speculative expediency that underwrote early modern treason prosecution.

Although it failed to attract the authorities' interest as a conspiracy, the scale of Murfin's forging enterprise and the range of techniques involved nevertheless provide us with a rare insight into forgery practice. Among his papers were found numerous forged letters in various hands as well as "sondrie blancks or shetes of whit pap[er], hauing the names of [various conspirators], ouer wch were to be written what soeuer Murfin wold."[70] Murfin had diligently gathered samples of particular hands to practice, persuaded parties to sign incomplete letters or documents with spaces left unfilled, produced false seals, obtained special stocks of paper, and experimented with special inks. The working methods recoverable from the contents of Murfin's study point to forgery as a professional operation. Many of the incidents of forgery pursued by the Privy Council and prosecuted in Star Chamber involved repeat offend-ers. Some, such as Richard Shute, a "very cunninge and subtill fellowe" sus-pected of producing numerous dubious documents over a long period, or Richard Billborough for whom "forgery . . . hath byn the best p[ar]t of his maintenance longe tyme" were clearly career counterfeiters.[71] Most cases in-volved professional textual specialists: the cast of defendants includes public notaries, scriveners, attorneys of the Common Pleas, and clerks from London and Canterbury, demonstrating that forgery involved a particular application of skills commonly present within the writing classes.[72] As noted above, the Crown had the expertise of its own textual professionals to call upon. Sir Fran-cis Walsingham had been a pioneer in the use of forgery techniques in the service of the state, supervising Mary, Queen of Scots' entrapment with a team of specialists using forgery techniques to infiltrate her correspondence. The key figure was Thomas Phelippes, a multilingual code breaker, decipherer, master of different hands, and maintainer of multiple epistolary identities, who supervised the Babington investigation.[73] He was assisted by Arthur Gregory, a skilled counterfeiter of seals who could open, copy, and reseal letters with such skill "that none could iudge them to haue beene vnsealed."[74] Walsing-ham's investment had produced innovative research into the art of epistolary duplicity. A 1586 request for resources sees Gregory showcasing new techniques for the composition of secret ink, his letter including a specimen text box and quantity of powder for Walsingham to rub in and reveal the hidden message.[75] The death of Walsingham in 1590 left his protégés pitching for employment from the most active courtiers and counselors in a developing intelligence market. Gregory soon offered Sir Robert Cecil "the use of my secret services," and we find him doing urgent forgery work for the secretary of state in 1596, when he complains to Cecil, "I find my self utterly unfitt to [do] a sodaine Counterfait for I scarse dare keepe it in my hands."[76]

Such glimpses into the activity of counterfeiters connected to the court demonstrate the vulnerability of the early modern letter to subversion, pro-viding some justification for the widespread anxiety of contemporaries. In the final years of Elizabeth's reign the development of forgery techniques and their increased availability for employment combined with a competition for influ-ence that encouraged ambitious courtiers to exploit treason accusations for their own advancement and the destruction of their rivals. That climate of textual distrust around the Elizabethan court made its mark on the wider cultural imagination and even found an audience in the public playhouse. As Alan Stewart has shown, Shakespeare's dramaturgy is marked by a concern

with the material processes of letter writing and particularly the material subversion of textual strategies. Hamlet's intervention as forger, framing the
death warrant of his erstwhile fellow students, shows the skills of the Danish
prince in the pragmatic arts of penmanship, while Maria's forging of Olivia's
hand in *Twelfth Night* applies the textual services routinely performed for her
mistress to her own comic ends.[77] These acts of secretarial subterfuge—
mastering the hand and wielding the tools of epistolary authority (the seal
and the signature)—play on contemporary anxieties over the vulnerability of
letter writing to imitation of a malicious kind. Nor was this concern confined
to Shakespeare. Perhaps the most extreme example of epistolary deception in
Elizabethan drama occurs in *The Blind Beggar of Bethnal Green* (1600), a collaboration between the author-printer Henry Chettle and the sometime Inns
of Court man John Day for the Admiral's Men. Popular enough to spawn a
succession of sequels the following year, the play's central plot features a
warrior-nobleman brought down by the machinations of rival factions, reflecting contemporary cynicism over courtly corruption in the late Elizabethan
period. The play mixes elements of comic romance with a quasi-historical setting in the reign of Henry VI, and draws on an established Admiral's Men
device in the banished nobleman Momford's use of a blind beggar disguise.[78]
What makes the play particularly noteworthy, however, is the complex intrigue
that brings about his fall—a device not present in the play's conventional
sources. Momford is accused and summarily sentenced to a permanent exile
for treasonous dealings over the town of Guines, and the proof against him
takes the form of counterfeit letters. The rudiments of the plot are revealed by
his double-dealing brother, Sir Robert Westford, who confesses how Young
Playnsey:

> counterfeited certain Letters,
> Subscribing them with Lord *Villiers* his name;
> In gratulation for betraying Guynes,
> The Post surpriz'd, examin'd where he had them.
> He answered from *Villiers* his Secretary:
> For in his habit Playnsey was disguis'd.[79]

The plan involves a complex chain of epistolary deceit that encompasses multiple forms of counterfeiting from the material production of letters to infiltrating practices of textual transmission. After getting himself captured by the
French, Playnsey impersonates the governor's secretary to dispatch a counterfeit

letter implicating Momford in an imagined agreement to yield the town, before arranging the interception of the letter and the messenger's interrogation. The kind of comic confounding of letter delivery that the Renaissance stage typically borrowed from Plautus is here converted to more sinister political skulduggery. While *The Blind Beggar of Bethnal Green* shares with the Shakespearean examples an interest in secretarial duties, its use of forgery involves a more convoluted form of letter deception, in which the balance of the counterfeiting hinges on misdirection: it is not Momford's hand that is forged but that of a French lord. The treasonable act is brought to light by the letters of an unverifiable third party in a material form subjected to no scrutiny. Where the actions of Maria and Hamlet apply the benefit of their serviceable skills, Playnsey's ploy seems designed rather to highlight the blatantly flawed justice meted out to the nobleman. Dramatizing the cunning confection of treason by epistolary means, we find the letter discredited as an evidentiary device. In its place, the play suggests, the letter is a vehicle for material fictions that perform and display the corrupt character of the Elizabethan court.

Daniell's Disasters

Chettle and Day delivered their dramatic take on epistolary treason to Philip Henslowe in May of 1600. Despite the deviousness of its device, however, a series of events were unfolding at court at this time that provide a more complex interpretive challenge than the theatrical representation of letter deceit from the Admiral's Men. This episode of malicious letter work centers on the correspondence of the Earl of Essex and constitutes the single most significant case of the period for understanding how the rich polyvalence of the letter was exploited in the material fictions of forgery and speculative construction of treason. The affair came to public prominence at Essex's trial for treason in February 1601, when the earl interrupted the prosecuting counsel to recount how "Bales the Scrivenor in the old Bailey hath confessed under his hand that he hath bene delt w[th]all and forced to forge and counterfett my hand in at least twelue serverall lres."[80] "Bales the Scrivenor" is none other than the noted author of *The Writing Schoolemaster* famed for his feats of miniature writing (he produced a copy of the Bible small enough to fit within a walnut shell) and for gaining the prize of a golden pen in a public writing competition held in 1595, and thereafter immortalized in his shop sign.[81] Essex's interjection drew on a declaration made by Bales in April 1600, with which the earl sought to color the prosecution's case with the taint of forgery. But Attorney General Edward Coke countered this with the suggestion that Bales "was hired therunto by one Iohn Daniell a seruant of the Earles to the end that if the Earles owen hand should be p[ro]duced to arrest him he might haue somewhat to say for him self."[82] The rival reading proposed by the Crown inferred a radical counterintelligence ploy on Essex's part to destabilize all textual evidence against him. The competing constructions aired at the trial demonstrate just how fertile the imagination of treason could be when its object was correspondence. Yet each is an expedient repurposing of a more complex and ambiguous series of events in which acts of copying form the central interpretive crux.

It was in June 1601, some months after the earl's execution, that John Daniell was found guilty in Star Chamber of having "procured" some of the earl's letters "to be Coppied, Counterfeited corrupted and forged."[83] Daniell had removed a selection of letters between the Earl and Countess of Essex from a casket entrusted to his wife, Jane, who was employed in the countess's service, but the profusion of terms in the judgment is a pointer to the variable constructions that might be placed on what he did with them. A quite remarkable array of materials survive to help us make sense of the affair. Although the original declaration from Peter Bales is not extant, various later written testimonies describe his dealings with Daniell (Figure 4.3).[84] Daniell brought a selection of Essex's letters to Bales's premises in the Old Bailey and paid him to produce multiple copies, apparently to assist him in reading the earl's difficult hand. Anthony Bacon, one of the earl's closest advisers, had called his script "as hard as any kypher to those that are not thoroughlie acquaunted therewith," and Bales himself testified that at the outset he "could not rede throse lres p[er]fectlie."[85] Rather than merely transcribe the letters, however, Daniell paid Bales 12d. to imitate them closely. According to the Star Chamber decree, he demanded Bales produce copies "as nere and like as he could posseblie to the Earle of Essex proper hande—wrytinge both in lynes, letters, And subscripcon as that the oryginall, and the Coppies might not be different or discerned."[86] To explain his possession of the letters Daniell provided a shifting backstory, first claiming that the copying project was undertaken at the countess's direction before subsequently telling Bales "that he ment to geue some a gull, wch words," recalled the writing master, "p[er]plexed mee greatlie."[87] When Daniell failed to reappear after this last meeting, Bales grew increasingly nervous and eventually confided in his acquaintance, the shadowy but well-connected figure of Peter Ferryman, who had formerly been a servant

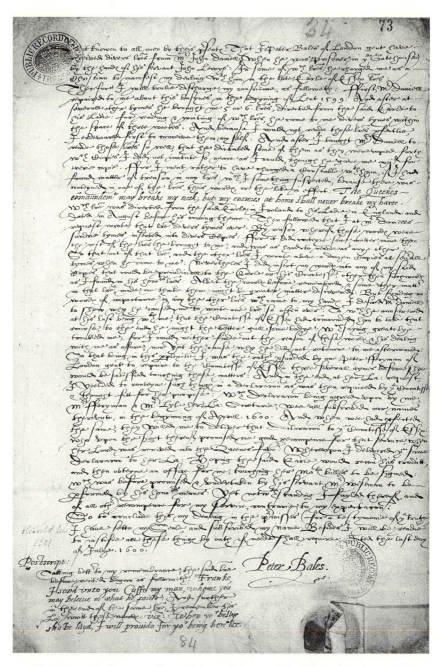

Figure 4.3. Declaration of Peter Bales, 31 July 1601. The National Archives, SP 12/281, fol. 73.

of both Sidney and Walsingham.[88] Throughout the period of his visits to Bales, Daniell had in fact been in contact with the countess, who had noticed a number of letters missing shortly after the casket's return. She was eventually persuaded to pay £1,720 for the letters' return after negotiations carried out through her secretary, George Lisle. Sometime after the deal was concluded Ferryman brought Bales to the countess, where, under Lisle's supervision, he produced the declaration of his dealings with Daniell that the earl would refer to at his trial.[89]

While Daniell was the one prosecuted, Peter Bales's involvement seems distinctly suspect. The writing master had a less public side. Linked to Walsingham, he may have been employed in the 1580s as part of his team of textual specialists.[90] In a petitioning letter to Burghley, he had signed himself off as "Cypherary," advertising the usefulness of his skills in matters of state, and in a later request for a royal pension he promised to supply both "a most secrett Cipher" and also a "maner of close conveyance of his M[ajes]ts lres of greatest imortance, that they shall passe without finding them about the messenger by any search whatsoever."[91] Bales can thus be classed as one of those textual artificers whose skill set covered the gray area between artful copying and artificial manipulation of texts. In the Daniell case, the writing master may have deposed that he intended to send for a constable "yf I found matter of state in the lres," but he proceeded with the project of imitation as commissioned, well aware that he was dealing with the letters of a key court figure then in confinement at York House following his unauthorized return from Ireland—a time when he was the focus of a wave of illicit textual circulation.[92] Bales's dealings with Daniell were marked by mistrust and anxiety on both sides, signaling a mutual awareness of the dangerous constructions that could be placed on their actions. Yet whether because of his court contacts, the utility of his skills, or his declaration, the investigation appears to have been deliberately steered away from the role of Bales who would go on to become tutor to Prince Henry after the accession of James I.

Where Bales was edited out of the prosecution, Daniell was persuaded it was in his interests to offer no defense of his actions at the Star Chamber proceedings and found himself being sentenced to life imprisonment. During the years he spent in the Fleet, however, he would make up for this silence. He produced a wealth of documents centering on the affair, including a prose narrative of his life that he would seek to have printed, as well as endless letters and petitions.[93] His wife, Jane Daniell, also wrote an autobiographical account of her role, vindicating herself from any part in her husband's proceedings, and produced her own series of petitioning letters.[94] John Daniell's extensive writings offer some insight into the intent behind his actions, including the reasoning behind the copying he commissioned from Bales. "Bie taking Bales Imytacons," he explained,

> and using them as Caracters to the rest of the lres I found these benefetts, ffyrst bie p[er]using hys wrtying the lres often ouer, I was resonablie p[er]fecte in makyng the lres knowen to mee. Then before I leaft hym I Could reade those lres (I brought hym) soe p[er]fect that I dyd dyctate some lres as hee wrote them. Thyrdlie afterward being at Rytchmond I used the best of Bales Imytacons as Caractors to the rest of letters, wherof I wrote fowre or fyue ^bryffe^ Copyes wch I sent to the Contesse.[95]

Daniell's comments elucidate the idea of "character" within early modern script, a term that here encompasses the sense of both a legend and a pattern for a style of writing. Deciphering the hand, according to this logic, works through the act of imitating the composition of the letters. Yet in this practice to become perfect in the reading of the hand is evidently also to master the character: Daniell progresses from studying Bales's process of imitation, through dictating copy, toward ultimately producing his own imitations. This serviceable familiarity with the hand demonstrates the potential for slippage between the investigation and the production of texts.

In the Star Chamber proceedings, Daniell's trafficking in these texts is mysterious, seemingly the malice of a malcontent intent on injuring others. What is missing from this narrative is any connection between Daniell's scheme and the fortunes of the Earl of Essex. The prosecution took great care to domesticate events and present the countess as a blameless victim, paying Daniell for fear of the earl's displeasure if "theise priuate letters of Complementes of loue & affectyon betwene them were discouered to the worlde."[96] With Cecil's backing, the prosecution of Daniell suddenly became an expedient way of restoring the countess's position after her husband's death and a full year after the practice had first been disclosed. This was a carefully constructed representation of events. In fact Daniell's actions provide a rich example of the attempt to speculate upon the potential of letters at a pivotal moment in the career of a court figure as the timeline shows. The casket of letters itself was deposited with the Daniells in October 1599, in the wake of Essex's disgrace following his unsanctioned return from Ireland and amid fears of the search or seizure of his papers. Following the earl's censure in Star Chamber at the end of November, there was little doubt that his fortunes hung in the balance. It was after the request for the casket's return in January 1600 that Daniell approached Bales about the bundle of letters he had detained, working with him for several weeks until late February. The explanation of the timing Daniell explicitly links to mistrust of the earl:

> I had some specyall intelligence, and notyce that the Earle was very dyssyrous to accept of any Condycons to haue ffryndshippe wth some, whom before hee termed hys enymyes, wch thynge I thought Could hardlie proceede from hym, unlesse there were greatter cause then was gener'allie Conceyvid, or I before that tyme Could Imagyne, and therupon I began to feare the event, and a lyttle to looke aboute mee whether there were matter in the lres that myght endanger mee or my estate[97]

If Daniell's claim to feel in danger appears disingenuous, the context of the earl's troubles as a background to recognizing the instrumental potential of these letters was not. Indeed a rumor always denied by Daniell suggested he had touted the letters to Essex's enemies Ralegh and Lord Cobham. It is repeated in the decree as a threat made by Daniell to the countess (although there is no mention of it in the deposition of the countess's secretary), and it was further disseminated in the verse libel that has Ralegh confessing to the earl "by letters I procurde thy bane / which of a Perjurde villaine I did buy."[98] Although Daniell concluded his lucrative deal with the countess for return of the letters in March (and Essex signed a release of Daniell from any obligations on 7 April 1600), he had earlier explored other options.[99] He had spent some eleven days at the court in Richmond after breaking with Bales, seeking access to the queen. His purpose, he claimed, was to show her the letters among which was one containing the phrase "The Queenes com[-]mandmt in her Servyces may breake my necke. But my enymyes practyces shall never troble my hart" and another that noted "I trust or longe to reduce Ireland to a peacesible governmt yf the traytors of England be not Confederate wt the Traytours of Ireland." Daniell's comment that these phrases "sheweth great dyscontentmt in hys Lo" at this time is just the kind of interpretation invited by the earl's situation in early 1600 and closely resembles the kind of phrasing used against Perrot a decade earlier.[100] With no little irony, Daniell reports that he was accounted one of the disgraced Essex's followers and so barred

Figure 4.4. Star Chamber decree, June 1601, with John Daniell's annotations in left-hand margin. The National Archives, SP 12/279, fol. 231.

the queen's presence—his attempts to use the Earl of Worcester as intermediary would lead to Daniell's possession of the letters being revealed to the countess.[101] On a copy of the Star Chamber decree that is covered with his annotations contesting the narrative constructed by the Crown (Figure 4.4), Daniell offers his most forceful defense of his original motives: "Therles letters ware hardly wrytten & not counterfyted but ymytated for the Queenes Srvyce from w[ch] he was withdrawen bie the Countesse and her frendes."[102]

It is worth acknowledging that Daniell's representation of his intent entirely fits the profile of contemporary letter investigations. At the time of his sojourn in Richmond, Penelope Rich's distempered letter to Elizabeth was in circulation at court, and she was being called to account for both its contents and dissemination. The earl's own notorious letter to Egerton, as well as his disobedient letters out of Ireland, played an important part in both the York House hearing of June 1600 and his treason trial of February 1601.[103] In this context, Daniell's speculative investigation of matters of state, and potential willingness to amplify the issue, is no more than a highly topical attempt to exploit letters as an instrument to incriminate individuals, marketing intelligence materials to promote prosecution. As we have seen, the use of forged matter in treason prosecution had received high-level patronage on a number of occasions, but as it turned out the fall of Essex did not require the hand of Daniell.

✴   ✴   ✴

The case of Daniell reveals the blurred boundaries between licit and illicit techniques of imitation, exposing the dubious role of the writing master and his hireable skills. Daniell failed to exploit the overlap between intelligence gath-

ering and intervention, where Walsingham's team of specialists and the prosecutors of Sir John Perrot had been able to effectively frame their targets by
taking an active hand in developing the potential of material evidence. Instead Daniell worked on the anxiety of the countess to extort money with his
copies but was unable to control the subsequent construction of his actions.
If his projects were unsuccessful, it is precisely their failure and consequent
protrusion into the light that provides us with an insight into the speculation
on letters in a culture of copying. While investigative techniques and evalua-
tive argumentation in the assessment of documentary evidence developed significantly in the period, these methods were often subordinated to political
expedience, so we find discursive constructions evoking evidential criteria but
diverging from its implications. By paying attention to early modern forgery
and the scrutiny that the law brought to bear on the early modern letter, we
can enhance our understanding of early modern correspondence and of the
material considerations that informed understanding of the letter. Yet in doing
so we are reminded that within a culture of copying the materials of forgery
were nearly always to hand, and the context and intent behind certain textual
acts were subject to competing constructions in which the line between du-
plication and duplicity was both thin and wavering. Daniell strived to play
on this ambiguity to preserve his credit, and years later he was still complaining of the wrong done to him. Ascribing the legal crime of forgery to matter
touching "estate in landes, Creditt, or goods," he sought to distinguish this
from his own actions: "But for Copying of deedes or lres, I neuer understood
nor suspected to be forgery till this my late dysaster."[104] Like Sidney before
him, the idea that this textual deed could be "but copying" is deeply disingenuous and fails to persuade the reader there is no more sophisticated invention at work. Daniell's disaster was to misread the acute sensitivity of the early
modern court to the ways in which its cultures of correspondence had been
infiltrated by a culture of counterfeiting.

CHAPTER 5

Allegory and Epistolarity

Cipher and Faction in Sidney and Spenser

ANDREW ZURCHER

Near the start of the 1593 version of Sir Philip Sidney's *Arcadia*, the Macedonian prince Musidorus, having been cast up on the shore of Laconia and fallen into the tender care of the shepherds Strephon and Claius, having been taken into Arcadia to the hospitable seat of the lord Kalander, and having heard the whole history of the senescent folly of King Basilius, receives at Kalander's hands the full purport of a purloined letter. Kalander's letter is the copy of an original sent to Basilius by Philanax, now regent of Arcadia, urging the king not to retreat into a timorous retirement. The letter was earlier copied by Kalander's son, Clitophon, in a scene that would doubtless have raised hackles among Sidney's familiar readers. What moved Basilius to abandon his royal office, take his wife and daughters into the woods, and cut off all access to the court, admitting to his conversation only shepherds and poets, "hath bin imparted," says Kalander "but to one person liuing"; however:

> My selfe can coniecture and in deede more then coniecture, by this
> accident that I will tell you: I haue an onely sonne, by name
> *Clitophon*, who is now absent, preparing for his owne mariage,
> which I meane shortly shalbe here celebrated. This sonne of
> mine (while the Prince kept his Court) was of his bed-chamber;
> now since the breaking vp thereof, returned home, and shewed me
> (among other things he had gathered) the coppie which he had

taken of a letter: which when the prince had read, he had laid in a
windowe, presuming no body durst looke in his writings: but my
sonne not only tooke a time to read it, but to copie it. In trueth I
blamed *Clitophon* for the curiositie, which made him breake his
dutie in such a kind, wherby kings secrets are subiect to be re-
uealed: but since it was done, I was content to take so much profite,
as to know it.[1]

The substance of Philanax's letter divides into two parts: first he reproves the
king for "what should haue beene done," faulting him for having sent to the
oracle at Delphi to know his future; and thereafter he censures him for "what
is to be done," that is, Basilius's plan to withdraw from the court and his office and to confine himself and his family in a rural retreat. Clitophon's curiosity, and the curiosity of his father, Kalander, are both indirectly reproved
by Philanax's reproof of Basilius's own curiosity. As Kalander reads out the
letter to Musidorus, we hear its transposed condemnation of curiosity with
bemusement and delight and must inevitably involve ourselves, too, in its
reach, for we, like Clitophon, are readers of a manuscript text—the *Arcadia*—
which Sidney himself never licensed for public circulation. But the consequence is even more direct for, as he moves from criticizing Basilius's recent
actions to his forward determinations, Philanax condemns his decision to se-
quester his daughters in woodland lodges:

> Certainly Sir, in my ladies, your daughters, nature promiseth
> nothing but goodnes, and their education by your fatherly care,
> hath beene hetherto such, as hath beene most fit to restraine all
> euil: geuing their minds vertuous delightes, and not greeuing them
> for want of wel-ruled libertie. Now to fal to a sodain straightning
> them, what can it do but argue suspition, a thing no more vnpleas-
> ant, then vnsure, for the preseruing of vertue? Leaue womens
> minds, the most vntamed that way of any: see whether any cage
> can please a bird? or whether a dogge growe not fiercer with tying?
> what doth ielousie, but stirre vp the minde to thinke, what it is
> from which they are restrayned?[2]

The source and wellhead of Sidney's romance history, the whole sprawling narrative of *The Countess of Pembroke's Arcadia*, rises here from a short vignette
about epistolary security. Insofar as Philanax's moral—that conspicuously

guarded secrets only excite curiosity—rubs against the history of Clitophon's curious transcription of Basilius's carelessly guarded correspondence, the story is a humorous one: young men, perhaps, will do it if they come to it, in what casement soever you drop your letters. But Kalander's story suggests something important, too: just as Musidorus's love for the princess Pamela begins here, with the first mention of her concealment, so the long, playfully allegorical narratives of Sidney's masterwork invite our interpretation merely for their habit of concealment; like letters left by great men in windows, they provoke curiosity. In this revised text of his romance, Sidney has taken pains to present a pastoral romance built on interpretative habits native to early modern epistolary security. In this essay, I want to take his suggestion seriously and ask how anxieties about the security of correspondence, and the strategies writers developed to cope with them, might have informed literary models of allegory and allegoresis. In what follows, I will concentrate on the works of Philip Sidney and Edmund Spenser, the two greatest English romance allegorists of the sixteenth century—and two men who also had considerable experience of diplomatic correspondence in the subtle and dangerous political landscape of Elizabethan Ireland.

Copying in Casements and Arguing Suspicion in *The Countess of Pembroke's Arcadia*

At about the same time Sidney began to write the *Arcadia*, in the spring of 1578, he developed a vehement suspicion that his father's secretary, Edmund Mollineux, had been opening his letters. Sidney's famous accusation, delivered by personal letter but in our period widely copied, was short and aggressive:

> Few woordes are beste. My lettres to my Father have come to the eys of some. Neither can I condemne any but yow for it. If it be so yow have plaide the very knave with me; and so I will make yow know if I have good proofe of it. But that for so muche as is past. For that is to come, I assure yow before God, that if ever I know yow do so muche as reede any lettre I wryte to my Father, without his commandement, or my consente, I will thruste my Dagger into yow. And truste to it, for I speake it in earnest. In the meane time farwell. From Courte this laste of May 1578.[3]

Mollineux denied the charge, and he and Sidney appear to have patched up their differences with some speed, but the incident must have placed a particular kind of pressure on the opening of the *Arcadia* for its knowledgeable manuscript readers among Sidney's close friends and family—as it does for us today.[4] In transcribing Philanax's letter to Basilius, Clitophon takes a serious, even mortal risk; what would have incited him to go so far? Clitophon's copying arises not just from curiosity but from some notion, even if only inchoate, that he might *use* the letter; did he intend to bring it to the "eys of some"? This is a question that becomes clearer at the end of the romance, when Kalander and Philanax end up on different sides of a factional struggle over the fates of Pyrocles and Musidorus, and the custody of the princesses Pamela and Philoclea. With hindsight, Clitophon's theft of Philanax's letter and his delivery of the transcription to his father look like a factional political strategy. This makes sense of Kalander's immediate admission to Musidorus that he has carried the letter on his person since it was given to him—a letter too valuable to destroy, but too dangerous to leave exposed.[5] Kalander needs the letter because it might one day prove useful in his relations with Philanax; Philanax, we know, does not know he has it and does not know that Kalander knows what Philanax has written to Basilius.[6] Kalander must keep the letter and must protect his son the copyist from the dagger that Philanax might well thrust in him, but he must also use the letter—as he does here with Musidorus—to build new and advantageous alliances.

Sidney's *Arcadia* begins, then, with a sustained allusion to a well-established complex of anxieties turning on patronage, factional politics, and epistolary security, all of which depend on material sheets of paper. The complicated concerns on which his romance draws are palpable more or less throughout the correspondence surviving from this period in the State Papers Ireland—papers of a kind that Sidney and his father, Sir Henry, twice lord deputy in Ireland, knew well. For example, Hugh Bradie, bishop of Meath, wrote to Sir Francis Walsingham in December 1581, from his seat at Ardbraccan, near Navan, in County Meath. He wanted to complain about the post:

> There is now such cleanlie convayance in convayeng of l[ett]ers as hardlie can any scape vnserched. vppon opening yf any thynge mislike the sercher the l[ett]er is supprest and never delivered[.] this practise as I know it to be vsed: so it maketh me thynk that those often l[ett]res w[hi]ch I wrote came never to yo[u]r hono[u]rs hand[es].[7]

Given the correspondent to whom his letter was addressed, the complaint might seem to us tinged with irony: Walsingham's own reputation for collecting and managing information, and above all the manifest witness of thousands of surviving letters from correspondents and informants in England, in Ireland, and abroad during the 1580s, may suggest that at least some of the intervention was at the secretary of state's own orders, or conducted with his interests in mind.[8] But Bradie's complaint hints at the complexity of the security problem facing members and adherents of the New English administration in Elizabethan Ireland: who were these searchers? In whose interests did they act? How could letter writers anticipate and thus negotiate the complex network of interested bearers, carriers, and interceptors through which their correspondence would surely have to pass? To these anxieties and questions Bradie gives witness, as he elaborates on his complaint to Walsingham; having acknowledged his fear that his letters miscarried, he continues:

> I am the rather so perswaded for that I sent you a goshauk inned which amongst our haukes here had name to excell but never could heere whether ever she was delivered or noe. the gent[leman] who rec[eued] her of me was appoyncted so to doe by S[i]r Henrie Wallop. I besech your honour not take this as that I sought for thankes but onlie to enfourme you of the dealinges of some that carrie and rec[eue] packquettes.[9]

Goshawks can sometimes be embezzled, or perhaps the bird flew away. But in reporting his misadventures in avian donation, Bradie seems to imply that a more sinister manipulation of patronage and information networks might have taken place. To divert his gift was to prevent, or break, the bond between Bradie and his patron Walsingham, the implications whereof could be pervasive. His own loyalty to Walsingham was earlier warranted, as Bradie informs Walsingham at the start of the letter, by the patronage of the deceased chancellor of Ireland, Sir William Gerrard, who had originally introduced the two men. The bearer carrying the hawk was recommended by Sir Henry Wallop, the treasurer of the wars in Ireland. Walsingham will know, Bradie implies, what to make of these men's influence and credit, and the loyalty of the clients and servants depending from them; from this, he will be able to make a judgment about the security of his epistolary networks. But the missing goshawk might be symptomatic of something.

Bradie's letter to Walsingham is typical of the anxieties over epistolary security that often surfaced in court-centered correspondence during the Elizabethan period. In fact, Bradie's letter might be said to be especially typical precisely because he was writing from Elizabethan Ireland, a kind of exaggerating incubator for the complex social, political, and religious tensions that dominated court politics and intrigue under Elizabeth, and for the material-textual strategies designed to negotiate them. Distance from London; the constant threat of rebellion and international intervention; factional politics in Ireland, in the intervening counties, and in the court; and a host of other factors compromised the security of correspondence between Dublin and London, requiring writers on either side of the Irish Sea to deploy heightened care and ingenuity in assuring the safety of their letters. Messengers and bearers were sometimes entrusted with delicate or secret communications,[10] but most loyalties could be purchased or otherwise compromised; and a properly written, ciphered, sealed, and packeted letter might well make a stronger claim to reliability. Bradie's letter is typical in another way, too. The patronage networks to which he appeals, and the legitimacy of which he questions, reflect the factional politics of the Elizabethan court. Over and over during this period, the politics and conspiracies of the New English administration in Dublin revealed the strong impression of the same factional divisions that defined court life in Westminster and London. Possibly the most spectacular example of factional intrigue and the manipulation of epistolary networks in Elizabethan Ireland was that which resulted in the disgrace and recall of Arthur, Lord Grey of Wilton, the lord deputy, in the summer of 1582. This plot, effected entirely through careful control of the post, saw the secretary of state Geoffrey Fenton join forces with Adam Loftus, archbishop of Dublin, and Sir Nicholas Malby, president of Connaught, to give Lord Burghley and the Privy Council a decidedly biased account of Grey's supposed "abuse" of the customary practice of distributing "custodiams," or temporary benefits in land, to his associates and servants.[11] These men played upon the queen's, and her councillors', fear that any one faction (for example, that of Grey, who thought himself a coreligionist and the "brother" of Walsingham, the Earl of Leicester, and Sir Henry Sidney) might gain a stranglehold on power in Ireland, a fear that would resurface two decades later when the Earl of Essex was sent as lord lieutenant to engage the rebel Hugh O'Neill, Earl of Tyrone. In Grey's case, it was his association with Walsingham and Leicester during the delicate marriage negotiations with Monsieur, the Duke of Anjou—which Elizabeth pursued in part to keep the various court factions in balance—that made his alleged construction of an Irish client base dangerous. But where it was thought Grey might use lands, and Essex might use armies, Fenton maneuvered himself into power through a thorough understanding of the materiality of epistolary networks.

Fenton appears to have achieved his putsch against Grey by turning various members of the Irish Council against the lord deputy and by managing the dispatches carefully to prevent Grey and his adherents from discovering the source of the allegations being seeded against him. A key ally in this attempt was the auditor Thomas Jenyson, who reported on Grey to Burghley, but Fenton also sought to induce the treasurer Sir Henry Wallop to switch sides and begin to inform for Burghley—an approach that Wallop grudgingly accepted.[12] Lodowick Bryskett, another former secretary of the council, also offered to become an informant in exchange for preferment, though whether or not his offer was ultimately accepted remains unclear (in the short term, he was passed over for promotion in Fenton's favor).[13] Grey fought back by trying to control the security of his own correspondence by sending to Walsingham copies of his letters to the queen and by requiring the rest of the Irish Council to cosign his letters to the Privy Council back in England—effectively forcing them to toe his party line. None of this was effective, and by August 1582 Grey had been recalled—a solution he desired, but in circumstances that humiliated him. As 1582 wore on, Jenyson recorded for Burghley in increasingly worried tones the scrutiny to which his letters were becoming subject; by the end of the summer, Grey's allies on the Irish Council were attempting to ferret out the informers.[14]

The experiences of Bradie, Jenyson, Fenton, and Grey suggest how early modern correspondents manipulated and even constructed factional politics by carefully managing their letters—letters of all sorts, from those they themselves wrote and sent, to letters they bore, handled, or received, and letters they copied both licitly and illicitly. It is impossible to know exactly how Sidney would have revised the later parts of the *Arcadia* had he lived to complete the project; but the conclusion of the unrevised fourth book, and the opening of the unrevised fifth, throw up tantalizing possibilities that seem consistent with the introduction of Kalander's purloined letter and what we have so far seen of Elizabethan epistolary intrigue. One of the most curious and important details about Kalander's initial production of Clitophon's letter is that he has it handy at all: "Now here is the letter," he tells Musidorus, "that I euer since for my good liking, haue caried about me."[15] The phrase, "for my good liking," which a modern reader might casually construe as "because I felt like it," means in the period something closer to "as a matter of prudence";[16] and indeed, close keeping, as the letter itself argues, argues suspicion. Later, when Basilius is discovered apparently dead, and the princes Pyrocles and Musidorus have been apprehended, the renowned civil order of Arcadia is thrown into disarray:

> And this was the generall case of all, wherein notwithstanding was
> an extreame medly of diuersified thoughts; the great men looking
> to make themselues strong by factions, the gentlemen some
> bending to them, some standing vpon themselues, some desirous to
> ouerthrowe those few which they thought were ouer them, the
> souldiers desirous of trouble, as the nurse of spoile, and not much
> vnlike to them, though in another way, were all the needy sorte,
> the riche fearefull, the wise carefull. This composicion of conceytes,
> brought foorth a daungerous tumulte, which yet woulde haue bene
> more daungerous, but that it had so many partes, that no body well
> knew against whome chiefely to oppose themselues.[17]

Though still in the shape of a "dangerous tumulte," this civil disorder has at its core the "factions" of the great. Within short time this potential is realized, as Philanax finds himself the target of an attack by the ambitious and factious nobleman Timantus. Timantus uses his eloquence to stir up a party against Philanax, calling him ambitious and deceitful.[18] No sooner has he launched his attack than Philanax hears that the Mantineans, under Kalander, have besieged the prison and intend to enlarge the princes. The fourth book ends as Philanax tries to spirit the princes away to an extrajudicial execution, only to be foiled by Sympathus, their jailer, who has adopted a position independent of each of the three factions. The arrival of Euarchus will eventually relieve this stalemate, and the fifth book concludes with his judgment and Basilius's miraculous recovery; but meanwhile it is clear to modern readers—encountering Sidney's unrevised conclusion after the preparation of the revised opening—that Kalander could here use Clitophon's purloined letter to the princes' advantage. One of the plot details that Sidney does *not* explain in his unrevised text (now encountered as the *Old Arcadia*) is why Timantus and his adherent lords consent to Philanax's determination to throw all matters on the judgment of Euarchus. Kalander's independent witness of Philanax's earlier selfless, innocent, and wise counsel to Basilius, counsel that if followed would have avoided the whole plot and seriously curtailed Philanax's own

power, would give him the moral authority and political power to bring about
the final trial. It would, simply, disarm Timantus's assault on his probity and
honor. As the holder of the letter, Kalander would in the to-be-revised *Arcadia* become the powerbroker and arbitrator between factions, and on his
decision to wield or suppress the letter could depend the whole revised conclusion. I want to argue the suspicion that, had the revisions to the *Arcadia* been
completed, Clitophon's copy of Philanax's letter would have made an important reappearance at this moment of factional stalemate; moreover, it could
have come not to only to dispel but also to symbolize the factional tumult
into which Arcadia nearly sinks.

Ciphers and Allegorical Interpretation in *The Faerie Queene*

Factional struggles like that which brought down Lord Deputy Grey were conducted entirely through covert correspondence, the use of codes and ciphers,
reliance on trusty bearers and (therefore) on patronage networks, and resort
to the basic security achievable through sealing wax, bands, enclosures, and
other stratagems. Probably no Elizabethan writer knew more about such epistolary security than the poet Edmund Spenser, Grey's private secretary in
Ireland between 1580 and 1582, who frequently copied, certified, docketed, subscribed, sealed, addressed, and dispatched Grey's correspondence for him.
Spenser's experience of the material exigencies of epistolary security would have
been deep and constant in the years preceding or during his composition of
The Faerie Queene (published 1590, 1596). Grey employed Spenser to produce
fair copies of important letters, which Spenser prepared in a range of hands:
an elegant secretary for private letters to Walsingham, a mixed hand for Latin
text, and a gorgeous Italian hand for letters to the queen. Spenser also produced fast copies for administrative and security purposes. Even when Grey
sent autograph letters, though, and even when other secretaries drafted
or copied letters, Spenser appears to have handled the complex process of
authenticating, recording, sealing, addressing, and dispatching his master's
correspondence.[19] All the material evidence provided by Grey's extant correspondence in the State Papers Ireland, and in the Cecil Papers at Hatfield
House, suggests that Spenser alone had access to Grey's personal seal.[20] In a
political environment in which faction divided Grey from his counselors, and
spies reported on his doings to Burghley, it was important for Grey that his
secretary should keep a tight hand on his letters, including drafts and copies,

and on the seal. Even Grey appears not to have had access to the seal, for though he occasionally superscribed letters himself, he also left even sensitive letters (for example, those with extensive passages in cipher) for his secretary to address and, presumably, to process. When he did so, he often made small marks either at the foot of the first page of the letter, or on the (blank) verso of the folded sheet, indicating to whom the letter ought to be addressed—a fact not always entirely clear from the letter's contents, because the salutation and subscription were often generic.[21] So Grey and Spenser did not always work together, or even meet one another, in the course of their daily business, but nonetheless Grey relied on, and authorized, Spenser to prepare, secure, and dispatch his correspondence on his behalf.

The record of Spenser's involvement in the Dublin secretariat, then, shows us a man whose daily routine was dominated by close attention to the material details of safeguarding the integrity of his master's correspondence. With the evidence of Spenser's addresses and subscriptions, seals and folds fresh in mind, I want to consider two ways in which epistolary culture impinges on the experience of reading *The Faerie Queene*. Perhaps the most obvious thing about the dedication to Queen Elizabeth, which was affixed to the poem shortly into its print run in 1590 (Figure 5.1), and appears on most surviving copies of the poem, is its formal similarity to the addresses that Spenser habitually supplied for Grey's letters (Figure 5.2). Allowing for the inclusion of Elizabeth's full style, the affixing of this dedication to the front of the poem *after* its completion and, indeed, after its delivery to the press must have struck the secretary as an act of addressing roughly comparable to that he had carried out in hundreds, probably thousands, of other instances in the epistolary context. The subscription and signature, too, obviously reflect letter-writing conventions. There is perhaps little in these details—after all, many books in this period were published with dedications—but the similarity in both form and content to Spenser's regular secretarial practice seems exact, especially when you consider that this dedication has strikingly little *content*. That is, it is simply an address, devoid of the usual compliments, requests for patronage or protection, and so on—blandishments that would feature in the 1596 dedication, which was also stylized to achieve a much different visual impact (Figure 5.3). The point of this address was, presumably, to package *The Faerie Queene* as a letter the reading of which was to be governed by much the same codes as letters issued from the secretariat: to get the message, one had to think like the intended recipient. In other words, to say that *The Faerie Queene* has been *addressed* to the queen is slightly more than to say that it has been *dedicated*

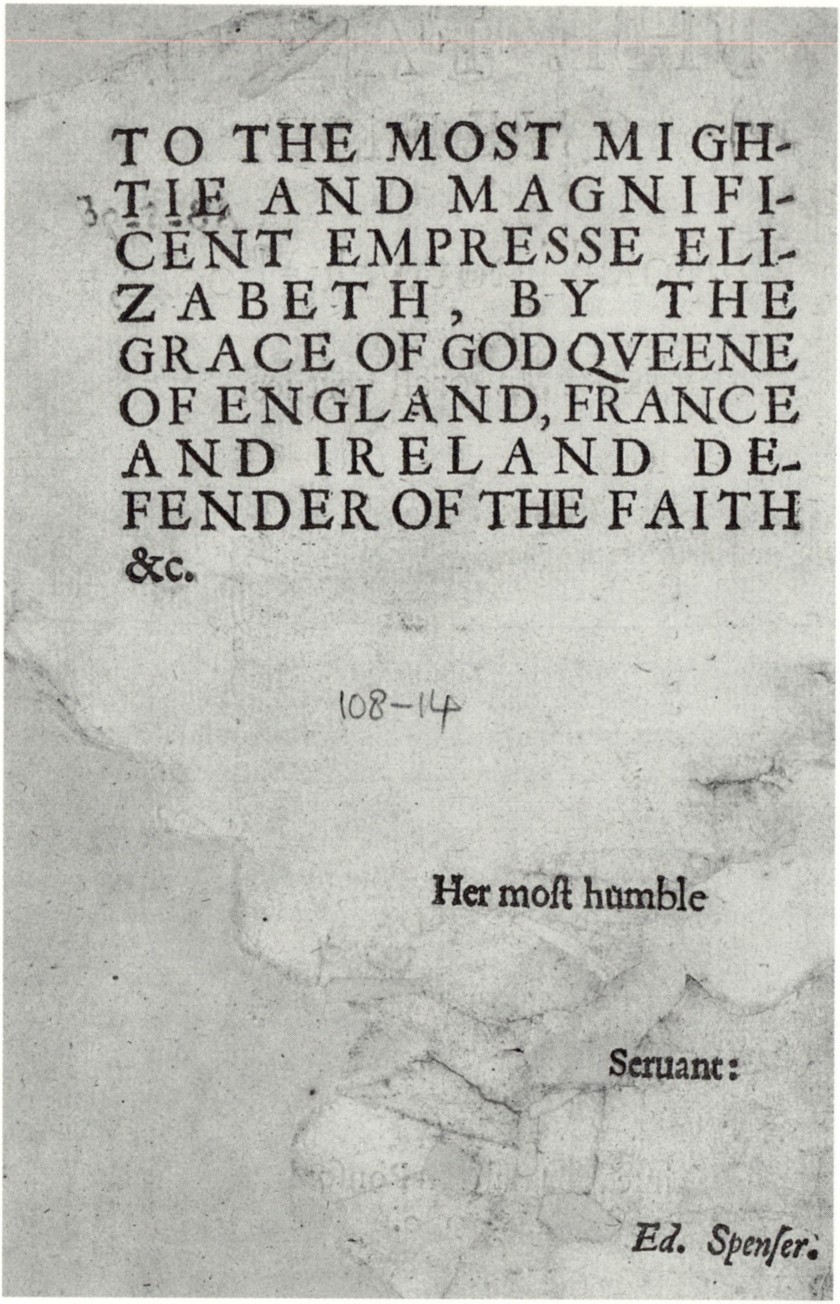

TO THE MOST MIGH-
TIE AND MAGNIFI-
CENT EMPRESSE ELI-
ZABETH, BY THE
GRACE OF GOD QVEENE
OF ENGLAND, FRANCE
AND IRELAND DE-
FENDER OF THE FAITH
&c.

108—14

Her most humble

Seruant:

Ed. Spenser.

Figure 5.1. The dedication to Queen Elizabeth inserted as a stop-press correction in Edmund Spenser, *The Faerie Queene* (John Wolfe for William Ponsonby, 1590), sig. A1ᵛ. Reproduced by kind permission of the Syndics of
Cambridge University Library.

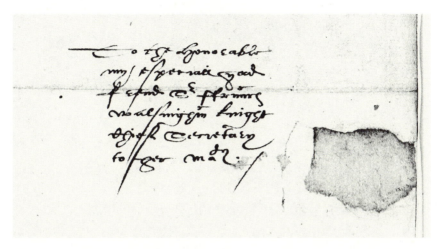

Figure 5.2. The address of a letter sent from Arthur Lord Grey, lord deputy of Ireland, to Sir Francis Walsingham, 5 July 1581, written in the secretary hand of Edmund Spenser. The National Archives, SP 63/84/3.

to her; the latter indicates that the book has been presented to her as a gift ("dedicate" derives from Latin *dare*, "to give"), while an address suggests, as it does for a letter, that the document enclosed contains something directed to her. Spenser thus achieves more economically what Sidney had earlier done, in combining his dedicatory letter to his sister, Mary, Countess of Pembroke, with the story of Clitophon's letter at the opening of the *Arcadia*: if you look in these sheets, he implies, you will be reading a work that has been directed to another. Both Sidney and Spenser construct their public readers as priers.

Historians of early modern epistolarity tend to think of addresses as significant primarily for those to whom letters were intended; that is, the purpose of an address is to single out the intended recipient. In fact, of course, the address also identifies a much larger group of people to whom a letter is not addressed and excludes them. In both these ways, the addressing of letters (like all the other strategies for securing them, noted above) reflects existing social networks between correspondents and their familiars and seeks to navigate them safely. As we saw before with Clitophon's copy of Philanax's letter, though, a letter's address comes to have important consequences when the letter is overseen and copied; in that case, the address acts to factionalize or to inculpate the bearer of the copy, for the letter has either been circulated to that bearer in trust (for example, by Clitophon to his father, by Kalander to

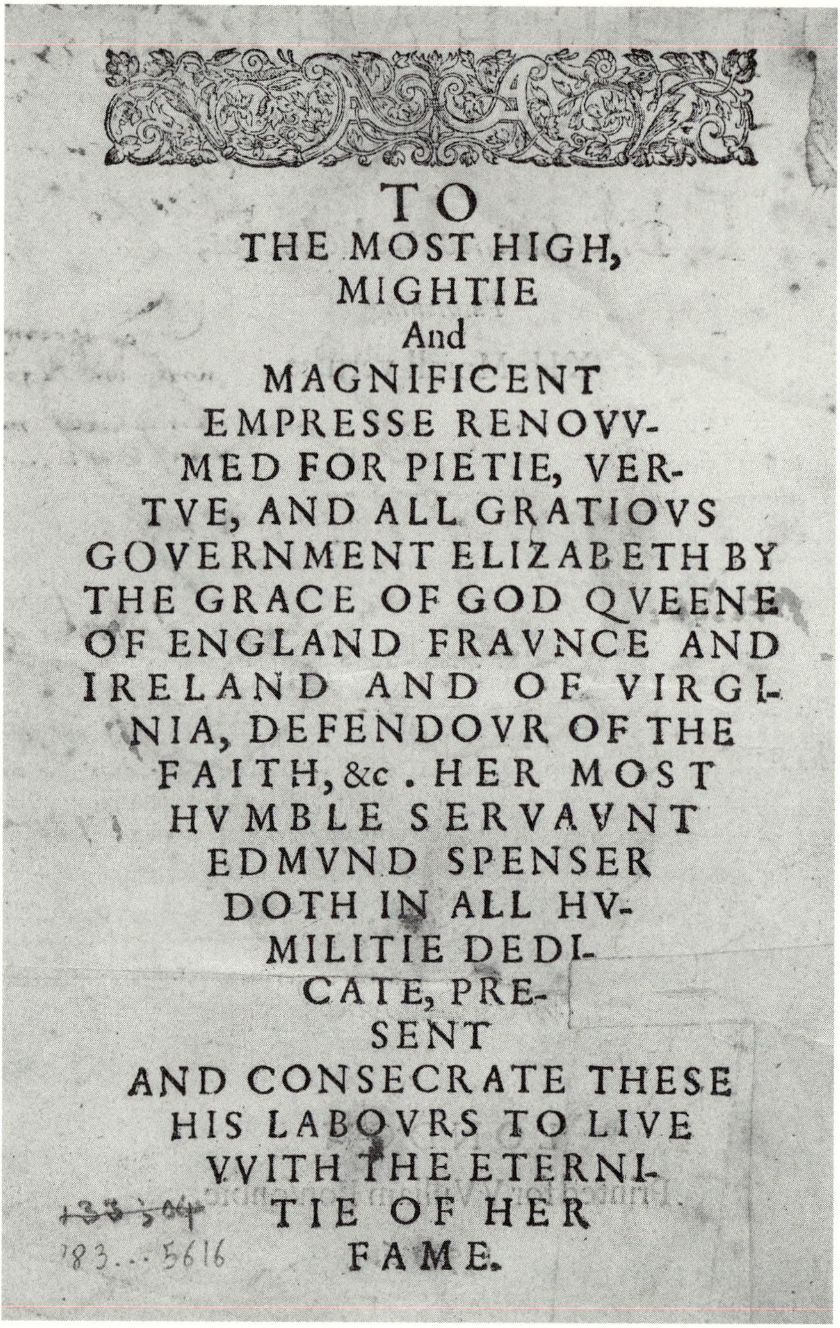

TO
THE MOST HIGH,
MIGHTIE
And
MAGNIFICENT
EMPRESSE RENOVV-
MED FOR PIETIE, VER-
TVE, AND ALL GRATIOVS
GOVERNMENT ELIZABETH BY
THE GRACE OF GOD QVEENE
OF ENGLAND FRAVNCE AND
IRELAND AND OF VIRGI-
NIA, DEFENDOVR OF THE
FAITH, &c. HER MOST
HVMBLE SERVAVNT
EDMVND SPENSER
DOTH IN ALL HV-
MILITIE DEDI-
CATE, PRE-
SENT
AND CONSECRATE THESE
HIS LABOVRS TO LIVE
VVITH THE ETERNI-
TIE OF HER
FAME.

Figure 5.3. The dedication to Queen Elizabeth printed in Edmund Spenser, *The Faerie Queene* (Richard Field for William Ponsonby, 1596), sig. A1ʳ. Reproduced by kind permission of the Syndics of Cambridge University Library.

Musidorus) or stolen by the bearer as an instrument (for example, by Clito-phon from Basilius, or in turn by Kalander from Philanax). In this sense the letter's address does not simply reflect an existing social structure; it can *create* that structure. Kalander may have had no notion that Clitophon would give him a dangerous letter; indeed, he blames him for it. But once he and his son are implicated in the copying of the letter, his wisest move ("for my good liking") is to hold it. Simply by learning about and receiving the letter, Ka-lander is forced into a new relation to Philanax, one in which it becomes pru-dent for him to retain it, as insurance.

This use of material letters to create and interpret faction plays an impor-tant role in at least two places in *The Faerie Queene*—both of which involve Duessa, a transparent figure in some parts of the poem for Mary, Queen of Scots, and both of which turn on ciphering. The practice of ciphering sensitive passages of diplomatic and even private correspondence was widespread in the Elizabethan period, and Spenser was well versed in its use as an instrument of faction.[22] For all this, "cipher" is not a word that Spenser explicitly uses in con-nection with his allegory, or the interpretative activity required to make sense of it. Sidney, by contrast, uses the verb "decipher" at various points throughout *Arcadia* to describe acts of interpretation, in ways that make it very clear that the verb was being borrowed from the epistolary context—as in an early moment in which Pyrocles (Zelmane) watches Musidorus (Dorus) dissemble his identity, shortly after their arrival in Arcadia: "And this *Dorus* spake, keeping affection as much as he could, backe from comming into his eyes and gestures. But *Zelmane* (that had the same Character in her heart) could easily discipher it."[23] Pyrocles and Musidorus are true friends, one heart in two bodies. Spenser may never speak so explicitly of ciphers or of deciphering, but this practice of securing cor-respondence makes a profound impact on Spenser's allegoresis. After visiting the House of Holinesse and defeating the dragon, Redcrosse celebrates his victory with the king and queen of Eden, who betroth him to their daughter Una. Archimago interrupts the triumph, disguised as a messenger bearing letters:

> But ere he thus had said,
> With flying speed, and seeming great pretence,
> Came running in, much like a man dismaid,
> A Messenger with Letters, which his message said.[24]

Archimago seeks to ingratiate himself, "falling flat" before the king of Eden and kissing the ground at his feet, "then to his hands that writ he did betake,

/ Which he disclosing, read thus, as the paper spake." (I.xii.25.8–9) Spenser insists on the material nature of the message that Archimago bears; he is a messenger, it is a letter, and Duessa's "sad lines" are "addrest" to the king. The purpose of the letter is to prevent Redcrosse's marriage to Una, and the grounds, a prior contract to Fidessa (Duessa); in other words, Duessa seeks to establish that Redcrosse has other friends, that he is part of a different faction:

> Therefore, sith mine he is, or free or bond,
>   Or false or true or liuing or else dead,
>   With-hold, ô soueraigne Prince, your hasty hond
>   From knitting league with him, I you aread;
>   Ne weene my right with strength adowne to tread,
>   Through weakenesse of my widowhed, or woe:
>   For, truth is strong, his rightfull cause to plead,
>   And shall find friends, if need requireth so:
> So bids thee well to fare, Thy neither friend, nor foe,
>
>

Fidessa. (I.xii.28)

Archimago's entrance and behavior here, like the formal organization of Duessa's letter (salutation, main body, subscription, and signature), borrows directly from epistolary conventions of the period; we might almost expect her (and him) to conclude the letter with the words, "from my House of Dissimulation, this twelfth day of Holinesse," and so on. Unprevailing silliness aside, the materiality of the letter that Archimago bears and reads is important to its function in the allegory. Duessa's false signature—a kind of cipher for her real identity—is the only word in the whole of *The Faerie Queene* that does not participate in the poem: it is not part of an argument, not part of the rhyme scheme, not part of the meter, not part of a stanza. It is also a lie, and one told in order to claim Redcrosse for her party, and force a break between him and Una. The implication is that the false materials used to disguise identities in the poem—the doublenesses that lie athwart the project of hermeneutical holiness in Book I—are, like ciphers, faction-building elements.

This implication is not surprising; just as the addresses of copied letters can bear witness against illicit copyists, so a ciphered letter, a cipher key, or a cipher casket could in the early modern period implicate its bearer in any conspiracy to which it was attached.[25] Una goes so far in this episode of the poem to suggest that the import of Archimago's and Duessa's ruse is *that it is a cipher*: as Una "discouer[s]" (I.xii.34.7) the truth of the "couer[ed]" "cryme," (I.xii.30.9) she notes that Duessa "suborned hath / This crafty messenger with letters vaine" (I.xii.34.1–2).[26] "Suborn" in this period can mean both "to commission (another) in one's place," and "to furnish, equip, adorn."[27] The cipher who with letters has taken her place is Archimago, for "cipher," from the Arabic * çifr*, "empty, void," is here rendered periphrastically by "letters vaine," literally (!) *litterae vanae*, "empty characters." Caught red-handed with one last cipher ("Fidessa"), one last allegorical identity, Redcrosse is implicated in Duessa's faction; only Una's truth can "uncase" the impostor and break the implied "band." In other words, one of allegory's potential products is the social organization native to epistolary culture. The first book of *The Faerie Queene* allegorizes allegoresis, as it follows the uncertain allegorical referent Redcrosse on his journey from unknown knight in symbolic armor (I.i.1.1) to his unified and resolved identity as St. George; Archimago's failed attempt once again to "part / The Redcrosse Knight from Truth" (I.ii.Arg.1–2) by menacing him with the culture of correspondence here reveals what the last canto of the book seems to conceal, that allegory like epistolary culture constructs and negotiates faction.

Early modern epistolary culture returns to the poem in its fifth book, with Duessa, in a second passage about ciphers. The maiden messenger Samient, sent by Mercilla in Book V to treat with the Soldan and Adicia, seems to have been named for a cipher: her name derives from the Greek word σημεῖον, "sign or token," which was regularly used in the classical period—for example, by Plutarch—for "cipher."[28] The queen of justice, Mercilla, sends Samient to her neighbor monarch, Adicia, as a messenger charged with mending fences; because Adicia ("injustice") is unable to read Samient's meaning, she dismisses her discourteously, and then sends two knights after her to deflower her. This episode immediately precedes one of the most sensational pieces of historical allegory in the entire poem, Mercilla's trial and execution of Duessa, a thinly veiled version of Elizabeth's execution of Mary, Queen of Scots. This was an episode of the poem over which Spenser clearly fretted, because it was bound to polarize his readers, dividing them into just those factions of which Grey had warned Walsingham. For this reason, the episode includes one of Spenser's most famous self-reflexive images, that of the tongue of the poet Bonfont, nailed to a post, whose name has been defaced and reinscribed, "Malfont." The juxtaposition of the ciphering messenger Samient with the lightly ciphered trial of Duessa as Mary, Queen of Scots, could not (and this is Spenser's irony) be clearer: the reader will get the message if, and only if, the reader has the key. The function of Mercilla's trial of Duessa is not, of course, so much to conceal the political history that it ciphers—everyone knew what Spenser meant—as to offer the reader, by the cipher, a choice on how to construe it. How the reader chooses to read this episode will identify her or him as one of these or one of those.

Following the work of recent critics such as Harry Berger, Jr., Gordon Teskey, and others, we are used to thinking of the allegory of *The Faerie Queene* as a hermeneutical playspace in which the reader is licensed to experiment with different kinds of reading and different interpretations; according to this dialectical reception of the poem's meaning, the reader achieves philosophical insight through a play of construction and conferral.[29] The epistolary context, by contrast, as it intrudes into Books I and V of the poem, may suggest we (also) think otherwise. Perhaps we can instead think of Spenser's allegory, at least in part, as a system designed to exclude some readers from participation in its addressed and ciphered allegory. That is, the historical allegory may be constructed in such a way—as a kind of cipher—that it permits the participation only of those readers—those noble and virtuous ones—whose social experiences and affiliations make them apt to receive the imprint of Spenser's moral and political teaching. This may be the force of that strange and famous tautology in Spenser's "Letter of the Authors . . . to Sir Walter Raleigh," where he claims that the "generall end therefore of all the booke is to fashion a gentleman or noble person in vertuous and gentle discipline";[30] what need teach a gentle and noble person how to be gentle and noble? It is certainly the force of Spenser's proem to Book IV of the poem, in which he condemns "the rugged forhead that with graue foresight / Welds kingdomes causes, & affaires of state," saying that "such ones ill iudge of loue, that cannot loue, / Ne in their frosen hearts feele kindly flame" (IV.Pr.1.1–2, 2.1–2). To see Spenser's allegorical method as akin to the conventions of epistolary culture is to take him seriously, then, when he immediately claims, "To such therefore I do not sing at all, / But to that sacred Saint my soueraigne Queene" (IV.Pr.4.1–2). The poem, like a ciphered letter, will choose its readers. In much the same way, in a passage from Spenser's *A View of the Present State of Ireland* (1596) that reeks of factional tension, Irenius shocks his friend Eudoxus by pointing out that, in times of crisis, a law must choose its subjects. There is no point in instituting good laws when no one will keep them, says Irenius, and therefore the unamenable must be "cut off."

Eudox: How then doe ye thinke is the reformacion thereof to be
    begonne yf not by Lawes and Ordinaunces /
Iren: Even by the sworde.[31]

So, says, Irenius, "sithens we Cannot now applie Lawes fitt to the people as
in the firste institucion of Comon wealthes it oughte to be we will applie
the people and fitt them to the Lawes as it moste Convenientlye maye be."[32]
For Spenser, colonial reformation shares its logic with the factional reading of
his historical allegory: times of crisis require a fit between people and the law,
between readers and a ciphered text that is addressed only to them. When
Duessa goes to the block, *The Faerie Queene* can mean only one thing—and
to only one kind of reader.

PART III

Genres and Rhetorics

CHAPTER 6

Mixed Messages and Cicero Effects in the Herrick Family Letters of the Sixteenth Century

LYNNE MAGNUSSON

This essay draws upon the Herrick Family Papers in the Bodleian Library, an extensive manuscript collection of correspondence exchanged among a large family of ironmongers and goldsmiths originating in Leicester, to build up a case study within a local community illustrating a larger issue for sixteenth-century letters in English: that is, clashing cultures of English correspondence growing out of grammar-school education in Latin, focused especially on Cicero's letters.[1] The correspondence affords unparalleled access to the lively epistolary culture in the later sixteenth century of a socially aspirant mercantile family, a family actively engaged in civic affairs, including the town corporation's work—in concert with its Puritan patron, Henry, Earl of Huntingdon—to provide improved schooling on the classical humanist model.[2] Historians have attributed an "evident transformation in the cultural and intellectual life of English society" to an "educational revolution" occurring between 1560 and 1640, a transformation, according to Victor Morgan, that can be read in "the unlaboured facility of expression which emerges over the years within large collections of family correspondence."[3] Nonetheless, despite considerable scholarship on humanist theory and instruction in Latin letter writing and on its impact in courtly, administrative, scholarly, and literary circles, important questions about its wider practical impact on vernacular correspondence, especially among the middling and merchant classes, have not been adequately addressed.[4] Did the citizens' investment of capital in Latin education and the town boys' investment of disciplined time and energy result in new epistolary styles being translated into use in English? Did translated epistolary scripts introduce altered modes of self-presentation and sociability? If unaccustomed linguistic styles and forms of sociability were indeed adapted to use in the everyday life of provincial towns like Leicester, did the symbolic capital of these educated paradigms accrue tangible benefits to their users?

This essay focuses on the contrasting epistolary styles of two boys writing from Leicester in the 1570s and 1580s to William Herrick, the family member whose retention of letters when he migrated to London as a goldsmith's apprentice accounts for this valuable collection. The correspondents singled out in this study are John Herrick, William's brother and an ironmonger's apprentice who eventually ran a shop in Leicester, and Tobias Herrick, William's nephew and, initially, a student at the Leicester Free Grammar School, eventually a university-trained cleric who returned to a small living outside Leicester. Whereas John's letters illustrate vernacular norms and individual creativity, Tobias's letters adapt Ciceronian imitation to English correspondence. The comparison exemplifies how the "educational revolution" of the later sixteenth century touched the lives of this local mercantile community. For a boy like Tobias it afforded an expanded repertoire for communication, although, as we shall see, it did not necessarily match the elite learning with the effective social rhetoric or the enhanced opportunities it seemed to promise, and it left him frustrated about its reception.

The first section of this essay sketches out the general context and the promise of Ciceronian epistolarity as a mainstay of sixteenth-century humanist education. The second section develops the case study, exploring Tobias's practice of Ciceronian imitation in relation to his efforts to transfer this educational capital gained through grammar-school education into regular use as a communicative instrument and, potentially, to embellish his English and advance his economic and social standing. In comparison, I show how the more utilitarian correspondence of the budding ironmonger and shopkeeper John Herrick draws fairly effectively upon a well-developed and prolific mercantile culture of vernacular letters and mode of literacy that, while informed by a petty-school education and probably some basic Latin, also taps into habits shaped by orality. The comparison of styles between the grammar-school boy and the merchant apprentice invites a distinction between high literacy, linguistic mastery, and elite educational capital, on the one hand, and situated rhetorical and communicative competence, on the other hand.

Translatio Epistolarum: Mixed Messages

The sixteenth century should have been a great epoch for English letter writing. Humanist educators placed an enormous emphasis on Latin letter writing, especially on Cicero's letters, and their concerted study and imitation took hold over the course of the century not just in elite grammar schools like St. Paul's and Westminster but in town and village schools. There was good reason to expect that the education in classical literature and culture that supplied the impetus for the flourishing of English Renaissance literature would also transform the English letter. The rediscovery of Cicero's letters has been heralded as a defining event for the European Renaissance, and the English grammar schools of the sixteenth century brought to English schoolboys the revelatory possibilities of these texts. So great had been the effect on Petrarch of reading a freshly discovered manuscript of Cicero's letters to Atticus that he had written back, as to a friend, exclaiming with pleasure and excitement, "as I read I seemed to hear your bodily voice, O Marcus Tullius, saying many things, . . . ranging through many phases of thought and feeling."[5] Not only were these potentially transformative epistolary models made readily available in humanist classrooms, but also the wherewithal to analyze, imitate, and reproduce their eloquence and immediacy was disseminated through grammatical and rhetorical training.[6] Yet, although traces of rhetorical virtuosity are certainly evident in the elaborate linguistic arabesques, for example, of Elizabethan petitioning or suitors' letters, it is harder to discover in everyday English correspondence of this period the effect of intimacy, the direct access to emotion, the sense of immediate human contact, or spontaneous thought that Petrarch attributed to Cicero.

Reviewing Dorothy Osborne's mid-seventeenth-century letters, Virginia Woolf claimed that "in English literature we have to wait till the sixteenth century is over and the seventeenth well on its way before the bare landscape becomes full of stir and quiver and we can fill in the spaces between the great books with the voices of people talking."[7] She was not alone in suggesting a curious belatedness in England in the appearance of the kind of letters we readily recognize as "familiar." John Donne, writing around 1604 about models

he regarded as important for letter writing, mentioned classical, biblical, Je-
suit, and patristic sources, but nothing in English. He was clearly aware of a
disparity between contemporary continental developments in vernacular letter writing and English practice, commenting pointedly on Michel de Montaigne's claim he had seen more than a hundred "volumes of Italian letters."[8]
No one's collected letters had been printed as a separate volume in English. Judith Rice Henderson comments astutely on the relatively isolated experiments
with a full-blown Ciceronian model in the English scholarly and literary correspondence of Roger Ascham, Gabriel Harvey, and Edmund Spenser, noting
that what the "Spenser-Harvey correspondence heralds" is "the development
of the English familiar letter *in the next century*."[9]

This situation is all the more surprising given the insistent focus that
sixteenth-century schools placed on achieving just such effects in letters. As
their most basic writing practice, schoolboys were trained to think of the letter
as "a conversation between two absent persons."[10] Certainly, for some humanist teachers following Erasmus's educational programs early in the century, the
principal aim in imitating Latin letters was to perfect their charges' mastery of
the Latin language, with no thought about developing English. If training in
this genre was valued more than as a means to this end, it was because accom-
plishment in the Latin letter potentially granted admission to an elite international community of learning. Yet, from the outset, many humanist educators
like the founder of St. Paul's school, John Colet, articulated pragmatic goals,
imagining young scholars as future counselors and governors, and, as the
century progressed, teachers like John Cheke and Roger Ascham and linguistic reformers like Thomas Smith and Gabriel Harvey increasingly looked to
Latin for what students could bring to the perfection of the English tongue.
The evident will of some of these English humanist educators to effect a kind
of *translatio epistolarum*, to appropriate the "bodily voices" heard in classical
letters and transfer their articulacy and their directness into English contexts,
and the surprisingly unpredictable results, is part of what makes the sixteenth
century a crucially important period in the formation of English letters. How
deep-seated in the understanding of many important figures was a belief in
the continuity between Latin learning focused on Cicero's models and English benefit can be illustrated by Lord Burghley's characterization of double
translation in his letter of 1578 to the young John Harington at Cambridge:

> if you follow the trade of Sir John Cheeke . . . you can not doe
> better. [He would] . . . appoint those that weare under hym . . . to

take a peece of Tullie, and to translate it into Englishe, and after,
layinge theire bookes asyde, to translate the same againe into Latine,
and then to compare them . . . how neare Tullies phrase was
folowed in the Latine, and the moste sweete and sensyble
wrytinge in Englishe; contynewinge with this kinde of exercise
once or twice a weeke, for two or three yeres, you shall come to
write (as he dyd) singularlie in both tongues.[11]

For Burghley, the profit to be taken from translating Cicero's epistles into English was entirely continuous with the lessons in moral philosophy or civics to be gained from transferring Tully's *De officiis* from Rome to Britain: together these can make you "a fytte servaunte for the Queene and your countrey, . . . a good staie to your self, and no small joye to your freends."[12]

The insistent educational effort to cultivate the expressive styles of Latin letter writers and to theorize their rhetoric had both profound and strange effects on English letter writing of the sixteenth century. It did not, however, produce in that century the transformation or rebirth in the English letter that might have been expected. Too many things ran interference, tangling English letter writers in contradictions. Chief among these obstacles were the tension between theory and practice in education, the situation of the English language, the highly conventionalized formality of inherited models for English letters, and, above all, a social and political structure at odds with the structures of relationship promoted by classical paradigms. Instead, it created the conditions for clashing cultures of correspondence in the period.[13] It is of course an oversimplification to say there were two opposing traditions of letter writing affecting English vernacular letters.[14] Even in imitating the style of Cicero's letters, some few might produce the immediacy of language Petrarch praised, others ornate eloquence, more still its shadow or parody. Nonetheless, there was, roughly, on the one hand, the tradition of classical letters, associated especially with Cicero and what came to be known as the "familiar" letter, a tradition mediated through humanist theories and pedagogy and taught to schoolboys as training in Latin composition. It mapped out social (and potentially political) relations in a distinctive way, often modeling interaction in terms of forceful self-presentation and close social bonds of equal power.[15] On the other hand, there were various vernacular traditions. Best known because most readily available in state archives are the courtly, petitionary, and administrative letters that cultivated deference and condescension to strongly demarcate social stratification and hierarchy.[16] Norman Davis has shown how the principal model migrated from French letters of the fourteenth-century English court and chancery into practices of vernacular letter writing of the fifteenth century; it was developed and complicated in Elizabethan practice.[17] Thus, at least two registers were often simultaneously available to educated writers from socially elite backgrounds, by far the largest group of letter writers whose correspondence survives from this period. Even among those interested in translating the educational capital of Latin into English, some were acutely aware of their contrary pulls. For example, the educator Richard Mulcaster, contrasting the linguistic propensities of Cicero's republican Rome and Elizabethan England, wrote, "Our state is a *Monarchie*, which mastereth language, & teacheth it to please."[18] Roger Ascham dramatized the conflict of epistolary styles in a bizarre suitor's letter to Queen Elizabeth pleading for the continuance of a pension: "as I daily wish and pray that you may long and long remain both highest sovereign and greatest friend unto me, so for this time of reading of this letter, I humbly beseech your majesty to imagine that your highness were absent in some withdrawing-chamber, and your goodness only present to read the same; for I write now . . . as to my dearest friend to ask some counsel in a suit I would fain make to the queen."[19] He addressed her in two clashing styles aimed at putting her in a dialogue with herself, as if she were two separate persons, the one addressed according to classical usage, as his familiar friend, the other, according to courtly and vernacular usage, as "your highness." His "friend" was urged to mediate on his behalf with "her highness," herself pursuing the desired outcome of the petition to herself.

Clearly, the long coexistence in Tudor England of contrasting paradigms caught English letter writers up in a host of contradictions. Grammar-school boys, encouraged by their teachers to transfer styles across languages, learned to write letters in Latin according to the first model; then, required to write English letters in the practice of their professions, their everyday business or social encounters, their correspondence was regularly judged and interpreted along the lines of the second model.

It would be difficult to overemphasize the omnipresence in the English grammar schools of the sixteenth century of the genre of the Latin letter and Cicero's letters in particular. While there were certainly continuities in the teaching of Latin between medieval schools and early modern English schools, the shift from teaching through simple invented sentences and printed *vulgaria* to the use of classical texts to illustrate grammar and serve as composition models helped to bring the user-friendly genre of letters to the forefront of education.[20] From early on, letters became a primary training ground as boys were instructed to parse and construe the Latin grammar in selections from Cicero's letters; to memorize and recite; to exercise their facility in "double translation," translating from Latin to English and later recomposing in English; to record useful commonplaces and figures in copybooks; to digest the material thus gathered for imitation according to topics and rhetorical genres. From the existing statutes and curricula of various schools, we have a good idea at what age or in what form boys typically studied simplified and selected Ciceronian letters to learn grammar and when they advanced to the study of *Epistolae ad familiares* with accompanying instruction in letter manuals and rhetoric by Erasmus, Macropedius, Mosellanus, and others.[21] Cicero's letters or classical epistles made continual reappearances in an incredible variety of guises at different educational levels, even in years where Cicero's epistles were not the explicit object of study. For example, at Harrow, between study of Cicero's *Selected Epistles* to illustrate grammar in the first year and use of *Epistolae ad familiares* in the third, no explicit mention of letters is made in the statutes for the second form.[22] Yet, the boys practiced everyday conversation in Latin using Erasmus's *Colloquies*, and here they were likely to encounter casual talk about letters, for example, copious variations on conversational gambits like "No news from home? . . . Have you received no letter?" "What good's a letter without money?" is one query subjected to repeated variations such as "What do useless, empty letters matter?"[23] In Erasmus there is an answer for everything, and Peter, Christian's friend, responds that "they're good for cleaning your behind. For wiping your buttocks. For cleaning your rear."[24] If the boys missed out on these conversations, they might still encounter the dialogue *Brevis de copia praeceptio*, which, encapsulates the basic principles and most famous examples from Erasmus's well-known rhetorical treatise *De copia*, which the boys would study in the fourth year together with *De conscribendis epistolis* ("On the Writing of Letters"). In the dialogue the characters play out many of the more than 150 examples from *De copia* of how to vary the Cicero-like letter opener "Literae tuae magnopere me delectarunt," "Your letter pleased me very much. Your epistle gladdened me wonderfully."[25] In later forms, rhetoric training further highlighted the making of letters, and the "making of an eloquent epistle" was both a university entrance requirement and the most common composition exercise at every grammar-school level. The ubiquity in the Tudor grammar schools of the letter genre, with the Ciceronian epistle as its chief exemplar, is very striking, and yet analysis of how—in actual everyday practice—this prized educational capital might have been translated (or mistranslated) within vernacular epistolary cultures has been limited to the social or the scholarly elite.

The Apprentice and the Schoolboy

Restricting the focus to elite schools like Harrow or Eton, or to exceptional figures like the educators Roger Ascham or Gabriel Harvey, may lead us to underestimate the wider—and perhaps more interesting—cultural impact of Latin letter-writing instruction in Tudor grammar schools. Can we find persuasive evidence that grammar-school boys trained in Latin letter writing in provincial schools actually did transfer styles across languages? Was the impact restricted to academic exercises in double translation recorded in their notebooks? Or did schoolboys carry over linguistic scripts or modes of self-presentation into their everyday lives and interactions within communities outside the schoolroom or university? Can we identify local contexts in which clashing cultures of correspondence arise when Latin-educated letter writers interact with family or community members employing vernacular paradigms?

The sixteenth-century correspondence of a large Leicestershire family of ironmongers preserved in the Herrick Family Papers (Bodl., Eng. Hist. MSS, b. 216 and c. 474–81) affords a fascinating case study. All of the letters in this collection were addressed to (and preserved) by the boy, or young man, who left his home in Leicester at approximately sixteen years of age in 1578 to apprentice as a goldsmith to his elder brother Nicholas in London. This boy was to become Sir William Herrick, one of the most prosperous goldsmiths and financiers in Jacobean London. A fruitful way to explore clashing epistolary paradigms that reflect variations in education is to compare the letters sent to him in a steady stream during his early years in London by two young relatives, his brother John Herrick—an ironmonger's apprentice—and his nephew Tobias Herrick—a schoolboy at the newly refounded Free Grammar School of Leicester and then among the earliest students to attend the newly established Emmanuel College, Cambridge, where he matriculated in 1588.[26] John and William were near contemporaries, the tenth and eleventh children in this very large family, John being the boy who stayed in Leicester to work for their elderly father in the ironmonger's business run out of their family home. Tobias, the son of their eldest brother Robert and only eight to ten years their junior, seems to have become the first in the family to attend university, even-

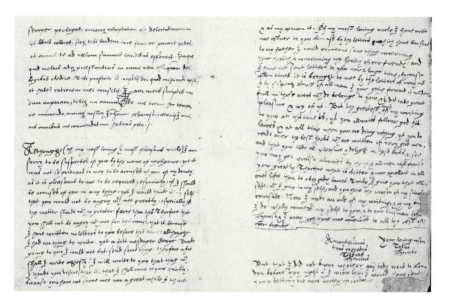

Figure 6.1. Tobias Herrick's bilingual letter to his uncle William (second and third page), Bodl., Eng. Hist. MS, c. 475, fol. 124ᵛ–125ʳ. Reproduced by permission of the Bodleian Library, University of Oxford.

tually attaining a bachelor of divinity, moving to Oxford, and ultimately returning to the area as rector of Houghton.[27] Tobias's first extant letter written about 1584 as a grammar-school boy to his uncle William,[28] an elaborately developed letter in Latin followed by a complete English translation, offers a very direct example of "Cicero effects," traces of the Latin epistolary scripts being transferred into English (Figure 6.1). In subsequent letters that Tobias sent over two decades, all in English, it is clear that elements of the classical epistolary script identifiable in this letter migrated to shape his self-presentation and construction of relationships, not always to happy effects. Bringing to life, through imitation and identification at a very young age, these relationships with and from the past, Tobias not only learned habits of style but shaped what Bourdieu would call his language habitus, or disposition toward interaction.[29] For better or worse, the school practice inculcated patterns of social exchange that would stay with him throughout his life.

How does imitation of Cicero shape Tobias's schoolboy letter? Tobias finds his Latin voice by appropriating quotations representing specific kinds of speech acts from the printed pages of his text of Cicero's epistles. In the words of Shakespeare's Sonnet 23 suggestive of the surprising changes wrought by literacy, he "hear[s] with eyes": that is, from the printed word and his master's recitation of it, he relives a version of Petrarch's experience, hearing Cicero's absent voice, right there in the Leicester Free Grammar School. It speaks to excuse dilatoriness in communicating with letters, and Tobias reuses it as his own, directly appropriating the precise words of the opening of Cicero's letter to Curio in *Epistolae ad familiares* (II.1, italicized below) to address his uncle in London:

> *Quanquam* (mi amantissime iucundissimeque auuncule) *me nomine negligentiæ tibi suspectum esse doleo: tamen* mihi *molestum fuit accusari abs te officium meum,* quam mihi *iucundum requiri,* præcipue, si abs te in aliqua re accusatus essem, attamen mecum putarem te mihi irasci noluisse mag[n]opere, præsertim, si res se habeat nulla maiore vi, quam hoc.

> Althoughe (oh my most louing & most pleasant vncle) I am sorry to be suspected of yow by the name of negligence: yet it was not so grieuous to mee to be accused of yow of my dewty as it is pleasaunt to mee to be required, especially if I should be accused of yow in any thing, yet I would thinke with my selfe that yow would not be angry w[i]th mee greatly, especially if the matter stande w[i]th no greater force than this.[30]

The appropriation of Cicero's words to fit generic situations like excuse making would have been facilitated by school texts like those the Earl of Huntingdon prescribed in 1574 in the new statutes for the Free Grammar School of Leicester, including "the epitome of Tullie his epistles" for use in the fourth year and "Tullie his familyare epistles" together with "*de conscribendis epistolis*" of "Erasmus or Brandeline" in the fifth year.[31] In mid-sixteenth-century texts of Cicero's selected letters like *Epistolæ aliquot selectæ,* the letters are classed or annotated according to use, occasion, or rhetorical genre to facilitate imitation.[32] The letter to Curio that Tobias imitates here to open his message and flesh out his excuses about dilatory letter writing is specifically classified in *Epistolæ aliquot selectæ* among excusatory letters, described as offering patterns for defense, excuse, and justification.[33] The direct invitation for the student to suit extracts from Cicero to his own similar situation, his reborn context, is even clearer in textbooks like Erasmus's *De conscribendis epistolis*, where Erasmus's *sylva*, his abundant collections of exemplary material for every variety of epistolary speech act, signal which letters and extracts by Cicero are appropriate for virtually any occasion. In theory, Erasmus's epistolary manual may not have encouraged such pedestrian imitation of Cicero, but his ample storehouse of well-classified extracts certainly contributed to the convenience of the practice.

A patchwork of other Cicero quotations from a variety of letters is rejiggered to Tobias's purposes, as he builds up the structure of his letter, moving from eloquent excuse making, to a search for suitable subject matter, to praise for his uncle's progress in his craft, and finally to counsel for his uncle to read and to obey divine law:

> *etsi quid scriberem non habebam:* tame[n] apto nuncio Georgio Bruxo *ad te eunti, non potui nihil dare. quid ergo potissimum scribam?* ad te scribam, *quod velle te puto, cito me ad te esse venturum* . . . (Bodl., Eng. Hist. MS, c. 475, fol. 124ʳ; italicized phrases from *Ad fam.* IX.3, to Varro)

> althoughe I had noe thing to write: yet a fitt messenger George Brook going to yow I could not but send some thing. therefore what shall I write chiefly? I will write to yow that thing w[hi]ch I thinke yow desire, that is, that I shall come to yow quickly . . . (fol. 124ᵛ)

◊ ◊ ◊

> . . . *ex litteris multorum et sermone* quoque *perfertur ad me* tuum progressum in ijs artibus quæ ad te pertinent *incredibilem* esse, ex eoq[ue] magnam lætitiam voluptatemq[ue]rapiebam. (fol. 124ʳ; *Ad fam.* XIV.1, to Terentia and Tullia)

> it is brought to mee by the letters of many me[n] & by the spech almost of all men th[a]t your going forward is wo[n]derfull in these artes wh[ich] do belonge to yow, & I did take great pleasure & ioy of yt. (fol. 125ʳ)

◊ ◊ ◊

> et omnes te *ad coelum summis laudibus* efferent. (fol. 124ᵛ; *Ad fam.* IX.14, to Dolabella)

> & all men will praise yow greatly. (fol. 125ʳ)

et *habes rationem mei consilij.* (fol. 124ᵛ; *Ad fam.* IX.2, to Varro)

Truly I giue yow that cou[n]saile. (fol. 125ʳ)

As well as borrowing from the Ciceronian translation a degree of stylistic ele-
vation, the English text stands out for the special way that it articulates social
relation: its imitated speech acts dramatize an assumed intimacy or "familiarity," apparent in the equalizing presumption that the uncle would value
the praise and counsel of his nephew. To the letter's recipient—a goldsmith-
in-training more likely to focus on the English than the Latin in this bilingual letter—it is hard to imagine that it would not sound more than a little
pompous.

Before analyzing in more detail how Tobias transfers and adapts the Ciceronian style in his English letters, it is instructive to consider the English
vernacular style in prevalent use within the familial context. What kind of
letter does John Herrick, a sixteenth-century ironmonger's apprentice, write
to his brother in London? The young John's letters are interesting in themselves and instructive for how they exemplify the vernacular paradigm of his
immediate social community. Of the twenty-one extant letters John sent in
his own handwriting between 1578 and 1586, this one addressed circa 1579 "to
his louing brother william herick att the Sine of the grasshopper In cheap-
side" (Figure 6.2) illustrates characteristic features:

> After moste humble and harty commenddations vnto yow louing
> brother [/] william & trusting In god that yow be In good health
> with all my brothers [/] And sisters. As wee were all att the
> making heare of prease be to god. [/] to lett yow vnderstand of my
> necklygense of riting to yow. I haue not bene [/] well att ease but
> since yow send me by rogar lanford your last letter I am [/] well a
> mendid. hoping to writ to yow more hearafter. giuing yow [/]
> moste harty thankes. for the trunck and the mooles which yow sent
> me [/] And all other things being sory I haue not as yett to make
> yow amens. [/] But hoping hearafter to requit one good torne
> for anothere. [/] my mother geueth yow harty thankes for her
> cowcombar which yow sent hir [/] Cristian giues yow thankes
> allso for sending hir word what mari [/] Ablesones mind wear. for
> she did ^not^ mind to come to dwell at my brothers house [/] but

now she will not come att all to dwell att London for she thinketh
[/] that she could not lick london so well as lesester. being loth to
trubble [/] yow any farther with my rewde hand att this time. by
your loving

Bedfello to commaund to his power Jhon herick:/

from Jhon herick to william herick [*flourish with
drawing of chain and reindeer*]

I haue sent yow a simpill token a
boke of plaster being sori I haue
no better a thing to send yow.
but I hope It be good enough
betwene ~~yoy~~ yow and me.[34]

First, while the Herrick family letters of the sixteenth century do create the
impression of a distinctive localized epistolary community, the opening and
close of the letters are virtually always built on a standardized and recognizable template, illustrated in John's four moves of commendation, address, trust
expressed of the addressee's health, assurance about the sender's health, and
praise to God for continuance of health. The beginning and end of the letter
incorporate a note of humility, placing agency in God's hands. This opening
sequence draws upon a long-lived template: it only slightly varies and abbre-
viates what Norman Davis identified as the norm of fifteenth-century English
correspondence "of a formal, respectful kind," a template itself borrowed from
Anglo-Norman correspondence circulating in England in the fourteenth
century. Davis described seven divisions, beginning with a form of address
structured like "Right well-beloved mother" and proceeding through various
formulaic assurance and wishes of health and welfare.[35] In relying on these
formulas (which on the whole disappear in the seventeenth-century Herrick
letters), young John's letter resembles the correspondence of his elderly father,
John, who is also his master, and hence a model he would be expected to emu-
late for business and other epistolary communication.

As a second feature, despite the formulas, John's letters often signal his
own delight and playfulness in the correspondence, a wish to individualize it
in one way or another. This is manifest, in this instance, in material ways.[36]
John has folded the paper about 8 by 10 inches on which he wrote the letter
in an original way, almost like origami, into a small square about 2 7/8 by

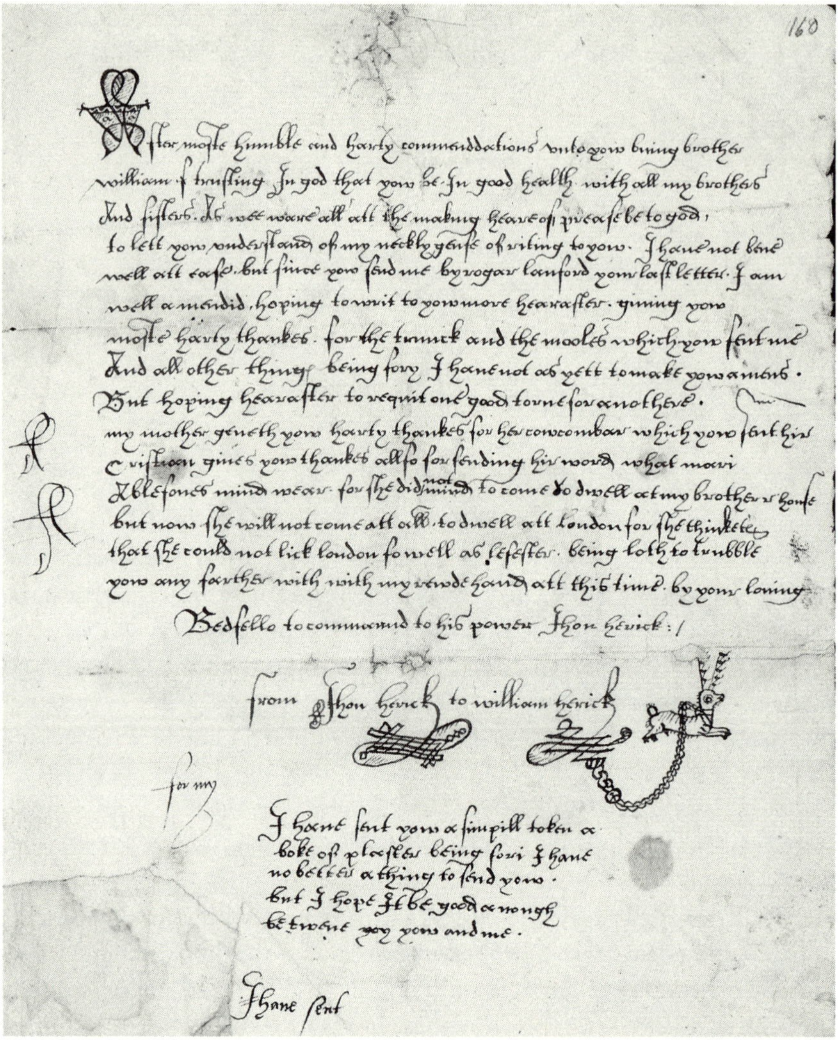

Figure 6.2. John Herrick's letter (c. 1579) to William Herrick. Bodl., Eng. Hist. MS, c. 474, fol. 160ʳ. Reproduced by permission of the Bodleian Library, University of Oxford.

2 7/8 inches, on which he addressed it; while his recipient could unfold the square to read the letter, it could also be partially unfolded into a three-dimensional shape and manipulated somewhat like a modern-day children's origami bird or fortune teller (Figures 6.3 and 6.4). This playful style of folding does not feature in other Herrick letters, but some do include small ink drawings like John's adornment of this letter: as if to signal the magical conveyance of the letter "from Jhon herick to william herick," a reindeer is linked by an ornamental chain to William Herrick's surname, poised in flight apparently en route to London (Figure 6.2). The chain might well be read as John's own indirect compliment to the goldsmith's craft in which his younger brother (as Tobias explicitly claims) is making progress. Furthermore, correspondence as an act of material exchange is accentuated by acknowledgment of an accompanying exchange of gifts, or "tokens," from the trunk and cucumbers William has sent home to the "boke of plaster" John indicates in a postscript he is sending in return. While the artistry stems from John's own creativity, the exchange of tokens is entirely characteristic of the sixteenth-century Herrick correspondence: few letters fail to mention an accompanying or missing token.

A significant feature reflecting social relations and complex social networking in this epistolary community is the messaging by a number of different family members in Leicester to close relatives in London that takes place right within this scripted letter transmitted from one brother to another. We saw that print voices from the past are inscribed in Tobias's manuscript letter. In contrast, John's letter serves as a kind of clearinghouse for spoken messages (mainly to and from female family members), making the letter a meeting place of oral and literate communication.[37] John's ostensibly personal communication presents or re-presents the spoken words, the voices, indeed the minds of other family members, extending the communication network far beyond the "I"/"you" axis of its nominally two-way exchange. Traversing the oral/literate divide, it also traverses the gender and corresponding educational divides, as John includes not only his mother's simple message of thanks for her cucumber but also, on the level of much more serious life choices, his sister Christian's "thankes . . . for sending hir word what mari Ablesones mind wear. for she did not mind to come to dwell at my brothers home but now she will not come att all to dwell att London for she thinketh that she could not lick london so well as lesester." The early modern culture of sixteenth-century England is a society in marked transit between orality and literacy, with close friends and family members constantly traversing this divide in their everyday

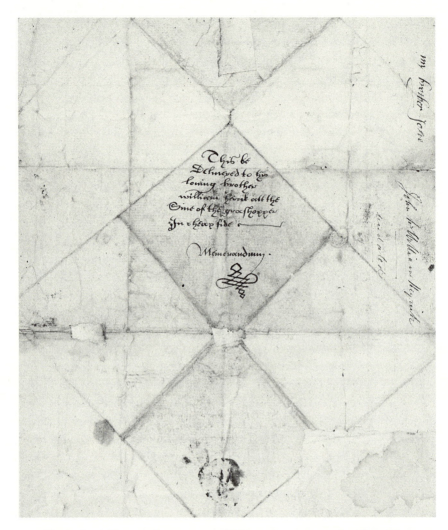

Figure 6.3. Address, endorsement, and fold marks on the verso of John Herrick's letter to William Herrick, Bodl., Eng. Hist. MS, c. 474, fol. 160ᵛ. Reproduced by permission of the Bodleian Library, University of Oxford.

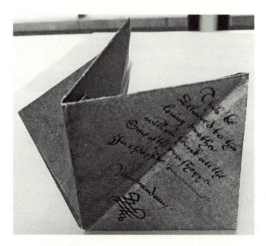

Figure 6.4. Facsimile of John Herrick's letter to William Herrick, illustrating folding.

interactions in ways quite alien to current-day experience, and the messaging and networking practices of the Elizabethan Herrick family letters provide rich illustration of how such negotiations were effectively managed.[38]

This Leicestershire family needs, values, and makes good use of what John Donne imagines as the frozen words "not heard till the next thaw" of letter writing's peculiarly material form of conveyance and conversation with absent loved ones. In a letter of 26 January 1584, John Herrick strives to articulate the value of written communication between himself and his loving brother: "i pray yow att your leasuer writ a word or tooe and I will writ to yow again so all though we bee absent In boddy wee may declar to bee present in mind one to warde a nother."[39] We should not underestimate the access to literacy and the expressive abilities of Leicester's ironmonger's apprentices on display in this correspondence—for, despite Woolf's disclaimer of "voices of people talking" and despite the delayed emergence of the full-fledged "familiar" letter in English until the seventeenth century—we do find shared intimacies and articulations of hope, anxiety, and longing that go well beyond conventional formulations in this understudied Herrick correspondence. At the same time, a frequent theme is the letter writer's frustration with the struggle for articulation in epistolary form and a strong preference expressed for communication John describes not as "face to face" but as "mouth to mouth": "I wish my selfe with yow that I might spack w[i]th yow mouth to mouth," he writes to his brother in a letter confiding about both marriage and shop-opening prospects.[40] Else-where, his frustration with the conditions of epistolary communication in the vernacular for serious disclosures—conditions including the prying eyes of the messenger or carrier, the heartily embraced expectation among family mem-bers that letters will be shared, and probably above all the genuine difficulty of achieving clear and easy expression in a vernacular in which no one had exten-sive education and people struggled to spell as they spoke—found expression as his "lovnging to see yow that wee might tavlck our myndes together."[41] It is fascinating, in these letters, to be able (as it were) to step into the mental frame of a speech or writing community at this liminal stage, where vernacular letters are inclusive of the voices and minds both of literate and oral subjects, where the level of literacy is sufficient to open up precious access to sustained com-munication maintaining and developing close relations among this large and loving family across distances. It is also fascinating to see how the correspon-dence gives expression to a combined sense of the pleasure and the frustration of social interaction in the written vernacular.

The vernacular literacy of these letters is fueled by the Leicester town cor-poration's evident attention to petty-school education in English in the later sixteenth century around the same time that the Free Grammar School was refounded (1564) and rehoused in a new building (1574). In 1574, a gift from Sir Ralph Rowlatt provided for a yearly salary of £3 6s. 8d. for an under usher, or "usher of the petits," to teach writing, reading, and catechizing in

English, with the grammar-school statutes specifying that the mayor and bur-
gesses appoint a separate "place" for this instruction. John's older brother and
Tobias's father, Robert Herrick, an ironmonger, small manufacturer, and a
man who took pleasure in wearing scarlet on feast days as a long-serving alderman and twice mayor, explicitly left money in his will to increase the
salary of "the schoolmaster that teacheth the petties, or under-usher."[42] Thus,
the town fathers provided carefully not only for the grammar-school education in Latin for boys like Tobias who could devote seven years to a daily attendance that required arriving at five o'clock in the morning in spring and
summer and seven o'clock in fall and winter, but also for the vernacular skills
that invigorate John's letter. Even if the statutes preserved the grammar
school as a separate culture in the town's discourse community, where "none of
the . . . cheifest foormes shall speake englishe one to another,"[43] at the same
time (pulling in two directions), they acknowledged the foundational importance of basic English education. Regular practice as a shopkeeper in routine
correspondence would have developed John's epistolary skills further. This arrangement is consistent with David Cressy's findings that ironmongers were
among the commercial elite of the country towns who were "almost completely in possession of 'literacy'" (at least insofar as literacy could be measured by writing one's own name).[44] Nor is it likely that the education of the
Herrick brothers, William and John, was limited to the petty-school year of
the Leicester Free Grammar School curriculum, provided off-site by the under
usher. From the 1490s, goldsmith's apprentices (like John's brother William
and elder brother Nicholas) were expected to demonstrate ability to read and
write in English and Latin, however limited.[45] Indeed, John signs off one letter
to William, "vale frater."[46] It is likely that both boys progressed to at least a year
or more in the three forms with instruction provided by the head usher, where
boys not only progressed in writing English but started Latin grammar and
learned short Latin sentences in *Pueriles sententiae* and *Pueriles confabulatiun-
culae*.[47] John, William, and their family certainly took pleasure in literacy in
many ways evident in the correspondence—for example, William frequently
sends gifts of sermons to his father, and the boys get excited about printed bal-
lads and prize a copy of the Grand Turk's letter to Queen Elizabeth, an example of the scribal publication of letters described by James Daybell.[48]

To point forward to where this lively, functional, sociable, and sustained
practice of vernacular correspondence among these sixteenth-century ironmongers of varying literacies seems to be heading, an expressive short extract

from a retrospective letter written in 1613 by John's eldest brother and Tobias's father will serve. Robert Herrick had been touring his Midland manufacturing enterprises, including an early paper mill, when he wrote to his brother William:

> Tovching ovre progres and ovre busynes in to the frontyres of the covntes, of Warwike and Staffordshire, I wovld yow had bene w[i]th vs. . . . yow know th[a]t suche yovthes as I am, doe more delyte in the pleasavnt woods of Kanke, &, to heare the sweet birds sing, the hammers goe, and betells in the papar myllns at the same place allso. for him th[a]t hathe got most of his wealth for this 50 years or nere that way, and now fynd as good Iron as was there this 40 yeare, as good wayght, as good woorkmen, as onest fellows, as good Intartaynment, what woolld yow have more[?][49]

This inspired English stylist, finding within the frame of the vernacular letter an uncomplicated expression of joy in the clanging of iron, the pounding of paper fibers, and the voices of laborers, is the father who sends his boy, Tobias, to be trained up at the Leicester Free Grammar School to write letters like Cicero. Robert's vivid and effective style seems to owe much of its vitality to the sociability and spirit of the preceding century's vernacular style, though it has dropped the formulaic conventions of early English letters described by Norman Davis. Yet, while the style contrasts strongly with his son Tobias's ponderous Latinity, Robert's ear for syntactic balance and parallelism ("as good wayght, as good woorkmen") may nonetheless owe a debt to the structures he has repeatedly encountered in his learned son's Ciceronianism.

Turning back to develop the comparison between John's community-inclusive vernacular epistolary script and Tobias's scripting of his bilingual letter, it is readily apparent how this Ciceronian imitation constructs the exclusivity of the social relation. While, as we have seen, the letter has been occasioned, at least ostensibly, by a long hiatus in communication and a lack of mutual engagement, as Tobias develops his copious amplification upon his excuse for failing to correspond, an ongoing and fully engaged dramatic interaction between the two correspondents is constructed. Tobias vividly projects the reactions, demands, and desires of the absent epistolary conversationalist, and represents himself as answering the other's suspicions and accusations, allaying anger and anticipating desire:

Althoughe (oh my most louing & most pleasaunt vncle) I am sorry
to be suspected of yow by the name of negligence: yet it was not so
grieuous to mee to be accused of yow of my dewty as it is pleasaunt
to mee to be required, . . . Therfore that yow shall not be angry w[i]th
mee for this cause, that is, because I haue written no letters to yow
before this time: althoughe I had noe thing to write: yet a fitt
messenger George Brooke going to yow I could not but send some
thing. Therfore what shall I write chiefly? I will write to yow that
thing w[hi]ch I thinke you desire, that is, that I shall come to yow
quickly bicause yow haue not seene mee now a great while I think
& as my opinion is.[50]

The immediacy and the intensity of the constructed engagement is accented
in the English translation by the foregrounding and repetition of the first and
second person pronouns, the "I"/"you" axis of exchange. A heightened sense
of performative exchange is also injected into the discourse by the Ciceronian
habits of direct vocative address ("oh my . . . uncle") and by the deployment
of the question-and-answer sequence ("what shall I write chiefly? I will
write . . ."). Also striking is the posture or rhetorical self-presentation of authority that Tobias borrows together with Cicero's speech acts and rhetorical
strategies. A highly mannered pretentiousness is especially evident where the
schoolboy, who has heard news from London of his uncle in his father's letters,
appropriates the Roman's statesmanlike posture of receiving and responding to
epistolary reports: "often times it is brovght to mee by the letters of many men
& by the spech almost of all men that your going forward is wo[n]derfull in
these artes w[hi]ch do belonge to yow, & I did take great pleasure & ioy of yt."
This stance is reinforced as he undertakes to counsel his uncle, advising him to
read and delight in good books and "to obey gods lawes. Truly I giue yow that
cou[n]saile."[51]

In style as in rhetorical self-presentation, one can readily see the effects of
school exercises in double translation. Clearly the boy has worked earnestly
to transfer the Latin stylistic capital of his school lessons to the English context of his letter. At the level of attention to language and style, a constant
focus of grammar-school education, one can readily identify qualities beyond
the "I"/"you" exchange, vocative address, and question-answer series not in
John's letter that Tobias has transferred from his Latin models. These include,
first, a more complex sentence structure building upon subordinate clauses

and a range of syntactic ligatures marking off logical development ("Al-thoughe . . . yet . . . especially if . . . Therfore . . . bicause . . .") and, second, an additional level of rhetorical structure marked off by parallel, balanced, and antithetical phrases and clauses ("it was not so grieuous to mee to be ac-cused . . . as it is pleasaunt to mee to be required"). But Ciceronian imitation in the sixteenth century is too frequently imagined as merely stylistic, and it is well worth underlining the extent to which this schoolboy's imitation of Cicero comes across primarily as a matter of rhetorical ethos, as authoritative self-presentation, as what would likely come across to his interlocutor—whether or not Tobias realizes it—as relational "attitude." The educated cul-tivation of familiarity sounds like condescending superiority and is out of place from a junior family member, comic and awkward at best and potentially of-fensive.

I have elsewhere called this dialogic script one of "aggressive familiarity,"[52] a manner associated with the Latin epistolary writing both of Cicero and Eras-mus. Its style of forceful self-presentation is quite different from the hearty vernacular style of Robert Herrick, let alone the deferential version of it that Tobias's addressee, William, might have reason to expect from his nephew. Instead, in constructing relation as reciprocal and essentially equal it proceeds by what modern-day linguistic pragmatics would identify as a version of pos-itive politeness: that is, a presumptuous and pressing manner of expressing mu-tuality that eschews deference and constructs friendship out of unmitigated speech demands.[53] Highlighted are boldly asserted assumptions about the de-sires of the other and acceptability of counsel and an epistemological coding that foregrounds rather than deprecates the writer's own acts of knowing (here, the ludicrously puffed-up locution, especially for a speaker imitating Cicero, "I think & as my opinion is").

One might, of course, ask if this is not merely a school exercise, an act of proud display of learning for his uncle, not really an English letter. But To-bias clearly regarded it as a vital communication, as is evident from his next letter, his only extant letter in a style I would identify with the vernacular mode, beginning with the formulaic "After my most humble & harty com[m]endations . . . trusting in god that yow be in good health" and ex-tending the greeting in the usual family pattern to "all the rest of my vncles & aunts and kinsfolkes w[i]th yow." Code switching into a humble version of the family's vernacular register, Tobias's letter of 10 January 1585 expresses his confusion and disappointment that his uncle made no reply to the bilingual letter, which, he explains, he wrote without ulterior motive, not pursuing any business intent, his own or anybody else's, but "euen for mine owne goodwill & loue that I haue borne allwayes towardes yow."⁵⁴ This is pretty well the last extant letter in which Tobias, always disappointed in life, is *not* asking his increasingly prosperous uncle for assistance, in money or in influence. There are a dozen or so fascinating letters he writes from Cambridge, Oxford, and Leicester, mixtures of art and pathos, which I can only glimpse at here. In each, there is no Latin preamble, but the style and self-presentation transferred from his Ciceronian imitation shapes his English correspondence for the rest of his life, with its keynote self-assertion accompanied by the repeated expression of frustration about his progress in life and the reception of talents and petitions.

Consider, as an example, Tobias's Roman style of demand shaping a letter sent from Emmanuel College, Cambridge, about 1588. Here he lectures his uncle on "obligations" and "benefits" (themselves topics closely associated with Cicero and grammar-school instruction in civics by way of *De officiis*) as he strives to sustain communication and to obtain money to pay his tutor for his university gown:

> I graunt I haue more iust occasion to write, but I write oftner to
> London than yow to Cambridge: I graunt also that (for any thing I
> knowe) you haue great businesse to let yow, w[hi]ch I am not so
> much troubled with: & finally I graunt that it is my dewty more to
> write to yow, than it is yours to write to me. Why? Therfore I desire
> but one answere for many letters, one short one, for two large ones,
> & 2 lines for 20. And how I [inquire] yow do yow think that I can
> write? how can you expect any thing from me, when as you yo[u]r
> self gaue noe matter to write yo[u]r courtesy, all other things layde
> aside, is a sufficient occashon To w[hi]ch reply I yeild: but yet if to
> this yow add the writing of a letter, then the occasion is made more
> favrible. ffor you knowe that ingratitude, & oblivion of benefitts
> done vnto vs is so fast cleft to o[u]r nature, th[a]t it is an hard thing
> all waie to call to mynde former benefitts & menes to let them
> slipp out of o[u]r mynds. This I saye not that I would haue yow to
> think, that I do, will, or possibly can forgett y[ou]r benefitts, but to
> signify vnto yow, that I lack whetting on by some externall meanes,
> that I maye shew my self gratefull for them. But of this thusmuch I
> understoode by my tutor that in y[ou]r letter w[h]ich yow sent to
> him you writt th[a]t forasmuch as I should haue a gowne, if he

would write, yow would send him so much mony as it came to.
Now my gowne is made & my tutor willed me to write vnto yow
what it coste.[55]

Here the distinctive traits exhibited in Tobias's schoolboy letter are strongly
foregrounded and even intensified, including the authoritative stance ("I
graunt"), the question-and-answer sequences, the insistent "I"/"you" interchange, the logicality of the syntax, and the structures of rhetorical repetition
and parallelism. Significantly less in evidence, however, is the confident construction of the interlocutor's engaged actions and responses, as if registering
a consciousness that desired reactions and outcomes cannot be guaranteed.
As a final example, after considerably more experience of life's defeats, including Tobias's miserable battle over election to a fellowship at Oxford, and later
his losing struggle for advancement in the church, consider the recognizable
Roman style (with a small intermixing of vernacular humility) that shapes the
articulation of his frustration and disappointment:

> And for you, if, after all yo[u]r endeavours for me, and expectation
> from you, you neither now, nor ever procure me any preferment,
> but all your labour be lost, all mine hopes frustrate, and yet you in
> the eie of the world so powerfull, so convenient, and so hopefull a
> meanes, and my self so fit, so approved and well accepted of an
> obiect: let it suffice you that I give you humble thanks for yo[u]r
> great goodwill, and I praie God it maie satisfy me, that God seeth
> an other estate better for me. Only give me leave to wonder th[a]t
> you should be so fortunate in yo[u]r owne businesses, and so
> vnfortunate in mine.[56]

In this final instance the Ciceronian manner is most pronounced in the rhetorical figures of repetition, balance, and parallelism. Here they emphasize the
antithetical oppositions of which Tobias complains, culminating in the ac-
cusatory wonder at how the prosperous goldsmith and banker Sir William
Herrick has turned out to be "so fortunate in yo[u]r owne businesses, and so
vnfortunate in mine."
        Whether we describe the manner of Tobias's lifelong Ciceronian episto-
lary style as reflecting his personal formation or malformation, his case shows
in detail how the Latin styles inculcated in sixteenth-century grammar-school
education brought a new form of communication and new inflections for

social relationships into the epistolary culture of a mercantile family. Just as significant is the bittersweet comedy that resulted as these "Cicero effects" entered into dialogue and at least indirect conflict with the forms of community and sociability informing the lively vernacular culture of correspondence illustrated in John Herrick's letter. This case study does not invite the simple conclusion that the direct importation into the English sphere of the Ciceronian epistolary styles so widely studied and imitated in Tudor grammar schools led to the "unlaboured facility of expression" that Victor Morgan finds in seventeenth-century collections of family correspondence, a facility that is, nonetheless, in evidence in many Herrick family letters. The trajectory is surely less direct, and the overall trend more likely derives from the heterogeneity and dialogue of styles that both the cultivation of letters in provincial grammar schools and the collisions of epistolary scripts occurring within localized communities both helped to foster.

CHAPTER 7

John Stubbs's Left-Handed Letters

CHRISTOPHER BURLINSON

The epistolary career of John Stubbs's left hand was invigorated when his right hand was publicly cut off in November 1579. Earlier that year, Stubbs had published *The Discoverie of a Gaping Gulf Whereinto England is Like to be Swallowed by an Other French Mariage*, a pamphlet attacking the proposed union between Queen Elizabeth and François, Duke of Anjou, that had been under negotiation throughout 1578 and 1579. Such a marriage to a Catholic prince, Stubbs argued, would not only flout God's law, and therefore surely be punished, but would also benefit neither Elizabeth nor her nation. Anjou was too young (twenty-two years younger than Elizabeth) and of the wrong religion to please the queen personally; Elizabeth was in her mid-forties, too old to ensure the English succession by safely conceiving a child; and the volatility of French politics meant that any stability achieved by the match would be a mirage. The projected marriage, in short, reeked of an anti-Protestant plot comparable with the St. Bartholomew Day massacre that had followed the contentious marriage between Henri of Navarre and Marguerite Valois in France only seven years previously. Stubbs presents the counsel contained in the *Gaping Gulf* as a "necessitie," a consequence of his loyalty; he writes not as "a busie body," he says, but as "a true Englishman, a sworne liegeman to her Maiestie."[1] But Elizabeth was incensed, and on 27 September she published a proclamation condemning the book as a "fardel of false reports, suggestions and manifest lies" and denouncing the "manifest lies and despiteful speeches" that had been made seditiously, by Stubbs and others, against Anjou.[2]

On 3 November 1579, then, Stubbs found himself in Westminster marketplace. In the speech that he delivered to the crowd before his punishment was carried out, he drew repeated attention not only to his own two hands, but also to those of his onlookers, of the queen, and of God. "What greif it is to ye bodye," begins the only surviving contemporary copy of his speech, "to lose one of his members yow all knowe."[3] Stubbs quickly turns his attention to his audience, remarking (and urging them to reflect) on the godly uses of the hand, as well as the seditious: "I pray God it may be an example to yow all that being so dangerous to offende the lawes wthout an evell meaninge as breedeth ye losse of a hande that yow may vse yor handes holyly." His own right hand, he says, is incidental to his person and yet capable of making him guilty by attachment; he regrets its loss, but it is nothing compared to Elizabeth's displeasure: "I am sory for ye loss of my hande & more sory to lose it by iudgem^t but most of all wth her m^{tyes} indignacion & evell opinion whom I haue so highely displeased. . . . For my hande I esteeme it not so muche, For I thincke I could haue saved it & might do yet But I will not haue a giltelesse hart & an infamous hande." Stubbs subsequently claimed in a letter to Sir Christopher Hatton that after the punishment had been carried out, he had called out "God save the Queen" before falling unconscious and being hauled back to the Tower of London, where he had been a prisoner for the past year.[4] And in another, perhaps apocryphal description of the scene, Stubbs was said, at that very moment, before he fainted away, to have lifted his hat from his head—with his left hand: "I can remember that standing by *Iohn Stubbes*, so soone as his right hand was off, put off his hat with the left, and cryed aloud, *God saue the Queene*."[5] This particular account appears in William Camden's *Annales*, and not in any of Stubbs's own letters or papers, but in the connection that it makes between the different roles of the hand—an instrument of writing, of offense, and of loyal subjecthood—it certainly resonates with the shorter speech given on the same scaffold by William Page, bookseller of the *Gaping Gulf*. Page, according to the copy of his speech preserved alongside that of Stubbs, "holding vp his right hand sayde This hand did I put to ye ploughe & got my lyving by it many yeres," but after the punishment, "so lifting vp the stumpe sayde to ye people I haue lefte there a true englishe mans hande." Which, though, was the hand of the true Englishman? The right hand ("lefte there" on the chopping block) that had distributed Stubbs's good and loyal counsel or the left hand ("lefte there" in place on his arm) that could thenceforth live a holy and reformed life?

Stubbs's correspondence from late 1579 onward, both before and after his hand was hacked off, insists upon the connection between the violence done (or shortly to be done) to his right hand, the agency of his left hand as well as his right, and his loyalty, which he continues to protest to the queen. In a letter, for instance, written to Queen Elizabeth in October 1579 (but according to the manuscript in which it survives in copy, "not dd" [that is, not given or delivered]), Stubbs offers a "supplycatory submission & peticion vnto yor mercyfull hands."[6] While he would "most willingly have redeemed the paine of one hande wth bothe handes," he writes, "my poore harte never conceyved malycious thoughte or wicked purpose against yor m^{ty}." Turning round the trope of heart and hand with which he protests his innocence, he writes of his hope that Elizabeth will be influenced by God to pardon him: "I pray him y^t is ye revealer of secret thoughts & who hath ye princes harte in his hand to woorke euen that perswasion wch is according to ye simple & sincere truthe of that I write." But his letter seems resigned, and the resignation expresses itself in anticipation of the loss of his right hand, as well as despair that this hand can perform any act of reparation: "ther is nothinge in me alredy to move yow, neyther can I promyse any newe & woorthy recompense of service due for so great a grace. For alas what can my poore hande perfourme?" All that he can do with his two hands, it seems, is pray, and it is with this that he concludes his letter: "the Lorde God cut of both their handes & he shorten their armes who do not wth all their harte pray for yor everlasting lyfe in heaven."

Stubbs's lost right hand, though, went on to provide him with a new textual—in fact, a new epistolary—identity, an identity that resided overwhelmingly in his left hand, even while it looked back to the deeds of his right. The nature of his punishment in November 1579 (violence enacted upon the writing hand for the crimes of the printed word) points out, with gruesome irony, the mechanical distance between the handwriting of a sixteenth-century author and his printed works, but the epistolary identity that emerges after Stubbs's punishment is disproportionately invested in his left hand, and in his handwriting, even if (as I will argue later) that handwriting is not quite so personally and uniquely expressive as it is occasionally claimed to be. Stubbs, in fact, printed little or nothing else until his death in 1592,[7] but he did carry on writing, and his new writing hand determined not only the material appearance of the letters that he writes to his friends and patrons but also the ways in which he and his friends come to speak to him, of him, and of their relations to one another. The violence done to John Stubbs's hand creates him; not, I will argue, in spite of his mutilation, but because of it. It creates him as a left hand writing.

The account that I offer of Stubbs's left-handed epistolary career makes use of many of the insights offered by Jonathan Goldberg's *Writing Matter*, now more than twenty years old but still luminescent and challenging.[8] Goldberg's study does not mention Stubbs, but in many ways Stubbs seems a paradigmatic subject for his Derridean reading of early modern writing practices. In the wake of the violence done to his hand, Stubbs positions himself as a hand: a secretary, a letter writer who gains an identity, but only in his subservience to the words of others—those whom he copies and those whom he obeys. Stubbs invests his own epistolary identity in that left writing hand, a hand (and a way of writing) that is both disembodied and declared to be fundamental to (even a metonym for) his bodily and ethical identity. This same paradox seems to shape his right hand in the time before it is removed, both an appendage that Stubbs would rather lose than be guilty in his heart and yet the instrument of his petitions for clemency, both written and prayerful. In all of this, Goldberg's reading remains remarkably perceptive, and remarkably apposite to Stubbs's career.

But bringing Stubbs into dialogue with Goldberg allows us to focus on something that Goldberg does not quite say, and perhaps also what he does not quite see. For although *Writing Matter* leads toward the figure of the secretary, and implicitly toward the epistolary practices in which secretaries constituted their professional identities—as the hands of their masters, so to speak—it has surprisingly little to say about letters themselves. And what this means is that it attends neither to the material lives of letters—their circulation, their transmission, their reception, and so on—nor to the various handwritten marks that these histories leave upon them: the different hands that compose them. In many ways, it is by reading the endorsements of Stubbs's letters, not only evidence of their material lives after transmission and reception, often into storage and archive, but also the written contributions made to those letters by other hands—by reading their versos as well as their rectos, their left-hand sides as well as their right—that we understand what, and how, Stubbs's left hand came to mean. Stubbs's left-handed identity not only depends upon his correspondents (in the sense that it emerges in letters written to them and stored, often ostentatiously, by them) but is also created by them.

*   *   *

Being deprived of his right hand provided John Stubbs with a new hand, a new script—and it is in his letters that it comes into use and into being. The earliest surviving document in this hand (which I will henceforth call "Hand

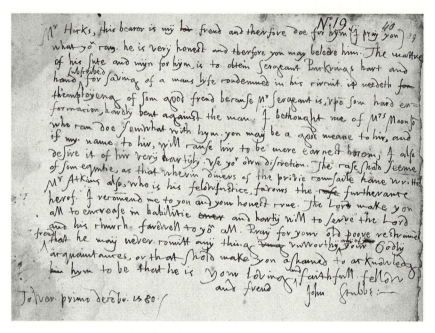

Figure 7.1. Letter from John Stubbs to Michael Hickes, 1 December 1580, BL, Lansd. MS, 31, fol. 19. © British Library Board.

L") is a letter written on half a sheet of paper to Stubbs's closest friend, Michael Hickes, secretary to William Cecil, Lord Burghley, from the Tower of London, and dated 1 December 1580 (Figure 7.1).[9] It is not the first letter that Stubbs wrote after November 1579—copies survive of letters to Christopher Hatton (mentioned above), William Cecil, and the Privy Council, all written in December 1579, as does a copy of a further letter that I shall describe below, as well as a letter to Cecil written in August 1580[10]—but it is the earliest to survive in this distinctive hand, which may suggest that until then, Stubbs was writing through an amanuensis. Hand L (which Stubbs must therefore have taught himself in the space of about one year) is an upright and rather plain mixed hand, jagged and broken in this particular letter but later increasingly fluent, with generally rather short ascenders and descenders, and its letters somewhat separate from one another. Its most distinctive letterform—unusual if not perhaps unique to Stubbs—is its minuscule *y*, which is regularly (though not always) written with two dots above the body, rather like a German umlaut, so that it has something of the appearance of *ij*; those two dots occasionally appear above majuscule *I*, and I shall return to them at the end of this essay. Stubbs's letterform, in fact, most clearly resembles the double-dotted *y* that is a feature of Dutch scripts of the sixteenth and seventeenth centuries, and which arises from an orthographical interchangability between *y* and *ij*.[11] It is an unusual letterform in English scripts of the late-sixteenth century, though, and equally unusual among the contemporary printed types renowned for their similarity to German and Dutch fonts.[12] So Hand L's adoption of a paleographical feature common to Dutch handwriting does not seem to come from a more widespread imitation of Dutch typefaces (in print, for instance): it appears to have been a quirk of Stubbs's hand and, as I shall show later, was widely recognized as such.

To judge from the folds and marks in the letter from Stubbs to Hickes (distinct from the customary folds that were subsequently made in the letter as it was filed), it appears to have been folded, or even rolled up rather tightly and untidily, perhaps for hasty removal from the Tower. After commending the bearer of the letter, Stubbs asks Hickes to obtain the "hart and hand" of John Puckering, sergeant at law, in the case of a man's life, perhaps the life of a fellow resident of the Tower; Stubbs offers some thoughts about the best way to approach Puckering and the legal precedents that might pertain in the case. The phrase "hart and hand" returns to the language of Stubbs's petition to Elizabeth, not only a reminder that legal and political will and agency might be substitutable with the writing and signing of documents, but also resounding with the reference to heartfelt religious devotion—not his own but that of Hickes and his brothers—with which Stubbs finishes. "The Lord make you all to encrease in habilitie," he writes, "and harty will to serve the Lord and his church. Farewell to you all. Pray for your old poore restrained frend that he may never committ any thing vnworthy any of your Godly acquaintances, or that shold make you ashamed to acknowledg hym to be that he is your loving and faithfull fellow and frend, Iohn Stubbe."

Stubbs's friendship with Hickes originated from their association at Cambridge and then Lincoln's Inn in the 1560s and 1570s, within a circle of Puritans that included Thomas Cartwright, Vincent Skinner, George Blyth, and more peripherally Arthur Hildersham, to whom I shall return later. But even within that godly circle, the epistolary relationship of these two men seems to have been unusually close. Many of Stubbs's surviving autograph letters are written to Hickes; many of these are now kept in the Lansdowne Papers at the British Library. A smaller number of letters also survive from Stubbs to politicians of the Privy Council, including five to Cecil, one to Walsingham, and one to Queen Elizabeth herself, and others, now kept in the Ancaster

Papers, written to Peregrine Bertie, Lord Willoughby de Eresby, for whom Stubbs worked as secretary in the 1580s after his release from the Tower—losing his right hand allowed Stubbs to reenter official public life as a professional writer. The correspondence between Hickes and Stubbs has attracted the critical attention of historians such as Alan Bray, who notes the long-standing jealousies that seem to be played out between them, and also the "combination of convention and affection," in Bray's words, that determines their epistolary expressions of friendship.[13] After Stubbs's mutilation, one of the subtexts of their letters becomes Stubbs's desire to reinforce his friend's piety and godliness: so, for instance, a letter from Stubbs to Hickes, written in Hand L on 30 July 1582 from his new home near Norwich, notes that "I might find mattre yenough to deplore the foly and idleness of oure mispent youth together, with som warm exhortation to the redeeming of tyme passed in passtyme, the redeemyng of it, I say, by spending the rest with more conscience to our building vp in faith and faithfull conversation, wherby we may in som Godly vocation glorifie our God and benefit our brethren, and withall lyve lyke Adams children."[14] The letter is signed "Your loving and assured Ihohn Stubbe Scęva"; more of that word in a moment.

The Lansdowne Papers also contain an undated copy of a letter that Hickes seems to have sent back to Stubbs, perhaps in response to the very words of advice mentioned above. And it is in this correspondence from Hickes to Stubbs—more than in the letter from Stubbs to Hickes—that we are forcibly reminded of Stubbs's one-handedness and forced also to equate his left hand, and its material role in writing letters, with his identity as Hickes's friend and counselor. Or to put it another way: it is Hickes's references to Stubbs's friendship and counsel that keep returning us to his hand—both his mutilation and the handwriting of his letters. Hickes, for instance, responds to Stubbs's request for a left-handed knife: "I send yow by this bearer a lefte handed knife, well handeld, as yow did desire I would yow could handle it as well. Such as it is, accept of it I pray yow, as a poore token of our old freindshipp and this new yeare."[15] And he gives thanks for Stubbs's counsel: "I will onlie note," he writes, "with hartie thankes that notable note of freindship in yow, (that is) to be remorste at the former folies of your freind, and to lend him both your hand & Counsell"—yet another yoking of hand, letter and agency—"to reduce him into a better course."

The letter filed immediately afterward in the very same volume of the Lansdowne Papers, is another undated copy of a letter from Hickes to Stubbs;[16] it contains some of the same allusions as the former (such as a reference, for instance, to Stubbs's son as Hickes's "playfellow"), and so may either be a different draft of the letter that Hickes sent in reply to Stubbs, or perhaps a different letter sent back to Stubbs as part of the same correspondence. (Although it has been folded letterwise, it has no address, no signature, and no remnants of a seal.) Here again, Hickes seems to place the spiritual and moral advice that he has received from Stubbs in the agency of the hand, writing that "it is sufficient, nay it is to muche, to have spent the former even almost 40 yeares in vanitye without either vocation or profitt in my vocation: so that besides my sorrowe & shame for it, it would wounde me further if I did not fynde many playsters of good Comfort in the swete garden of godes woorde, & namly one, by that excellent & blessed gardiner St Paule, which is lett hym that hath stolne steal no more, butt rather labour both his owne handes." Remorse through the labor of the hands. Furthermore, Hickes identifies Stubbs, and the mutual affection that they feel for one another, with the hand in which Stubbs's original letter was written. "I thanke god," he writes,

> I neither lack wytt to accept of your freindly & godly advise thankfully, and I pray god I never want grace to followe and make fruyte of it effectually. I have receyved from yow since our first accquayntaunce, many good & freindly letters, which beare testimony of the goodwill yow beare me, these I retayne, and many tymes do reade, to recorde, that longe & mutuall goodwill betwixt vs. Butt I assure yow, these few lynes, in this ragged pece of paper, and wrytten with the lefte hande, do more rightly expresse me and more truly declare yow to love me, then, those many shetes. albeit I remember, I have good lessons in some of them and am beloved in them all.

The materiality of Stubbs's letter of advice, then—and which letter is this "ragged pece of paper"? A surviving letter, perhaps even the "ragged" document of 1 December 1580, or a letter now lost?[17]—its very materiality and its origin in Stubbs's "lefte hande," perhaps in opposition to his former letters, written with his right, are taken as guaranteeing the authenticity of his friendship. It is not that writing with the left hand denotes a new turn in Stubbs's life (in the sense that he was reborn as a true friend after his mutilation on the scaffold, and that he now writes in that context), but that this scrap of left-handed writing declares their long-standing friendship as it "truly" is. What's more, the letters of Stubbs's left hand reveal his true care for his friend, but they also reveal Hickes: they "rightly expresse me," as Hickes writes, "and more truly declare yow to love me." Stubbs's left hand seems to be a token of the way he is received by Hickes, rather than (or as well as) the way that he writes to Hickes. It bespeaks Hickes as well as bespeaking Stubbs; it almost seems to belong to both of them. The agency and the subject of these letters of the left hand are produced in their receipt, as well as in their penning.

This mutuality also governs the use of the word mentioned above: "Scæva." The first extant letter written in Hand L, Stubbs's December 1580 letter to Hickes from the Tower, is subscribed and signed "your loving and faithfull fellow and frend, Iohn Stubbe," but on the reverse side, the first line of the endorsement reads "Mr Stubbs Scæua." *Scaeva* is the Latin word for a left-handed person (the adjective *scaevus* describing something that goes from right to left), and Stubbs's use of the word seems to allude to the account in Livy's *Ab urbe condita* (II.xii–xiii) of Gaius Mucius Scaevola, a young Roman who in 508 B.C. attempted to assassinate Lars Porsena, the Etruscan king of Clusium, who was besieging Rome. Scaevola, Livy tells, concealed a sword beneath his cloak and made his way into the Etruscan camp, but unsure of Porsena's identity (and in a further Stubbsian echo), he assassinated a secretary (*scriba*) by mistake. He was seized and brought before Porsena, but Livy writes that in a show of bravery, he called out "Look, that you may see how cheap they hold their bodies whose eyes are fixed upon renown," thrust his right hand into a fire, and held it there impassively as it burned.[18] Porsena was so impressed by his courage and endurance that he freed Mucius, and shortly afterward led the Etruscan army in retreat. Scaevola's status as a humanist exemplar of loyal service and fortitude is attested by the frequent allusions or references to him in a number of sixteenth-century English authors, not to mention the direct quotation from Livy's account ("Facere et pati Fortia") on Marcus Gheeraerts's portrait of Captain Thomas Lee.[19] The association between Stubbs and Scaevola (both of them being given their names as a result of their sufferance) clearly has a political as well as an ethical register, although the use of the mere name in isolation leaves it ambiguous: it construes Stubbs's act as that of a loyal subject, but positions him somewhere between loyalty to Elizabeth, regardless of the misery of his punishment, and stoically steadfast and defiant in the face of that very punishment, loyal in opposition, and resolved to continue in his ways.[20]

Stubbs appends the word "Scæva" (in this or some other spelling) to his name in a succession of documents, such as his letter to Hickes of 30 July 1582 (BL, Lansd. MS 36, fols. 212^r–213^v). But in that particular letter, the word ap-

pears once again in the receiver-side endorsement: "Mr Stubbs Scæua / 1582."
In the December 1580 letter from the Tower (BL, Lansd. MS 31, fol. 40), the
word does not appear in the signature, but it *does* appear in the endorsement,
which begins "Mr Stubbs Scæua," and then continues in a different hand:

> to Mr Mich. Hicks
> writ wth his left
> hand: his right Cut off
> for writing a seditious
> Book ag. ye Qns mariage
> wth Monsieur

The juxtaposition of these two hands makes it difficult to decide the order in
which the endorsement was written and also who was responsible for writing
it. The letter has no separate address, so it could be that the lines beginning
with "to Mr Mich. Hicks" are in fact the address itself (written not in Hand
L and therefore presumably by an amanuensis), to which Hickes has prefixed
"Mr Stubbs Scæua" on receipt—or, vice versa, that the first line was the de
facto address (written, therefore, by Stubbs or someone in his company) and
that the subsequent lines were added on receipt. Or it may be that the first
line was written first, upon receipt, and that the others were added later, perhaps when the letter was filed, as a kind of docket of the information contained in it. These suggestions can only be hypothetical, but they are not
trivial—the way in which this endorsement was written affects the point at
which (and the way in which) Stubbs's left-handed writing was acknowledged
and taken up into his name. For it is striking that although Hand L is clearly
a self-evident material feature of the letter, and although it pertains directly
to the conditions of Stubbs's imprisonment, he does not acknowledge it in the
letter itself. Is it only when Hickes receives the letter that he identifies Stubbs
with the left hand that wrote the letter? Does Stubbs become Scaeva only at
the hand of Hickes? And how do we translate the word "Scæua"? As a cogno-
men (in other words, "Mr Stubbs, the left-handed man"), or synonymous with
the rest of the endorsement, a kind of ablative of instrument ("Mr Stubbs, written with his left hand")? Just as the name and the left-handed subjecthood
seem shared between writer and recipient, the word "Scæua" seems to bridge
both the identity of Stubbs as a writer and the physical instrument of his writing. His new hand gives him a voice, but a voice that is defined, and defines
itself, as the mere instrument itself. His very will, of which only a copy survives,

treats it in both of those ways, beginning "I Iohn Stubbe Scæva of Thelmton in Norfolk gentleman do in good healthe of Bodie and quyet of mynde declare this my shorte and laste will and testamente," but ending with a scribal copy of his characteristic signature: "By me Iohn Stubbe Scæva."[21]

Stubbs customarily signed his letters "John Stubbs, Scaeva" from the early 1580s until his death, the only exception being a letter written to Hickes in French in 1590, shortly before he died: Stubbs appears to have been with Peregrine Bertie, Lord Willoughby de Eresby, in France at the time (in the aid of the king of Navarre, according to the endorsement on a letter written to Burghley at the same time), and in his letter to Hickes he jokes about having used up all of his French ("j'ai dépensé et consumé toute mon français") in the many diplomatic letters that he had been forced to send. This particular letter, uniquely for Stubbs's career after 1580, is not written in Hand L: since Stubbs begins it by implying that he has written it himself ("mettant la plume à la papier pour la faire"), it seems to imply that he wrote it in draft, at least, but the different hand suggests that another secretary has copied out and corrected his French in his own hand. And this letter, unlike all the others, is not signed or endorsed "Scaeva" or "with his left hand."[22] Many, though not all, of them are endorsed in an equivalent way;[23] the exceptions, however, corroborate the reading that suggests that "Scaeva" was an identity not only partly created by Stubbs's close friends such as Hickes but fully meaningful only within that circle of friends. Four letters, for instance, survive that Stubbs wrote in 1585–86 as secretary to Willoughby.[24] All four are written in Hand L, and Stubbs retains the word "Scaeva" in his signature, but neither the secretary who receives the letters, nor Drue Drury—another member of Willoughby's household who worked with Stubbs on the household financial affairs and who mentions him by name in his own letters[25]—either refer to Stubbs by his nickname or mention that he is writing with his left hand. Outside of the circle that seems to define Stubbs as Scaeva, the endorsements no longer style him in that way, even though Stubbs himself continued to do so.

The creation and functioning of the name Scaeva within an epistolary network receives its final confirmation in a further document—paradoxically, both the first and the last time in which the word "Scaeva" is appended to a signature. Parts of an academic and theological commonplace book (BL, Harl. MS 3230), compiled, with textual excerpts, Ramian diagrams, and so on, in several stints between about 1584 and 1613, may have been written by Arthur Hildersham, a Puritan divine younger than Stubbs but peripherally connected to his Cambridge group through Thomas Cartwright; Hildersham is certainly

Figure 7.2. Later copy of a set of poems by Stubbs replicating Stubbs's hand. Commonplace book associated with Arthur Hildersham, compiled 1584–1613. BL, Harl. MS. 3230. © British Library Board.

closely associated with the book's compilation. The book contains texts copied from Cartwright and others, and also a set of twenty psalm translations, composed by Stubbs himself while he was a prisoner in the Tower and transcribed in no other place. The psalms are preceded by a copy of a letter from Stubbs, apparently to Cartwright, signed and dated "16. Iune 1580, Your bounden brother Scęva"; almost six months before Hickes uses the term in his endorsement to a letter of Stubbs's—in which even Stubbs doesn't sign his name in that way. Was Stubbs already Scaeva in June 1580? Or does the owner of this book himself supply a signature that came into common use later in 1580 and beyond? We know that these poems and letter were copied out in 1592, two years after Stubbs's death, because the scribe includes notes of the dates on which he has copied them. But what he has also done is to mimic Stubbs's handwriting in his copy of the letter and poems, using the same double dots above his minuscule *y* that appear in Stubbs's Hand L (Figure 7.2.).

Stubbs's unusual double-dotted Dutch *y* appears neither in his right-handed writing nor in the autograph letters of Hickes, Hildersham, or any other member of that Puritan circle, nor in any other text transcribed in the commonplace book, and yet it appears again in this posthumous copy of his poems. If this is indeed an attempt to replicate the paleographical features of Hand L, two years after Stubbs's death and twelve years after the translation of the psalms and their transmission in a letter to Cartwright, it shows how intimately the one-handed John Stubbs was associated with his hand. If those translations were not written in Hand L, but (like the letter written immediately after his mutilation) by an amanuensis, it would show that very identity being superimposed onto a set of Stubbs's epistolary writings, at the moment that they are received into and cataloged alongside other writings from his circle. Either way, it shows John Stubbs's left-handed letters—both his epistles and his script—being created and preserved by the social and religious group that receives them, either in endorsement or in their commonplace book. And it shows that the materiality and the distinctiveness of his left hand was once again to become the property of his readers, and the receivers of his letters, even after his death.

CHAPTER 8

"An Uncivill Scurrilous Letter"

"Womanish Brabb[l]es" and the Letter of Affront

MICHELLE O'CALLAGHAN

"Secretaries," or collections of model letters, such as Angel Day's *The English Secretorie* (1586) or William Fulwood's *The Enemie of Idlenesse* (1568), fully expected that those consulting their manuals may, at some stage, need to compose a letter to complain of an injury received or to take an acquaintance to task for behavior or actions that had caused offense. The model that was provided was the vituperative letter, which set out the decorum to be observed when dipping one's pen in gall. The vituperative letter was intended for situations in which an individual's reputation or that of his or her family had been besmirched or to voice grievances, particularly in disputes over property or money. Thomas Cohen, writing of sixteenth-century Italy, locates the rituals and vocabulary of affront, including the letter, firmly within the symbolic systems of an honor culture.[1] Renaissance courtesy books set out standards of civil behavior and speech that the gentle classes should abide by and expect to be observed by others in social exchanges. Maintaining honor and reputation was therefore at the heart of civil conversations; deviation from these standards was liable to cause affront, and so could provide just cause for response. This reflexive model of honor meant that if an individual was insulted then his or her reputation was damaged unless the insult was countered.[2] An analogy can be made between the letter of affront and the duel within this framework of reflexive honor since, in both cases, violence, verbal or physical, could be justified as a legitimate response to an affront to one's honor. There are, however, limits to this analogy. Certainly some letter writers, as we shall see, did use the language of the duel and posited an equivalence between abusive words and physical assault. That said, letter-writing manuals advocated a careful balance between attack and conciliation and continually reminded their readers to observe decorum when using the rhetorical forms of vitupera-tion. Displaying anger in the letter, as Linda Pollock has shown, was only acceptable if there were reasonable grounds for complaint, if it was used constructively to seek redress and conciliation, and, most important, if its expression was moderate and violent words were avoided. Hence, while mod-erate, constructive anger could be justified and the temperate letter of affront had a place in civil conversation, immoderate, destructive anger and violent, abusive words were not to be tolerated and were deemed uncivil.[3]

A distinction therefore can be made between temperate and intemperate uses of vituperation in the letter; and, yet, this distinction itself is not always clear-cut.[4] The point when dispraise that was civil, legitimate, and excusable became abusive language that was uncivil, scurrilous, and blameworthy was not always easy to judge. A writer may have sought to control a letter's inter-pretation by imposing a particular reading on his or her words. However, the recipient's response could not be fully determined, and the letter writer's justification could be rejected and offense taken at its tone.[5] The use of vitu-peration in the letter was thus not without its social risks. Vituperative lan-guage, if too violent, could quickly rebound on the speaker or writer to threaten his or her own character. In the cases that I shall explore in this essay, vituperation was either deliberately intemperate or perceived as such by the recipient, and the letter writer, in a number of instances, threatened with legal action. Some of these letter writers were women. It is often argued that women's use of vituperation carried more risks than male letter writers, in Cohen's words, they "more readily gained shame than honor" compared to their male counterparts: feminine models of decorum enjoined modesty rather than violence of speech, which tended historically to be coded mascu-line.[6] Yet, despite these particular gendered difficulties, women did use vitu-perative rhetoric in letters.[7] When Lady Bridget Willoughby wrote letters of affront, vituperation was used constructively to compel the addressee to check his behavior and to seek redress. However, she also viewed vituperation as a form of revenge and wanted her words to do harm. The response to her letter also demonstrates the risk that the use of such violent words carried given that Willoughby was threatened with prosecution before the Privy Council.

Arguably Willoughby was censured because her words were perceived to be too violent, not necessarily because women were per se precluded from writing vituperative letters. As others have noted, there is extensive evidence that elite women could and did employ vituperative rhetoric without damaging their reputation.[8] Men were also censured for their use of violent words in letters. When Christopher Brooke wrote a scandalously vituperative letter in response to Lady Eleanor Davies's verbal attack on his wife's honor, the case was brought before the Star Chamber. As John Chamberlain noted, Brooke had written "an uncivill scurrilous letter," that was deliberately vulgar and offensive.[9] Both Brooke's letter and the letters exchanged between Lady Mary Wroth and Sir Edward Denny in the 1620s display a heightened awareness of the culture of verse libels that, in turn, not only shaped their use of vituperative rhetoric but also rendered their use of its forms scandalous. Taken together, these letters provide examples of how vituperation could cross the line between civil and uncivil discourse, the various ways in which violent words could be deployed within the letter, and the risks involved. Vituperation, whether moderate or immoderate, carried a risk that can itself be viewed as a means of dealing with the insecurities induced by early modern society, particularly those relating to disputes over social standing and property. But, the use of violent words significantly increased the risk of censure, and so prompts questions about the social calculations involved. If, as Lynne Magnusson suggests, letter writers took "speech-act risks" according to an "estimation . . . of one's chances of success in any particular field of action," then, in the case of violent words, the chance of success was difficult to determine because of the inherent volatility of angry speech.[10]

*　　*　　*

Vituperation belongs to the demonstrative or epideictic forms of rhetoric, which incorporates the forms of praise and blame. The ability to use vituperative rhetoric effectively as a mode of opprobrium and to defend one's honor, as David Colclough notes, was "an important part of one's identity as both *homo rhetoricus* and *vir civilis*."[11] Hence just as the topics of praise and dispraise are grouped together in rhetoric manuals, the laudatory and vituperatory letters are grouped together in letter-writing manuals. Day is not atypical in advising the letter writer in his *The English Secretorie* simply to write the opposite of praise when writing vituperatively.[12] Panegyric and vituperation share the same topics: both address the subject's birth, education, achievements;

his or her physical attributes; and virtues, or their inverse. As in other arenas of public oratory, such as the law court and pulpit, vituperation had a recognized place in the civil conversations promoted within letter-writing manuals—but, only if it was moderate and observed decorum, and this is a key qualification.

The manuals point to a clear social etiquette governing the use of vituperation. William Fulwood advised the letter writer to write honorably and dispraise honestly. Vituperation within civil conversations required its participants to follow a rhetorical strategy that enabled the letter writer to maintain the ethical upper hand:

> First, to get good will vnto our selues, declaring that indeede we
> doe not loue, neither that it is our common vse to write euill of any
> man, but that nowe we are vehemently vrged and constrained
> thereunto, &c. Secondly, wee muste dispraise the partie in honest
> and couerte termes, so placed, that to be not plainly perceiued that
> we speake for enuie, anger, or such like: but onely that in verie
> deede of great pride which is in him doth cause vs to say it, to the
> end to abate his presumption and to reforme him.[13]

The onus was on the letter writers to retain credit in the exchange, to "get good will vnto our selues." To accomplish this, the writer needed to maintain an internal distance within the letter from the negative emotions—envy, malice, or anger—associated with vituperation. Such a disinterested stance was a marker of the letter writer's integrity and credibility. Instead, the motivation should be said to arise from the faults of the addressee, and thus from the civil imperative to reform the offender's character. Fulwood warns that the letter writer must be seen to write in honest terms. When Fulwood wrote *The Enemie of Idlenesse* the word "honest," alongside its current meaning of truthful and free from disgrace or reproach, was also a term firmly rooted in an honor culture and dependent on reputation. The honesty ascribed to a person was reliant on his "honourable position or estate; high rank."[14] The "honest" terms used by the letter writer therefore established his or her claim to a good moral character and also confirmed a social identity that was worthy of respect. In the case of women, honesty was not simply a synonym for chastity; instead, sexual honesty was one aspect of female honor and operated alongside other factors, such as status and reputation.[15]

When dispraising, the letter writer is advised to write not just in honest terms, but also covert, so "that to be not plainly perceiued that we speake for enuie, anger, or such like."[16] The civil conversations promoted in courtesy manuals, a genre that incorporated letter-writing manuals, sanctioned artful dissimulation, lying in order to maintain the appearance of politeness—at stake was the need to maintain face and gain social advantage over an opponent.[17] Whether an insult was true or not was not the primary concern. Ciceronian models for the use of invective in judicial oratory did not require that attacks on character of the accused be true, although blatant falsehoods could backfire, while the *perceived* truth of the allegation did help to strengthen the prestige of the attacker at his opponent's expense.[18] The letter writer was expected to dissimulate honesty, given that the letter may well be written out of envy or anger, in order to maintain rhetorical advantage in a dispute. The civil use of vituperation thus placed particular demands on the letter writer, requiring subtle maneuvering. Such care was necessary because one of the pitfalls of using invective is that it can easily recoil on the speaker to damage their claim to "honesty" if it is perceived to be intemperate.

Sir Francis Bacon's letter to Sir Edward Coke is a very good example of dispraising "in honest and couerte termes." The two men were long-standing enemies.[19] In some copies, this letter is dated December 1616, in others 1617, placing it in the period immediately after Bacon had orchestrated Coke's removal from his office of chief justice of the King's Bench. To avoid the accusation of triumphing maliciously over the downfall of an opponent, Bacon needed to proceed carefully and to demonstrate he is dispraising in "honest" terms from the outset. Part of his strategy is to incorporate vituperation within the format of the letter of advice, thereby enabling him to cast his attacks on Coke's character in the form of moral censure rather than malicious insult. Integral to the mode of invective employed in the letter, and its strategies of dissimulation, is Bacon's repeated recourse to the authorial persona of the "true friend." In Coke's "time of . . . affliction," Bacon seeks to take

> this seasonable advantage like a true frend (though farr unworthy
> to be accounted soe) to shewe you your true shape in a glasse and
> nott in a false one to flatter you nor in one that is oblique and
> angular to make you seeme worse then you are and soe offend you
> butt in one made by the reflection of your owne words and
> actions . . . yet of this resolue you self itt proceeds from loue, from

a true desier to doe you good. . . . mende whatt you finde amisse in
your self, and retain what yo[u]r iudgement shall approue.

In Ciceronian style, Bacon equates the attack on Coke's character that follows this opening address with frankness of speech, which, in turn, is offered
as a healthy and necessary antidote to the flattery Bacon implies Coke has
previously attracted and encouraged. The guise of the friend allows Bacon to
add weight to his professed aim in writing the letter, which is to encourage
Coke to reform his character and behavior by honestly showing him a mirror
in which he may see his vices. There is a further sting in the tail in the coda
that Coke does not have enough true friends to do this office for him: "since
I feare both your selfe and all great men want such beinge themselues true
frends to few or none."[20] The letter is certainly frank in relating Coke's faults.
That said, particularly in the framing passages of the letter, Bacon is careful
to stay just on the right side of the very thin line dividing just censure and
malign abuse. Bacon points out Coke's character defects in very stark terms,
but frames these attacks as moral advice, which claims to wound only in order
to cure. The letter exemplifies the type of artful dissimulation that is intended
to maintain the appearance of "honest" censure, while delivering covert,
although easily discernible insults.

   Vituperation was used by women letter writers to intervene in family disputes and to remedy perceived insults or complain of injustices. And some of
these women letter writers did not always use such arts of dissimulation. On
the contrary, they appreciated the linguistic violence of vituperation, particularly the instrumentality of the curse. Lady Bridget Willoughby resorted to
using invective in the letter as part of the armory available to defend herself
as a gentlewoman against those seeking to undermine her standing with her
father. Bridget and her husband, Sir Percival, were the principal heirs of her
father, Sir Francis Willoughby, which left them vulnerable to the predations
of her father's servants and friends, as well as her siblings, in the competition
for his favor. Sir Francis's own behavior was particularly volatile: he was heavily in debt, easily manipulated, and continually altered the arrangements for
the settlement of his estate. This situation reached a critical point in 1595 when
the widowed Sir Francis remarried, and Bridget and Percival stood to lose
much of their inheritance if his new wife bore a male heir. Family relations
were further strained by a quarrel between Percival and Francis over the latter's mortgaging of six manors, part of the couple's marriage settlement, heavily encumbering them with debt.[21] The couple's loss of Sir Francis's favor is

evident in his angry letter addressed to Bridget in September 1595, when he takes Bridget to task for insulting his friend, Sir Clement Fisher, by publicly refusing to accept his greeting, saying that "she bid him spare that courtesie for others that had a better opinion of him." Sir Francis concluded his letter warning he would throw them out of the manor at Middleton because "he would no longer permit such contrary and rebellious humours to be in his house."[22]

Sir Francis Willoughby's household had long been fractious. He and his first wife, Elizabeth, were embroiled in bitter disputes throughout their marriage that were aggravated by Sir Francis's servants and friends.[23] His household supported a large number of gentlemen servants, who, according to the later assessment of Bridget's great-granddaughter, Cassandra Willoughby, Duchess of Chandos, writing in the early eighteenth century, had "gained his friendship so much as to have thereby a power to persuade and influence him in the affairs of his family" and exploited family divisions for "their own advantage."[24] There were substantial rewards for such influence, including property or financial settlements. Thomas Willoughby wrote to his son, Percival, soon after his marriage to beware of Sir Francis's servants and friends, since he is "so followed by Markham, Fisher, Cludd and Marmion, that he hardly does any thing without them."[25] When Lady Bridget wrote a letter to Fisher prompted by his recent act of fomenting discord between father and daughter, the stakes were therefore extremely high. The risk she took in using violent words in her letter was calculated in relation to the immediate threat to her financial security posed by Fisher's manipulation of her father. Part of her justification of her angry words rested on the long-standing disruptive role of gentlemen servants and friends in her father's household, and she is at pains to illustrate how Fisher has insinuated himself into her father's favor in collusion with these servants. Bridget accuses Fisher of attempting to marry her to his cousin, Thomas Cludd, "a poor cozening knave of my father's."[26] Given that Bridget was the eldest child and potential heir, such a marriage would have been lucrative to both men and illustrates the social aspirations of gentlemen servants. Cludd was one of Sir Francis's favorite servants and had considerable authority within the household. In one incident, when Lady Elizabeth Willoughby had attempted to throw her husband's servants out of the house in his absence, Cludd confronted her with "his sword under his arm," leaving her fearing for her life. Lady Elizabeth was subsequently confined to the house under the authority of Cludd.[27] He was also instrumental in setting Sir Francis against Percival by fabricating a letter in which it was claimed that Percival aimed to murder his father-in-law once he had secured his estates. Percival and Bridget were thrown out of her father's house—this may be the incident Bridget refers to in her letter when she claims that "I was once before for thy pleasure and perswasions little better then hurled out of this house, being great bellied, when thou didst hope both by that means might have perished."[28]

Lady Bridget aims to show that Fisher's actions in denouncing her to her father proceed from malice and self-interest, casting herself as one of the many innocent victims of his slanderous tongue, which "is so busie in all matters, and spareth not ladys and gentlewomen of greater account then myself."[29] This accusation justifies her anger and her own invective since such a powerful rhetorical weapon is required to check his slanderous assault: "Malicious knave thou art that canst not spare poor gentlewomen and infants with thy tongue and practices; gentleman thou know'st thyself to be none, and tho' at this instant I have no better means of revenge then a little ink and paper, let thy soul and carkes be assured to hear and tast of these injuries in other sort and terms then from and by the hands of a woman."[30] Bridget does present her gender as a constraint—as a woman, she may only wield "a little ink and paper." Nonetheless, she assumes violent words are a means available to her to "revenge" her honor as a gentlewoman. Gary Schneider has argued that letters were chosen over face-to-face encounters in such conflicts to act "as a social buffer" and so "preserve civility."[31] Yet, Lady Bridget closes this distance by equating the textualized injury she can inflict with her "ink and paper" with the physical injury she may call on others, presumably male kin and friends, to inflict on her behalf. This passage resembles a curse in that it is a ritualized and instrumental verbal assault intended to injure the recipient—this is not a display of temperate anger. Such textualized violence might be seen as excusable if it is in response to an injury that is serious enough to justify the harshness of the words used.[32] Hence Lady Bridget's efforts in the letter to give ample just cause for her grievance against Fisher.

But Lady Bridget was taking a risk with her violent words. She may have been compelled to take that risk because her already fraught relationship with her father had been so badly damaged by Fisher's accusations and her inheritance jeopardized. Success, however, could not be guaranteed. Upon receiving the letter, Fisher threatened "to trouble her for it" and to call her before the Privy Council. Lady Bridget did assume responsibility for her actions, defending herself in a letter to her husband, which included a copy of her letter to Fisher, insisting that "there is nothing [in the letter] but what may be well answered if he were far better then he is, seeing it is all too true." Yet, she was also concerned that her letter might shame her in the eyes of her husband: "Come what may of it, I hope for your part, being a common enemy to us both, you will think no otherwise then well of/Yours/Brigitt Willoughby."[33] While Lady Bridget took an active role in managing the conflict, nonetheless there is also an awareness that she must answer for her actions to her husband. The case does not seem to have gone before the Privy Council. Instead, it was Fisher's wife, Mary, who responded to Lady Bridget and used vituperation in her husband's defense. Mary Fisher denied Lady Bridget's accusations against her husband, hence the grounds of her anger, and also criticized her "untemparate letter," arguing that Lady Bridget's uncivil use of invective "hardly beseemed a gentlewoman."[34] Although Mary Fisher was, in a sense, acting as proxy for her husband and writing in his defense, presumably with his support, she did assume an active role in defending the collective honor of the family.[35] Even so, it raises the question of why Clement Fisher did not respond himself. It is possible he sought to claim the moral advantage by refusing to engage directly in a war of words, and so not risk his own standing as an elite male through an intemperate, angry letter. In the case of Lady Bridget, the counteraccusation made by Mary Fisher was that she had damaged her own standing through her intemperate and violent words, which were not only unfit for a woman, but, more important, for someone of her class.

*   *   *

Vituperation, as Alastair Bellany points out in relation to verse libels, was viewed with a fundamental ambivalence: on the one hand, its instrumentality was valued; but, on the other hand, its use was stigmatized and considered shameful.[36] In the following examples, the connection between the vituperative letter and the verse libel is particularly close. Both sets of letters were produced during the early 1620s, at the time of the Bohemian crisis, when verse libels circulated with renewed vitality in this period of unrest, and suggest an acculturation to the libel's stylized language of abuse and a sophisticated understanding of the instrumentality of violent words.

Christopher Brooke penned a letter of complaint to Lady Eleanor Davies in 1622, accusing her of insulting his wife, that is deliberately intemperate in its expression of anger, exuberantly stepping over the line between just censure and scurrilous abuse. In this case, a man of lower status, albeit a gentleman, directs his anger at an aristocratic woman and selects her sense of honor as his main line of attack, rather than her gender. Brooke, a lawyer, long-standing

member of Parliament for York, and author of literary works, had married
Lady Mary Jacob, the widow of Sir Robert Jacob, in December 1619. It seems
their son, John, was born in the months before the marriage, given he was
"eight years and more" when Brooke wrote his will on 8 December 1627.[37]
Brooke alludes to two encounters in which he claims Lady Eleanor was vio-
lently abusive to his wife; the first incident also involved a child, possibly
Lady Jacob's daughter, Mary, by her first marriage, or perhaps more probably
her infant son, John, who would have been just over two years of age. Brooke's
accusation that Lady Davies has lied about his wife toward the end of his letter suggests a sexual slander, possibly that John was a bastard.

The two women had been acquainted for a number of years through their
husbands. Sir Robert Jacob, as solicitor general in Ireland, had worked under
Lady Eleanor's husband, Sir John Davies, the attorney general; both women
returned to London in 1619, the year after Jacob's death. Sir Robert seems to
have been on good terms with the Davies family, visiting Lady Eleanor when
in England in 1617, and passing on news of their son to Davies.[38] However,
the Jacobs were new gentry; he had been knighted in Ireland, and there seems
to have been some resentment of their newly acquired status in Dublin. Barnaby Rich, in a confidential report written for Sir Julius Caesar on Ireland's
governance, claimed that Mary was a Southampton sailor's widow, and that
Robert, before arriving in Ireland, "never [had] a foote of lande, neuer a house,
nor so much as a bedd of his own to lye upon." Robert, in fact, was the son of
a Dorset gentleman, and it is likely that Mary's family, like that of Christopher Brooke, belonged to the prosperous middling classes.[39] Lady Eleanor, by
contrast, was the daughter of an earl, and this difference in social status un-
derpins the dispute. Brooke's response to the injury to his wife's reputation
assumes that he and his wife are the social equals of Lady Davies and dismisses
the notion of aristocratic honor. The quarrel was serious enough to go before
the Star Chamber in July 1622. Details of the proceedings no longer survive,
and it is possible that the case was not concluded because Lady Jacob became ill;
she died in November 1622, three months after the action commenced.

Brooke's letter to Lady Eleanor contrasts with the majority of personal
vituperative letters through its deployment of the language of abuse in a self-
consciously stylized manner, and it is this that reveals the letter's artful af-
finities with the verse libel. Brooke unleashes the authorial persona of the
Juvenalian railing, biting satirist. There is no attempt to temper the language
of insult, rather it owns its abuse—it is a letter that aims for the heightened
rhetorical affects of malice and intemperate anger. The opening section of the

letter, in which Brooke relates the cause of the quarrel, claims the indignation
of the moralizing satirist: "Did not I intreat you my Lady Tryfle to make some
mannerly amends for you^r impudence & causeles abusing my wife, & that
innocent childe. And is not it true that, my wife tells me that you are an in-
corrigible Malkyn, & have sett upon hir againe with you^r base coxcomicall
braveries." Brooke is employing the rhetorical device Puttenham calls "the
questioner," *erotema*, which involves asking many questions and looking for
no answers, "speaking indeed by interrogation."[40] Rhetorically, it puts Lady
Eleanor on trial and allows the speaker to adopt a stance of righteous anger,
pointing out that her abusive behavior was without just cause and directed
at an "innocent childe." Fury and malice, however, quickly overwhelm the
speaker. This is, of course, deliberately crafted. To gain a sense of the effect of
the gratuitousness of the insults and the sheer quantity and violence of the abusive words that are amassed in the following sentences, they must be quoted
in full:

> thou abominable, stinking, greasie, symnell faced excrement of
> hono^r, since (abandoning all goodnes & modesty) thou wilt stand
> upon that vaine glorious foote stoole, what a notable sluttish
> ornament of Bedlam wouldst thou bee if thou hadst thy right, that
> art so habitually madd for it is yet a moneth & more to Midsum-
> mer moone; what a scorne & shee block of laughter is that scurvy
> contracted purse mouth of thine, & those black patches of ugly
> deformities, wch makes thee ridiculous to all men, weomen &
> children, except thy shitten selfe, for the eyes of the body are
> allwayes hoodwynckt ^&clouded^ wth Cypres & vales & Mercury
> cloutes most filthily putt on. And the eyes of thy minde have ever
> bin bleared & blinded wth fastidious punctualities, & the humo^r of
> my Lady Woodbee in the play. Is it not a wretched thing that thou
> art naked & hast no figleaves to cover thy shame but the titles of
> thy house, are there no higher considerations, doth not a Brickbatt
> of Babel in that respect goe twenty times beyond thee. Is not a
> china dish more worth then twenty such glazed & sized pitchers as
> thou art if thy husband did not cover thee, but againe hoysted on
> his blatant beast bid him expound these verses Malo pater tibi sit
> Thersites, dummodo tu sis Aeacidæ similis vulcaniq[ue] arma
> capescas quam te Thersiti similem producat Achilles. If he did and
> thou yet remaine an incorrigible unperfumed peece of Egyptian

Mummey then I will vouchsafe to interpret them my selfe to thee, but gentlye & not according to the rigor of the letter. Better Thersites were thy father farre, so thou wert vertuous wife & debonayre, Then that Achilles had thee (Monster) made as now thou art, a sorie & lying Jade, but I will spend no more terme time upon thee Hecate, Medusa, Legion, Cloven footed Gorgon, yet if I meete thee in the vacation, assure thy selfe, I will kick thee & scratch a mynced pye for a dogg from thy ill kept filthy dunghill arse. And be ever what thou art, wch is the most horrible curse that can be laid upon thee.[41]

Brooke's letter is a ritualized venting of spleen in which terms of abuse pile up in a deforming *copia*. But this is not simply a rant, in which emotions run wild, instead the insults are carefully organized around the theme of the nature of true nobility. Hence, Brooke cites Juvenal's eighth satire on this topic, which opens with the questions "What's the use of pedigrees? What's the advantage, Pontius, of being valued by the length of your bloodline, of displaying the painted portraits of ancestors . . . if . . . the life you live is rotten?"[42] The lines cited in the letter come from the conclusion, the gist of which is that it would be better if Lady Eleanor's father were baseborn and she virtuous, than her father worthy and she base. Underlying the abuse in Brooke's letter is the premise that nobility of blood does not necessarily equate with virtue and that ancestry is not a guarantee of individual worth, which, in turn, functions as a defense of his wife's, and his own, social standing against Lady Eleanor's insults. The curse that closes the letter makes manifest the letter's ritualistic element. The desecrating violence unleashed by the language of abuse in Brooke's letter is designed to deform what Lady Eleanor is said to hold sacred, her family honor, a public image in which her self-worth and virtue reside in the "titles of thy house." To do so, Brooke subjects her to a process of abjection in which images of excrement, filth, and disease abound—she is metaphorically full of shit. The language of the grotesque, Laura Gowing argues, was "a particularly fertile way of undermining superior bodies," although, in the case of women, it focuses "overwhelmingly" on sexual honor.[43] Yet, Brooke's insults impugn Lady Davies's sexual honor—the "Mercury cloutes" imply the pox, and he calls her a "Jade," or prostitute—as an aspect of her misplaced sense of family honor, not necessarily as a target in itself.[44] In any case, there is no propriety to this letter. Brooke closes by imagining a scene of face-to-face physical violence in which abjection and brutality go hand in hand in his threat to "kick thee & scratch a mynced pye for a dogg from thy ill kept filthy dunghill arse."

What is notable and disturbing about the letter is this combination of extreme textualized violence with the self-consciously literary form of its abuse. As we have seen, Brooke ostentatiously quotes from Juvenal's eighth satire. Throughout the letter, he draws on satiric topoi, shared with Juvenal's satire, which contrast extrinsic trappings of nobility, such as the reliance of the decadent nobility on monuments to their ancestors, with intrinsic quality, exemplified by virtuous men of humble birth. Brooke also turns to the texts of his friend, Ben Jonson, a master of a form of ridicule that viciously deformed its victim and moved the reader to scornful laughter. He addresses Lady Eleanor with the Jonsonian epithet "Lady Tryfle," and likens her to Lady Politic Would-be. In *Volpone*, Lady Would-be's humor is vanity, her loquacity identifies her as an empty vessel, making much sound but little sense, and signifying her pretentions to learning. Brooke estimates Lady Davies's worth is less than "a Brickbatt of Babel," a piece of human folly that was an affront to God, and associated with linguistic confusion. The letter then adds a Spenserian note, seating Sir John Davies on Spenser's Blatant Beast, an archetypal figure of the public voice of envy and detraction and of rancorous speech. The Latin verses Davies is invited to "expound," as we have seen, come from the end of Juvenal's eighth satire. This is a carefully crafted letter. Its literary intertextuality, which continually locates the text in a tradition of satire, reshapes the vituperative letter, aligning it with the forms of the verse libel.

The highly self-conscious literary aspect of the epistle suggests that it was not intended solely as a "private" letter, meant only for the eyes of Lady Eleanor and Sir John Davies, but wider circulation was envisioned. There is a "surplus value" to the invective generated by the vicious laughter of ridicule, which interpellates a readership who enjoys these jokes and shares these values—the letter was intended to entertain as well as defame.[45] Chamberlain certainly knew of Brooke's letter when he wrote to Dudley Carleton in July 1622 with news of "a hot suit commenced in the Starchamber twixt Sir John Davies Lady and the Lady Jacob about womanish brabb[l]es, and an uncivill scurrilous letter written by Kit Brooke in his wife's behalf."[46] An autograph copy survives among the papers of the Conway family and may have come into the hands of Edward, the first Viscount Conway, as part of the Star Chamber inquiry in his official capacity as a recently appointed member of the Privy Council, or it may have been collected by his son, who had a taste for burlesque and satire. Brooke was part of a network, which included John

Hoskins and Richard Martin, known for its composition of burlesque poetry and verse libels, including "The Censure of a Parliament Fart." It is probable the libelous letter was written, in part, for the entertainment of this group of wits. Lady Jacob seems also to have participated in these games of licentious wit and is credited with authorship of a bawdy burlesque answer poem. Intriguingly a number of rare verses associated with Brooke and Jacob, such as the epithalamium written for the couple, survive in the Conway papers.[47] Brooke's letter does not appear to have circulated beyond these close associates and so there is no evidence it was copied into manuscript miscellanies as was so often the case with verse libels. And yet, this "scurrilous letter" is highly conscious of a tradition of verse libels, which inflects its use of the forms of vituperation. Brooke's letter aimed to injure Lady Davies in revenge for her attack on his wife's reputation. He may have risked using the mode of the verse libel in this dispute because he shared the view of his close friend, John Donne, who wrote in a letter of "witty and sharp libels" that, "for the elegancie and composition, would take deep root, and make durable impressions in the memory."[48]

The letters exchanged between Lady Mary Wroth and Sir Edward Denny in early 1622 are structured by a far more intricate social dance, in this case, directly prompted by the circulation of verse libels. Denny had taken offense at passages in Wroth's pastoral romance *Urania*, which he believed were a thinly veiled libelous account of the marriage of his daughter, Honora, to James Hay, the Scottish favorite, that covertly accused him of violence toward his daughter. Denny is said to have counterattacked with a verse libel addressed to Lady Mary, and she responded with her own verse libel. Both Wroth and Denny equate the libel and its conventions of vituperation with the duel, particularly, the language of the lie. Calling another a liar or giving the lie questioned one's gentle status and was therefore grounds for a challenge to a duel.[49] Wroth's verse libel answers Denny's verse libel by returning his insults blow by blow in an act of mocking mimicry: "How easily now do you receave your owne/Turnd on your self from whence the squibb was throwne."[50] She gives Denny the lie, thus challenging his honesty and honor.[51] Her letter, which was sent with the verse libel, is less intemperate. While the letter also gives the lie, it makes skillful use of the forms of dissimulation, associated with vituperative rhetoric, in a ritualized game of prestige. Two different forms of lying operate in the letters: giving the lie, and so challenging the others' honor, and the civil use of lying. There is a studied politeness to this exchange that contrasts dramatically with Brooke's libelous letter of affront. Much use, for example, is made of the civil complimentary lie in the subscriptions to the letters by both Denny and Wroth: "Your most well-wishing frend Edward Denny who for the great honor I bear somme of your noble allies and my deerly honored frends doe forbeare to write what I might"; "Your as well wishing frend Mary wrothe"; "Your truly well wishing frend if you could think so Edward Denny."[52]

Given that Denny-Wroth verse libels were already in circulation, these letters are framed by the particular issues raised by libelous discourse. Wroth's opening letter plays with the status of the verse libel as a deliberately unauthored text: this can be an advantage in that authorship can be disavowed; however, since the text is unowned, this very openness means that authorship can be attributed to an individual by others. The letters of both Wroth and Denny involve a complex negotiation of authorship in which words are owned and disowned. Wroth's initial letter is characterized by a deliberate disingenuousness, by lying in order to maintain the social veneer of politeness that should structure the exchanges of the gentle classes:

> This day came to my handes some verses under the name of the
> Lord Denny's but such vile, rayling and scandalous thinges, as I
> could not beleeve they proceeded from any but some drunken poet;
> and they [the] rather bycause they so feelinglie speak of that vice
> and sinne; but to think my Lord Denny who hath professed so
> much Religion, Justice and love of worth, should fall into so strange
> a disposition as to slander and revile a woman-frend who hath ever
> honour'd him; I was loath to creditt it; especiallie knowing mine
> own innocencie; which is as cleare and pure as new borne; what
> ever such like slanderous conceipts have layed upon mee.[53]

Insult is delivered in the very loose guise of praise: since Wroth says the verses could only have been written by a drunk, she initially could not credit Denny's authorship because of his own professed virtue. The use of the word "professed" is, of course, double-edged, both meaning avowed and implying insincerity, and it is mirrored in her own professed admiration for him. At first, Wroth seems to be offering Denny a face-saving bargain: if he will not accuse her and her book of libel, then she will not attribute the verse libel to him.

If Wroth had left it there, she would have maintained the dissimulation on both levels. But she does not. Instead, in an act of deliberate affront, Wroth breaks cover and gives him the lie by openly attributing authorship of the verse libel to Denny. Why does she do this? One possible answer is that this is an affair of honor in which Wroth expects to take an equal part and does not represent herself as disadvantaged by her gender. Instead, as a member of the nobility, she is ready to own her own words in a simulated face-to-face encounter and eschew forms of politeness when it is to her advantage. The language of the duel permeates the verse libels and is mirrored in the reflexive notion of honor that structures these letters, particularly Wroth's letters. In this epistolary duel, Wroth parries, as she says, by returning the accusation that he has thrown at her, point by point. While both insist on their differences, what these letters affirm is their similarities—they are both combatants in the complex and highly charged social games of prestige among the early modern elite.

The letters exchanged between Wroth and Denny are alert to the risks of vituperation and obsessed with who said what to whom. The question of who has the king's ear is of vital concern to both parties, and both fear being brought into discredit with James. This is a world in which reputations were made and damaged, sometimes irrevocably, by others' words. Wroth demands to be put on trial at a type of court of honor and challenges Denny to "Produce your wittnesses."[54] She pointedly reminds him of her high aristocratic status, of "my ranke below the Kings Majestie and his," and that she can call on her "noble allies" to speak and act in her defense.[55] Denny was also of the nobility, descended from courtiers, and a wealthy man. Yet, Denny's last letter bows out of the quarrel. He ends by acknowledging that Wroth's "best frends" and "noble allies" at court necessitate his withdrawal.[56] He has lost face at court, been made a fool of in front of the king, and his final letter conveys a sense that either he has been outmaneuvered in this game of reputation or perhaps he made the calculation that the quarrel with Wroth was just not worth the further risk.[57]

The use of vituperation was a risky business, especially when violent words were employed. Shame did not just attach itself to women in these disputes, as we have seen in the case of Christopher Brooke. When Chamberlain expressed his disapproval of Brooke's "uncivill scurrilous letter," he also implied that Brooke had transgressed the codes of elite masculinity not only through his intemperate words, but, relatedly, by engaging in "womanish brabb[l]es." Here, gendered language is deployed to describe a situation—a dishonorable and demeaning squabble—rather than simply the gender of the individuals involved. There is an uneven relationship between the gendered discourse around anger and the gender of those who used its rhetorical forms in letters, rather than a straightforward equivalence. In cases of intemperate letters, what appears to have attracted the most censure was the incivility and scurrility of words, rather than necessarily the gender of the letter writer. For both men and women, the risky business of writing vituperative letters was a response to the insecurities of early modern society—the vagaries of patronage, the instability of property rights, and the centrality of reputation in a society based on credit. While, as Pollock argues, moderate anger may have "had a valued place in the regulation of everyday personal interaction in early modern England," vituperation was not always used so constructively.[58] Individuals also wanted their words to do harm and to inflict injury. What the cases in this essay demonstrate is the strategic investment in violent words by both elite men and women and a sophisticated understanding of the instrumentality of vituperation in its various forms.

PART IV

The Afterlives of Letters

CHAPTER 9

"Burn This Letter"

Preservation and Destruction in the Early Modern Archive

ARNOLD HUNT

> There is a story that Sir Robert [Peel], in the last year of his last administration [1845–46], appeared late at night in the bedroom of [Edward] Cardwell [financial secretary to the treasury], and paced up and down without saying a word, Cardwell watching with amazed perplexity from his bed. At last he broke silence. "Never destroy a letter," he oracularly said. "No public man who respects himself should ever destroy a letter." He then turned on his heel and left the room.
>
> —Lord Rosebery, *Miscellanies Literary and Historical*

"Never destroy a letter"—Peel's maxim could be the motto of the modern bureaucratic state, and nowhere more so than in nineteenth-century Britain, where the vast increase in official business and the need for swift and efficient communication between imperial center and periphery demanded new technologies of record keeping and retrieval.[1] Six years after Peel's midnight visit to Cardwell's bedroom, John Stuart Mill, giving evidence before the House of Lords on behalf of the East India Company, conjured up a utopian vision of a perfect archive in which every act of government was recorded and every item of correspondence preserved. "The whole Government of India is carried

on in writing," he told the Lords, "and the whole of the original correspondence is sent to the Home Government; so that there is no single act done in
India, the whole of the reasons for which are not placed on record."[2] And
once preserved, it was hoped, the records would endure forever. Lord Palmerston, another stickler for archival order and control, justified his obsession with
good handwriting on the grounds that "those who wrote despatches or letters
which were to be preserved for all time should take care to write them well."[3]

This ideal of total preservation, which Mill regarded as "a greater security for good government than exists in almost any other government in the
world," was carried over into the new discipline of archive administration that
grew up to serve the bureaucratic state. Hilary Jenkinson's *Manual of Archive
Administration* (1922), the founding text of modern archive management, argued that the archivist was essentially a custodian, whose role was to catalog
and preserve records, not to tamper with what Jenkinson, in a revealing choice
of words, called the "impartiality" of the archive. Writing soon after the end
of the First World War, Jenkinson was aware that the proliferation of official
papers made some weeding of the public record almost inevitable. Modern
administrators, he complained, had fallen into a "slipshod manner of archive-
making," aided by new forms of copying technology: "Why exert oneself to
decide whether four copies of a letter are necessary when the difference in
labour is only that of putting five sheets instead of one into a machine? why
go to the trouble of adding a cross-reference from one file to another when it
is so easy to slip a copy into each?"[4] Yet Jenkinson argued that destruction
could only be justified in the comparatively rare cases where two records precisely duplicated each other. Anything beyond this made him profoundly
uneasy. He was left, he wrote, with "a growing conviction that destruction of
any of the Archives we have received from the past is a course that a conscien-
tious Archivist must find it difficult to commend."[5]

But if we step back to an earlier period, we find a very different attitude
to archival preservation and destruction. In the early modern period the destruction of letters was frequently taken for granted. As John Donne remarked
in a letter of 1608: "with how much desire we read the papers of any living
now (especially friends) which we would scarce allow a boxe in our cabinet,
or shelf in our Library, if they were dead?" Since letters were a form of speech,
Donne considered that they no longer had any value when the writer was no
longer alive to speak through them, "for the writings and words of men present, we may examine, controll, and expostulate, and receive satisfaction from
the authors; but the other we must beleeve, or discredit; they present no mean."[6]

It comes as no surprise to find Donne asserting the familiar Erasmian commonplace that letters are speech at a distance, but what is far more surprising, to our eyes, is his matter-of-fact assumption that the letters of friends will be discarded after their death. There is no expectation here that the letters of others might form part of a personal archive, nor even that they might be preserved in memory of the dead. As John Donne the younger observed in the preface to his father's *Letters to Severall Persons of Honour* (1651), cremation by fire was "the fate of most letters," so that to edit and publish a collection of letters amounted almost to a form of bodily resurrection.[7]

In this essay I want to explore some of the empty spaces in the early modern archive by looking at letters that draw attention to their own mortality or even invite their own destruction. The surviving evidence is, of course, only fragmentary. We can never know how often the request to "burn this letter" was complied with; all we have to go on are the instances where it was disregarded. Enough survives, however, to suggest that early modern letter writers were acutely conscious of the afterlife of their correspondence and sought as best they could to control—and limit—what would be preserved. As a result, the early modern archives that have come down to us are very often the product of a deliberate but largely invisible process of selection. This not only challenges the assumed impartiality of the archive, it also requires us to rethink the relationship between preservation and destruction. One recent textbook on archive management declares that "the mirror image of the impulse to save records is the impulse to destroy."[8] At first glance this might seem obvious: what could be more antithetical to good archival practices than the burning of letters? Yet another view is also possible: that it is the impulse to save that generates the impulse to destroy. The emergence of more systematic archival practices in the early modern period, which led to more letters being preserved, also led to more being burned precisely so that they would not remain in the archival record.

The request to "burn this letter" also needs to be read with sensitivity to early modern epistolary conventions. Some letters, it is true, were genuinely dangerous to preserve.[9] But letter writers could also play with the conceit of burning a letter as part of what might be termed a rhetoric of intimacy, a way of signifying that they were opening their true mind and admitting their correspondent to a level of trust from which others were excluded. Thus Donne, writing to Sir Henry Goodere in 1614 to confide his disappointment in what he considered the ungenerous conduct of his patron the Countess of Bedford, could add, as an afterthought, "I would you could burn this letter before you read it," as if wishing he could cancel the words he had just written and that Goodere had just read. Donne may have been sincerely anxious that the letter should not remain, as he put it, "upon record" (though Goodere kept it anyway), but the plea to burn the letter, with the wry suggestion that burning *before* reading would be even safer than burning after reading, also serves to admit Goodere to a deeper level of intimacy.[10] Francis Bacon, writing to King James in 1616, apologized for writing "soe longe a letter, which yet I wish may have a short continuance, and be punished with fire," yet the letter survives in scribal copies that Bacon himself seems to have put into circulation at a later date.[11] Here the request to burn the letter functions retrospectively as a way for Bacon to demonstrate his trusted position as the king's confidential adviser.

These references to letter burning are also a reminder of the materiality of the letter. Paper has many useful qualities that make it ideally suited for confidential correspondence: it can be easily burned or torn, but it can also be cut up into separate pieces, or folded inside another sheet. Again, the letters of Donne and Bacon supply some revealing examples. In another of his letters to Goodere, Donne passes on a tidbit of gossip about "an honourable person (whose name I give you in a schedule to burn, lest this Letter should be mis-laid)"; the implication is that the letter itself will be preserved and perhaps circulated to other readers, while the enclosure will be taken out and burned.[12] Bacon, in a letter to George Villiers (later Duke of Buckingham), acknowledges the receipt of "two letters by the same bearer" and ends with a postscript: "Sir, I humbly thanke you for your inward letter. I have burned it as you commanded; but the flame it hath kindled in mee, will never be extinguished."[13] It seems likely that Bacon intends a double meaning here: Villiers's letter is "inward" in that it deals with inward or secret matters, but also literally inward in being folded up and enclosed inside the other letter. The tension between public and private—or between the letter as ephemeral speech and the letter as documentary record—is thus manifested in the material form of the letter itself.

What did it mean for a letter to be "private" in the early modern period? Clare Brant, writing on eighteenth-century correspondence, has challenged the idea of a binary public/private divide as too rigid to accommodate the "varied and often unpredictable circulation of letters."[14] As she rightly points out, many letters that appear private or personal actually had a wider circulation beyond the original recipient. Privacy in the early modern period was configured very differently from privacy today.[15] But this does not mean that early modern letter writers had no concept of privacy at all. Indeed, it was the very fluidity of the public/private distinction, the ease with which letters composed for a single reader could find their way into the hands of others, that made letter writers so anxious to control their circulation. "Burn this letter" has sometimes been taken as a purely conventional request, routinely made and just as routinely ignored. I wish to argue that it deserves to be taken more seriously. I also want to look more closely at the survival of early modern letters, and particularly at those cases where letters intended to be burned have in fact been preserved. What did it mean to preserve a letter, in an age when the natural fate of most letters was to be discarded? The letters that have survived have survived not by accident or default but by a set of deliberate decisions to withhold them from destruction. By making those decisions more visible we may be able to learn more about how early modern writers protected their privacy—and in doing so, perhaps we can also learn a little more about those "unknown unknowns," the letters that have not survived.

"Else Shall I Be Afraid to Write": Letter Burning in the Late Elizabethan Period

Simon Adams has argued that "the reign of Elizabeth I marks a major transformation in the composition and extent of English archives," with far more material preserved among the papers of the nobility and gentry.[16] This explains why requests to "burn this letter," which turn up occasionally in fifteenth- and early sixteenth-century correspondence (there are several examples among the Paston Letters), start to appear more frequently in the Elizabethan period. Not only were letters more likely to be kept, but the likelihood of their being kept generated more anxiety about their preservation. Two groups of letters from the very end of Elizabeth's reign—Rowland Whyte's letters to his patron Sir Robert Sidney, written between 1595 and 1602 when Sidney was governor of Flushing, and Sir Robert Cecil's letters to Sir George Carew, written between 1600 and 1603 when Carew was lord president of Munster—stand out as being particularly concerned with questions of preservation and destruction.[17] Both touch on highly confidential matters of state and court politics, which could have caused considerable embarrassment if their contents had become widely known. Both were written to correspondents abroad, which forced their writers to commit to paper information that they might have preferred to transmit orally and also increased the risk of loss or interception. Protecting the security of the correspondence was therefore of paramount importance.

As Sidney's agent at court, one of Whyte's main duties was to take delivery of his master's letters as they arrived, usually sealed together in large packets, and distribute them to their recipients. This was not always an easy task, as letters might have to pass through several intermediaries before reaching their intended destination. The potential pitfalls were illustrated by an incident in 1597 when Sidney sent a letter to Robert Cecil to pass on to the Privy Council, with instructions to Whyte that he was to obtain a receipt before handing the letter over. Cecil took offense at the implication that he could not be trusted to deliver the letter without a receipt, and Whyte had to smooth the matter over as tactfully as he could by telling Cecil that the request for a receipt was merely "desired to assure [Sidney] I had delivered it, being as it should seem of such great importance and rather a distrust had of me, servants being for the most part careless of their master's service."[18] In this climate of uncertainty, with no guarantee that he could even get his letters delivered, Sidney relied heavily on the Earl of Essex to promote his interests at court. Whyte's letters give us a few glimpses of the secret correspondence passing between Sidney and Essex: in February 1597 he informed Sidney that "when my Lord of Essex read the 2 letters you sent him, Mr Pickford told me that he burnt the one, and sent the other to Mr Reynolds [his secretary] to keep." The following year, when Sidney was negotiating for a period of home leave, Whyte reported: "My Lord of Essex read all your 4 letters, and burnt 3 of them and so he bid me tell you. The other he imparted to the Queen which hath brought you over."[19]

Essex's departure for Ireland in March 1599 was therefore ominous for Sidney, leaving him, as Whyte warned him, with "no assured friends to prefer you." His return in September, and subsequent banishment from court, left Sidney even more exposed. Whyte immediately grasped the changed situation, and his letters to Sidney after Essex's return are full of urgent warnings about the dangers of newswriting. On 30 September 1599, after reporting on Essex's appearance before the Privy Council, he urged Sidney to "burn my letters, else shall I be afraid to write. And I beseech you be very careful what you write here, or what you say where you are, for I have some cause to fear that many things are written here that might very well be omitted. . . . If you write by post, take heed what you write, for now letters are intercepted and stayed." In another letter a few days later he noted that he was "bold to write all things that I hear, because I know you will burn my letters, else would I not do it for anything."[20] On 4 October 1599, reporting the news of Essex's arrest, he added a self-exculpatory postscript to guard against the possibility of interception: "These are matters that I have nothing to do withal, far above my reach, but unto you, that do live abroad, whose wisdom I know to be such, as you will pray as all men pray, for the safety of our most gracious princess, I write what I hear of this matter." Writing again the following week, he thanked Sidney for his promise "to burn my letters," a promise that, fortunately for us, Sidney did not keep.[21]

Whereas the Sidney-Whyte relationship was very much a relationship of master and servant (albeit a trusted and confidential servant), that between Cecil and Carew was more a relationship of social equals, linked by a mixture of friendship and self-interest. When Carew was posted to Ireland in December 1599, Whyte commented in one of his letters to Sidney that "he hath very good friends at court," clearly referring to Cecil though without mentioning him by name.[22] It was a friendship that benefited both men. Cecil protected Carew's interests at home, much as Essex had done for Sidney, and was not above reminding Carew how much he needed a well-placed friend at court. When John Herbert was appointed secretary of state in November 1600, Cecil advised Carew to cultivate his friendship by writing to him regularly, in order to "prepare his minde to respect you hereafter, when peradventure death, sycknes, or other accident, may throw you into his hands, as you now are in myne." In another letter he reminded Carew pointedly that men never needed to safeguard their reputation more "than when they are in forrain imployments." In return, Cecil relied on Carew for accurate information on the military situation in Ireland and the opportunity, when needed, to exert a countervailing influence to Mountjoy, the lord deputy.[23]

The letters passing between Cecil and Carew were of two types, some intended to be kept on file, others to be burned after reading. Writing to Carew on 8 November 1600, Cecil directed him to separate the "public" and "private" sections of his letters, so that the public material could be shown to the Privy Council without having to be recopied, while the private material was reserved for more limited circulation:

I pray you also remember to direct your advertisements of things done, of publicq purposes in future, and (of your demands and necessities) to the whole Consells, and not to me in particuler, for

I am much absent from Court, where God doth know (excepting her
Maiestyes favour,) I take no comforte: and therefore in my absence, it
is some trouble, because I am fayne to delivre the publicq advertisements out of your letters singly directed to me, wherein are commonly
some private things, which being ouvertures of some plotts intended,
or hopes of some services to be done by some speciall men (which are
things to be carried more privately) are not to be read by others, then
by the Queen and my self. I pray you therefore make separation of
these things when there is cause, otherwise lett no dispatch come
from you, but that my lords may see themselfs written unto, yf they
contayne only things of that nature abovesayed.[24]

Cecil assured Carew, "I burn all your particuler letters," and seems to have kept
his promise; both men, in fact, appear to have burned the private letters they
received from each other.[25] The correspondence only survives because Cecil
kept drafts or copies of his letters that were later obtained by Carew, probably
after Cecil's death in 1612. Other files of correspondence were removed from
Cecil's archive at the same time: Dudley Carleton petitioned Cecil's executor,
Sir Walter Cope, to destroy his letters to Cecil, "for now they are out of the
Secreta, which is theyr proper element, I know not into whose hands they may
one day fall accidentally, and turne more to my preiudice then yf they had
never been sequestred."[26] Carew, however, preserved the letters he obtained
from Cecil's archive and later quoted some of them in his self-justifying history
of the Irish wars, *Pacata Hibernia*, to illustrate Cecil's "deare affection" for
him.[27]

     Putting the general and "particular" correspondence side by side sheds a
great deal of light on Cecil's epistolary practices. The letter dated 25 March 1602,
for example, is in a secretarial hand, but enclosed with it is a second letter in
Cecil's holograph, with the names in cipher, beginning: "If in my particuler
you desire to know how I do, I say thus shortly to you that of all our Number
(God knoweth it) excepting 3002 and 2050 I have none but vypars." Cecil goes
on to warn Carew to be wary in writing to other persons at court, particularly "3006 and 2048" (possibly Ralegh and Cobham), noting with obvious
disapproval that "they shew all mens letters to evry man."[28] It was even possible for Cecil to give instructions in the main letter that he then counter-
manded in the particular letter. Writing to Carew on 24 October 1602, he
recommended a certain "gentleman" (unnamed in the main letter) for the post

of vice president of Munster, urging Carew: "when you come to Dublyn, shew your extreame affection to place him (whom I have named unto you) in your Government." In the particular letter, he identified the gentleman in question as Sir Oliver St John, "whom I have so assured of my desire to have him placed . . . as he will imploy all his might to my Lord [Mountjoy] to perswade it," but advised Carew that he need do no more than "humour" him. "When you come, therefore, use all accordingly, and referr the success to the Queen and to his freends, and that is all which you need do, for I hope you think I like not such an election nor think it feisible."[29]

Another letter in the collection, addressed to Mountjoy but apparently copied to Carew, concerns the peace negotiations with the Earl of Tyrone. Cecil reported that the queen had laid down strict conditions for any treaty with Tyrone, including the demand that he should be stripped of his earldom and addressed by the lesser title of Baron of Dongannon. This was highly unwelcome to Cecil, Mountjoy, and Carew, who were all desperate to bring the war in Ireland to a speedy conclusion. Cecil's retained draft of the letter, with its extensive revisions and convoluted syntax, shows him wrestling with the impossible task of obeying the queen's orders while simultaneously instructing Mountjoy to disregard them:

> Now, Sir, know, I pray you, hereby, that this is her owne and neither our proposition nor conceipt, But rather suffred pro tempore then wee would loose the former warrant, by contesting toe long against yt, which will dye as soone as she is satisfied from you, that wee have obeied her, and that you find the Impossibility of these things, which she would be glad of, but so as not to prevent the rest, and therefore now I have done all, and sayd all. I~~feare me for fruict~~ I know in these last I have said nothing, and yet in obeying I have done much.

Cecil requested Mountjoy to send him two separate letters in reply, one containing "that which is fytt to be shewed her Maiesty," and the other, "that which is fytt for me to know (aparte) in which kind all honest servants must strayne a little when they will serve Princes." He ended with a heartfelt postscript—"I wold not do this to 2 men living, and under my hand to no man if otherwise it cold be"—and asked Mountjoy to return the letter to avoid "accidents unlooked for."[30]

It is no coincidence that all these letters date from the last years of Elizabeth's reign, a period of factional crisis and political instability overshadowed
by the awareness of impending regime change. Essex's intelligence-gathering
activities made him particularly sensitive to the danger of letters falling into
the wrong hands. Much of his incoming correspondence was burned, either
immediately after receipt or in the general destruction of compromising papers after the failure of the Essex Rising in 1601, but there are a few surviving
traces of what has been lost. In July 1596, Anthony Bacon wrote to the newly
appointed lord keeper, Thomas Egerton, offering to supply him with intelligence on the same terms as he had done for Essex. As a sample of what he had
to offer, Bacon supplied an impressively well-informed report on the queen's
meeting with the Scottish ambassador the previous day, but requested "that
your Lordship would vouchsaffe me the same favour I alwaies received of my
singular good Lord the Earle of Essex when I sent him anie private advertisements, whiche was, either to returne them backe yf his Lordships leisure served
or els to burne them himself, his most inward Secretaries having bene mere
strangers to the contents of suche my lettres."[31] Egerton evidently complied
with this request, as his copy of the letter, returned to Bacon, is preserved in
the latter's papers along with Bacon's own retained draft.

Yet these precautions cannot simply be attributed to the peculiar political circumstances of the late Elizabethan period. They also reflect the tension
generated by the emerging news culture of early modern England between
the letter as personal communication and the letter as social currency. News,
like money, was a valuable commodity, and, like money, it existed to be spent
rather than hoarded. There is a telling acknowledgment of this in Bacon's letter to Egerton. In the copy he sent to Egerton, Bacon boasted that Essex had
withheld the contents of his newsletters even from his own secretaries, but in
his earlier draft he wrote that Essex had withheld "the most parte of my letters," a small but significant difference that suggests that even Bacon himself
was uncertain how private his letters to Essex had been. The liminal nature of
news, straddling the public/private divide, explains why requests and promises to "burn this letter" tend to cluster around newsletters in particular.
"You may safely wryte us some newes if it please you," the Earl of Shrewsbury
wrote to Sir Michael Hickes in November 1603, "and I assure you your letter
shall be burnte immediately after we have redd it over." But when Hickes
wrote back a week later, with a long account of the trial and sentencing of
Ralegh and Cobham, Shrewsbury kept the letter on file.[32] Judging by his

surviving papers, Shrewsbury seems to have been in the habit of keeping letters that should have been destroyed. But if this tells us something significant about Shrewsbury, it also tells us something significant about the value attached to news.

"The Safest Secretary in the World": Letter Burning in the Early Stuart Period

With the expansion of this news culture in the early seventeenth century, newswriters increasingly came to accept that their letters might be copied or circulated to a wider circle of readers.[33] Requests to burn a letter therefore tended to focus not on the circulation of news as such but on the moments of political tension when news became more highly charged. One such episode occurred in 1614–15 with the failure of the Addled Parliament, the imprisonment of several MPs for sedition, and the power struggles at court culminating in the fall of Robert Carr, Earl of Somerset, as the king's favorite. In July 1614, a month after the dissolution of Parliament, Thomas Lorkin wrote to Sir Thomas Puckering reporting on Somerset's influence at court, and ending: "I beseech when you have read these letters burne them."[34] Another newsletter the following month includes an oblique reference to factional struggles at court that, in the writer's opinion, were too dangerous to be reported openly: "I could inlarge upon this theame but the less the better: common messengers are no sure depositoryes of secrets: and truthe may be told wyth danger."[35] Sir George Carew, sending a roundup of the year's news to Sir Thomas Roe in Constantinople in January 1616, also made it clear that there were some things he could not put in a letter: "You may nott expect from me any other than vulgar intelligence, res gestae, and no further I meane nott to treat of; the distance betwene England and Mogor is to muche, and into whose hands these may fall is uncertayne, wherefore so muche as I may not safelie speake in publique, itt were no discretion to committ to paper."[36]

The dangers of letter writing were forcefully expressed by John Holles, first Earl of Clare, writing to his son John in December 1625. Holles chided his son for a letter to his brother-in-law Thomas Wentworth, which he had refrained from forwarding to Wentworth because of its indiscreet remarks on "state matters." Such remarks were all very well in spoken conversation, Holles observed, but should not be set down in writing under one's own hand:

> Yow sent to your mother a letter superscrybed to your brother
> Wentworth, which shee shewed me; what you writt, yow might
> better have spoken, and therefore I thought better not to send
> it, for though I presume yow may safely open your pack there,
> yet why should yow putt your self into any mans curtesy, under
> the wittnes of your owne hand, espetially to be a critike in state
> matters. Remember that morall aphorisme, bene vixit, qui bene
> latuit: a councell of infinite latitude, to be understood in many
> sences, and to be applyed to this particular, viz hyde your self, lett
> none know your opinion of any men, which our Saviour insinuateth,
> saying, iudge not, least yow be iudged; for as yow measure to others,
> so shall it be measured to yow agayn.

The Ovidian maxim "bene vixit qui bene latuit" (he has lived well, who lives
well hidden) was commonly used to express the pleasures of a retired life, but
Holles here gave it a more politic application, to argue that the wise man con-
ceals his true opinions. "More have been hurt by their words then by their
deeds," Holles reminded his son, and even the gentlemanly virtue of liberal-
ity could be dangerous: "liberall speeche overthrew the Lords Gray, and Cob-
bam, Sir Walter Rawly, and many others."[37]

This sense of a dividing line between public and private, or, as Holles suggested, between what could be written and what could only be spoken, could
also be expressed in the format of the letter itself. James Palmer, writing to
his kinsman Sir John Scudamore in December 1625, began his letter with greet-
ings and compliments to Scudamore and his family, followed by a note at the
foot of the first page, "turne over thes leafe, which keepe to your selfe as much
as you thinke fitt." He then continued on the verso with political news, ending on a second sheet with a request to "keepe the first part secret" and a strong
hint that there was more to be said than could safely be written: "this being
the text the observations is left to your iudgment; I longe to see you, for though
thes is all the substantiall newes movinge heere, yett there are particulers that
would hould an howeres walke upon the pavementes of the nine worthies."[38]
In some cases this division was taken to its logical conclusion by making the
two parts of the letter physically separable. Sir Simonds D'Ewes, writing to
Sir Martin Stuteville in May 1626, reported the imprisonment of Sir John Eliot and Sir Dudley Digges in a separate postscript of "private newes," which
he instructed Stuteville to "keepe to your selfe as your owne by separating this

halfe sheete and burning itt or concealing it though there bee nothing in it unlawfull or unfitt to be saied."[39]

The dissolution of the 1626 parliament was another moment of political crisis that prompted a sudden rash of requests to "burn this letter." Palmer's letter to Scudamore on 16 June, the day after the dissolution, included a highly pessimistic commentary on the event: "I protest I knowe not what could have happened worse, for the manner is so unhappie as it is good for noe party." Palmer believed that it damaged the king's reputation "abrode and at home," deepened the Duke of Buckingham's unpopularity, and was "ill for the people, for they have gotten the kinges displeasure, and may feare the effectes." On receiving this letter, Scudamore immediately copied it almost verbatim in a letter to his uncle, but added a cautionary postscript: "Sir, I beseeche you, when you have reade this letter, burne it."[40] This does not mean that Scudamore considered the news too dangerous to be shared outside the family circle, but rather that he did not want his own letter kept on record or put into wider circulation. The risk lay in the preservation of the letter rather than the transmission of its contents. In the same way, D'Ewes took it for granted that Stuteville would pass his letters on to others, but asked him to have the letters transcribed before forwarding them: "lay upp my lettre and lett your clarke onlie write out the newes that soe none to whome you communicate it may see my hand or name."

Again, two sets of letters stand out for their concern with preservation and destruction. These are Elizabeth of Bohemia's letters to the diplomat Sir Thomas Roe, mostly written after 1632 when the widowed Elizabeth took over her husband's political activities, and William Laud's letters to Thomas Wentworth, written between 1632 and 1639 when Wentworth was lord deputy of Ireland.[41] Both of these were sent to correspondents abroad, which—as with Whyte's letters to Sidney, and Cecil's to Carew—meant that the writers had to take special precautions to keep their letters secure. Elizabeth was based in The Hague, Roe in England, and each repeatedly urged the other to burn their letters after reading. Roe ended his letter of 30 June 1633 "with a suite to your Maiestie to burne this letter: for ther is nothing els I will trust at the Haghe, but your Maiestie and fire to enterprett me," while Elizabeth's letter of 20 March 1634 ends: "I pray burne this letter and give your best councell to this bearer," suggesting that some information was being transmitted orally, via the messenger, rather than put on paper.[42] It is therefore remarkable that the letters survive at all. Elizabeth seems to have burned Roe's letters to her, as none of the originals survive, but Roe kept her letters to him, as well as copies of his own letters, making it possible to reconstruct both sides of the correspondence.

Given the survival of the letters, it is reasonable to ask whether the requests to "burn this letter" were intended to be taken literally. In letters to other correspondents, both Roe and Elizabeth were capable of invoking the idea of letter burning for strategic purposes. Writing from Constantinople in 1622, Roe asked the Duke of Buckingham to pass his letter on to the king, "and though matters of this distance seeme unworthy of his enterruption, yet if he vouchsafe to accept my duty, the papers are easely condemned to the fire." Here, as in Donne, the written letter is seen as ephemeral and disposable except insofar as it serves to cement the relationship between writer and recipient.[43] Elizabeth, too, could use letter burning to denote friendship and intimacy: in a letter to the Marquess of Hamilton in 1634 seeking his support for a proposal to raise troops for the recovery of the Palatinate, she told him: "I have written this particullar to none but to yourself besides my Brother because I trust you and I know but a few that I have cause to doe so . . . you see I write freelie to you, and therefore I pray burne my letter, and lett no bodie see it."[44] The request to burn the letter had symbolic value as an expression of her trust, and Hamilton's decision to keep the letter suggests that he understood it more as a rhetorical gesture than as an instruction to be literally obeyed.

Yet Elizabeth had good reason to be sensitive about the preservation of her letters, particularly in 1634, when her correspondence with her secretary Sir Francis Nethersole had recently been seized by the Privy Council. Both she and Roe were deeply disturbed by the seizure of Nethersole's papers, which threatened to expose their meddling with matters of foreign policy where the king had made it clear he brooked no interference. Elizabeth defiantly claimed that she did not care who saw her letters and merely resented the insult to her honor, but her letters to Roe reveal a heightened concern with security. Writing in January 1635 after a temporary lapse in their correspondence, she explained that she dared not write by every messenger, "for though there is nothing in my letters that I need feare who sees, yett I doe not love anie shoulde see them but those they are directed to," ending with the usual request: "I pray burne this letter."[45] Roe was alarmed by reports that some of his letters had been found among Nethersole's papers and demanded to know whether any of them had come from Elizabeth. She insisted, "I never gave him anie of them, nor shewed them him, for most of them that have anie thing in them I burne, and this I assure you upon my word," but Roe had learned his lesson and became far more cautious in his letters to her. As he wrote to Elizabeth in 1636, "I must leave much to your wisedome to picke out meanings that I would not write."[46] Whatever his reasons for keeping her letters unburned (as he did those of other correspondents who also asked him to burn them), this was clearly a calculated decision, and not without an element of risk.[47]

Laud and Wentworth went to even greater lengths to secure the privacy of their letters. Wentworth relied on Laud's access to the king to ensure that his voice was heard at court, and Laud in turn kept him informed of current affairs in a series of highly personal letters reporting, often in indiscreet detail, on the machinations of their political rivals and enemies.[48] At the same time Laud fretted constantly about the risks of writing with such "mirth and freedom" and feared that their letters might get into the wrong hands. Although they communicated partly in cipher, Laud complained that the chore of deciphering letters was "miserable vexation to me that have so little time" while being too confidential to entrust to a secretary. He also feared that the cipher key might survive among their papers, and "by that cipher all our letters may be read when we are dead. Some things you know are personal, and such as, though not hurtful, yet such as neither of us would have some men see."[49] He kept no copy of his own letters to Wentworth and urged him to burn the letters he received, but Wentworth had other ideas. As Julia Merritt has acutely observed, there was a conflict between the letter-burning tendency typified by Laud and the archive-keeping tendency typified by Wentworth, for whom information was power and not to be lightly thrown away.[50]

This conflict was played out in an exchange of letters in 1635–36, as Laud and Wentworth debated the best way to keep their correspondence secret. Laud, predictably, wanted to burn the letters after reading. Wentworth pointed out that it was sometimes necessary to keep letters to prove they were acting on the king's orders. Laud objected that the king might deny giving the orders: "Should the king deny it, all these letters could not be produced. So for that, keeping and not keeping comes much to one." Wentworth suggested that if either of them were suddenly taken ill, they should seal up their letters and send them back to the other. Laud replied that it would be safer to burn them immediately. "The more I think of the business of our letters, the more I am still convinced in my own way of burning them so soon as their business is answered and ended." For "I am most confident if either of us fail, our letters will be fingered. And I would not have any sport made either with myself or my friends after my death." He agreed that it was prudent to keep "all such letters as bring in them any instructions or commands from the King, that if anything be doubted of at present, or in future, you have your warrant to show." But private letters, he insisted, were a different matter: "I can never hold it fit to keep such letters anywhere but in the fire."[51]

In the end it was Wentworth who came up with the solution, reinventing the method that Cecil and Carew had used in their correspondence forty years earlier of putting private material in a separate enclosure or "side paper." Laud wrote on 23 January 1636 approving this new procedure:

> As for that which you have found out for the future, I like it
> extreme well to break our letters into two, and in the one to write
> nothing but barely the King's directions, which may be kept, and
> in the other all things personal and private, which may be burnt.
> And this I will most religiously perform, and expect the like from
> you. And then let me add for that which is past, you may without
> any great labour cause to be transcribed all the passages which are
> in my letters that are fit to be kept, you may send them to me, and
> I will subscribe them and send them back to you, and when they
> come transcribe them for myself. This done, your Lordship may
> burn all my letters already received, and so will I all yours, save
> duplicates and such public business as being seen can make no
> reflection.[52]

All these precautions were, however, rendered useless by Wentworth's decision to keep the side papers instead of burning them. Laud could not have known this, though his repeated injunctions to Wentworth—"I hope you burn all these side papers"; "This is a side paper, and ergo you must burn it"—suggest that he may have suspected it.[53] He was also critical of Wentworth's habit of giving the side papers to his secretary to transcribe: "I hope you cannot distrust your transcriber, but I am sure I take the safer way. Here you have it in my own hand. And God is my witness, I keep no copy of my own, and I burn yours so soon as I have answered it."[54]

Outside the realm of high politics, Edward Conway, second Viscount Conway, was also exercised by the problem of security in his letters to George Garrard. On 14 July 1636 he half-humorously reproved Garrard for circulating his letters around his social circle: "You shew my letters, I send you Virgins and you prostitute them." Conway's chief concern was that his jesting letters might give him a reputation for frivolity: "you shew them to my Lord Deputy [Wentworth], peradventure to other Statesmen, they when I think I am fooling, will thinke I am foolish."⁵⁵ But he also hinted that Garrard had committed a deeper breach of order and decorum by putting private letters into public circulation: "All things in heaven and under the Moone keepe theire order, the Starres goe not out of theire Spheares, and the elements keepe theire places, doe you likewise in the shewing my letters keepe within due limits; let the reader be adaequated to the writing . . . and let not my letters goe out of your hand unlesse it be into the fire, who is the frend I only trust with all the secrets written to me; for allthough I know not very well what to speake, I know very well what not to speake."⁵⁶ In reply, Garrard tried to excuse himself by assuring Conway that his letters were good enough to be printed, but Conway was having none of this. "You are pleased to make your selfe merry with me in saying that you would print my letter," he wrote to Garrard, "but if you intend me a favour doe it not." He went on to reflect in the same half-humorous vein on the ill-fated afterlives of all letters ancient and modern. Cicero's letters were "blotted by schoole boyes," Seneca's letters corrupted by critics, while as for the moderns, "if the Cardinals Ossat and Perron had not traces of history in theire letters they might goe into the fire with Balzac who is only thought well of by those that love wordes and hardly matter to uphold them." Letters between friends, Conway implied, had no life or meaning outside that friendship, and thus it was with his letters to Garrard: "My letters to you are private assurances of my love and to you onely particular not Epistles generall."⁵⁷ Letters were ephemeral and not to be preserved, far less published for the whole world to read.

Yet Conway's comments also seem to reflect a more general mood of anxiety among letter writers in the 1630s. The newswriter John Pory, in a letter to Lord Scudamore in 1631, requested him to do as "other mine honourable patrones use to do" and "comitte all the letters I have or shall write to you, to the safest secretary in the world, the fire."⁵⁸ This does not mean that all letter writers lived under the constant threat of interception or the long shadow of censorship. Pory, as a professional newswriter, did not wish to have his wares cheapened by being made too widely available and may have exaggerated the risks in order to persuade his clients that they were getting their money's worth. However, Kevin Sharpe's breezy dismissal of such passages as merely intended to add a little spice to the letter, or "sauce to the indiscretion," does not give full weight to the fears expressed by very many letter writers that their private correspondence might come back to haunt them. "That such news served to polarize the realm or foster an oppositionist stance," Sharpe concludes, "must remain at best a conjecture, which the evidence we have would seem to undermine."[59] But we also need to confront the possibility that "the evidence we have" is not telling us the full story.

"Things Which Are Not Proper to Put into Despatches": Letter Burning Beyond the Early Modern Period

We can never know how many early modern letters were burned after reading, but we can guess that it was a considerable number. Even when a series of letters appears to be complete, there may be private letters or other enclosures that are now missing from the archival record. As historians are now coming to recognize, the basic unit of early modern correspondence was not the single letter but the packet, which might contain multiple letters, "side papers," and separates. The contents of these packets are now widely scattered, and in some cases, such as Donne's letters to Goodere, the only surviving clue to their existence is that the letter is addressed "to your self," showing that it was originally sent under cover with other letters to be forwarded to other recipients.[60] As a result, reconstructing early modern correspondence can very often feel like trying to assemble a jigsaw puzzle with an unknown number of missing pieces.

These hidden gaps may affect our understanding of early modern letters in unsuspected ways. For example, the tone and affect of private letters can be hard to interpret because we have so little with which to compare them. J. S. Brewer, the nineteenth-century editor of the Carew Papers, was taken aback by Cecil's letters to Carew, which seemed to him to exhibit a depth of feeling "rarely found in any man, never, so far as I have seen, in the correspondence of prime ministers" and more reminiscent of "the warm and disinterested attachment of a woman than the measured and tempered regard of the other sex."[61] Laud's letters to Wentworth have come in for similar treatment from one of his modern biographers, who interprets them as an "outlet for his most personal worries," reflecting his sexual insecurity and his desperate need for intimacy.[62] The same might be said of the letters from Henry Howard, Earl of Northampton, to Robert Carr, Earl of Somerset, another highly personal correspondence with homoerotic overtones that shocked contemporary observers when it was made public at the Overbury trial in 1615.[63] But what we may be encountering here is a language of elite male friendship and homosocial bonding that is not easy for us to "read" because we have so few other examples. "My letters are feminine; weake," Conway wrote to Garrard in 1636.[64] It was precisely this element of gendered vulnerability that made Conway so reluctant to expose the letters to the critical gaze of other male readers.

I began with a contrast between the early modern tendency to destroy letters and the modern tendency to preserve them. The cultural shift is perfectly captured, almost at the very moment of transition, in Sir William Wentworth's advice to his son Thomas, future Earl of Strafford, in 1607. Wentworth's advice on writing letters was simple: "wryte as few as yow can." Letters from social inferiors should not be answered in one's own handwriting: "either do it by word of mouth, or cause one of your servants to write to him your answear." Letters from enemies should also be answered orally, by a message delivered in the presence of two witnesses, and "nott in wrytinge." But even letters to friends should be written sparingly and with discretion, "for itt is a common custome of men to kepe letters safelie and sometymes many yeares after to produce them for evydence against the author of them, either in open courtt or otherwise."[65] This preference for face-to-face communication, well suited to Wentworth's needs in dealing with his Yorkshire tenants and neighbors, clearly could not have worked for his son in Ireland, where written communication was essential. But Wentworth's advice carries a further implication: that if other people were likely to keep your letters to them, prudence dictated that you should keep their letters to you. While harking back to an older era of oral intercourse, his advice also looks forward to the modern era of government at a distance in which it was expected that letters would remain on file.

But if the early modern period saw the adoption of some distinctively modern archive-keeping practices, it also saw the evolution of some more shadowy counterpractices for keeping sensitive material out of the archive. Among these, as we have seen, was the habit of putting private information into a "particular" letter or "side paper," which could be withheld from the official file. In the eighteenth century this became an increasingly widespread custom. In April 1718 the English ambassador in Paris, John Dalrymple, second Earl of Stair, wrote to James Craggs, the newly appointed secretary of state in London, promising to send him regular letters for private consumption: "I shall from time to time continue to write you Epistles of this kind for your self only, which will give you hints sometimes of things which are not proper to put into despatches that must in the first place be communicated to a cabinet counsell and after lye in offices on record. There is no need of keeping such letters and the best is to burn them on both sides."[66] In April 1752 the Earl of Holdernesse wrote to Joseph Yorke, British minister plenipotentiary at The

Hague: "I have received the Favour of Your private Letter in Your own Hand . . . and shall be very glad to be favoured with Your Correspondence, whenever any Thing arises, of a Nature not to appear in the Office Letters."[67] The two types of letter were physically distinct, the private letter on quarto-sized paper and the official letter in a larger folio format, a relic of the days when one letter had been enclosed inside the other, which continued to be observed even when, as often happened, the two letters were sent by separate posts.

In the nineteenth century this system of dual public/private correspondence was gradually institutionalized and the private letter took on a more official character, becoming, in the words of one commentator, "as much a part of the recognised correspondence as are the numbered official despatches."[68] Defenders of the system argued that the private letter was an essential instrument of diplomacy that allowed ministers to express themselves more freely and confidentially. Yet it was rooted in an older tradition of secret correspondence that had a distinctly darker side. One notorious example occurs in the correspondence of Jeffrey Amherst and Henry Bouquet, two of the British commanders in North America during the Seven Years' War, who plotted to distribute smallpox-infected blankets in the hope of starting an epidemic among the Indians fighting on the French side. "Could it not be Contrived to send the Small Pox among those Disaffected Tribes of Indians?" Amherst inquired in July 1763. "We must on this Occasion, use Every Stratagem in our power to Reduce them." Bouquet replied that he would try to "inoculate" them "with some Blankets that may fall in their hands, and take Care not to get the disease myself."[69] Amherst's remarks were written on the inside of the letter wrapper, and Bouquet's on a separate enclosure, to conceal them from the prying eyes of clerks in the office and to ensure that they could be easily destroyed without leaving any trace in the records. It was a technique that would have been instantly familiar to the statesmen, diplomats, and newswriters of the early modern period.

Archivists and historians have always understood, at least in theory, that important correspondence may fail to find its way into the files. As Hilary Jenkinson admitted, the system of "making the Administrator the sole agent for the selection and destruction of his own documents" was not without its dangers. "We have to make sure that he destroys enough," but, at the same time, "we must see that [he] does not revert too completely to primitive habits and destroy unreasonably."[70] Jenkinson's ideal of archive management was founded on the belief that it was possible to strike the perfect balance between these two extremes. Yet the ideal of the total archive, so cherished by Mill,

Palmerston, and their nineteenth- and twentieth-century successors, was only ever an illusion. The India Office archive, for example, underwent sporadic purges, notably in 1867 when many of the commercial records of the East India Company were destroyed in order to reinvent the India Office as an arm of territorial government.[71] At the Indian end of government, this culminated in "the pall of smoke which hung over Delhi during the mass destruction of documents in 1947," which was still fresh in the memories of colonial administrators in the 1950s and 1960s as they prepared to incinerate their own archives in the countdown to the end of empire.[72] As Sir John Tilley and Stephen Gaselee remarked in their 1933 history of the Foreign Office, in an ironic riposte to Jenkinson's well-meaning archival positivism: "The attempt to make everything public and available will either dry up some sources of information or drive that information farther underground."[73] How right they were.

In his magisterial history of British official secrecy, David Vincent suggests that the mid-nineteenth century marked "the beginning of a tradition of public secrecy," which led in due course to the Official Secrets Act. But the roots of this tradition can be traced much farther back. It is founded, I suggest, on an older tradition of epistolary secrecy inherited from the more systematic record-keeping culture of the early modern period, a culture of archival preservation that in turn generated a culture of archival destruction. And this early modern culture may strike us as strangely familiar. We live in an age where, thanks to electronic technology, the dream of the total archive has come far closer to being realized, yet this has generated its own set of anxieties. As the *Financial Times* observed in 2004: "It can be tempting to regard e-mail as ephemeral—easily deleted without leaving any obvious physical presence. Yet many have come to realise that e-mails provide a record more permanent and indestructible than many older forms of communication." This parallels the conceptual shift that took place in the early modern period as it became apparent that letters were not merely an ephemeral adjunct to speech but might leave a permanent trace in the archives. In response, the *Financial Times* hinted that managers wishing to protect the privacy of their correspondence should consider reverting to older forms of material technology: "an e-mail," the writer pointed out, "leaves traces that may return to haunt the writer long after the event," but "paper documents can be burnt."[74] In this as in other respects, the electronic revolution turns out not to be such a revolution after all. The long-lost letters of the early modern period still have a spectral presence in the modern digital archive.

CHAPTER 10

Gendered Archival Practices and the Future Lives of Letters

JAMES DAYBELL

In his now classic mediation on the nature of archives and memory, *Archive Fever*, Jacques Derrida posits a very male-dominated model of the archive in which his "archons" are "patriarchs," and women play an ambivalent role, at once central but also marginalized and excluded from the "economic" work of the archive.[1] He introduces, however, the term "matriarchive": "Without the . . . force and authority of this transgenerational memory . . . there would no longer be any question of memory and of archive, of patriarchive or of matriarchive, and one would no longer even understand how an ancestor can speak within us, nor what sense there might be in us to speak to him or her."[2] Quite what is the nature of a "matriarchive" is not actually explained. Yet in his recent study of marginalia, William H. Sherman responds to this suggestive neologism by conceptualizing such an archive, by looking at "the role of women in organizing goods, information, and history in the early modern household," the role they played in early modern "archival practices," as well as "the place they have traditionally occupied in the archives we now use to access their lives and works." In asking "What does a matriarchive look like?" Sherman suggests that printed books (as sites for marginal annotation and record keeping) and manuscript compilations form two distinct types of female-oriented archive.[3] The kinds of activities outlined by Sherman reveal more about women as producers of texts, as writers, compilers, and as readers, rather than their involvement with archival practices and the ways in which early modern women's writings survive to us today. As a way of looking at the relationship between women and archives, this essay focuses on the preservation of women's letters. Building on Sherman's work, it will be argued that any working definition of a "matriarchive" needs to move beyond textual production, and female writers' own efforts to preserve their writings, and be sensitive to wider archival practices that preserved, privileged, or purged letters penned by women. As such this essay is interested not only in women's direct involvement with early modern archives as repositories of "transgenerational memory" but also in what might be described as the *gendered* politics of archival survival and its impact upon the afterlives of texts produced by early modern female letter writers.

Scholarship to date has shown that women have complex relationships with early modern archives and the transmission of knowledge. Traditionally women have been identified as repositories of oral knowledge, the custodians of genealogical, family, and household memory and tradition bequeathed from one generation to the next.[4] This is a notable feature of sixteenth- and seventeenth-century family histories, produced mainly by the family patriarch, who upon occasion relied on ancient female family members for details. Such women were especially useful as transmitters of transgenerational knowledge of the maternal side of the family.[5] Other studies, however, have emphasized women's exclusion from archives, in particular their lack of access to key records relating to property (normally held by the family patriarch) during litigation cases. These obstacles clearly disadvantaged women involved in disputes over property and inheritance, and it was something that equity courts, such as the Court of Requests attempted to circumvent.[6] Beyond their function as living archives of memory, women, as Jan Broadway argues, in some cases controlled access to archives, particular papers of heirs in their minority and those belonging to their late husbands.[7] Wives might also have access to their husbands' papers, lockable desks, studies, or closets.[8] A glimpse of the clear ordered habits of archiving within households is provided by an examination of the preservation of letters; it is clear that many women were involved in the archiving of their own incoming and outgoing correspondence. The existence of personal items of furniture owned by women (listed in inventories) attests the prevalence of epistolary archival practices among female correspondents. The closet of Lady Margaret More contained "a fayre deske" and "a borded capcas," or small trunk for holding letters; Mary Walpole wrote of "all the writtin[g] in the stude wiche belong to me & all those that were in the flatte boxe"; the Countess of Essex in 1599 stored letters in a casket under her bed; while in the mid-seventeenth century, Elizabeth Pepys kept a bundle of papers including all the letters she received from her husband in a locked trunk.[9] Lady Hoby described a morning spent in her closet "sorting out papers."[10] The inclusion in household manuals of instructions for how to preserve paper indicates the importance of record keeping within the early modern household.[11] In many ways, such practices are short-term archival strategies with the intention of safeguarding papers for everyday use rather than future-proofing them for posterity. It is the latter in which this essay is particularly interested. A key issue is the status and value of letters (and in particular women's letters) as a category of document. Fundamentally, how and why were they preserved? To what extent were letters considered ephemeral, throwaway, not worthy of preservation, in contrast to the way that documents concerned with land and lineage (pedigrees, deeds, rental agreements, and other legal papers, usually produced on vellum for durability) were viewed as a crucial form of patrilineal inheritance. Among those groups associated with record keeping, what was the relationship between women's personal papers and family and household archives and muniments rooms?

Survival of women's letters was sometimes a matter of happenstance. An early seventeenth-century letter from Lady Gower to her undergraduate son Thomas was discovered serendipitously in 1836 under a floorboard in Wadham College, Oxford.[12] Doubtless other letters remain hidden from memory, concealed in buildings or books, or moldering in attics. In the majority of cases, however, women's outgoing letters are preserved in institutional archives, among the State Papers; papers of government officials; within legal archives, such as the courts of Chancery, Exchequer, Requests, and Wards, where they are classified as exhibits; among the records of educational and philanthropic bodies; as well as among the working papers of physicians and astrologers. Here survival relies upon the institutional impulse for record keeping, with letters preserved as documents relating to matters of state, law, property, and profession, which necessarily restricts the kinds of letters that survive, inflecting their nature and purpose.

The other main category of repository containing women's letters is family and household archives, where correspondence survives in muniments rooms alongside other evidences and papers relating to the household and estate. As landowners in their own right, certain elite women amassed records connected to estates. Thus, as lord of the manor of Stanford-in-the-Vale, Berkshire, Margaret Knollys received numerous suits and complaints.[13] Survival of such "papers" and "evidences" is related to the concept of archives that the Dutch professor of archivistics Eric Ketelaar terms "cultural patrimony" (an anachronistic term for the early modern period, but useful conceptually nonetheless), in other words, the idea that "records created for current business be transferred as a heritage to future generations who will value those records as cultural assets." Borrowing from the theoretical work of Jean-Michel Leniaud, Ketelaar outlines four main features that identify a "paradigm of *patrimoine*":

> (1) Conservation: the intentionality of the creator of a monument; the scientific, artistic, etc., interest; the importance for social life; the economic value. (2) Motivations that lead one to accept the past or to reject it: a patrimony needs not only a testator and a will but also an heir who accepts the conditions. (3) The modalities by which *patrimoine* has been appreciated, preserved, and transferred: inventorying, restoring, reusing. (4) The media and means for diffusion within society: publications, tourism.[14]

Such a concept explains the bequests of a range of materials that are passed down to future generations, including but by no means limited to family books of remembrances, family histories and memoirs, family Bibles, pedigrees, and genealogies, advice literature, recipe books, commonplace books, and miscellanies. A strong feature of all of these forms of manuscript is the desire to transmit knowledge (often related to genealogy), usually accompanied with a hefty dose of advice, to the next generation.[15]

In assessing the nature of family archives one of the main questions is about the impulses to preserve different sorts of documents, and where letters (and letters by women) fit into these bureaucratic practices. In other words, why did families preserve family correspondence? One of the driving forces behind the organization of evidences was the practical purpose of recording land ownership and compiling documentation for use in litigation, which sometimes meant that very little in the way of personal materials survive.[16] The organization of archives in this manner stems from medieval cartularies, which evidence collective and communal habits, but also translated into a family context, as well as family books of remembrances, as paper repositories of deeds and other documents deemed important for future generations of the family. Letters that did not relate to estate business were often discarded, not thought worthy of preservation; correspondence archived with estate records contains very few letters by women. Others destroyed letters that shed a poor light on the family; Edward, fourth Earl of Dorset (1590–1652), burned incriminatory papers in the aftermath of the Civil War.[17] The destruction of letters (as discussed by Arnold Hunt in his essay in this volume) clearly played a role in constructing family identity and memory and may explain the lack of sex in the archives! Other families, such as the Verneys and Thynnes, preserved vast caches of family correspondence.[18] As suggested by the example of cabinets and chests, private letters may have been kept outside the muniments room, where the charters, title deeds, and most of the manorial and estate management records were preserved, although at a later date they obviously gravitated toward family archives, and were "monumentalized," considered worthy of preservation, and assumed a particular status within the household.[19] As Marie-Louise Coolahan has demonstrated, wives' writings (including letters) were sometimes edited and "scribally" published by widowed husbands, as an act of remembrance, a form of literary memorialization.[20] The manuscript memorial volume of Lady Anne Southwell (Folger MS V.b.198), organized posthumously by her husband Captain Henry Sibthorpe, includes two letters, one to Cecily Ridgeway, Countess of Londonderry, and one to Viscount Falkland.[21] Roger Ley, the early seventeenth-century curate of St. Leonard's, Shoreditch, copied ten letters of his wife Anne (including two in Latin) into a miscellany of writings by both of them, which included her commonplace book, verse, and funerary texts.[22] The late seventeenth-century minister Anthony Walker published his wife's manuscript writings posthumously in print in 1690 under the title *The Holy Life of Mrs. Elizabeth Walker*, with a series of letters and papers contained in an appendix, including several consolatory epistles and a letter of advice to her grandchild.[23] In the case of "missing texts," where manuscript originals do not survive, Coolahan argues that attention be directed toward the reception of early modern women's writings as part of the construction of a posthumous literary reputation.[24] Thus, we move from studying the letter and letter writer per se, connected to an essential moment of composition or production, toward focusing instead on the later transmission, reception, archival journey, and textual afterlife of individual or corpora of letters.

The remainder of this essay looks at the survival of women's letters outside of formal institutional archives, through a trio of case studies that examine the status, treatment, and archival afterlife of three distinct groupings of letters within family archives. The first example concerns a manuscript at Lambeth Palace Library that has always intrigued me, Talbot MS 3205, a volume composed almost entirely of women's letters, which was assembled and bound by the physician-antiquary Dr. Nathaniel Johnston (1629?–1705) and bequeathed to the College of Arms in the late seventeenth century, a collection later transferred to Lambeth Palace Library. The second case study concerns the preservation of Mary Baskerville's letters by her son, the antiquarian Hannibal Baskerville, and the use of correspondence as a material site for family biography. The third relates to a letter book of Margaret Clifford, Countess of Cumberland, assembled by her daughter Anne Clifford, as an act of memorialization.

Lambeth Palace Library, Talbot MS 3205

To begin with, Lambeth Palace Library's Talbot MS 3205 is a folio volume of some eighty-nine letters, almost all from or to women connected to the earls and countesses of Shrewsbury covering the period 1506 to 1615.[25] Its intrinsic interest lies not only in the fact that it is a seventeenth-century assembly of women's correspondence, but also because of what it tells us about the provenance and history of family papers, early modern archival and antiquarian practices, and the treatment and categorization of identifiably *women's* letters within a larger collection of papers, separately from men's letters and those connected with the earls of Shrewsbury. The volume is one of fifteen volumes of Talbot manuscripts, the raw materials of which came down to Henry Howard, sixth Duke of Norfolk (1629–84), who inherited them as part of the Talbot estates through his grandmother Aletheia Talbot after the death of Edward Talbot, eighth Earl of Shrewsbury, in 1617 ended the male line of George Talbot.[26] After the destruction of the Talbot's principal seat, Sheffield Castle, the papers were left lying untended in a hunting lodge, Sheffield Manor, in the great park, several miles from the castle. It is here that the Yorkshire-born physician-antiquarian Nathaniel Johnston had access to the papers along with the elderly antiquarian John Hopkinson of Lofthouse near Wakefield. The two men were responsible between 1671 and 1675 for reading, sorting, and transcribing the papers, and Johnston records that "at severall tymes, from amids the multitudes of waste papers, and the havock that mice, ratts, and wet, had made I rescued these letters, and as many more as I have bound up in fifteen volumes, and have more to gett bound."[27] Johnston persuaded the Duke of Norfolk to deposit the Talbot manuscripts at the College of Arms "for the use of posterity"; they were purchased by Lambeth Palace Library in 1983.[28] Johnston was an antiquary of some standing, who spent more than three decades from the 1660s collecting materials for his intended history of Yorkshire along the lines of Dugdale's *Warwickshire*.[29] It is through his antiquarian industry and interest in family and local history (which were inextricably intertwined during the seventeenth century) that the papers survived. His manuscripts compiled for his *Antiquities of Yorkshire* incorporated notes on leading families, including "Volumes in folio of Transcripts or Extracts of Deeds of the families of Gentlemen in Yorkshire."[30] This example illustrates the ordering of a family archive by Johnston following the discarding of papers. While it is not direct evidence of familial habits of archiving, it reveals the imposition of archival organizing principles upon a body of family correspondence.

In the ordering of the Talbot manuscripts, Johnston organized the 6,404 numbered leaves into fifteen separate volumes, each volume labeled *A* to *P*, with the letter *J* omitted. Overall, the organization of the papers was largely chronological, the first twelve volumes following the lives of the earls Francis, George, and Gilbert, the subjects of Johnston's family history of the Shrewsburys; these volumes are largely connected with office, while two remaining volumes contain miscellaneous papers relating to the lord lieutenancy. The first four volumes (A–D, or LPL, MSS 3191–94) are largely concerned with the public service of Francis Talbot, fifth Earl of Shrewsbury (1500–1560), with the fourth volume dominated by papers relating to his role as lord president of the Council of the North, an office he assumed in 1549. The next three volumes (E-G, or LPL, MSS 3195–97) overlap with the earldom of George Talbot, sixth Earl of Shrewsbury, and highlighted his guardianship of Mary, Queen of Scots, as well as the souring of his marriage to Bess of Hardwick (G, or LPL, MS 3197).[31] Volumes H to M (LPL, 3199–3203) cover the earldom of Gilbert, seventh Earl of Shrewsbury (1552–1616), although with some chronological license, and highlight the earl's attendance at court, his interest in news, and his disputes with the Stanhope family.[32] The final three volumes in the collection are rather miscellaneous. Volume N (LPL, MS 3204) contains papers relating to the earls of Shrewsbury as lords lieutenant during the period 1546 to 1608, while volume P (LPL, MS 3206) contains a range of documents (more than one hundred numbered leaves) dating from 1499 to 1580.[33]

Volume O (LPL, MS 3205) is unusual in its organization since it contains letters mainly by women, indicating an archival policy to separate women's letters from the other volumes. With the exception of volume M (LPL, MS 3203), which contains a significant number of letters from and to women, there are relatively few letters bound into the other volumes: indeed the first eleven volumes contain only twenty-seven letters (of these only fifteen were by women, four were to women, and eight were to or from married couples), with many of the letters addressed to men in their official capacities as officeholders: Anne Molyneux and Elizabeth Neverell, for example, both ask the sixth earl to remit the sum imposed on them by the privy seal.[34] Only eleven women's letters are contained in volumes N (LPL, MS 3204) and P (LPL, MS 3206). Of the letters contained in MS 3205 about a third are what might loosely be termed letters of petition or recommendation, requesting favor in personal suits or soliciting on behalf of family and servants. The remaining letters are from female family members, and these often treat practical matters (inheritance, jointures, land and household administration) but nonetheless a large proportion throw light on the more intimate side of family life, exposing relationships, including a series of letters from Anne Howard, Dowager Countess of Arundel, which deal with various matters, health and illness, household provisioning, hospitality and gifts, offer condolences, as well as news of pregnancies, children's progress (one letter describes their "littell jewell," her grandson, James Howard's teething; and another grandson Henry Howard is described as "a most ernest criar"), and we also have repeated descriptions of her son's toothache.[35] The inclusion of letters from women to the earls of Shrewsbury in MS 3205, rather than volumes connected with their lives, suggests Johnston made a distinction between letters connected with "public" office and those concerned with "private" affairs, though these categories are extremely blurred. Lady Pope wrote to George, sixth Earl of Shrewsbury, in 1560 a letter mixing condolence with business.[36] Although they were archived separately from men's letters, the survival of these women's letters within the broader Talbot collection suggests they were considered worthy of preservation for future generations by an antiquarian with a general fascination with past artifacts, rather than being purged as "unimportant"; that they were deposited at the College of Arms connects them to the lineage and heraldry of the Shrewsbury family. Moreover, Johnston's salvaging of the entire collection, which had been effectively discarded by the family once the male line had become extinct, illustrates the perils of archival loss and decay, as well as the long-term importance of antiquarian interest in preserving collections of papers and institutional repositories as custodians of family papers.

The Letters of Lady Mary Baskerville

The second case study examines the survival of a small corpus of letters relating to Lady Mary Baskerville (d. 1632), wife of the Elizabethan naval commander

Sir Thomas Baskerville (d. 1597) and daughter of Sir Thomas Throckmorton of Gloucestershire. The letters were preserved in a manuscript miscellany, now Bodleian Library Rawlinson MS D 859, by her son Hannibal Basker-ville, the "antiquarian dilettante" or "eccentric antiquarian," as he has been variously termed by the *Oxford Dictionary of National Biography*.[37] They in-clude a letter from her maternal grandfather, Sir Richard Berkeley, to accept a suitor recommended by her father; nine letters to her son Hannibal; a letter to a feoffee of her Sunningwell estate; and a letter from her brother Sir William Throckmorton.[38] Among this correspondence is also collected various other documents connected to Mary Baskerville: a list of furniture and an epitaph in Mary's hand of her own mother, Elizabeth Throckmorton.[39] The volume thus partly operates as a repository of family documents and includes numerous letters from other family members (notably Hannibal Baskerville's cousin Margaret Brook and his son Thomas Baskerville, the topographer) as well as other social contacts, although it is not an archive of Hannibal Baskerville's own correspondence, which is organized alphabetically by let-ter writer in Bodleian, Rawlinson MS, Letters 41. The remainder of Rawl-inson MS D 859 is made up of miscellaneous materials; in addition to various family notes, it includes transcripts of letters and papers of Sir Walter Ralegh (fols. 80–87) and other letters of notable figures, such as the Great Mogul to James I, as well as parliamentary speeches, verse and antiquarian and topographical notes, including names of colleges, halls, and churches in Oxford (fol. 83), description of the ruins of Tewkesbury Abbey (fol. 98), and fragments of Baskerville's private accounts and memoranda. Basker-ville's antiquarian pursuits are suggested by Anthony Wood's description of a visit to his house in February 1659, where he found him a "melancholy and retired man."[40] Although dismissed by Ian Mortimer as no "scholar," his antiquarian interests as "little more than dabblings, predominantly re-lating to his own family," this fundamentally misunderstands the nature, purpose, and complex series of impulses—biographical, autobiographical, and antiquarian—that underlay Baskerville's activities in annotating and preserving family documents.[41]

A key feature of Baskerville's miscellany is his habit of using the cor-respondence itself as a material site for family biography. This practice of annotating the blank space of letters and other documents is witnessed throughout the volume and attests a later engagement with or rereading of cor-respondence, with an eye to family history. Mary Baskerville's epitaph of her mother includes in the grandson's hand an account of the habits and character of Lady Throckmorton. She was an early riser, given to private prayer, relieved the poor, and provided hospitality to all comers, and she "was a greate student euer readinge one sacred booke or other and heere is not to be forgotten yt shee understoode the Latin, French; Italian and I have heard could reade the Greeke Tongues."[42] Potted biographical sketches of this kind were often assembled to form more official family histories or memorials, in the manner of the *Memorials* of the Rodney and Holles families, and Baskerville's notes may represent working papers or raw materials to be incorporated later into a more ambitious project of memorial.[43]

By far the most sustained exercise in biographical writing, however, is the annotations made on the series of letters Hannibal received himself from his mother in the years after the breakdown of her second marriage to Sir James Scudamore (d. 1618).[44] Mary, whose first match had been to the Elizabethan naval commander Sir Thomas Baskerville, was treated quite monstrously by Scudamore and his father Sir John—the marriage deteriorated in 1604 and was repudiated in 1608 although no formal divorce was arranged—and Hannibal and his mother spent almost two decades seeking redress.[45] Complaining that she had been turned out of her house by her father-in-law and maltreated by her husband, refused justice by the bishop of London, and reduced to penury, she petitioned Robert Cecil, Earl of Salisbury, for his protection in 1609, but with no success.[46] Throughout this period, Baskerville kept up a regular correspondence with his mother and her servant Thomas Clerkson, the latter writing to him in 1619 conveying his mother's advice that he take to court his "adversaries," in other words, his stepfather who claimed both Hannibal's wardship and his mother's dower.[47] His mother's letters during this period register materially her separation from her husband by the unusual nature of their signatures. In several letters dated after 1608, Mary appears to have dissociated herself from Scudamore by signing herself "Marie B" or "Marie Baskeruile" immediately after the text, followed by the name Scudamore struck through at the bottom of the page, materially registering separation from her husband (Figures 10.1 and 10.2).[48]

More important, her misfortune was chronicled by Baskerville in narrative form in a series of notes written on the back of her letters.[49] The biography starts with details of his mother's first separation from James Scudamore, their subsequent reconciliation and return to Holme Lacy, and the death of her father, Sir Thomas Throckmorton (d. 1607), before sketching in

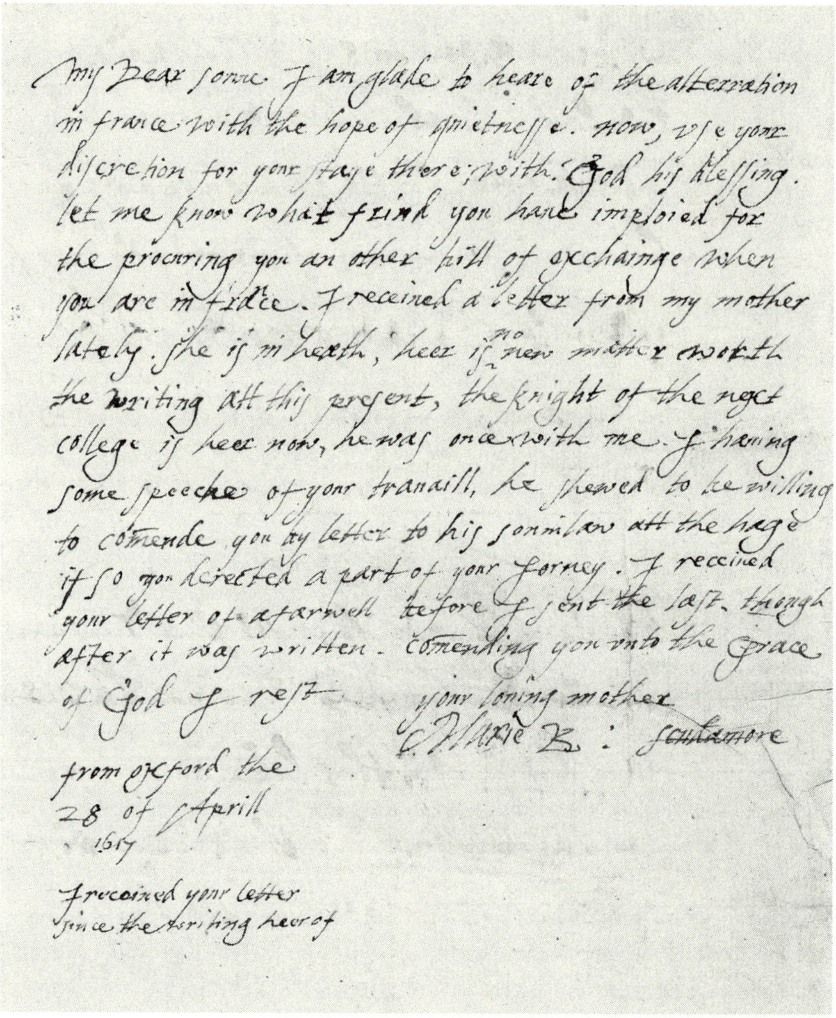

Figure 10.1. Letter of Mary Baskerville to Hannibal Baskerville, 28 April 1617, Bodl., Rawl. MS D 859, fol. 3ʳ. Reproduced by permission of the Bodleian Library, University of Oxford.

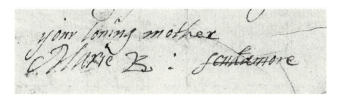

Figure 10.2. Letter of Mary Baskerville to Hannibal Baskerville, 28 April 1617, Bodl., Rawl. MS D 859, fol. 3ʳ; detail of deleted signature. Reproduced by permission of the Bodleian Library, University of Oxford.

more detail his stepfather's and Sir John Scudamore's determination to "put her away":

> they brake open her closet doore and tooke there hence all her
> jewels chaines of goald pearle and other riches wch was of no
> smalle valewe but God preserved to vs the euidences of sonningwell
> for if they had seene them or thought of them they would have
> tooke them and by theyr deeds afterward doen unto vs the greatnes
> of the doinges may bee discerned both unto vs and likewise to all
> our succeedinge posteritye they sued my mother for them in ye
> names of Sr JC and R Scud Esq.[50]

The narrative continues (with the year noted in the margin) describing the itinerant life of Hannibal and his mother as they sought refuge and support from family and friends. Her "friends," her brother William and brother-in-law Sir Barnabus Samborne, persuaded Scudamore to pay his wife a £100 annuity. Here Baskerville interjects his own autobiographical fragments into the narrative; while they were staying with her sister in Somerset, Hannibal Baskerville "was at Bristoll at the free school in the house of Mr Swyft the schoole master"; at the age of twelve he returned to his mother, and at this stage Scudamore refused to pay the annuity but was ordered by Salisbury to pay it to his mother, who had been before the "council table" to seek redress. They then stayed with his grandmother for four years in the house of John Stevenson, before moving to Oxford when Hannibal was sixteen and where he lived until he was nineteen years of age; he traveled in France when he was nineteen, returning to Oxford in the summer, staying there until he was twenty-two. The death of James Scudamore in 1618 created a "pecke of troubles and suites in lawe" since he had leased the lands of Sunningwell and Bayworth to Sir James Crofts and

Rowland Scudamore for sixty years, but after three years in the courts Hannibal and his mother came into possession, Hannibal living at Bayworth until he
married. In recording his mother's final return to Bayworth and subsequent
death, Hannibal wrote: "If she liued in pleasure here it was eyther in her
childhood or the summer yt shee dyed," adding she "could not haue ioye
her mother beinge gone." Summing up her life and marriages he concluded:

> In her first marriage though it might be greate
> yet it was short for within a moneth after
> mariage my father was sent to ye indies.
> wher and at london he was one y[ear] from her
> and after he was sent to france and he
> was but 2 y[ears] married
> In her 2d she tooke no content.[51]

In a very real sense, the letters assume a new function, becoming a site of family
and personal history, recording not only his mother's life, but also the rudimentary contours of his own early years. Elsewhere Baskerville pens autobiographical
fragments, under the headings "The Times and Places where I haue Soiourned
all the daies of my Lyfe" and "A computation of all somes of monye yt I have
giuen according to my vowe made in Nouember 1619 vnto pious vses."[52] Baskerville also records the circumstances of his birth and the death of his father:

> April ye 5, 1597, I was born at a town of Piccardy, called St Vallery
> where was a deadly plague among ye French, but it did not infect
> the English soldiers. I was christened by one Mr Man ye preacher,
> and I had all the captains about 32 to be my godfathers, it being
> the custome so of the wars, when the generall hath a son (they say)
> but two only stood at the font or great bason, one was Sir Arthur
> Savage, the other I can not remember his name. Sr Arthur Chich-
> ester was there, and other great men that have been since my father
> Sr Thomas Baskerville died of a burning feavour at a town called
> Picquency. I was then 9 weeks old.[53]

As documents, the letters attain a dual purpose: they are personal letters in
the hand of his mother (and are objects valued as such), as well as records of
her struggles, character, and marriages. A large part of Baskerville's activities,
therefore, lies in his impulse to leave a corrective record for posterity, and he
reframed the letters through his own paratextual additions.

A further clue to Baskerville's activities is a printed summons from Elias Ashmole, the Windsor herald at the College of Arms at a time when he was executing his "Visitation of Berkshire" in 1665. The letter itself is interesting materially, since it represents an early example of a printed pro forma letter of the kind used by the state in 1633 to issue instructions for the king's loan, and a precursor of the kind of printed questionnaires developed by learned societies of the later seventeenth and eighteenth centuries about which Adam Fox has recently written.[54] The summons asks Baskerville to appear before Ashmole in Abingdon on 16 March, and "there to enter your Descent and Arms, and to bring with you such Arms and Crests as you bear."[55] Baskerville recorded payment to "Elias Ashmole windsore Herald of Armes 37s 6d," adding that "Hee tooke the names of all my children dead and Alive, the names of my father and Grandfather"; Ashmole refused, however, to accept the evidence of the 1629 pedigree given to him by his father-in-law, asking for original documents.[56] Thus a very practical purpose lay behind the assembling of family genealogies and documentation relating to property and land (including a presentation copy of his will), which reveals a further layer of understanding of archival practices.[57] Throughout the miscellany Baskerville recorded details of his extended kin. On one of his mother's letters are details of his wife Mary's previous marriage, the children arising from it, and their own offspring; another was appended with an account of Sir William Throckmorton's three wives, their parentage, offspring, and the ancient inheritance of the family.[58] Elsewhere he records "The names of my kindred by consanguinitye and aliances yt I have seene and knowen in my life tyme," while a letter sent to his mother contains on the back of it a family genealogy.[59] This interest in family was continued by his son, the topographer Thomas Baskerville (1630/31–1700), who may have inherited the volume, since there survives in his hand an account of Constance Baskerville and her mother, including details of the poesies on their wedding rings.[60] Here, then, the letters survive preserved by a son with antiquarian interests in recent history and topography, as well as in family history, who was engaged in registering the family pedigree but also wished to bequeath to posterity autobiographical and biographical fragments.

Margaret Clifford's Letter Book

The final case study relates to the survival of the correspondence of Margaret Clifford, Countess of Cumberland, which is now dispersed across several archives, reflecting previous distinct activities of collection at specific points in time. The countess was involved in various patronage activities, acting as an intermediary and petitioner on behalf of her daughter, Anne Clifford, during her disputed inheritance, which necessitated writing to various Privy Counsellors and the monarch. Original sent versions of the countess's business letters survive among the State Papers and the papers of administrators and officials such as Julius Caesar, Lord Keeper Puckering, Robert Cecil, and Thomas Sutton, founder of Charterhouse Hospital, as well as among the papers of the earls of Rutland and Shrewsbury.[61] Copies and heavily revised drafts of some of these outgoing letters were preserved as records among the countess's papers now held at Kendal Record Office among the Hothfield manuscripts.[62] Among these family papers, which descended to Anne Clifford on her mother's death is a much broader range of Margaret Clifford's correspondence, including letters between the countess and her husband, George Clifford, an extensive correspondence with Anne, and incoming letters from Lord Willoughby, the Countess of Shrewsbury, and her sister, the Countess of Warwick.[63] For Margaret Clifford, the preservation of a series of letters to Privy Counsellors was part of wider archival activities connected with assembling documentary evidence as part of her daughter's legal battle; she kept her papers in a "great trunk" "full of writings of Craven and Westmoreland and other affairs with certain letters of her friends and many papers of philosophy," which Anne Clifford recorded taking to Knole House in January 1619 as a way to "pass away the time."[64] There is evidence of Anne Clifford having read her mother's letters in earlier periods of her life in connection with her claims to land. Two of her mother's letters to her are annotated with similar notes about her inheritance. A letter dated 30 May 1605 contains the note, "Of Brougham Castell to bee mine heerafter"; another undated letter, which details the death of Lady Arbella Stuart (so written after 25 September 1615), contains two annotations, one dating from 1 June 1655 (to which I will turn later) and another, which appears to have been written much earlier, that reads, "which [letter] showes thatt Brougham Castell should be mine Heareafter." The preservation of correspondence here had a utilitarian purpose.

Anne Clifford, however, had interests in her mother's correspondence extending beyond their legal significance. More broadly, Anne actively preserved and annotated correspondence related to her and played an important part in the archival process of her family and in the construction of a transgenerational memory. Letters she received in the 1650s and 1660s from her own daughter Margaret and her son-in-law James Compton, third Earl of

Northampton, were annotated either in her own hand or by a secretary at her dictation, sometimes commenting on national news contained in the letter, but more commonly recording family events to which the letters refer. On the address leaf of one letter she wrote, "My daughter of Thannetts Letter to mee the 19 day of Juley in 1653: by whiche I cam furst of all to know that the day beefor her now eldest Daughter was Married, butt the day beefor to Mr Gorge Couentreys eldest soone to the now Lorde couventrey"; another dated 24 September 1661 was endorsed by a secretary "touching the death of my deare Grandchild Wm Lord Crompton at Castle Ashby the 14th of the same month"; another, "A lre from my Daughter of Thanet dated. ye 23 of February 1664: 1665. By which I came first to know yt her daughter Lady Frances Tufton was marryed the same day in the Chappell in Thanet House in Aldersgate Street London, to Mr Henry Drax./ which lre I received the first of March 1664: 1665"; another letter from her son-in-law the Earl of Northampton was annotated "My Lorde of Northamptones letter to mee wherin hee writtes mee word of the Dethe of his furst Sonne May 22 1648." Here Anne Clifford's interest was in recording the rites of passage connected to the lineage of her family, and thus the annotating and archiving of her correspondence was a key part of the family history activities in which scholars have shown that she was engaged.[65]

In many instances the process of annotating the letters was not one that took place at the time of receipt in the way that was commonplace for secretaries to endorse letters with date and brief notes on contents for easy archival retrieval. Instead Anne's annotations were made at a later date when the letters were reread for different purposes. This is evident in the way she approached her mother's correspondence, which she systematically worked through in the mid-1650s long after her mother's death and after Anne succeeded to her long-awaited title and lands. Clifford's interest at this point was not in the letters for practical legal purposes, but rather in archiving and mining them for information connected to preservation and the production of family history. In some cases, Anne Clifford's annotations of her mother's correspondence are concerned with the archival process in a conventional manner, summarizing contents: a letter from the Countess of Shrewsbury was endorsed "Most of itt beeing of the Dethe of her Neece the Ladey Arabella who died in the Tower of London about the beegining of October in 1615." An undated letter from Anne Clifford sending her mother a new year's gift contains a later note in Anne's handwriting indicating that it was written from London in 1615.[66] The dating of a letter from her father to her mother dated 23 February is completed in Anne Clifford's hand adding the year "1594" with the explanation "as the yeare beegines on nwers day"; another "as 1590 as the yeare beegines on Nwers day."[67] Other annotations suggest a more personal interest in family history. One letter was endorsed "the last leter whiche I reseued from my dere mother of her o[w]n hand writinge, it beeing towards the later end of Aprell 1616"; another, "the Letter my Father writt to my Mother presenttlay after my berthe when hee then laye att Bedford howse att London"; while a letter from her father to her mother was endorsed by a secretary, "A very kind letter of his Lordship, written in the tyme of great sickness, wherein he offereth satisfaction for wrongs, comforteth her Ladyship agaynst his death, intreateth her to think well of his will, and requesteth her to conceyve rightlie off his brother."[68] Anne's interests here seem to have been much more biographical and autobiographical. The arrangement and annotation of these letters then should be read as a clear act of family history writing in the later stages of her life when she had other works compiled, including her "Great Books of Record," two histories of her ancestors compiled by the judge and antiquary Sir Matthew Hale, two copies of Earl George's voyages, a book of heraldry and genealogies.[69]

As part of these textual and historical activities, in the mid-1650s Anne Clifford also had a letter book drawn up of her mother's correspondence. This is clear from Anne's other annotations on her mother's letters, which often include the date when the letter was copied and the nature of the transcript made. For example, annotations include: "This letter was cop[i]ed into my Blessed Mother her Booke of Letters the 4: of June in 1655"; "some part of this Longe letter was written into my Blessed Motheres Booke of Letters the furst of May in 1655"; "onley on sayinge in this letter is written into the Booke of Letters, The furst of June 1655." And occasionally mention is made of letters not included: "this is not written into the Booke of Letters at all," she wrote of one of her mother's letters to her, "because ther was so little in itt." Most of the letters that Anne received from her mother were copied into the letter book, along with letters to Sir Robert Stabilton, the Duke of Lennox, letters to Robert Cecil, a letter and petition to King James, and several letters from the countess to her husband, including a draft of a rather spiritual letter of rapprochement sent to the earl before their reconciliation on his deathbed. Judging from these annotations, Anne Clifford had a policy of partial inclusion, privileging her own letters from her mother, key letters to Privy Counsellors and the monarch, and letters that shed light on her mother's role as reconciler in a difficult marriage. The precise nature of Anne's policy of excluding letters—which was circumscribed by what her mother chose to retain in the first place—is hard to reconstruct but is hinted at in the endorsements of original copies. Several letters including to her servants and a letter to her husband, which opens with discussions about the king's coronation, are annotated as "not put into the book of letters." Quite why this particular letter to the Earl of Cumberland was not included is hard to discern. Presumably letters to servants were not considered important enough for inclusion, yet also excluded was a letter to the Countess of Warwick, which suggests that Anne Clifford was not merely interested in including letters to correspondents of elevated social status. Nevertheless in many ways, then, the volume represents a highly selective letter book, which memorializes the countess in a particular way, emphasizing her relationship with her daughter. The countess's letters thus have a rather complex and layered archival afterlife: first, they were composed and dispatched and on receipt subsequently archived by their recipients, with some copies retained for legal purposes by the countess herself; second, those received by Anne Clifford herself were read at the time for utilitarian reasons; third, Anne Clifford archived, annotated, and preserved for posterity original copies of the letters as documents connected with the Clifford family; and, last, she had particular examples of her mother's correspondence collected together and transcribed into a memorial volume.

Frustratingly the letter book, which was drawn up between 1 May and 4 June 1655, appears to no longer be extant. Instead what survives is a late eighteenth-century copy of a collection of Margaret Clifford's letters gathered among the Portland manuscripts now held at Longleat House.[70] The relationship between these later copies and the volume that Clifford commissioned is unclear. Of the seventeen original letters among the Hothfield manuscripts endorsed as "inserted" or written into Margaret Clifford's letter book, only ten appear in Portland MS 23: two letters to her husband (fols. 13–14, 27–28), five to Anne Clifford (fols. 63–64, 67–68, 69–70, 73, 74), and a letter to Robert Stabilton (fols. 23–24), one to the Duke of Lennox (fols. 44–45), and another to King James (fols. 50–51). The manuscript letter book contains a further forty-nine letters (fifty-nine in total), which among the most celebrated include the countess's long autobiographical letter to her spiritual adviser Dr. Leyfield, a letter from the poet Samuel Daniel, who tutored Anne Clifford, and a series of other letters to her husband and daughter. Other correspondents include her daughter's first husband, Richard Sackville, Earl of Dorset, her niece Anne Russell, Lady Herbert, and her nephew Francis Lord Russell, Sir Anthony Shirley, Sir Thomas Erskine, Lord Henry Howard, King James and Queen Anne, Salisbury, and Edward Bruce, Lord Kinloss. For all these letters the only textual witness is an eighteenth-century copy, possibly based on the missing 1655 letter book. Indeed, there are scribal clues suggesting

the Portland manuscript was based on a volume compiled by or for Anne Clifford. On folio 35 is written the heading "The coppies of several letters written by
my blessed mother Margaret Countess of Cumberland when she was a widow to
my noble father George earl of Cumberland to King James to several Councellors of note & other great lords to come officers of Judicature in this nation
about the business of my inheritance," while folio 55 contains the heading "Several letters written by my Blessed Mother to my selfe, to my first lord Richard
Earle of Dorsett and to others of her kindred in her latter times." This strongly
suggests that the copyist had access to an original letter book, or it was intended
to give that impression; however, elsewhere there is evidence of the eighteenth-
century copyist intervening to construct some kind of narrative history. After a
series of letters to the Earl of Cumberland, King James, Anna of Denmark, and
various Privy Counsellors, the copyist interjects to provide a framing commentary: "But notwithstanding all this vertuous Lady's intreaties her daughter and
only childe the Ladye Anne Clifford was carrye from her about the middle of
July, from her house in Austin Friars in London by the earl of Cumberlands appointment down to the old house at Grafton." This episode is alluded to in "A
summary of the records and a true memorial of the life of me the Lady Anne
Clifford."[71] The volume is then at the very least a hybrid somewhere between
a letter book and form of personal history, and there are suggestion of an intertextuality between the letter book and other Clifford-related texts.

Examining the letter book alongside other items bound within Portland
MS 23 sheds further light. It survives as one of five distinct manuscript fragments written in four different hands: first, a transcript of "A Summary of the
History and a true Memoriall of the Life of me, the Lady Anne Clifford"; second, a manuscript entitled "Of the Countess of Pembroke"; and third, an
account of the siege of Brampton Bryan Castle and related documents including numerous of Brilliana Harley's letters. Fourth, and more important, the
volume includes transcripts of Anne Clifford's diary for 1616–19, which is preceded by autobiographical notes from 1603, and followed by two of her letters
to the earls of Bedford and Arlington. This last item is in the same hand as
the countess's letters, which Katherine Acheson has tentatively identified
as that of Margaret Cavendish Harley Bentinck (1715–85), Duchess of Portland, and granddaughter of the manuscript collector Robert Harley.[72] The
broader collection of Portland papers represent the remains of the Harleian
manuscripts sold to the nation in 1753, including autograph letters of notable
persons and the papers of Robert Harley and Margaret, Duchess of Portland.
The Harley material in Portland MS 23 suggests the duchess's interest in her

own family history, as does her collecting of an autograph volume of Gervase Holles's *Parentela et parentalia Hollesiorium* (Portland MS 24), reflecting her maternal connections to the Holles family. Her interest in the Clifford material perhaps stemmed from her grandfather Robert Harley, who visited Appleby Castle in 1725 and was allowed to examine the Clifford manuscripts and commissioned in 1737 an abridgment of *The Great Books of the Clifford Family* now in the Harley collection at the British Library.[73] Acheson also speculates that the Duchess of Portland may have identified with Anne Clifford, since "she too was an embattled heiress unjustly dispossessed of her rightful inheritance"; Margaret Clifford's letter book represents a mother battling for her daughter's rightful inheritance and wrestling with a difficult marriage.

The survival of Margaret Clifford's letters, then, as a later copy identifies a further archival life as they are consumed by an eighteenth-century noblewoman well known as a patron of the arts and sciences, a collector of art and natural history specimens, and a correspondent of Jean-Jacques Rousseau, Mary Delany, and Elizabeth Montagu.[74] Yet a comparison of the original letters among the Hothfield manuscripts with those in Portland MS 23 highlights a form of copying little concerned with producing an accurate, authentic copy. Surviving letters reveal frequent scribal errors, simplifications, and modernizations. However, certain letters were embellished to the extent that they are fictionalized. An undated original letter from Sir Robert Stabilton is partially transcribed and dated "Clerkernwell Aug 1st 1604." The eighteenth-century copy follows the opening lines of the letter, but fails to transcribe the second part offering his wife a cloak belonging to the Countess of Warwick (Figures 10.3 and 10.4). Instead the copy provides an account of a supposed illness suffered by Anne Clifford, which is without any corroboration or basis in the letter text: "My only childe Anne Clifford is lately recovered of that burning feaver which she tooke with a surfeit of cherryes, of which it was a hundred to one but she had dyed, but yet mercifull providence maintained her life; she and I are shortly to remove from this House for altogether but wheresoever I am I will still bee your assured true frend Margaret Clifford."[75] Likewise, an undated letter to George Clifford complaining of financial difficulties is copied with significant additions, including "yor Lop cannot but know what great charges I was at the last year with meeting the queen at her first coming to England," and glossing mention of her "friends" as "my brother William Lord Russell and my nephew Edward Earl of Bedford."[76] The Duchess of Portland intervened in these two cases partly for purposes of clarification, but also in an emphatic fashion, blurring the boundaries of "fact" and "fiction," with

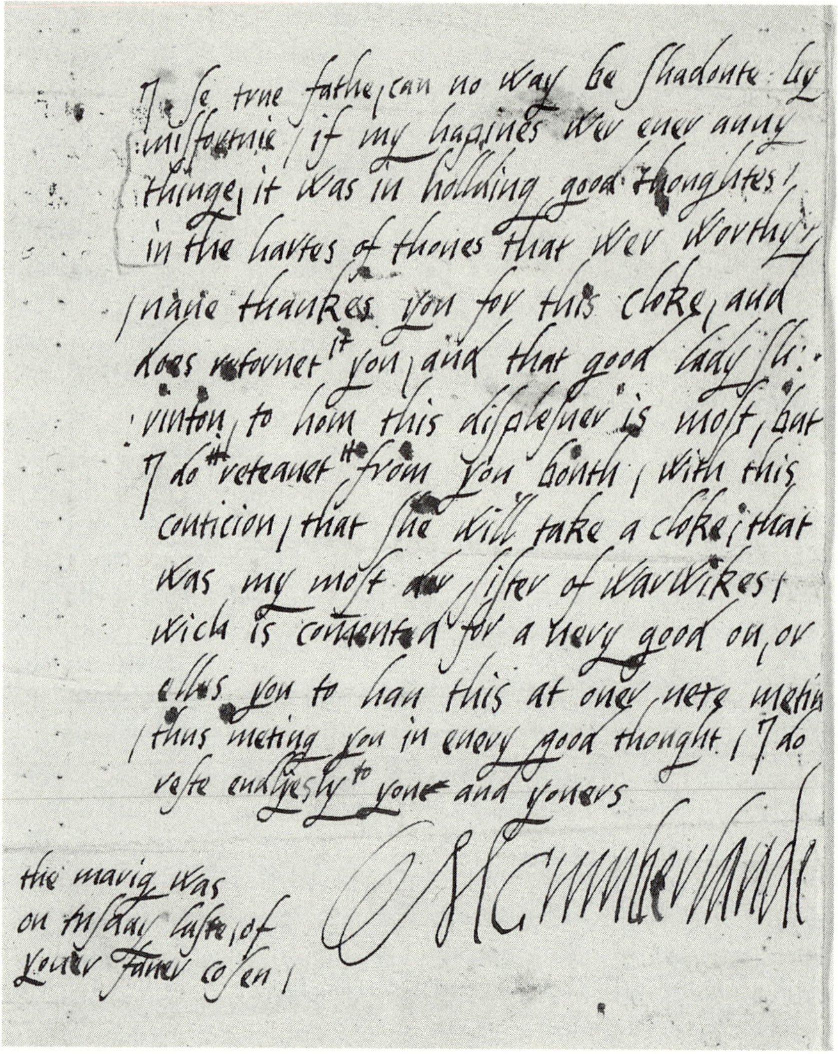

Ye se true fathe, can no way be shadowe by
misfortune / if my hapines wer ever anny
thinge, it was in holding good thoughtes,
in the hartes of thoses that wer worthy
manie thankes you for this cloke, and
does returne it you, and that good lady Sk:
:vinton, to hom this displesuer is most, but
I do retaine it from you bouth, with this
condicion, that she will take a cloke; that
was my most dere sister of Warwikes,
wich is commended for a very good on, or
elles you to hav this at our nete meting
thus meting you in every good thought, I do
reste endlesly to yours and youers

M Cumberlande

the mariag was
on tusday laste, of
youer faire cosen,

Figure 10.3. Copy of Margaret Clifford's letter to Sir Robert Stabilton, Kendal Record Office, Hothfield MSS, WD/Hoth/Box 44. Reproduced by permission of Lord Hothfield.

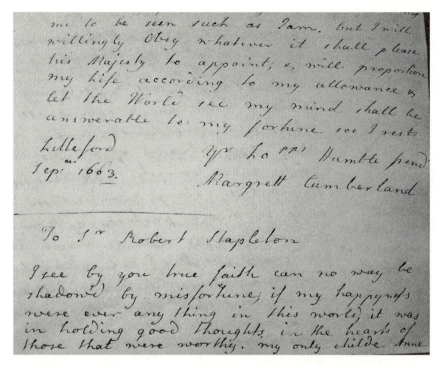

Figure 10.4. Copy of Margaret Clifford's letter to Sir Robert Stabilton, Long-leat House, Portland MS 23, fols. 23–24 (24). Reproduced by permission of the Marquess of Bath, Longleat House, Warminster, Wiltshire.

interventions designed to produce a certain kind of affect in the reader, as with the paratexts framing the response of the reader to Anne and Margaret. It is also conceivable that the Duchess of Portland or someone else added anec-dotal material that corresponded with the same date as the letters, as suggested by the possible inclusion of events from Clifford's "Summary of the Records and a True Memorial."[77] The reference to "fever" in the Stabilton letter echoes descriptions of various fevers or agues suffered by Anne Clifford in her autobio-graphical writings, including an occasion in June 1603 at Hampton Court, where according to Clifford she "fell extremely sick of a fever so as my mother was in some doubt it might turn to the plague"; and cherries are certainly men-tioned elsewhere in the diary.[78] Again, this suggests a degree of intertextuality, an awareness of biographical background informing the copying, amending, and commentary of the letters. Given that this was her practice with these letters, it then destabilizes other letters within the volume for which originals

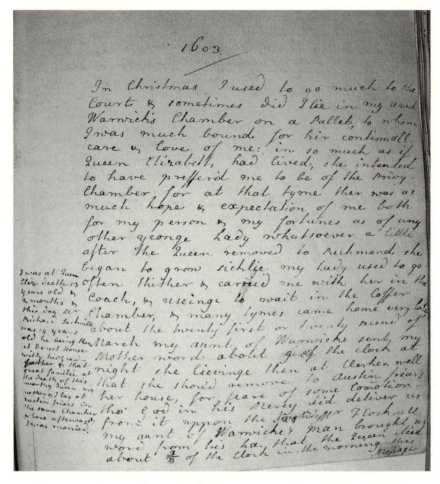

Figure 10.5. Extract of Anne Clifford's 1603 memoir, Longleat House, Portland MS 23, fol. 74ʳ. Reproduced by permission of the Marquess of Bath, Longleat House, Warminster, Wiltshire.

do not survive. Furthermore, and perhaps more important, it prompts questions about the "authenticity" of Anne Clifford's autobiographical fragments and journal for 1603 and 1616–19 (in the sense of being an exact replica of autograph texts), which are similarly in the duchess's hand and for which the Portland manuscript is the earliest surviving copy (Figure 10.5).[79]

The textual discrepancies in different versions of Margaret Clifford's letters as they were copied from original sent letters and transcribed into letter

books in the seventeenth and eighteenth centuries destabilize our understand-
ings of early modern letters as fixed texts, especially in their later reincarna-
tions. As Andrew Gordon argues in his examination of epistolary forgeries
(Chapter 4 of this volume), cultures of copying were bound up with the material act of copying as well as social anxieties about fidelity to the original
text. The relationship between early modern letter books and manuscript letters sent is a complex one. While secretaries might produce accurate "fair" copies of outgoing or incoming correspondence, surviving copybooks evidence
enormous variations in copying practices, and it is often hard to distinguish
between fair copies and drafts. In many cases, copyists reproduced solely the
main part of a letter, sometimes only copying key passages, and often leaving
out modes of address and closing, dates and location. Indeed, Anne Clifford
on occasion had "some part" or "most part" rather than the entirety of her
mother's letters copied. Other examples produced précis of missives; sought
to convey the flavor of a letter; or merely listed correspondence sent or received,
rather than rendering a carbon copy of a manuscript original.[80] Overall, there
is a slippage between copies retained and those that were sent that is related
to the material practices of copying. Moreover, there are suggestive parallels
between Margaret Clifford's letter book and the way in which John Donne
the younger printed a highly edited selection of his father's correspondence in
Letters to Severall Persons of Honour (1651; reissued 1654). Although only two
holograph originals survive of Donne's letters that were later printed, there
are marked variations between the manuscript letters and their printed descendants. The polished virtuoso prose letters that were printed differ significantly from the perfunctory missives that survive solely in manuscript.[81] While
one cannot assess the accuracy of Clifford's scribal publication of her mother's
letters—in that the volume does not survive—the act of selecting correspondence, by its very nature an editorial intervention, as in Donne's case, appears to
have been concerned with orchestrating the literary legacy of a parent. Thus,
while the eighteenth-century copies of the Countess of Cumberland's letters
betray textual infidelities suggestive of creativity and artifice, so too it might be
argued that earlier assemblies of her letters might be viewed as "fictions."

Conclusion

In closing I would like to draw together the various strands offered by these
rather intricate case studies and reflect on where we began with Derrida's

notion of the "matriarchive" and the ways in which women's letters as texts fit into the process of transgenerational and archival memory. Here I am interested in the gender politics of the early modern archive, the survival or nonsurvival of *women's* letters, and the changing status, meaning, and cultural afterlife of letters. Clearly early modern women were regular letter writers; correspondence was a quotidian activity connected to household and family in the broadest sense. They were thus producers of documents that might be archived, although to a lesser extent than men for reasons of literacy, utility, and power. However, only a small fraction of letters once written by women survive, since the main categories of documents preserved relate to office and law, areas that excluded or marginalized women; though women are represented as petitioners and intermediaries in the state papers and papers of officeholders. Within family collections, women's correspondence to male heads of households (fathers, sons, and uncles) is most likely to survive, which privileges these sorts of relationships and power structures; equally runs of letters from husbands, since they tended to write to the household, survive in greater quantity than those from wives. Women did engage in archival activities, endorsing and preserving correspondence, and they had access to family papers; many preserved their own correspondence in trunks or desks, but these tended to be kept outside of muniments rooms and estate correspondence, only surviving beyond their lifetimes if they were inherited and gravitated toward more permanent archival spaces. Those that do survive within family papers assumed a particular significance, as a form of cultural patrimony, a mode of memorialization, remembrance, or family biography.

Furthermore, the preservation and survival of letters is a layered and ongoing process as new generations reevaluate and reinterpret the value of documents. Such later practices of preservation are separate from the initial decisions of recipients or writers first to preserve a letter. Future survival then rests on archival decisions of subsequent generations to retain letters for various reasons. In the case of state and legal archives there is a clear imperative to keep records intact, as part of a national or institutional heritage, and within the family there is a sense of patrimonial inheritance, documents including letters being passed from one generation to the next as a mode of transgenerational memory. In only one of the instances discussed, however, did the papers remain within the family or household with which they were associated: some of the letters of Margaret Clifford were at Appleby House until deposited at Kendal, while copies of others were acquired by the great manuscript collector Robert Harley and his granddaughter; here the interest is in Margaret Clifford as a notable historical figure. In the other two cases, antiquarians were at the root of the survival of manuscripts: Nathaniel Johnston recognized the importance of the Talbot manuscripts and rescued them from inevitable decay, ensuring their survival in the College of Arms; while the papers of Hannibal Baskerville ended up among the collections of Richard Rawlinson and are now part of the Rawlinson manuscripts at the Bodleian.[82] Johnston's ordering of the Talbot papers treated women's letters as distinct from those of the earls of Shrewsbury, while Mary Baskerville's letters were subsumed within the papers of a seventeenth-century antiquarian. Manuscript collectors, antiquarians, and record-keeping institutions, such as libraries, record offices, and private homes are fundamental to the long-term survival of manuscript letters, and the dispersal of collections throughout the world is extremely complex.

Beyond these broader patterns of archival survival and dispersal, and shifting preoccupations and interests, these case studies highlight the ways in which women's letters attained complex future lives, which changed significantly over time. Letters acquired meaning and significance to later generations of readers, different from those intended by the writer at the moment of composition. By the eighteenth century letters were becoming the raw materials or historical sources for family histories, histories often written by women: Cassandra Willoughby, for example, kept a small quarto volume entitled "An Account of the Willughby's of Wollaton, taken out of the Pedigree, old letters and old Books of Account in my Brother Sir Thomas Willoughby's study, Dec., A.D. 1702," into which she transcribed family letters, many of the originals of which are no longer extant.[83] Letters thus acquired new meanings as they moved between archives, from those of the sender or recipient to new custodians; and as they moved from particular archival moments or contexts to be incorporated into larger collections, a process reorienting interpretations. The gendered politics of archival survival and the role that this plays in how we understand and value women's letters is mutable, altering over time with changing attitudes. While the past two decades have seen an explosion in scholarly interest in women's letters, with the production of numerous editions and online finding aids such as "Women's Early Modern Letters Online," previous generations of scholars and archivists were less interested. Thus, in the 1860s a British Museum archivist cataloging a volume of "letters and papers concerning the disputes between Anthony Bourne and his wife" described the collection as being "of no importance," although it included numerous letters by Elizabeth Bourne depicting the experiences of an Elizabethan gentle-woman separated from her husband.[84] The ways in which archives were constructed, organized, and ordered often overlooked rather than privileged women's records; archivists were often in effect gender blind, employing gender-neutral or more likely male categories of ordering, which influences the ways in which those archives are used, read, and understood.[85] It is these kinds of barriers and cultural conditionings that current digital initiatives and scholarship are seeking to overcome, giving greater visibility to early modern women's letters for future generations of readers and scholars.

CHAPTER 11

Familiar Letters and State Papers

The Afterlives of Early Modern Correspondence

ALAN STEWART

Critical approaches to early modern correspondence fall largely into two camps. The first approach concerns the content of letters—the information they contain, obviously, but also what we might see as their rhetorical or linguistic construction. Historians have for centuries mined letters for their record of empirical fact; biographers have read them for their insights into the minds of their writers; most recently, linguists and literary critics have examined their rhetorical formations to examine the place of letter writing within social relations.[1] The second, and recently dominant, approach focuses on the materiality of letters: the paper, pens, ink, wax and seals, penknives, whetstone, and sand required for the production of the physical letter; the multiple, coded possibilities of handwriting; the layout of the letter's page, and the ways in which its layout of text, or its deployment of "significant space," to use Jonathan Gibson's evocative term, encodes assumptions about the relationship between writer and recipient; the way the letter is folded and sealed; the mechanics of bearing or carrying letters; how the letter is refolded and filed.[2] Most scholarship today employs elements of both approaches, manipulating the textual evidence of early modern letters while paying at least some attention to its material form.

In this essay, I want to explore a third approach that to date has remained relatively underexplored, and that might complement the two we already follow. It involves looking beyond the letters themselves, as either rhetorical products or material objects, and asking instead about the *places* they occupy: Where have they been, in the three or four centuries since they were written? What was their journey after their initial function was exhausted? And what might that location mean for our understanding of them?[3] While attention to provenance is second nature to editors, it might be argued that the intense recent interest in the letter as material object—the minute focus on the physical aspects of how a letter looks *now*, in order to understand its function *then*—breeds in its apparent immediacy an odd lack of concern for the period between then and now, what we might call the archival afterlife of correspondence. That effect is exacerbated by the remarkable possibilities of online resources such as *State Papers Online*, Perdita, the Cecil Papers, Digital Scriptorium, and so on, which bring stunning digital images of letters and other manuscripts to us at our desks, erasing our need to go to (and therefore take into account) the archives that now house them.

Those archives are, of course, many and various in nature: from privately owned country houses, to the libraries of universities and corporate bodies, to civic and local records offices, to the personal libraries of modern collectors, to the national or state libraries and archives. We tend to expect the types of papers in these collections to be correspondingly differentiated: a country house would be most likely to house the family papers of its early modern occupants; London's Guildhall, to house the papers dealing with the capital's civil governance, and so on. By this logic, "state papers" would be expected to be found in what the early modern period called the Paper Office, and later generations have developed as the Public Record Office, latterly part of the National Archives, and now, virtually, available as *State Papers Online*. As Stephen Alford writes, in his excellent article accompanying the online database, "Most of the original documents we read in *State Papers Online* were the everyday working papers of the royal government." However, as Alford admits, "In reading *State Papers Online* we face too some intriguing matters of organisation. The wonderful thing about the resource you are reading is that it brings together documents which, though now in different archives in diverse collections and archives, once belonged together."[4] So the "state papers" bring together not only those papers filed under "SP" at the National Archives in Kew, but also papers that survive in collections such as Cotton and Yelverton at the British Library, and the Cecil Papers at Hatfield House, papers that have passed down through private hands.[5]

What does it mean that government papers that supposedly "belong together" lie scattered in private collections and have to be "brought together" to form *State Papers Online* (although they remain, in all reality except virtual reality, quite separate)? This chapter traces the origins of this situation. It demonstrates that there was an acute interest in the Elizabethan and Jacobean periods in the *place* of state papers: where they were kept, who kept them, and how their long-term survival should be achieved. In so doing, it challenges our commonsensical ideas of what constitutes state papers—or, for that matter, family papers—and, by extension, the notion that public office holding in the early modern period can be easily divorced from private, familial concerns. It also takes a fresh look at the role of letters among state papers. Among such papers, the place of correspondence is perhaps the most fraught, since letters are usually directed to a particular individual, and invested—even when dealing with the most "official" concerns—with a high level of personalized affect. Lying behind this inquiry, then, are two questions about letters: When does a familiar letter become a state paper? And when can a personally addressed "state" paper remain a private missive?

*   *   *

A key figure in the history of the state papers, and in "the evolution of archival practice" more generally, is Arthur Agarde, who was deputy chamberlain of the Exchequer—essentially the Exchequer's record keeper—from 1570 to 1616.[6] To Agarde we owe a remarkable account of "The repertorie of records: remaining in The 4. Treasuries on the receipt side at Westminster,"[7] and a fascinating consideration of the dangers to archives, part of a tract dating to around 1600 entitled "The Compendium of the Records in the Treasury."[8] In this tract, after detailing exactly what the records comprise, and how they are physically organized, Agarde itemizes what he describes as the "fower fould hurte that by necligence may bringe wracke to recordes," which requires the record keeper to have "a fourefould diligence and care" about his records. The first three are the banes of all paper records: fire, water, and rodents (specifically "rates, mice, weesels, &c."). But the fourth danger is "misplacing":

> it is an evill that riseth by thofficer that produceth the record for
> the search or service, and it is an enemye to all good ordre, and the
> bringer in of all horror and inconvenience a[m]monge records. For
> if there bee not had regard for ev[er]y record to be placed in its right
> or knowne chest or presse & in its nature, but one thrust into an
> others bagge or misplaced in its Kinges time &c. (as I sayd before,)

it is impossible to find any thinge certaine, yea, and thofficer shall bee discredited when it shall be pleaded against him, *Nul tiel record*.

But while these "fower inconveniences procuring hurt and losse to recordes" are bad enough, Agarde advises, "there followeth yet a last daunger woorse than some of the former, that is even plaine taking of them away." Agarde here pinpoints the two true threats to the Exchequer records: "the first when one Privie Counsellor or moe Justic[e]s or any of the Kinges learned Counsell direct a warrant to thofficers to bringe to them leages books or other records, and then the same must bee left w[i]th them, although thofficers come for them & demaund them never soe oft, yet shall he seldome or never get them out of their handes, as by experience I have found." The other is simple loan, without formal warrant, to those with power: "The second, is the lending of books roles or records, to great officers or others, wherein it appeared to me that sundry have failed, for I have hard many things asked for w[hi]ch have beene sent in [the] Threasaurie. But the[y] that bee officers and doe not respect the preserving of them, may be sayd to have but smalle regard to ther othes." Agarde's tract points us to the materiality of these records as papers and to their vulnerability. But it also highlights the porousness of this archive— theoretically with the power to keep records, but in practice always subject to the commands of the Privy Council and the whims of "great officers."

The Privy Council clerk Robert Beale foregrounded a more specific version of "misplacing" in his 1592 "Treatise of the Office of a Councellor and Principall Secretarie to her Ma[ies]tie":

In the Colleccion of thinges I would wish a distincc[i]on used betweene that w[hi]ch is publicke and that w[hi]ch is private,—that is, a separacion betweene those thinges w[hi]ch are her Ma[ies]ties Recordes and appertaines unto her and those which a Secretarie getteth by his private industrie and charge. Heretofore there was a chamber in Westm[inster] where such thinges, towards the latter end of K[in]g Hen[ry] 8, were kept and were not in the Secretaries private Custodie; but since, that order hath beene neglected and those thinges w[hi]ch weare publicke have bine culled out and gathered into private books, wherby no meanes are left to see what was donne before or to give anie light of service to yonge beginners, which is not well; and therefore I would wish a Secretarie kept such thinges aparte in a chest or place and n[o]t to confound them with his owne.[9]

Without that public/private division, Beale argues, an officer's papers are entirely at risk, as a recent example showed: "the want of so doinge was the cause that upon the death of Mr. Secretarie Walsingham all his papers and bookes both publicke and private weare seazed on and carried away, perhapps by those who would be loath to be used so themselves."[10]

Beale here attempts to maintain what he calls "a distincc[i]on . . . betweene that w[hi]ch is publicke and that w[hi]ch is private." By "publicke" he means papers that are official, related to the state, governmental; by "private," those papers whose content may have derived from public papers, but which were put together by the private industry of the secretary as a private individual. By confusing and confounding the two categories, not only does the private individual run the risk of losing his papers, as the recently deceased Walsingham apparently did; but the public officer runs the risk of denying crucial information to his successor in the post, "to see what was donne before or to give anie light of service to yonge beginners." The passage betrays the awkward situation of the man who works with state papers. Is his work his own, or does it belong to the office he holds? Is there a way of separating out some of it as his own (as Beale evidently hopes)? If so, how is it to be done? And does he leave his work to the record keeper who follows him in the post, or to his familial heir? This last question is, as I shall show, perhaps the biggest unasked question. When Robert Beale mentions Walsingham here, his choice of example is not random: Walsingham was Beale's brother-in-law, as the two men were married to sisters Ursula and Edith St. Barbe. When he died in 1590, Walsingham was survived by Ursula, to whom he gave total power as his executor, "Referringe vnto her in regarde of the truste I repose in her the whole and onlie interpretac[i]on of such doubt[e]s and ambiguities as maye arise in the penninge of the saide will."[11] He did not specify who should inherit his papers, or any part of his papers. And as a result, "all his papers and bookes both publicke and private weare seazed on and carried away."

Bearing Agarde's and Beale's wise words in mind, we can revisit the Jacobean State Paper Office. This period is routinely evoked by historians as the moment when the modern Paper Office emerges in a recognizable form: F. S. Thomas's 1849 *A History of the State Paper Office* is typical in claiming that "It was not . . . until the time of King James the First, that these papers were reduced to the form of a library, having before been kept in chests."[12] In perhaps the best recent account, written for *State Papers Online*, Andrew Thrush similarly affirms that "during the early years of James I's reign the formal archive created in 1578 for the papers belonging to the secretaries of state began to take shape."[13] Hubert Hall's 1908 *Studies in English Official Historical Documents* gives a typical "chronology of the custody of the state papers" under Elizabeth and James:

> 1578–1603.   Traditional establishment of a State Paper Office at
> Whitehall, and appointment of Dr Thomas Wilson and
> Dr James successively as Keepers of the Papers of State.
>
> 1603.   Grant of an Annuity of £50 to Sir Thomas Lake in consideration of his custody of the Papers of State.
>
> 1610.   Grant of the Office of Keeper of the Papers of State to
> Levinus Munck and Thomas Wilson.
>
> 1614.   Further grant of the same office to Thomas Wilson and
> Ambrose Randolph.
>
> 1614–1618.   Construction of a repository for the State Papers at
> Whitehall.
>
> 1619.   Destruction of certain Papers by a fire at Whitehall.
>
> 1619.   Removal of the State Papers to the Whitehall Gateway.
>
> 1629.   Grant of the Office of Keeper to Ambrose Randolph, on the
> death of Sir Thomas Wilson.[14]

As the repeated mentions of his name suggest, the hero of this timeline is the second Thomas Wilson; Hall writes, "To the zeal and energy of Sir Thomas Wilson the permanent establishment and organization of the State Paper Office has been justly ascribed."[15] After an academic career at Cambridge and some diplomatic work abroad, around 1605 Wilson became a private secretary to Robert Cecil, Earl of Salisbury, himself then principal secretary of state.[16] It was Salisbury who procured for Wilson the post of keeper of the records at Whitehall, probably in 1606, with a salary of £30 per annum.[17] In 1616, after a decade in the post, Wilson described to the king his early years, claiming that "I was apointed to peruse, register, abstract, & putt in order, all your Maiesties papers for buisnes of state, w[hi]ch I found in extreame confusion, & haue reduced them into that due order & forme, that yo[u]r Ma[ies]tie and most of the lords haue seene and aproued, wherin I haue spent more then ten painfull yeares."[18] The nature of the extreme confusion is suggested by James's 15 March 1610 patent concerning the preserving and well ordering of papers and records, appointing Levinus Muncke (a clerk of the signet and another Salisbury man) and Thomas Wilson keepers and registrars of these papers. It notes:

> The careful endeavours of Robert Earl of Salisbury, our Principal Secretary and our High Treasurer of England, to reduce all such papers, as well those that heretofore remained in the custody of Sir Thomas Lake, Knight, being the papers of some of the Principal Secretaries of our Predecessors, as also some such papers as he shall think fit to depart with, being either such as he hath collected of his own times, or such as were left to him from his late father the Lord Burleigh, then Lord High Treasurer of England, into a set form or library, in some convenient place within our palace of Whitehall, to be at all times the readier for our use, and for the use of any of our Principal Secretaries hereafter, for the better enabling them to do us service.[19]

Salisbury is presented as having three kinds of papers—the papers once in the custody of Lake, which derive from previous secretaries of state; Salisbury's own collected papers; and some papers he was left by his father, Lord Burghley. Here we see how Burghley differed from Walsingham, or perhaps how he learned from Walsingham's mistake. Lord Burghley indeed bequeathed to his son "my writings concerning the Queenes causes either for hir Revenue or for affayers of Counsell or state, to be advisedly perused by him."[20] When Burghley wrote this, his son was already secretary of state, but the writings do not reach Sir Robert as a result of his office holding, but as a result of a private, familial bequest. In other words, state papers—these are emphatically "writings concerning the Queenes causes either for hir Revenue or for affayers of Counsell or state"—are passed on via his family papers, an odd mingling that bears out Beale's concerns.

Wilson continued to fight to maintain control of the office and to augment its function. When Salisbury died in 1612, Wilson and Muncke swept in to clear his papers. An undated memorial by Wilson, probably from 1614, describes how the Paper Office now contains "2 sort of papers viz. those that haue ben long kept at Whytehale of long tyme by dyuers officers and lastly by sʳ Tho. lake & before him by Dʳ James or other and thos brought from Salisbury howse [Salisbury's waterfront house on the Strand] by my selfe since the late l[ord] Treas[urer]s death," with the Salisbury House papers "farr the greater in number." Wilson records that having "spent 8 yeares in reducing them out of extreame confusio[n] and brought them into order" by binding "the most part vp into books according to ther subiects, heads & years," he must shift to a second mode of organization: "nowe those bookes must be all broken and the papers therin thus deuyded in place must be made up all in one according to ther heads & contryes." These heads are largely "domesticall" and "foreign," but "Irish" occupies its own category—and necessarily so, since the Irish papers are "soe many as noe other countrye hathe so much." In order to do this, Wilson urges that he should have a great room, "to haue them orderly sorted and deuyded into theyr seu[er]al contries years and head[e]s," an immense task that will take "a year or two labourious paynes."[21] Over the following years, new physical space for the Paper Office was indeed located in Whitehall, and this work undertaken.

  In addition to putting in order what he already had, Wilson went in energetic pursuit of additional state papers, not waiting to pounce when he heard a government officer had died or been disgraced. While this may strike us as being in somewhat poor taste, a kind of archival ambulance chasing, Wilson reminded the king in 1617 that this was how the system was meant to work: "This paper is only to putt yo[u]r Ma[ies]ty in mynde that at the death of Secretaries and men imployed for the state, the clerke of your papers for buisnes of that subiect, is bound by oth for the carefull looking to such papers as belong to yo[u]r Ma[ies]ty and to procure them to that office." But the system was not working: "I am only bold to lett you knowe [tha]t in my obseruac[ion] for the tyme I haue serued in cort, the seru[an]ts of secretaries or such men haue embesseled & reserued to ther own vse those things."[22] It is striking that after this appeal, Wilson was demonstrably more successful in seizing papers. Three days after the execution of Sir Walter Ralegh on 29 October 1618, for example, Wilson sent to the king a wish list of Ralegh's remains: "a great MS. book in parchment, near a yard square, containing the descriptions of all countries in the world, and a great sort of excellent sea cards done by hand"; three sea cards of the West Indies, "which he would not have given for 300*l*.," which had instead been delivered to Sir George Calvert; a book in Ralegh's own hand teaching the art of war by sea; and "300 or 400 very fair books of all sorts of learning" that would fit very well into the king's library, plus a thousand books belonging to Ralegh's friend and Tower of London companion Henry Brooke, Lord Cobham, now gravely ill ("who they say now is never likely to make use of them").[23] In January 1622, Wilson provided a list of papers belonging to Sir Edward Coke—then under investigation on charges of failing in his official duties—papers "as are fit to be kept in the Office of His Majesty's Papers and Records for business of State and Council." Two years later, he received papers from Sir Robert Naunton, after he had been suspended from his post as secretary of state; in January 1625 some from George Calvert, who resigned from the same post, and so on. Moreover, on occasions when he felt papers were in the wrong hands, Wilson acted to right that wrong. In 1618, noting that the late Secretary Ralph Winwood had failed to deliver to him some "older papers," Wilson petitioned George Villiers, Earl of Buckingham, to correct the situation.[24] When the following year the collector Ralph Starkey acquired a wealth of papers that had formerly belonged to Elizabeth's secretary of state William Davison, Wilson succeeded in obtaining a warrant (dated 10 August 1619) that authorized him to search Starkey's house and seize the Davison papers; four days later Wilson brought back to the office forty-five parcels of manuscripts in a sack.[25]

There are signs that, despite his energetic endeavors on behalf of the Paper Office, Wilson may have become disillusioned with his mission. Writing to King James in 1616, he asks for an alternative position: "I am not desirous of place, nor preferment, I am content to see yonger men, and of less meritt goe before mee; the highest bound of my ambition is, to doe yo[u]r Ma[ies]tie such acceptable seruice, as yow might take more knowledge of." Part of this disillusionment was undoubtedly financial, "hauing but poore 30^{li} a yeare wages from yo[u]r ma[ies]tie to maintaine my self, and all my seruants that I emploie therin." Wilson repeatedly petitioned to be made master of requests, and, more pitifully, asked the king "to bestowe on mee some smale dyett, of a dish, or two a meale, att Whitehalle wherby I may goe forward in the busines I am in w[hi]ch otherwise I am not able to doe."[26] But some of his anxiety was also about the utility of his project. In his bid to the king to be given other employment, Wilson asked that he "not bee buried amongst dead papers, wherof ther is not soe much vse made, as the treasure therin hidden deserues."[27] Wilson himself attempted to remedy this underuse, by making clear what that hidden treasure involved. In August 1616 he provided Lord Chancellor Ellesmere with a "collection of treaties regulating commercial intercourse with the Netherlands"; on 4 October 1617 he presented to James I a "Rhapsody concerning the marriages of princes' children"; in 1619, he helped George Villiers with collections relating to the history of his latest title (Marquess of Buckingham) and on his hoped-for appointment as earl marshal. Other collections dealt with the military government of Ireland, and a history of the revenues of the chief powers in Europe—all produced by Wilson from the papers in his custody.

Thus far this narrative appears to show Wilson's conduct to be admirable, as he ensures that important papers do not disappear into private collections, but are kept in the Record Office to be of use to the king and his ministers. But matters are not as simple as this. A bill survives, probably from 1613, awarding a grant in reversion of the office of keeper of state papers to one Edward Collingwood, Esq., on the event of the death, surrender, or forfeiture of the office by Muncke and Wilson. The bill is unsigned, and was not completed[28]—and the failure of Collingwood to receive this grant may have lain in Wilson's hands. For in the following year, on 25 July 1614, another grant was made to Wilson and one "Ambrose Randall" "of the office of Keepers of Papers and Records concerning matters of State and Council, for their lives, jointly on the surrender of Levinus Muncke, Esq. and Wilson, with the fee of 3s. 4d. per day."[29] But it turns out that "Ambrose Randall," or Ambrose Randolph, as he is more usually known, had, in the previous May, married Dorothy, the only child and heir of Thomas Wilson.[30] So in 1614 Wilson turned the Paper Office into a family affair.[31]

It is clear from surviving letters from Wilson to Randolph that the marriage and the Paper Office post were part of a complex arrangement between the two men. On 13 March 1613, Wilson wrote from Hertford Castle, asking Randolph

> to make all hast you may for caling y[ou]r mony into your hand,
> for mr leuynus must be payd yett before ester, if you haue [*paper
> torn*] and the other 300[li] must be presently imployed as we have
> agreed. this being done and the rest you are to doe, whatsoeuer is
> to be p[er]formed by me or myne shall be dispached soon after, but
> you must deale with yo[u]r m[*torn*] ernestly that you may haue the
> other 50[*torn*] speedily, for t[ha]t I wold wish you to bestowe it
> vpon a good bargayne nowe to be had neer the land you are to haue
> of me. you may bring with you whe[n] you come the drawght of
> our agrem[en]t w[hi]ch mr Hill hath drawne and soon after you
> and I will retorn to london to p[er]fect all.[32]

This letter witnesses a sequence of deals involving properties, offices, contracts, and, I would suggest, the bestowal of Wilson's daughter (hinted at in "whatsoeuer is to be p[er]formed by me or myne"). Two months later, on 20 May 1613, Randolph married Dorothy Wilson, but it was another year before he received Muncke's post. The delay may have been caused by Muncke's absence on Low Countries business, or the lack of a secretary of state to push for the appointment; Wilson tried to prevail on the unofficial secretary, Robert Carr, Earl of Somerset, to intervene, but it was only after a new secretary of state, Sir Ralph Winwood, was appointed on 29 March 1614 that Wilson's pursuit of the post was successful.[33]

A more worldly Wilson also emerges from his behavior upon the death of Arthur Agarde, who had been deputy keeper of the Exchequer for the past forty-five years. On the day of Agarde's funeral, 24 August 1616, Wilson wrote to Secretary Winwood to inform him that "of late I was entreted by Mr Agarde (who is this day I am accompanying [*sic*] to his burial) to p[er]use certayne of his manuscripts which were the labors of most part of his life." Among these manuscripts, Wilson "found one booke of the exemptions of the kings of England fro[m] the power of the pope and ther proceedings fro[m] tyme to tyme for recouering ther right w[hi]ch that iurisdicc[i]on had vsurped, and diuers other books of abbreviats of treatyes & other business of state." These, he determined, should not be left to Agarde's estate, but "are fit to be brought and kept in the office of his Ma[ie]styes papers." However, Agarde's papers had been claimed by another notable collector: "all w[hi]ch and all other I am told that s[i]r Rob[er]t Cotton makes chaleng vnto and means to sease the[m] into his hands." This situation, Wilson urged Winwood, had to be averted: "I need say noe more you know howe necessary it is that things shall be conserued & kept in good custody by such of his Ma[ies]tyes officers as are sworne to the due conseruatio[n] of the[m], w[hi]ch els may be suppressed whe[n] we may have most need of them." He therefore asked Winwood to consider "whither it be not fit [th]at a warra[n]t be procured fro[m] his Ma[ies]ty to cause those books to be comitted to some vntill they be seen & considered by his Ma[ies]ty to whom he thinks fit to comitt them." In the margin of the letter, he adds a postscript, in an attempt to preempt what he knew would be Cotton's argument: "he will say [th]at ma[ste]r Agarde hath geue[n] the[m] to him by his will but I heare he helped him to make [th]e will."[34]

In this episode, Wilson casts Sir Robert Cotton as his nemesis. Other evidence might suggest the men, with their shared interests in manuscript collecting, were close. Both had been at Cambridge: Wilson at Trinity Hall and Cotton at Jesus.[35] In 1614, the two men negotiated over a house that Wilson was selling, although the outcome is unknown.[36] But Wilson evidently saw Cotton as direct and galling competition. The previous October (1615), it had been alleged that Cotton, "having amassed together, diuers secrets of State, hath co[m]municated them to the Spanish Ambassador, whoe hath caused them to bee copied out, and translated into the Spanish tongue." James ordered that Cotton should be examined by the archbishop of Canterbury and others, but added: "we will and require yow, to seize vpon all his papers, and manuscript[es], in our name, and to our vse, and to cause them to bee brought into our paper Chamber at Whitehall there to be reserved and digested in order by him to whom that charge appertayneth."[37] That "him" would be Thomas Wilson: the king casts him as the legitimate holder of papers that Cotton has illicitly "amassed together."

Agarde's will, however, tells another story. Cotton was indeed involved in the making of the will, as one of three named executors, but Agarde makes a bequest to him: "Item I giue to S[ir] Robert Cotton knighte all myne owne Ligiar bookes and manuscript[es] whome I haue found a moste faithefull and deere frend, and from whome I do acknowledge I haue learned and receyued all my knowledge and Learning in Antiquities. Let hym therfore make choise of all to take what he please and deliuer to hym all his owne Bookes which are as I thincke aboue Twentie manuscript[es] of Antiquitie." While "take what he please" would seem to bear out Wilson's fears, Agarde's "all myne owne Ligiar bookes and manuscript[es]" comes with a rider attached:

> But for [th]e manuscript[es] of myne owne hand collected by me
> out of the King[es] Ma[ies[t[ies] Recordes in the late Abbey of
> Westminster and otherwise Let them be deliuered to my good
> frend M[aste]r Bingley to the end he may shewe them to my Lord
> Treasurer and M[aste]r Chancellor of the excheq[ue]r and their
> honors to giue order for theire preseruation, for they are necessarie
> bothe for the kynges seruice and readynes for the Subiect. And also
> a direction to the Officers that shall succeede me: And I doubt not
> but their honors will contribute somewhat to myne Executor for
> them and my diligence in Collecting.

Among those "manuscript[es] of myne owne hand" listed in the will, is "a booke intituled the Kynges booke of Recordes in opposic[i]on against the Pope and his favourites in England seeking to ympeache the kynges prerogatiue," the very volume that piqued Wilson's fancy.[38] Despite his gratitude to Cotton, Agarde is keen that this book, and several others, should be kept in *his* record office, in order to be of service to "the Officers that shall succeede me." Wilson thus overstates Cotton's claim on Agarde's manuscripts: Agarde had ensured that Cotton would not take certain manuscripts. But equally, he had specified that they should remain in his own office, and not migrate to Wilson's.

In reality, the story of Wilson's perusal of Agarde's manuscripts was a little more macabre than he revealed to Winwood. As Wilson told his son-in-law Randolph in a letter written the same day: "Good sone, I coming to London but yesterday to deale w[i]th m^r Agarde about certayne books & treatyes w[hi]ch I wold have gotten into our office; I found the good mans boddy breathless and this daye I haue accompanied it to the graue." Wilson apparently found Agarde's corpse and took the opportunity to go through his manuscripts. Without pausing, Wilson relays some urgent advice for his son-in-law: "his place"—a postscript clarified "I mean his office of keeping the records not the tallyes"—"is the only place in the kingdome to make an able sufficient man for great seruice it is in the guift of the chamberlayn s[i]r John Poignes I knowe will thinke you as worthy of it as if you will sue for it." But this is not only about Randolph: "it will doe you *and me* more pleasure then any other men for [tha]t therby *we* may make *our own* office perfect and doe the king seruice by it."[39] Wilson plans to place Randolph in Agarde's Exchequer post in order to bolster the influence of his own Paper Office.

But in gaining this post, Wilson wrote, Randolph would have to defeat the man who claimed Agarde's books:

s^r Rob[er]t Cotto[n] will claym he haue one ther [in the Exchequer office] att his deuocio[n] w[hi]ch you may consider howe dangerous it wilbe to the state you knowing what man he is as also howe preiudiciall it wilbe to our office to lett him have command ther who alredy by hauing such things as he hath coningly scraped together doth putt me out of all imploym[en]t by thrusting him-selfe into those things [tha]t belonges to me ^& you^ to doe in his Ma[ies]tys seruice; I pray slake it not but get it by all means possible.[40]

The implication is that Cotton's wielding influence in the Exchequer Office would be very detrimental to Wilson's Paper Office, "putt[ing him] out of all imployme[nt]."

Wilson and Cotton were thus fighting it out, sometimes by proxy, both for papers and for the positions that would allow them to procure papers. To modern historians, Wilson is supposedly a public records man, Cotton a private collector, but in truth they both dealt in state papers and they both desired to leave a dynastic legacy. On 16 April 1622, Sir Henry Bourgchier wrote to James Usher to inform him that "Sir *Robert Cotton* hath purchased a House in *Westminster,* near the *Parliament House,* which he is now repairing, and there means to settle his Library by Feoffment to continue for the use of Posterity."[41] And by "Posterity" Bourgchier means not the future of humanity but Cotton's descendants. In 1629, representatives of the State Paper Office closed up Cotton's library in order to scrutinize its contents and catalog it. While his will, made on 4 May 1631, two days before his death, bequeaths his "manuscript books and antiquities and other collections in my studies, being my labours for forty years," to his son Thomas, stipulating that they remain to his grandson John,[42] that will is merely confirming a 1629 indenture that did indeed enfeoff the library.

Wilson's plans for his own posterity, however, were compromised by his ongoing debt. He had made a promise to his son-in-law Randolph that, in lieu of a marriage portion, he would leave him the lease of the gatehouse of Hertford Castle, which he had acquired in 1615; in 1622, however, he was forced to sell the lease to pay off a debt.[43] Seven years later, Wilson was on the verge of selling off the one asset he had left to leave his son-in-law: the office of keeper of the records itself. But at the eleventh hour, to the undisguised delight of his daughter Dorothy, fate intervened. As she wrote to a friend in a wonderfully callous letter, "My father, to my great joye, made his last actions suitable to his former." Wilson apparently "came so neer it [selling the office] as the man [the buyer] was in the howse with money to paie for it, when at the instant he [Wilson] failed of words and breath, soe nothing was done." Despite her father's timely death, her husband was not yet assured of the office, however, as Dorothy recorded: "my Lord Carlisle [James Hay, Viscount Doncaster] co[m]mended one to the King, which he apointed to posses my father's plase, M[r] Randolph being such a stranger as I think they knew not what right he had to it." Finally, however, they compromised, having been "perswaded to let the man paie for it and be his partner, and reseave half the benefit." Dorothy berated her husband who "might have possesed [the benefit] alone had he not neglected it"; for his part Randolph was "glad ther is one to do the busines for him, that he [the new partner] may live like a drone as he did."[44] The man recommended by Lord Carlisle was William Boswell, a Privy Council clerk who had recently accompanied him on a diplomatic mission to Savoy.[45] One of Boswell's first tasks was to seize and catalog the library of Sir Robert Cotton,[46] and in time he did the same for the libraries of Captain Henry Bell,

Denzil Holles, John Selden, and Sir John Eliot—precisely the kind of aggressive intervention for which Wilson had long campaigned.

It would be wrong to see this narrative as a gradual emergence of an undisputed state monopoly on state papers. To the contrary: the battle of family versus state, private versus public continued. Robert Beale learned from Walsingham's mistakes, and on his death in 1601 left his collection to his only child, a daughter, who married Sir Henry Yelverton; their son inherited Beale's papers, and it became the Yelverton Collection, deposited in the British Museum.[47] Cotton's enfeoffed library did indeed make it to the third generation of the Cotton family, his grandson Sir John Cotton. But by the time Sir John died in 1702, he had ensured that the Cotton library would be bought for the nation by Act of Parliament 12 & 13 William III, c. 7 (1701). Apparently, this was to prevent the library falling into the hands of his "two illiterate grandsons."[48] (In this emergency, it seems, the familial imperative could be overruled.) And so, in time, the family papers of Yelverton and Cotton become part of the British Museum's (later the British Library's) collections, and eventually end up as "state papers online." But not all state papers ended up in a state collection. Wilson may have petitioned Sir Ralph Winwood to aid in his attempts to ascertain the preeminence of the Paper Office, but many of Winwood's own papers followed his family line, moving from his son Richard Winwood to Richard's nephew Ralph Montagu, later first Duke of Montagu, and eventually forming part of the Buccleuch manuscripts (now at Northamptonshire Record Office).[49] And while the imposition on the Paper Office of William Boswell may have seemed like a counterbalance to the dynastic office holding attempted by Wilson and Randolph, in 1640 a grant in reversion was made to set in line the next keeper, Thomas Raymond—who was Boswell's nephew.[50]

The story of the Jacobean Paper Office, Thomas Wilson, his family, and his rivals, is a salutary tale that reminds us that the line that supposedly separates public from private, state from family, is by no means a given, but one that is constantly confused and contested in the period. But, in concluding a narrative that focuses on the place of correspondence, I must say a word about the place of correspondence in mine. As the notes make clear, this story is constructed (a few probate documents aside) from a patchwork of letters. But where are these letters? Where have they been? What might their afterlives tell us? Much is drawn from a series of papers known as the "State Paper Office Documents," now SP 45/20 in the National Archives at Kew. These are letters and memorials relating to the formation of the office, and the story they tell is the one of the hardworking Wilson—which is hardly surprising because those are the records he chose to leave to form the archive of his office. Reading just these documents, we would know nothing of Agarde's corpse, the rivalry with Cotton, or even the fact that Ambrose Randolph was Wilson's son-in-law. SP 45/20 is the version of events that Wilson left for our posterity, alongside the office he left for his posterity. But a final irony lies in the letters I use to unpick that story. One of them, Dorothy Randolph's letter describing her father's death, remains in a family archive. But all the letters from Thomas Wilson to Ambrose Randolph, letters that reveal the maneuvering behind the keepership of the Paper Office, are in SP 14, the "State Papers, Domestic Series," of the reign of James I. They are there, presumably, because they were taken to the record office when their recipient, Ambrose Randolph, took up his post there—and there they remained. These are not "government working papers" of any kind—but these familiar letters may tell us a good deal more about the places occupied by state papers than the official papers left by Wilson ever will.

NOTES

INTRODUCTION

Epigraph. Michel de Montaigne, *Essayes*, trans. John Florio (1603), I.39, p. 126.

1. It is perhaps no surprise that the current perception of the letter as a dying form has generated several recent studies that attest the interest in the historical medium: Shaun Usher, *Letters of Note: Correspondence Deserving a Wider Audience* (Edinburgh: Canongate, 2013), a collection of facsimiles and images of letters by famous letter writers from Leonardo da Vinci to Mick Jagger; Simon Garfield, *To the Letter: A Curious History of Correspondence* (Edinburgh: Canongate, 2014).

2. Pliny the Younger, *Epistularum libri decem*, ed. R. A. B. Mynors (Oxford: Clarendon Press, 1963), 6.16. Author's translation.

3. See the letter to Septicius Clarius that opens the collection, *Epistularum*, 1.1.

4. Ilaria Marchesi, *The Art of Pliny's Letters* (Cambridge: CUP, 2008); Umberto Eco, *The Limits of Interpretation* (Bloomington: Indiana UP, 1991), pp. 123–36. Roger Ascham advocates study of Pliny's letters praising him as "the purest writer, in myne opinion, of all his age." *The Scholemaster* (1570), p. 34. For the influence of Pliny's letter writing in the Renaissance, see Peter Mack, *Elizabethan Rhetoric: Theory and Practice* (Cambridge: CUP, 2004), pp. 25–26, 77.

5. Michael Hunter, "How to Edit a Seventeenth-Century Manuscript: Principles and Practice," *Seventeenth Century*, 10 (1995), 277–310; Hunter, *Editing Early Modern Texts* (Basingstoke: Palgrave, 2006). Cf. Jonathan Gibson, "Significant Space in Manuscript Letters," *Seventeenth Century*, 12/1 (1997), 1–9.

6. *The Correspondence of Sir Philip Sidney*, ed. Roger Kuin (Oxford: OUP, 2012), p. xiv.

7. LPL, MS 653, fol. 293^r: Essex to Anthony Bacon, undated. On Essex's development of epistolary intelligence networks, see Paul Hammer, *The Polarisation of Elizabethan Politics: The Political Career of Robert Devereux, 2nd Earl of Essex, 1585–1597* (Cambridge: CUP, 1999).

8. LPL, MS 652, fol. 115^r: Edward Reynolds to Anthony Bacon, 21 October 1595.

9. Alan Stewart, *Shakespeare's Letters* (Oxford: OUP, 2008), pp. 14, 30.

10. Allan J. Stevenson, "Paper as Bibliographical Evidence," *Library*, 17 (1962), 197–212; Mark Bland, "Italian Paper in Early Seventeenth-Century England," in *Paper as a Medium of Cultural Heritage: Archaeology and Conservation*, ed. R. Graziaplena (Rome: Istituto centrale per la patologia del libro, 2004), pp. 243–55; Heather Wolfe, "'Neatly Sealed with Silk, and Spanish Wax or Otherwise': The Practice of Letter-Locking with Silk Floss in Early Modern England," in *In the Prayse of Writing: Early Modern Manuscript Studies; Essays in Honour of Peter Beal*, ed. S. P. Cerasano and Steven W. May (British Library, 2012), pp. 169–89.

11. Susan Whyman, *The Pen and the People: English Letter Writers, 1660–1800* (Oxford: OUP, 2009), p. 9.

12. For a classic account of epistolarity, see Janet Gurkin Altman, *Epistolarity: Approaches to a Form* (Columbus: Ohio State UP, 1982).

13. Erasmus, *De conscribendis epistolis* (1522), in *Collected Works of Erasmus*, vol. 25, ed. J. K. Sowards (Toronto: U of Toronto P, 1985), pp. 20, 51. For Cicero the letter was "amicorum colloquia absentium" (*Philippics*, II, 7); Seneca, in his letters to Lucillus, claims to write in his letters as he would speak "if you and I were sitting in one another's company or taking walks together" (Qualis sermo meus esset, si una sederemus aut ambularemus, inlaboratus et facilis, tales esse epistolas meas volo, quae nihil habent accersitum nec fictum). Seneca, *Ad Lucilium epistulae morales*, trans. Richard M. Gummere (Heinemann, 1920), vol. II, pp. 136–37, no. 75. On Erasmus's cultivation of letters in *De conscribendis epistolis* and elsewhere as "intimate conversations between friends," see Lisa Jardine, "Reading and the Technology of Textual Affect: Erasmus's Familiar Letters and Shakespeare's *King Lear*," in *Reading Shakespeare Historically* (Routledge, 1996), pp. 78–97 (pp. 78–82).

14. William Fulwood, *The Enemie of Idlenesse* (1568), sig. 3ᵛ; Angel Day, *The English Secretorie* (1586), p. 14.

15. Peter Stallybrass et al., "Hamlet's Tables and the Technologies of Writing in Renaissance England," *Shakespeare Quarterly*, 55/4 (2004), 379–419; Wendy Wall, "Constructing Authorship and the Material Conditions of Writing," in *The Cambridge Companion to English Literature, 1500–1600*, ed. Arthur Kinney (Cambridge: CUP, 1999), pp. 64–89.

16. Jean Robertson, *The Art of Letter Writing: An Essay on the Handbooks Published in England During the Sixteenth and Seventeenth Centuries* (Liverpool: UP of Liverpool, 1942); Katherine Gee Hornbeak, *The Complete Letter Writer in English, 1568–1800* (Northampton, MA: Smith College, 1934). See also Carol Poster and Linda C. Mitchell, eds., *Letter-Writing Manuals and Instruction from Antiquity to the Present: Historical and Bibliographical Studies* (Columbia, SC: U of South Carolina P, 2007); Alan Stewart and Heather Wolfe, *Letterwriting in Renaissance England* (Washington, DC: Folger Shakespeare Library, 2004), pp. 21–33; James Daybell, *The Material Letter in Early Modern England: Manuscript Letters and the Culture and Practices of Letter-Writing, 1512–1635* (Basingstoke: Palgrave Macmillan, 2012), chap. 3.

17. John Browne, *The Marchants Avizo* (1589), sigs. E2ᵛ–I2ʳ.

18. Lawrence D. Green, "Dictamen in England, 1500–1700," in Poster and Mitchell, *Letter-Writing Manuals*, pp. 102–26 (pp. 106, 116, 117).

19. Francis Bacon, "Of Negotiating," in *The Essaies of Sr Francis Bacon Knight, the Kings Solliciter Generall* (Iohn Beale, 1612), p. 194.

20. Such an approach has been pioneered by Christopher Burlinson and Andrew Zurcher in their exemplary edition of *Edmund Spenser: Selected Letters and Other Papers* (Oxford: OUP, 2009).

21. "Correspondence of Constantijn Huygens, 1608–1687," http://resources.huygens.knaw.nl/briefwisselingconstantijnhuygens (accessed 9 September 2014).

22. Christopher Burlinson and Andrew Zurcher, " 'Secretary to the Lord Grey Lord Deputie Here': Edmund Spenser's Irish Papers," *Library*, 6/1 (2005), 30–75.

23. Alan Bray, *The Friend* (Chicago: U of Chicago P, 2003).

24. John Donne, *Poems* (1633), pp. 353–55.

25. Stewart, *Shakespeare's Letters*, p. 5.

26. Stewart, *Shakespeare's Letters*, p. 128.

27. Folger, L.b.539.

28. Andrew Gordon, "*Copycopia*, or the Place of Copied Correspondence in Manuscript Culture: A Case Study," in *Material Readings of Early Modern Culture: Texts and Social Prac-*

tices, 1580–1730, ed. James Daybell and Peter Hinds (Basingstoke: Palgrave Macmillan, 2010), pp. 65–82; Gordon, "Essex's Last Campaign: The Fall of the Earl of Essex and Manuscript Circulation," in *Essex: The Cultural Impact of an Elizabethan Courtier*, ed. Annaliese Connolly and Lisa Hopkins (Manchester: Manchester UP, 2013), pp. 153–78.

29. BL, Add. MS 74286: Hulton MS (1590–1601).

30. Burlinson and Zurcher, "Spenser's Irish Papers," pp. 31, 36, 37, 49, 50; Spenser, *Selected Letters*, pp. xxx, xlviii–lvi.

31. Claudio Guillén, "Notes Toward the Study of the Renaissance Letter," in *Renaissance Genres: Essays on Theory, History, and Interpretation*, ed. Barbara Kiefer Lewalski (Cambridge, MA: Harvard UP, 1986), pp. 70–101, distinguishes at least seven kinds of writing associated with the letter: the neo-Latin prose letter, the vernacular prose letter, the neo-Latin verse epistle, the vernacular verse epistle, the tradition of the theory of the letter, practical manuals for letter writing, and letters inserted within other genres.

32. On recent approaches to Renaissance letters and letter writing, see James Daybell, "Recent Studies in Renaissance Letters: The Seventeenth Century," *ELR*, 36/1 (2006), 135–70; James Daybell, "Recent Studies in Renaissance Letters: The Sixteenth Century," *ELR*, 35/2 (2005), 331–62; James Daybell and Andrew Gordon, "Select Bibliography: The Manuscript Letter in Early Modern England," *Lives and Letters*, 4/1 (Autumn 2012), http://journal.xmera.org /volume-4-no-1-autumn-2012/articles/bibliography.pdf.

33. Roger Chartier, "*Secrétaires* for the People? Model Letters of the Ancien Régime: Between Court Literature and Popular Chapbooks," in *Correspondence: Models of Letter-Writing from the Middle Ages to the Nineteenth Century*, by Roger Chartier, Alain Boureau, and Cécile Daupin, trans. Christopher Woodall (Cambridge: Polity Press, 1997), pp. 59–111.

34. Graham Williams, *Women's Epistolary Utterance: A Study of the Letters of Joan and Maria Thynne, 1575–1611* (Amsterdam: John Benjamins, 2013); Melanie Evans, *The Language of Queen Elizabeth I: A Sociolinguistic Perspective on Royal Style and Identity*, Transactions of the Philological Society Monograph Series 45 (Oxford: Wiley-Blackwell, 2013).

35. David M. Bergeron, *King James and Letters of Homoerotic Desire* (Iowa City: U of Iowa P, 1999); Alan Bray, "Homosexuality and the Signs of Male Friendship in Elizabethan England," *History Workshop Journal*, 29 (1990), 1–19.

36. See also Toon Van Houdt et al., eds., *Self-Presentation and Social Identification: The Rhetoric and Pragmatics of Letter Writing in Early Modern Times* (Leuven: Leuven UP, 2002).

37. Marie Boas Hall, "The Royal Society's Role in the Diffusion of Information in the Seventeenth Century," *Notes and Records of the Royal Society of London*, 29 (1975), 173–92; Maarten Ultee, "The Republic of Letters: Learned Correspondence, 1680–1720," *Seventeenth Century*, 2 (1987), 95–112. On newsletters, see Richard Cust, "News and Politics in Early Seventeenth-Century England," *P&P*, 112 (1986), 60–90; F. J. Levy, "How Information Spread Among the Gentry, 1550–1640," *JBS*, 21/2 (1982), 11–34; Ian Atherton, "The Itch Grown a Disease: Manuscript Transmission of News in the Seventeenth Century," in *News, Newspapers, and Society in Early Modern Britain*, ed. Joad Raymond (Frank Cass, 1999), pp. 39–65.

38. James Daybell, *Women Letter-Writers in Tudor England* (Oxford: OUP, 2006); Daybell, ed., *Early Modern Women's Letter Writing* (Basingstoke: Palgrave, 2001); Jane Couchman and Ann Crabb, eds., *Women's Letters Across Europe, 1400–1700: Form and Persuasion* (Aldershot: Ashgate, 2005); James Daybell, "Select Bibliography: Women's Medieval and Early Modern Letters," Women's Early Modern Letters Online, http://blogs.plymouth.ac.uk/wemlo/resources/wemlo -bibliography/ (accessed 3 September 2014).

39. On material approaches to letters, see Daybell, *Material Letter*; Daybell, "Material Meanings and the Social Signs of Manuscript Letters in Early Modern England," *Literature Compass*, 6 (2009), 1–21; Stewart, *Shakespeare's Letters*, chap. 1; A. R. Braunmuller, "Accounting for Absence: The Transcription of Space," in *New Ways of Looking at Old Texts*, ed. W. Speed Hill (Binghamton, NY: Medieval and Renaissance Texts and Studies, 1993), pp. 47–56; Gibson, "Significant Space"; Sara Jayne Steen, "Reading Beyond the Words: Material Letters and the Process of Interpretation," *Quidditas*, 22 (2001), 55–69.

40. Harold Love, *Scribal Publication in Seventeenth-Century England* (Oxford: Clarendon Press, 1993); H. R. Woudhuysen, *Sir Philip Sidney and the Circulation of Manuscripts, 1558–1640* (Oxford: Clarendon Press, 1996); Arthur F. Marotti, *Manuscript, Print and the English Renaissance Lyric* (Ithaca, NY: Cornell UP, 1995); Peter Beal, "'Hoping They Shall Only Come to Your Merciful Eyes': Sidney's *Letter to Queen Elizabeth* and Its Transmission," in *In Praise of Scribes: Manuscripts and Their Makers in Seventeenth-Century England* (Oxford: OUP, 1998), pp. 109–46, 274–80; Andrew Gordon, "'A Fortune of Paper Walls': The Letters of Francis Bacon and the Earl of Essex," *ELR*, 37/3 (2007), 319–36; Gordon, "*Copycopia*, or the Place of Copied Correspondence in Manuscript Culture"; James Daybell "Women, Politics and Domesticity: The Scribal Publication of Lady Rich's Letter to Elizabeth I," in *Women and Writing, c.1340–c.1650: The Domestication of Print Culture*, ed. Anne Lawrence-Mathers and Phillipa Hardman (Woodbridge: York Medieval Press, an imprint of Boydell and Brewer, 2010), pp. 111–30.

41. Hunter, "How to Edit," p. 281; A. R. Braunmuller, "Editing Elizabethan Letters," *Text*, 1 (1981), 185–99. For recent editions that have sought to represent in print the material aspects of early modern letters, see *The Collected Works of Mary Sidney Herbert, Countess of Pembroke*, ed. Margaret P. Hannay, Noel J. Kinnamon, and Michael G. Brennan, 2 vols. (Oxford: OUP, 1998); *Elizabeth Cary, Lady Falkland: Life and Letters*, ed. Heather Wolfe (Tempe: Arizona Center for Medieval and Renaissance Studies: and Cambridge: Renaissance Texts from Manuscripts, 2001); A. R. Braunmuller, ed., *A Seventeenth-Century Letter-Book: A Facsimile Edition of Folger MS. V.a.321* (Newark: U of Delaware P, 1983); Spenser, *Selected Letters*; Nadine Akkerman, ed., *The Correspondence of Elizabeth Stuart, Queen of Bohemia*, 3 vols. (Oxford: OUP, 2011–), I and II.

42. Early Modern Letters Online, http://emlo.bodleian.ox.ac.uk/ (accessed 6 September 2014).

43. Folger LUNA Collections, http://luna.folger.edu/luna/servlet/FOLGERCM1-6-6; Folger Finding Aid Database, http://findingaids.folger.edu/; Huntington Digital Library, http://hdl.huntington.org/cdm/; Beinecke Digital Collections, http://beinecke.library.yale.edu/tags/digital-collections; all accessed 8 September 2014.

44. The downside of course is that many of these resources sit behind expensive paywalls, which limits accessibility.

45. Most notably at the Centre for Editing Lives and Letters directed by Lisa Jardine and Alan Stewart, which hosts a series of editing projects (including the correspondence of William Herle, Thomas Bodley, and Francis Bacon), http://www.livesandletters.ac.uk/projects; and Alison Wiggins's majestic Correspondence of Bess of Hardwick Project, Alison Wiggins, Alan Bryson, Daniel Starza Smith, Anke Timmermann, and Graham Williams, University of Glasgow, eds., *Bess of Hardwick's Letters: The Complete Correspondence, c.1550–1608*, web development by Katherine Rogers, University of Sheffield Humanities Research Institute (April 2013), http://www.bessofhardwick.org.

46. "Cultures of Knowledge," http://www.culturesofknowledge.org/; "Electronic Enlightenment," http://www.e-enlightenment.com/; "Mapping the Republic of Letters," http://republicofletters.stanford.edu/ (accessed 6 September 2014).

47. E. A. Wrigley et al., *English Population History from Family Reconstitution, 1580–1837* (Cambridge: CUP, 2005).

CHAPTER 1. FROM PALATINO TO CRESCI

1. This script style should not be confused with English "chancery hand," a "set" legal hand, which, originating during the reign of Henry VI, only finally ceased to be used in an official capacity in 1836. See Hilary Jenkinson, *The Later Court Hands in England from the Fifteenth to the Seventeenth Century* (Cambridge: CUP, 1927), pp. 68–71. Legal hands, claimed by the poet and writing master John Davies of Hereford to be as challenging as "Egyptian Hieroglyphicks" to most of his contemporaries (*The Writing Schoolemaster* [1631], sig. B2ᵛ), are not discussed in this essay.

2. Three books conveniently survey the field: A. S. Osley, *Luminario: An Introduction to the Italian Writing-Books of the Sixteenth and Seventeenth Centuries* (Nieuwkoop: Miland, 1972); A. S. Osley, *Scribes and Sources: Handbook of the Chancery Hand in the Sixteenth Century* (Faber and Faber, 1980); Stanley Morison, *Early Italian Writing-Books: Renaissance to Baroque*, ed. Nicolas Barker (Boston: Godine, 1990). See also Emanuele Casamassima, *Trattati di scrittura del Cinquecento italiano* (Milan: Il Polifilo, 1966); James Wardrop, *The Script of Humanism: Some Aspects of Humanistic Script, 1460–1560* (Oxford: Clarendon Press, 1963), pp. 36–49; A. F. Johnson, "A Catalogue of Italian Writing-Books of the Sixteenth Century," *Signature*, n.s., 10 (1950), 22–48. I am particularly indebted to Osley's lucid, generously illustrated works of synthesis.

3. Though Jenkinson (*Later Court Hands*) does map the model court hands of English writing manuals onto handwriting in the manuscript "common paper" of the Scrivener's Company.

4. Casamassima, *Trattati*, p. 38; Jonathan Goldberg, *Writing Matter: From the Hands of the English Renaissance* (Stanford, CA: Stanford UP, 1990), pp. 321–22; Peter Holliday, *Edward Johnston, Master Calligrapher* (British Library, 2007). As Holliday makes clear, the advocacy of italic was essentially a repudiation of Cresci's innovations (pp. 13–16). The blurring of description and prescription is particularly obvious in Fairbank's scholarly, popular, and influential italic/roman-focused surveys of the history of handwriting (e.g., *A Book of Scripts*, new ed. [Faber and Faber, 1977]), which scarcely mention widely used cursive "gothic" handwriting such as secretary hand.

5. The "Palatinian"/"Crescian" distinction outlined in this essay will be apparent in any substantial collection of early modern English letters.

6. For a short list of copies of continental writing manuals known to have been owned by early modern English people, see H. R. Woudhuysen, *Sir Philip Sidney and the Circulation of Manuscripts, 1558–1640* (Oxford: OUP, 1996), p. 32. For Edward VI's ownership of a copy of Palatino's book, see T. A. Birrell, *English Monarchs and Their Books: From Henry VII to Charles II* (British Library, 1987), p. 14; for women's use of English writing books, which, influenced by continental models, began to appear in the later sixteenth century, see Heather Wolfe, "Women's Handwriting," in *The Cambridge Companion to Early Modern Women's Writing*, ed. Laura Lunger Knoppers (Cambridge: CUP, 2010), pp. 21–39 (p. 24).

7. B. L. Ullman, *The Origin and Development of Humanistic Script* (Rome: Edizioni di storia e letteratura, 1960); A. C. de la Mare, *The Handwriting of Italian Humanists*, vol. 1, fasc. 1 (Oxford: OUP, 1973). Humanists referred to humanistic script as *littera anticha*, or "the old writing" (Wardrop, *Script*, p. 4). Arnold Pannartz and Konrad Sweynheym of Subiaco, the first printers in Italy, were also the first to use a typeface approaching a roman style, ca. 1465. The first italic type was cut in 1501 by Francesco Griffo for Aldus Manutius in Venice.

8. Sigismondo Fanti, *Theorica et pratica perspicacissimi Sigismundi de Fantis . . . de modo scribendi fabricandi omnes litteram species* (Venice, 1514); Ludovico degli Arrighi da Vicenza, *La operina di Ludovico Vicentino da imparare di scrivere littera cancellarescha* (Rome, 1522); Giovantantonio Tagliente, *Lo presente libro insegna la vera arte delo excellente scrivere* (Venice, 1524); Oscar Ogg, ed., *Three Classics of Italian Calligraphy: An Unabridged Reissue of the Writing Books of Arrighi, Tagliente, Palatino* (New York: Dover, 1953) (facsimiles of a 1522 copy of Arrighi's manual and of a 1530 copy of Tagliente's); *The First Writing Book: An English Translation & Facsimile Text of Arrighi's Operina*, ed. John Howard Benson (OUP, 1955). Other translations of Arrighi's concise primer, which is still very popular with calligraphers, can be found online. Tagliente and Arrighi seem to have been racing to produce the first illustrated writing book. Osley argues that Tagliente's book actually appeared first and that the dates given for Arrighi's *La operina* and its sequel on writing materials, *Il modo de temperare le penne* (Venice, 1524), are misleading (Osley, *Luminario*, pp. 35–39; see also Morison, *Early Italian Writing-Books*, pp. 156–63). Arrighi was born at Vicenza and is therefore sometimes referred to as "Vicentinus" or "Vicentino." For introductions to all three writers, see Casamassima, *Trattati*, pp. 37–49; Osley, *Luminario*, pp. 5–39; Osley, *Scribes*, pp. 47–80; Morison, *Early Italian Writing-Books*, pp. 44–69.

9. Accordingly, "Chancery cursive dominated Cinquecento correspondence and record keeping outside the merchant's ledger" (Paul F. Grendler, *Schooling in Renaissance Italy: Literacy and Learning, 1300–1600* [Baltimore: Johns Hopkins UP, 1989], p. 327). Cf. Brian Richardson, *Manuscript Culture in Renaissance Italy* (Cambridge: CUP, 2009), pp. 59–61. Italian merchants used a gothic hand, *mercantesca*, with similarities to English secretary hand.

10. Humanistic hands were also used for some literary texts. Although the poet Petrus Carmelianus, Henry VIII's Latin secretary, was long thought to have been the first person to have used humanistic cursive in England, earlier examples have been found in the register of Oxford University; see Alfred Fairbank and Berthold Wolpe, *Renaissance Handwriting: An Anthology of Italic Scripts* (Faber and Faber, 1960), p. 30. For Cambridge, see Alfred Fairbank and Bruce Dickins, *The Italic Hand in Tudor Cambridge* (Bowes and Bowes, 1962).

11. Cf. A. S. Osley, "Canons of Renaissance Handwriting," *Visible Language*, 13 (1979), 70–94 (pp. 80–81).

12. Ogg, *Three Classics*, p. 7 (Arrighi, sig. A3ʳ); Osley, *Scribes*, p. 75.

13. Osley, *Scribes*, p. 73.

14. Morison, *Early Italian Writing-Books*, p. 70. For Palatino, see James Wardrop, "Civis Romanus Sum: Giovanbattista Palatino and His Circle," *Signature*, n.s., 14 (1952), 3–39; Osley, *Luminario*, pp. 49–56; Osley, *Scribes*, pp. 82–96; Morison, *Early Italian Writing-Books*, pp. 70–79. One of the most intriguing of Palatino's manuscripts, BL, Add. MS 25454, contains love poetry addressed to an unnamed man.

15. Giovambattista Palatino, *Libro nuovo d'imparare a scrivere tutte sorte lettere antiche et moderne di tutte nationi, con nuove regole misure et essempe . . .* (Rome, 1540). My references to Palatino's Italian cite the facsimile of the 1561 edition reproduced in Ogg, *Three Classics*. Most of Palatino's text is translated in Osley, *Scribes*, pp. 87–96.

16. Ogg, *Three Classics*, pp. 132–34 (Palatino, sigs. A5^v–A6^r); Osley, *Scribes*, p. 87.

17. Ogg, *Three Classics*, p. 136 (Palatino, sig. A7^v); Osley, *Scribes*, p. 87.

18. Ogg, *Three Classics*, p. 105; Osley, *Scribes*, p. 61.

19. Ogg, *Three Classics*, p. 142 (Palatino, sig. B2^v).

20. Wardrop, "Civis," p. 20.

21. Osley, "Canons," p. 81; see Ogg, *Three Classics*, p. 149 (Palatino, sig. B6^r).

22. Ogg, *Three Classics*, p. 243 (Palatino, sig. H5^r); Osley, *Scribes*, pp. 94–95.

23. Palatino's *cancellaresca formata* is still slower, featuring less of a slope, fewer joins, and shorter, serifed ascenders and descenders (Ogg, *Three Classics*, pp. 169–71 [Palatino, sigs. C8^r–D1^r]).

24. Osley, *Luminario*, pp. 58–62, 85–86; Osley, *Scribes*, pp. 98–111, 126–47, 160–70. Amphiareo's letters are also wider than Palatino's; Augustino da Siena supplemented Palatino's three straight lines with a curved downstroke; Lucas's *bastarda*, constructed from six stroke types (including three curves), had a major influence both on later Spanish calligraphy and on the twentieth-century English italic revival.

25. Wardrop, *Script*, p. 46.

26. See note 6, above.

27. Jonathan Gibson, "The Queen's Two Hands," in *Representations of Elizabeth I in Early Modern Culture*, ed. Alessandra Petrina and Laura Tosi (Basingstoke: Palgrave Macmillan, 2011), pp. 47–65.

28. Osley, "Canons," pp. 86–87.

29. W. W. Greg et al., *English Literary Autographs, 1550–1650* (Oxford: OUP, 1932), vol. 3, no. xci (Elizabeth); Fairbank and Wolpe, *Renaissance Handwriting*, nos. 25 (Edward), 28 (Elizabeth), 32 (Fitzpatrick) and 33 (Grey); Francis Pryor, *Elizabeth I: Her Life in Letters* (British Library, 2003), nos. 3, 4 (Elizabeth). For more on Elizabeth's hands, see the important chapter by H. R. Woudhuysen, "The Queen's Own Hand: A Preliminary Account," in *Elizabeth I and the Culture of Writing*, ed. Peter Beal and Grace Ioppolo (British Library, 2007), pp. 1–27.

30. Fairbank and Wolpe, *Renaissance Handwriting*, no. 46; Fairbank and Dickins, *Italic Hand*, no. 13.

31. Grace Ioppolo, "Early Modern Handwriting," in *A New Companion to English Renaissance Literature and Culture*, ed. Michael Hattaway, 2 vols. (Chichester: Wiley-Blackwell, 2010), I, pp. 177–89 (pp. 178–79); Wolfe, "Women's Handwriting," pp. 21–39.

32. Goldberg himself expresses similar reservations (*Writing Matter*, p. 10).

33. A distinction should be made between men who aspired to work as secretaries—for whom an ability to write formal script was desirable—and such people's employers, for whom the skill was not to be flaunted.

34. Or, to use early modern terms, "set," "fast," and "facile" variations (Martin Billingsley, *The Pens Excellencie, or the Secretaries Delight* [1618], sig. C3^v).

35. For discussion and examples of all three of these script types, see Anthony G. Petti, *English Literary Hands from Chaucer to Dryden* (Arnold, 1977); Giles Dawson and Laetitia Kennedy-Skipton, *Elizabethan Handwriting, 1500–1650: A Guide to the Reading of Documents and Manuscripts* (Faber and Faber, 1968); Jean F. Preston and Laetitia Yeandle, *English Handwriting, 1400–1650: An Introductory Manual* (Asheville, NC: Pegasus Press, 1999). See also Harold Love, *Scribal Publication in Seventeenth-Century England* (Oxford: Clarendon Press, 1993), pp. 108–16; Ioppolo, "Early Modern Handwriting." Jenkinson, *Later Court Hands*, analyzes different varieties of secretary hand in both printed English writing books and in manuscripts (pp. 57–62), dealing with mixed hands more summarily (pp. 65–67).

36. An attitude that has been linked to the illegibility of doctors' handwriting, the motivation for which, it has been claimed, is "to show that [doctors] are no mere copyists" and that they know "that others will be prepared to make an effort" (Richard Dury, "Handwriting and the Linguistic Study of Letters," in *Studies in Late Modern English Correspondence: Methodology and Data*, ed. Marina Dossena and Ingrid Tieken-Boon van Ostade [Bern: Lang, 2008], pp. 113–35 [p. 116]). See also James Daybell, *The Material Letter in Early Modern England: Manuscript Letters and the Culture and Practices of Letter-Writing, 1512–1635* (Basingstoke: Palgrave Macmillan, 2012), p. 89.

37. Cf. Daybell, *Material Letter*, pp. 86–87.

38. Two examples from the Elizabethan court are the distinct hands of the very close friends Fulke Greville and Philip Sidney: Greville's, an "eccentric, mixed secretary and italic hand"; Sidney's, a "loose and flowing" italic (Woudhuysen, *Sir Philip Sidney*, pp. 214, 213).

39. Cf. James Daybell, *Women Letter-Writers in Tudor England* (Oxford: OUP, 2006), pp. 50–51; Daybell, *Material Letter*, pp. 87–88.

40. Christopher Burlinson and Andrew Zurcher, " 'Secretary to the Lord Grey Lord Deputie Here': Edmund Spenser's Irish Papers," *Library*, 6/1 (2005), 30–75.

41. Such as John Dee (e.g., Greg et al., *English Literary Autographs*, vol. 3, no. cii; Pryor, *Elizabeth I*, no. 44).

42. Thomas Nashe, *Haue with You to Saffron-Walden; or, Gabriell Harueys Hunt is vp* (1596), sig. I4ᵛ. Nashe calls it "a faire capitall Romane hand" (for the meaning of "Romane" here, see the discussion at note 64 below).

43. Ioppolo, "Early Modern Handwriting," p. 178.

44. Susan Frye, "Materializing Authorship in Esther Inglis's Books," *Journal of Medieval and Early Modern Studies*, 32 (2002), 469–91 (479).

45. Daybell, *Women Letter-Writers*, p. 39; cf. Daybell, *Material Letter*, pp. 58–63. Examples include the Palatinian letter of the eleven-year-old second Earl of Essex to his new guardian, Lord Burghley, that is reproduced and discussed in Roy Davids, "The Handwriting of Robert Devereux, Second Earl of Essex," *Book Collector*, 37 (1988), 351–65 (pp. 351–54).

46. Ioppolo, "Early Modern Handwriting," pp. 178–79.

47. E.g., Pryor, *Elizabeth I*, nos. 18 (Mary, Queen of Scots), 33 (Mary's formal Palatinian hand), 28 (Bess of Hardwick); Alison Wiggins, Alan Bryson, Daniel Starza Smith, Anke Timmermann, and Graham Williams, University of Glasgow, eds., *Bess of Hardwick's Letters: The Complete Correspondence, c.1550–1608*, web development by Katherine Rogers, University of Sheffield Humanities Research Institute (April 2013), http://www.bessofhardwick.org; Preston and Yeandle, *English Handwriting*, no. 19 (Cavendish).

48. Though some women wrote secretary hand, and many could read it (Daybell, *Women Letter-Writers*, p. 68; Ioppolo, "Early Modern Handwriting").

49. For an analysis of this hand, see Burlinson and Zurcher, "Spenser's Irish Papers," pp. 34–35.

50. Davids, "Handwriting," 351–54 (the early hand), 360–63 (the later hand); Pryor, *Elizabeth I*, no. 47 (1591).

51. See Gibson, "Queen's Two Hands," pp. 58–60; for examples, see Pryor, *Elizabeth I*, nos. 14 (with some similarities to her Palatinian italic), 25, 29; Preston and Yeandle, *English Handwriting*, no. 21.

52. Petti, *English Literary Hands*, no. 32. Unlike me, Petti finds the *d*'s similar.

53. A phenomenon related to Jacques Derrida's "iterability," chewed over in Goldberg, *Writing Matter*, pp. 236–38. I use the word "significance" (cognate with Latin *signum*, or "seal")

advisedly. For an introduction to the use of seals in early modern correspondence, see Daybell, *Material Letter*, pp. 105–8.

54. For other features of signatures, including their capacity for private significance, see Daybell, *Material Letter*, pp. 95–97. In this essay I do not discuss the other differences in hand (and scribe) that frequently occur between different sections of the same letter (for example, the salutation at the top of the letter, the main body of the letter, the subscription [the equivalent of "yours sincerely"], the "direction" [the name and address of the addressee that appears on the outside of a folded letter], the postscript, and so on): for this topic, see Daybell, *Women Letter-Writers*, p. 54; a case history is provided by Burlinson and Zurcher, "Spenser's Irish Papers."

55. Giovan Francesco Cresci, *Essemplare di piu sorti lettere* (Venice, 1560); I cite the facsimile of the 1578 edition printed in Cresci, *Essemplare di piu sorti lettere*, ed. and trans. A. S. Osley (Nattali & Maurice, 1968). James Mosley, "Giovan Francesco Cresci and the Baroque Letter in Rome," *Typography Papers*, 6 (2005), 115–54, prints important newly discovered material and critiques the choice of the 1578 edition for Osley's reprint. The first modern publication to highlight Cresci's importance was James Wardrop, "The Vatican Scriptors: Documents for Ruano and Cresci," *Signature*, n.s., 5 (1948), 3–28. See also Osley, *Luminario*, pp. 69–83; Osley, *Scribes*, pp. 112–25 (including partial translations); Casamassima, *Trattati*, pp. 61–74; Morison, *Early Italian Writing-Books*, pp. 96–111.

56. Cresci, *Essemplare*, pp. 30–31. He also says he holds his pen at less of an angle than his predecessors.

57. Cresci, *Essemplare*, p. 37.

58. As Osley points out, "There was a functional reason for this: it ensured that, when the pen had been lifted from the paper and moved up above the line of writing, the risk of its not depositing ink to start the letter could be avoided" (*Luminario*, p. 74).

59. Without mentioning Cresci, however: Petti, for example, records that "the most popular formal italic of the later 16th century is a fairly large rounded version of *cancellaresca* with curved and clubbed heads on the ascenders and therefore known as *testeggiata (headed)*" (*English Literary Hands*, p. 19). John Davies of Hereford calls these features "bells" or "bolts" (*Writing Schoolemaster*, sig. A2^r).

60. Osley, *Luminario*, pp. 76–78; Osley, *Scribes*, p. 116.

61. A. S. Osley, *Scalzini on Handwriting: An Essay from Marcello Scalzini's Writing-Book of 1578 "Il Secretario," Translated from the Italian* (Wormley: Glade Press, 1971); Osley, *Luminario*, pp. 93–98; Osley, *Scribes*, pp. 243–79. Cresci's reply oddly appeared two years *before* Scalzini's book.

62. Osley, *Luminario*, pp. 99–157; Morison, *Early Italian Writing-Books*, pp. 112–29. It is tempting to link the looseness of Cresci's cancellaresca to a change in the method of reproducing handwriting in printed books that occurred at about the time he was writing, the shift from relief printing (woodcut) to intaglio engraving (copperplate). Whereas a woodcut requires a craftsperson painstakingly to cut around letters drawn on a block of wood, copperplate engraving is a much freer process, involving the use of a burin to cut into wax: the artisan's actions are much more akin to those of a scribe, and therefore more likely to produce a fluid script. In his dispute with Scalzini, however, Cresci, whose books are illustrated with woodcuts, attacked intaglio reproduction, claiming it made the engraver a rival of the writing master (Osley, *Scalzini*).

63. John de Beau Chesne and John Baildon, *A Booke Containing Divers Sortes of Hands (London, 1602)* (Amsterdam: Johnson, 1977), "Italique hande" (Palatinian; sig. D1^r), "Italiq

letter" (Crescian; sig. D8ʳ). For a discussion of the English writing masters, see Woudhuysen, *Sir Philip Sidney*, pp. 29–45.

64. Thus, for example, Martin Billingsley's distinction between "Roman" and "Italian" hands (Billingsley, *Pens*, sig. C4ʳ) is reflected in the difference between plates 18–20 in his book, Crescian *cancelleresca formatella* that Billingsley clearly understands to be "Roman," and plates 21–24, more cursive (and thus "Italian") varieties of Crescian italic. The "Roman" samples are not "roman" in the strict sense as they slant and contain a single-bodied *a*. The misidentification of the more formal varieties of italic as "Roman" is understandable, as they were certainly stiffer and more upright than Crescian cursive. The script that Wolfe identifies as the usual early modern hand for English women, "a script that combined features of both Roman and Italic" ("Women's Handwriting," p. 21), I would rather identify as Palatinian or Crescian formal italic.

65. William Shakespeare, *Twelfth Night, or What You Will*, ed. Keir Elam (London: Arden Shakespeare, 2008), 3.4.27.

66. E.g., CP 46/59 and 75/53; BL, Harl. MS 5001, fol. 357ʳ. Gorges's scribes used a similar hand in his formal petitions (e.g., CP, Petitions 119). All of the letters by Gorges to use scribal italic postdate 1590, and thus use Crescian forms. The scribe who put together Gorges's poetry manuscript, BL, Eg. MS 3165, in about 1580, however, worked in a Palatinian italic: for reproductions of this hand, see *The Poems of Sir Arthur Gorges*, ed. Helen Estabrook Sandison (Oxford: Clarendon Press, 1953), plate facing p. xlviii, figures *a* and *b*.

67. E.g., CP 117/74, 251/45; Bodl., Ashmole MS 1729, fol. 177ʳ. For a reproduction of this hand in a different context, see *Poems of Sir Arthur Gorges*, plate facing p. 124.

68. E.g., CP 32/83, 35/97, 49/102.

69. Respectively, Fairbank and Wolpe, *Renaissance Handwriting,* no. 51 (1581); and Dawson and Kennedy-Skipton, *Elizabethan Handwriting*, no. 34 (1615).

70. *The Poems of Lady Mary Wroth*, ed. Josephine A. Roberts (Baton Rouge: Louisiana State UP, 1983), pp. 77–79 (formal), 80–81 (informal); for descriptions, see pp. 61–62.

71. Greg et al., *English Literary Autographs*, vol. 3, no. lxxxi.

72. R. H. Miller, "Sir John Harington's Manuscripts in Italic," *Studies in Bibliography*, 40 (1987), 101–5.

73. Davies, *Writing Schoolemaster*, sig. B2ᵛ.

74. Greg et al., *English Literary Autographs*, vol. 3, no. lxxiv (Ralegh; for rougher mixed and secretary hands, see no. lxxv); Alan Stewart and Heather Wolfe, *Letterwriting in Renaissance England* (Washington, DC: Folger Shakespeare Library, 2004), no. 56 (Donne).

75. It has been argued that Cresci's italic derives from Italian "mixed" notarial hands; see Julian Brown, "Recent Palaeographical Studies," *Library*, 5th ser., 31 (1976), 150–57 (156). The Franciscan writing master Vespasiano Amphiareo had anticipated Cresci by combining, in 1548, italic and "mercantile" forms in a single, if unfluid, model hand ("the Friar's bastard"); see Osley, *Luminario*, p. 62 (illustrated on p. 59); Osley, *Scribes*, p. 100.

76. Stewart and Wolfe, *Letterwriting*, nos. 19 (Bagot), 47 (Skipwith).

77. Dury, "Handwriting," p. 122; Osley says of Crescian clubbing, "once this technique became established, it led naturally to the looped letters of the copperplate hand" (*Luminario*, p. 76 n.1). While D. C. Greetham views the hegemony of copperplate, coeval with the development of the British Empire, as the "disciplined construction of a national style to bring a state-sponsored order and hierarchy back from the potential chaos of the profligate and idiosyncratic mixing of styles in the early Renaissance" ("Parallel Texts," *Text* 9 [1996], 408–29 [420]), Susan Whyman stresses its "revolutionary" and "levelling" effect (*The Pen and the People: English Letter Writers, 1660–1800* [Oxford: OUP, 2009], p. 27).

78. David Norbrook, "Memoirs and Oblivion: Lucy Hutchinson and the Restoration," *HLQ*, 75 (2012), 233–82.

79. For examples and methodology, see Daybell, *Material Letter*; Stewart and Wolfe, *Letterwriting*.

80. Jerome J. McGann, *The Textual Condition* (Princeton, NJ: Princeton UP, 1991). McGann's "bibliographical code" comprises "textual materials which are not regularly studied by those interested in 'poetry'"—"typefaces, bindings, book prices, page format, and all those textual phenomena usually regarded as (at best) peripheral to 'poetry' or 'the text as such'" (p. 13)—which nevertheless contribute to meaning. Although McGann is only interested in the bibliographical codes of literary texts, the concept is clearly also applicable to "nonliterary" genres such as sent letters.

CHAPTER 2. CONVEYING CORRESPONDENCE

1. Alan Stewart and Heather Wolfe, *Letterwriting in Renaissance England* (Washington, DC: Folger Shakespeare Library, 2004), pp. 121–23; James Daybell, *The Material Letter in Early Modern England: Manuscript Letters and the Culture and Practices of Letter-Writing, 1512–1635* (Basingstoke: Palgrave Macmillan, 2012), chap. 5, "Postal Conditions," pp. 109–47.

2. Post Office (Revenues) Act, 1710, 9 Anne, c. 11, II.

3. Thomas Todd, *William Dockwra and the Rest of the Undertakers: The Story of the London Penny Post, 1680–1682* (Edinburgh: C. J. Cousland, 1952), pp. 10–16, 22–30, 45–49.

4. York City Archives, Chamberlains' Accounts, CB3, 1535, fol. 132.

5. Canterbury City Archives, Account Books of the City Chamberlain or Cofferer, CC F/A/14, 1549–50, fol. 156, and CC F/A/18, 1577–87, fol. 118. Foot posts dispatched with letters to London in 1579 and 1580 received 3s. 4d.

6. City of Coventry Archives, Borough Accounts, BA/A/A/26/2, fol. 328.

7. *Devon Household Accounts, 1627–59*, part II, *Henry, Fifth Earl of Bath, and Rachel, Countess of Bath, 1637–1655*, ed. Todd Gray (Exeter: Devon and Cornwall Record Society, 1996), pp. 51, 52, 65, 77, 88, 95, 279.

8. Significant new work on the letter-carrying services provided by posts within a county has been carried out by Ian Cooper in his doctoral thesis research, "Networks, News and Communication: Political Elites and Community Relations in Elizabethan Devon, 1588–1603" (Ph.D. thesis, Plymouth University, 2012). See also Ian Cooper, "The Speed and Efficiency of the Tudor South-West's Royal Post-Stage Service," *History*, 99/338 (2014), 754–74.

9. Richard Carew, *The Survey of Cornwall; and An Epistle Concerning the Excellencies of the English Tongue*, new ed. (1769), pp. 85–86.

10. Cornwall Record Office (CRO), Truro, M484/1–3: Will and inventory of John May, 9 March 1627/28.

11. LPL, Carew MS 607, p. 76, [23 December] 1580; MS 618, p. 58, 1 October 1591; MS 612, p. 60, 6 July 1596; MS 621, p. 141, 11 July 1599; MS 615, p. 74, 23 June 1600; MS 615, p. 219, 26 January 1601; MS 624, p. 141, 13 May 1602.

12. LPL, Carew MS 624, p. 195, 7 August 1602; MS 624, p. 197, 18 August 1602.

13. Federigo Melis, *Intensità e regolarità nella difusione dell'informazione economica generale nel Mediterraneo e in Occidente alla fine del Medioevo*, Quaderni di Storia Postale, 2 (Prato, Italy: Istituto di Studi Storici Postali, 1983), pp. 11–60.

14. Luciana Frangioni, *Organizzazione e costi del servizio postale alla fine del Trecento*, Quaderni di Storia Postale, 3 (Prato, Italy: Istituto di Studi Storici Postali, 1983), pp. 4, 7–20; Mark Brayshay, "Post-Haste by Post-Horse," *History Today*, 42 (September 1992), 35–41 (pp. 37–38).

15. On the treaty, known as the Intercursus Magnus, see J. A. J. Housden, "The Merchant Strangers' Post in the Sixteenth Century," *EHR*, 21 (1906), 739–42 (p. 739); "House of Lords: Report from the Select Committee on the Post Office," *Parliamentary Papers*, 1844 sess., XIV (HMSO, 1844), appendix, pp. 30–31.

16. *Calendar of State Papers, Domestic Series (CSPD), 1547–1580, Edward, Mary and Elizabeth*, vol. 47, ed. Robert Lemon (HMSO, 1856), pp. 312–13, 316 (articles 21, 22, 24, 31, 32, 65).

17. *Extracts from the Records of the Merchant Adventurers of Newcastle-Upon-Tyne*, vol. II, ed. F. W. Dendy, Publications of the Surtees Society, no. 101 (Durham, 1899), p. xxi.

18. *The York Mercers and Merchant Adventurers, 1356–1917*, ed. Maud Sellers, Publications of the Surtees Society, no. 129 (Durham, 1918), pp. 160, 180, 183.

19. *York Mercers and Merchant Adventurers*, pp. 215–16, 224, 243, 254–55, 258.

20. Proclamation, Greenwich, 26 April 1591. *By the Queene. Whereas heretofore sundry wayes haue bene deuised to redresse the disorders among the postes of our realme* ([1591]). See also BL, Lansd. MS 78, fol. 93 (draft).

21. TNA, SP 14/50, fol. 45.

22. Useful sources on common carriers include J. Crofts, *Packhorse, Waggon and Post: Land Carriage and Communications Under the Tudors and Stuarts* (Routledge and Kegan Paul, 1967), pp. 22–41; Philip Beale, *England's Mail: Two Millennia of Letter Writing* (Stroud: Tempus, 2005), pp. 126–37; Dorian Gerhold, "Packhorses and Wheeled Vehicles in England, 1550–1800," *Journal of Transport History*, 3rd ser., 14 (1993), 1–27; Gerhold, *Carriers and Coachmasters: Trade and Travel Before the Turnpikes* (Chichester: Phillimore, 2005), pp. 19–30.

23. TNA, AO 3/868.

24. Canterbury City Archives, Account Books of the City Chamberlain or Cofferer, CC F/A/18, 1577–87, fol. 141ᵛ.

25. Plymouth and West Devon Record Office, Borough Account Book, 1569–1658, 1/133, fols. 57, 68, 142; Devon Record Office (DRO), Exeter, ECA Exeter Receivers' Accounts, 7/8 James I, 1609–10, fol. 5.

26. CRO, L345/1–3: Will and inventory of William Lane, carrier of Bodmin, 29 March 1632.

27. Hobson's death in 1631 prompted the publication of numerous short epitaphs as well as some lengthier eulogies; see verses "on Hobson the carrier" in George Herbert and William Marshall, *Witts Recreations Selected from the Finest Fancies of Moderne Muses* (Humphry Blunden, 1640), sigs. Aa3ʳ, 9–12; Cc1ʳ⁻ᵛ, 96.

28. Andrew Clark, ed., *Register of the University of Oxford*, vol. II (1571–1622), part 1 (Oxford: Clarendon Press, 1887), p. 316.

29. Eric Pawson, *Transport and Economy: The Turnpike Roads of Eighteenth Century Britain* (Academic Press, 1977), p. 43.

30. *Devon Household Accounts*, II, p. 141.

31. Mary C. Hill, *The King's Messengers, 1199–1377: A Contribution to the History of the Royal Household* (Arnold, 1961), pp. 8, 17, 22, 142.

32. *A Collection of Ordinances and Regulations for the Government of the Royal Household Made in Divers Reigns from King Edward III to King William and Queen Mary* (Society of Antiquaries, 1790), pp. 168–70.

33. TNA, E 351/541, fol. 128^{r-v}; TNA, AO 1/387/38, fol. 28^v. See also Frederick C. Dietz, *English Public Finance, 1558–1641* (Frank Cass, 1964), pp. 407–9.

34. *Collection of Ordinances*, p. 351.

35. TNA, LC 3/1 Lord Chamberlain's Books, fols. 5, 5^v, 36.

36. V. Wheeler-Holohan, *The History of the King's Messengers* (Grayson & Grayson, 1935), pp. 5, 10–11.

37. Wheeler-Holohan, *History of the King's Messengers*, pp. 241–49; 251; TNA, SP 46/3, 7, fols. 7–8.

38. TNA, SP 12/157, fol. 80: Petition of the posts for Flanders to Thomas Randolph (1582).

39. These were prized possessions; see TNA, PROB 11/71: 17 August 1587, Will of Roger Iveson, a messenger for the Duchy of Lancaster, stipulated that his "livery coate" and "boxe" were to go to William Lyon, but his "scuchene" was to remain with his wife. See also TNA, SP 12/125, fol. 61: August 1578 Supplication of Lawrence Dutton and Raffe Walton, Messengers of the Household.

40. Some may be found in TNA, E 407/38.

41. TNA, SP 78/24, fol. 300: Ottywell Smith to Lord Burghley, 30 June 1591.

42. TNA, SP 78/31, fol. 13: Ottywell Smith to Burghley, 7 May 1593.

43. J. W. M. Stone, *The Inland Posts, 1392–1672: A Calendar of Historical Documents, with Appendices* (Christie's-Robson Lowe, 1987), p. 2.

44. *The King's Book of Payments*, in *Letters and Papers, Foreign and Domestic, of the Reign of Henry VIII*, ed. J. S. Brewer et al., 21 vols. and addenda (HMSO, 1862–1932), II, pp. 1444, 1451–53.

45. *King's Book of Payments*, pp. 1458, 1460.

46. E. W. Puttkamer, *The Princes of Thurn and Taxis* (Chicago: Literary Club, 1938), pp. 21–23; Martin Dallmeier, "Il casato principeso dei Thurn und Taxis e le poste in Europa, 1490–1806," trans. Gaetana Gervasoni, in *Le Poste de Tasso, un impresa in Europa* (Bergamo, Italy: Published in association with the exhibition "I Tasso, l'Evoluzione delle Poste," 1984), pp. 1–85.

47. Beale, *England's Mail*, p. 144.

48. *The Lisle Letters*, ed. Muriel St. Clare Byrne (Chicago: University of Chicago Press, 1981), III, p. 628.

49. TNA, SP 12/78, fol. 128^r.

50. TNA, SP 12/78, fol. 128^{r-v}.

51. *Lisle Letters*, III, p. 431.

52. Stone, *The Inland Posts, 1392–1672*, p. 7.

53. TNA, E 164/50.

54. TNA, E 101/427/17, fols. 1–13. See also TNA, AO 3/868: "The monethlie chardges of the Postes."

55. TNA, AO 3/868. The rate was 20d. per stage for each packet of letters.

56. For example, Gascoigne was paid £10 14s. to lay posts for the 1564 progress to Cambridge (TNA, E 351/541 fol. 58).

57. TNA, SP 12/41, fol. 71.

58. TNA, SP 11/14, fol. 11; BL, Lansd. MS 78/92: "Ordynaunces deuised by the Kynge and Quenes Maiestie for the order of the Postes and Hackeneymen betwene London and the bordere of Scotland."

59. TNA, APC, 5, p. 315, 29 July 1556.

60. TNA, SP 12/96, fols. 109^r–110^v: May 1574.

61. BL, Lansd. MS 78, fols. 224^r–227^v, 1590; SP 14/73, fol. 45^{v-r}; CP 141/36, January 1590; *Orders for the Posts of our Realmes . . .* (1603).

62. TNA, SP 12/167, fol. 64: January 1584.

63. Mark Brayshay, *Land Travel and Communications in Tudor and Stuart England: Achieving a Joined-up Realm* (Liverpool: Liverpool University Press, 2014), pp. 284–88.

64. TNA, SP 52/17, fol. 23, 1570; SP 12/154, fol. 71, 1582; SP 12/157, fol. 28, 1582 or 1583; SP 12/158, fol. 56, 1583; SP 12/163, fol. 76, 1583; SP 12/170, fol. 7, 1584.

65. TNA, AO 1/1950/1–6 and E 351/2731–2736. In fact, accounts until 1 September 1637 survive (AO 1953/28 and E 351/2757). For a discussion of this evidence, see Brayshay, *Land Travel and Communications*, pp. 289, 298, 301–6.

66. George Walker, *Haste, Post, Haste! Postmen and Post-Roads Through the Ages* (George G. Harrap, 1938), p. 89.

67. William Taylor, "The King's Mails, 1603–1625," *Scottish Historical Review*, 42 (1963), 143–44. See TNA, AO 1/1951/12, April 1602–March 1605; AO 1/1951/13, April 1605–March 1607. See also Brayshay, *Land Travel and Communications*, pp. 293, 295, 298–302.

68. *CSPD, 1629–1631, Charles I*, vol. 161, ed. John Bruce (HMSO, 1860), pp. 199–200: February 1630; DRO, Ancient Letters H.H. 5, 329: 21 November 1629/30.

69. TNA, SP 15/42/34, fols. 60^r–64^v.

70. TNA, AO 1/1953/27–28.

71. R. T. Pritchard, "The History of the Post Road in Anglesey," *Transactions of the Anglesey Antiquarian Society and Field Club* (1954), 18–33 (p. 22).

72. "An Ordinance touching the Office of Postage of Letters, Inland and Foreign," in *Acts and Ordinances of the Interregnum, 1642–1660,* ed. C. H. Firth and R. S. Rait (HMSO, 1911), pp. 1007–111.

73. Nadine Akkerman, "The Postmistress, the Diplomat, and a Black Chamber? Alexadrine of Taxis, Sir Balthazar Gerbier and the Power of Postal Control," in *Diplomacy and Early Modern Culture*, ed. Robyn Adams and Rosanna Cox (Basingstoke: Palgrave Macmillan, 2011), pp. 172–88.

74. Edward Turner, "The Secrecy of the Post," *EHR*, 33 (1918), 131, 320–27.

75. British Postal Museum and Archive: The Royal Mail Archive, London, Post Office Archives, POST 114/1: 17 September 1657, Post Office: Acts and Warrants; see also Firth and Rait, *Acts and Ordinances*, pp. 1110–13.

76. 12 Chas. II, c. 35; "Charles II, 1660: An Act for Erecting and Establishing a Post Office," in *Statutes of the Realm: Volume 5, 1628–80*, ed. John Raithby (HMSO, 1819), pp. 297–301.

CHAPTER 3. ENIGMATIC CULTURES OF CRYPTOLOGY

This research has been made possible by a RUBICON grant from the Netherlands Organisation for Scientific Research (NWO).

When date of birth/death cannot be ascertained to a single year, I follow *ODNB* convention and indicate alternate years in the format 1603/4 and 1603x6 to indicate a greater range of years.

1. Nadine Akkerman, ed., *The Correspondence of Elizabeth Stuart, Queen of Bohemia*, 3 vols. (Oxford: OUP, 2011–), II (2011), "Appendix: Cipher Keys" (pp. 1055–76).

2. Sabrina A. Baron, "The Guises of Dissemination in Early Seventeenth-Century England: News in Manuscript and Print," in *The Politics of Information in Early Modern Eu-*

rope, ed. Brendan Dooley and Sabrina Baron (New York: Routledge, 2001), pp. 41–56 (p. 48). James Daybell suggests that secret writing was practiced throughout 1512 to 1635, the period under scrutiny in his study; see Daybell, *The Material Letter in Early Modern England: Manuscript Letters and the Culture and Practices of Letter-Writing, 1512–1635* (Basingstoke: Palgrave Macmillan, 2012), p. 149.

3. Ian Arthurson, "Espionage and Intelligence from the Wars of the Roses to the Reformation," *Nottingham Medieval Studies*, 35 (1991), 134–54 (p. 134).

4. Maurice Keens-Soper, "Wicquefort," in *Diplomatic Theory from Machiavelli to Kissinger*, ed. G. R. Berridge, Maurice Keens-Soper, and T. G. Otto (New York: Palgrave, 2001), pp. 88–105 (p. 97).

5. Arthurson, "Espionage and Intelligence," p. 142.

6. John Guy, *My Heart Is My Own: The Life of Mary Queen of Scots* (Harper Perennial, 2004), p. 82.

7. Nicholas Faunt, "Discourse touchinge the Office of principall Secretarie of Estate" (ca. 1592), in Bodl., Tanner MS 80, fols. 91–94. I cite the printed version in Charles Hughes, "Nicholas Faunt's Discourse Touching the Office of Principal Secretary of Estate, &c. 1592," *EHR*, 20/79 (1905), 499–508 (p. 502).

8. Robert Beale, "Instructions for a Principall Secretarie obserued by R: B for Sr Edwarde Wotton," in BL, Add. MS 48149, fols. 3^v–9^v. I cite the printed version: "A Treatise of the Office of a Councellor and Principall Secretarie to her Ma[jes]tie," in Conyers Read, *Mr. Secretary Walsingham and the Policy of Queen Elizabeth* (Oxford: Clarendon Press, 1925), I, pp. 423–43 (p. 428).

9. The keys are to be found in six bound manuscript volumes: TNA, SP 106, vols. 1–6.

10. David Kahn, *The Codebreakers: The Comprehensive History of Secret Communication from Ancient Times to the Internet*, rev. ed. (New York: Scribner, 1996), pp. 120–23. For Mary Phelippes, see James Daybell, "Gender, Politics and Diplomacy: Women, News and Intelligence Networks in Elizabethan England," in *Diplomacy and Early Modern Culture*, ed. Robyn Adams and Rosanna Cox (Basingstoke: Palgrave Macmillan, 2011), pp. 101–19 (p. 101, and esp. n. 5); and Daybell, *Material Letter*, p. 164. Similarly, Sir Anthony Desmarches was also assisted by his wife in deciphering correspondence for the royalists in 1658/59; see Doreen Cripps, *Elizabeth of the Sealed Knot: A Biography of Elizabeth Murray, Countess of Dysart* (Kineton: Roundwood Press, 1975), p. 55.

11. For Porta, see Kahn, *The Codebreakers*, pp. 137–43.

12. Lines 25–29 of Epigram 92, in *The Cambridge Edition of the Works of Ben Jonson*, ed. David Bevington, Martin Butler, and Ian Donaldson (Cambridge: CUP, 2012), V, pp. 158–59 (p. 159).

13. Margaret Ferguson, "The Authorial Ciphers of Aphra Behn," in *The Cambridge Companion to English Literature, 1650–1740*, ed. Steven N. Zwicker (Cambridge: CUP, 1998), pp. 225–49 (p. 227). Edith Snook, *Women, Reading, and the Cultural Politics of Early Modern England* (Aldershot: Ashgate, 2005), chap. 5, " 'Onely a Cipher': Reading and Writing Secrets in Lady Mary Wroth's *The Countess of Montgomery's Urania*," pp. 145–66 (pp. 153–54).

14. See Akkerman, *Correspondence of Elizabeth Stuart*, II, pp. 1056, 1059–62.

15. See the glossary of terms that precedes Kahn's comprehensive history of cryptology, in *The Codebreakers*, pp. xv–xviii (pp. xv–xvi). My explanation of cryptology used by Elizabeth's circle is heavily indebted to Kahn's glossary.

16. See Akkerman, *Correspondence of Elizabeth Stuart*, II, letter nos. 23 and 30.

17. See Akkerman, *Correspondence of Elizabeth Stuart*, II, pp. 1057–59.

18. Gerhard F. Strasser, "The Noblest Cryptologist: Duke August the Younger of Brunswick-Luneburg (Gustavus Selenus) and His Cryptological Activities," *Cryptologia*, 7/3 (1983), 193–217. Elizabeth also corresponded with philosopher, statesman, and cryptology expert Sir Francis Bacon (1561–1626); see Akkerman, *Correspondence of Elizabeth Stuart*, I (2015). As such, she might also have been familiar with Bacon's so-called "bi-literal cipher," which can only be detected by use of a magnifying glass. For this cipher see Alan Stewart, "Francis Bacon's Bi-literal Cipher and the Materiality of Early Modern Diplomatic Writing," in Adams and Cox, *Diplomacy and Early Modern Culture*, pp. 120–37.

19. Nadine Akkerman, "Cupido en de Eerste Koningin in Den Haag: Constantijn Huygens en Elizabeth Stuart," *De Zeventiende Eeuw*, 25/2 (2009), 73–96. Reprinted in the exhibition catalog *Vrouwen rondom Constantijn Huygens*, ed. Els Kloek, Frans Blom, and Ad Leerintveld (Hilversum: Verloren, 2010), pp. 76–96.

20. Karl de Leeuw and J. A. Bergstra, *The History of Information Security: A Comprehensive Handbook* (Amsterdam: Elsevier, 2007), p. 336.

21. A. G. H. Bachrach, *Sir Constantine Huygens and Britain: A Pattern of Cultural Exchange* (Leiden: Sir Thomas Browne Institute, 1962), pp. 9–10.

22. Constantijn Huygens's Latin autobiography *De vita propria: Sermonum inter liberos*, translated into Dutch as *Mijn leven verteld aan mijn kinderen in twee boeken*, ed. Frans R. E. Blom, 2 vols. (Amsterdam: Prometheus/Bert Bakker, 2003), I, pp. 136–37. Author's translation.

23. See, for instance, Akkerman, *Correspondence of Elizabeth Stuart*, II, letter no. 170.

24. S. Groenveld, "'Chijffre pour la communication avec Mr. Jermijn, de l'année 1647': Geheimschriftsleutels als bron voor netwerkreconstructies rond Prins Willem II," in *Jaarboek Oranje-Nassau, 2009–2010*, ed. C. R. van den Berg, et al. (Rotterdam: Barjesteh van Waalwijk van Doorn, 2010), pp. 55–78.

25. For a more detailed description of Elizabeth's cipher and code system, see Akkerman, *Correspondence of Elizabeth Stuart*, II, pp. 1055–56.

26. Nadine Akkerman, "The Postmistress, the Diplomat, and a Black Chamber? Alexandrine of Taxis, Sir Balthazar Gerbier and the Power of Postal Control," in Adams and Cox, *Diplomacy and Early Modern Culture*, pp. 172–88.

27. TNA, SP 12/256, fol. 186: P. Proby to Sir Robert Cecil.

28. Compare, for instance, letter no. 1966 to no. 4290 of Grotius's correspondence. The seventeen printed volumes of Grotius's *Briefwisseling* (1928–2001) were digitized by the Huygens Institute in 2009: *The Correspondence of Hugo Grotius*, http://www.grotius.huygens.knaw.nl.

29. Hannah J. Crawforth, "Court Hieroglyphics: The Idea of the Cipher in Ben Jonson's Masques," in Adams and Cox, *Diplomacy and Early Modern Culture*, pp. 138–54 (p. 144).

30. Key reconstructed from TNA, SP 29/167, fol. 209. The letter is also printed in W. J. Cameron, *New Light on Aphra Behn* (Auckland: Wakefield Press, 1961), as document no. 2. Cameron produced an immaculate diplomatic transcription of Behn's espial correspondence with various individuals. However, in respect to the words in code or cipher he regrettably abandons his diplomatic transcription policy for convenience's sake. Instead of, for instance, "he is so extreamly watch[ed] by 38. [Arlington decodes 38 as Bampfield]," Cameron renders the numbers immediately in italic plain text: "he is so extreamly watch by BAMPFIELD." In Cameron's edition the reader can no longer see which code system Behn employed or when she replaced one key with another. The social context of her spy network is thereby erased since it becomes impossible to see whether other spies employed the same system.

31. Akkerman, *Correspondence of Elizabeth Stuart*, I, letter nos. 301, 340, and 374. Roe often notes the Julian (Old Style) as well as the Gregorian (New Style) date for Elizabeth's convenience; 12 July and 22 July were in fact the same day, the calendar simply depending on where one found oneself.

32. Snook, *Women, Reading, and the Cultural Politics*, p. 155.

33. Akkerman, *Correspondence of Elizabeth Stuart*, I, letter no. 388.

34. Akkerman, *Correspondence of Elizabeth Stuart*, I, letter no. 324.

35. Harold Love, *Scribal Publication in Seventeenth-Century England* (Oxford: Clarendon, 1993), p. 177.

36. See for instance Kevin Sharpe, *Reading Revolutions: The Politics of Reading in Early Modern England* (New Haven, CT: Yale UP, 2000). For communal readings of manuscripts, see Daybell, "'I wold wyshe my doings myght be . . . secret': Privacy and the Social Practices of Reading Women's Letters in Sixteenth-Century England," in *Women's Letters Across Europe, 1400–1700: Form and Persuasion*, ed. Jane Couchman and Ann Crabb (Burlington, VT: Ashgate, 2005), pp. 143–61.

37. TNA, SP 14/163, fols. 72–73 (fol. 73ʳ): Carleton to Carleton, 15 April 1624, presumably Old Style.

38. Akkerman, *Correspondence of Elizabeth Stuart*, II, letter no. 328.

39. Julie C. Hayes, "Writing to the Divine Marquis: Epistolary Strategies of Madame de Sade and Milli Rousset," in *Writing the Female Voice*, ed. Elizabeth C. Goldsmith (Boston: Northeastern UP, 1989), pp. 203–18 (p. 207).

40. *The Queen's Maiesties Gracious Answer to the Lord Digbies Letter* (Printed at London: for Tho. Powell and averred by I. B. Cler., [1642]; Wing [2nd ed.] / H1458; Thomason Tracts / E.138[8]), sig. A1ᵛ.

41. Lucy Hay (née Percy), Lady Carlisle, for instance, communicated with her husband in cipher when he resided as a diplomat in France, as well as with her sister Dorothy, Countess of Leicester. See *The Correspondence (c. 1626–1659) of Dorothy Percy Sidney, Countess of Leicester*, ed. Michael G. Brennan, Noel J. Kinnamon, and Margaret P. Hannay (Farnham: Ashgate, 2010). For earlier examples, see James Daybell, "Secret Letters in Elizabethan England," in *Material Readings of Early Modern Culture: Texts and Social Practices, 1580–1730*, ed. Daybell and Peter Hinds (Basingstoke: Palgrave Macmillan, 2010), pp. 47–64 (pp. 53–54).

42. Ever since the sixteenth century, encryption and decryption had also been practiced by women, further strengthening my argument that cryptology spilled over from the domain of the diplomat in courtly circles. See also Elizabeth Mazzola, "The Renaissance Englishwoman in Code: 'Blabbs' and Cryptographers at Elizabeth I's Court," *Critical Survey*, 22/3 (2010), 1–20. Mazzola goes as far as suggesting cryptography was an art particularly suitable to the feminine, connecting it "to other early modern writing technologies like needlework, allegory, graffiti, and the masque, activities for which many women had great skill and made enormous investments of time and interests" (p. 10).

43. Lois Potter, *Secret Rites and Secret Writing: Royalist Literature, 1641–1660* (Cambridge: CUP, 1989), p. 39.

44. *Mercurius Aulicus* (Oxford: Printed by Henry Hall for William Webb; Thomason Tracts / 13:E.74[10], 42nd week, 21 October 1643), p. 598.

45. *Mercurius Aulicus* (42nd week, 21 October 1643), p. 598.

46. Kahn, *The Codebreakers*, glossary of terms, p. xv.

47. Akkerman, *Correspondence of Elizabeth Stuart*, II, letter no. 620.

48. Kahn, *The Codebreakers*, glossary of terms, p. xv.

49. Jacqueline Eales, "Patriarchy, Puritanism and Politics: The Letters of Lady Brilliana Harley (1589–1643)," in *Early Modern Women's Letter Writing, 1450–1700*, ed. James Daybell (Basingstoke: Palgrave, 2001), pp. 143–58 (p. 148).

50. Eales, "Patriarchy, Puritanism and Politics," p. 148. Four cutout letters were fully printed in a nineteenth-century edition by Thomas Taylor Lewis, *Letters of the Lady Brilliana Harley*, Camden Society Publications, no. 58 (Printed for the Camden Society, 1854), nos. 188 (pp. 191–92), 189 (pp. 192–94), 192 (pp. 196–97), and 195 (pp. 199–200). It seems that Lewis could not have made the transcriptions without the sheet, but it has not been recovered among Harley's papers in the British Library. The technique was invented by the Italian physician, astrologer, mathematician, and gambler Girolamo Cardano (1501–76); see Daybell, *Material Letter*, p. 164.

51. I am grateful to Karen Britland for sharing her unpublished article with me in 2012. It has since appeared as "Reading Between the Lines: Royalist Letters and Encryption in the English Civil Wars," in "Missing Texts," ed. Adam Smyth, special edition, *Critical Quarterly* 55/4 (2013), pp. 15–26.

52. John Donne, "A Valediction Forbidding Mourning," in *Complete English Poems*, ed. C. A. Patrides (Dent, 1994), line 19.

53. In his study *Sentences: The Memoirs and Letters of Italian Political Prisoners from Benvenuto Cellini to Aldo Moro* (Toronto: U of Toronto P, 1999), Charles Klopp mentions several imprisoned writers who wrote with brick dust and their own urine.

54. BL, Add. MS 31022, fol. 68.

55. According to the calendar in the *Second Report of the Royal Commission on Historical Manuscripts* (HMSO, 1871), appendix, p. 83, these secretive letters in invisible ink are among the private manuscripts of the Cotterel–Dormer family.

56. Abraham Cowley, lines 31–42 of his "Written in Juice of Lemmon," in *The Collected Works of Abraham Cowley, 1618–1667*, ed. Thomas O. Calhoun, Laurence Heyworth, and J. Robert King, 2 vols. (Newark: U of Delaware P, 1989–1999), II, pp. 28–29 (p. 29). Line 37 "seely" should be glossed as "harmless."

57. Ann Geneva, *Astrology and the Seventeenth Century Mind: William Lilly and the Language of the Stars* (Manchester: Manchester UP, 1995), chap. 2, "'Aenigmaes, Metaphors, Parabols, and Figures': Seventeenth Century Encrypting," pp. 17–55 (p. 18).

58. Lewis, *Letters of the Lady Brilliana Harley*, no. 189 (p. 194).

59. Lewis, *Letters of the Lady Brilliana Harley*, no. 192 (p. 197).

60. René van Stripiaan, *Leugens en vermaak: Boccaccio's novellen in de kluchtcultuur van de Nederlandse renaissance* (Amsterdam: Amsterdam UP, 1996), pp. 21–27.

61. Theresa M. Kelley, *Reinventing Allegory* (Cambridge: CUP, 1997), p. 44. More generally, see also Potter, *Secret Rites*.

62. Marsha S. Collins, *The Soledades: Góngora's Masque of the Imagination* (Columbia: U of Missouri P, 2002), pp. 15–17, 41, 46–48, 133–34, 140, 142, 154, and 225n.

63. See also Elisa Oh, "'[T]he art to desifer the true Caracter of Constancy': Female Silence in Wroth's *Urania*," *Early Modern Women: An Interdisciplinary Journal*, 5 (2010), 45–75 (pp. 47 and 50).

64. Marcy L. North, *The Anonymous Renaissance: Cultures of Discretion in Tudor-Stuart England* (Chicago: U of Chicago P, 2003), pp. 164–65.

65. Cecile M. Jagodzinski, *Privacy and Print: Reading and Writing in Seventeenth-Century England* (Charlottesville: UP of Virginia, 1999), p. 86.

66. *Collected Works of Abraham Cowley*, II, p. 243.

67. Jagodzinski, *Privacy and Print*, p. 86.

68. See also Daybell, " 'I wold wyshe,' " pp. 153–54.

CHAPTER 4. MATERIAL FICTIONS

For comments on earlier versions of this essay I am grateful to James Daybell, Adam Smyth, Alan Stewart, and Adelyn Wilson, as well as to audiences in Aberdeen, London, Montreal, and Plymouth.

1. Philip Sidney, *Astrophel and Stella*, in *The Major Works*, ed. Katherine Duncan-Jones (Oxford: OUP, 1989), Sonnet 3, lines 12–14.

2. Peter Bales, *The Writing Schoolemaster* (1590), sig. R2^v. On the formative effects of Bales's method, see Jonathan Goldberg, *Writing Matter: From the Hands of the English Renaissance* (Stanford: Stanford UP, 1990), pp. 111–69.

3. On *copia*, see Terence Cave, *The Cornucopian Text: Problems of Writing in the French Renaissance* (Oxford: Clarendon Press, 1979), pp. 3–34.

4. As Wendy Wall has argued, the marked interest in the materiality of manuscript circulation in sonnet sequences was reinforced with the translation of the sonnet craze into print in the 1590s. Wall, *The Imprint of Gender: Authorship and Publication in the English Renaissance* (Ithaca, NY: Cornell UP, 1993), pp. 23–110. On the complication of the act of writing in Sidney, see also Andrew Strycharski, "Literacy, Education, and Affect in *Astrophil and Stella*," *Studies in English Literature, 1500–1900*, 48/1 (2008), 45–63.

5. Anon., "Canzon 18," *Zepheria* (1594), sig. D1^v.

6. Margaret Christian, "*Zepheria* (1594; STC 26124): A Critical Edition," *Studies in Philology*, 100/2 (2003), 177–243 (pp. 177–90). On manuscript circulation at the Inns of Court, see Arthur Marotti, *Manuscript, Print and the English Renaissance Lyric* (Ithaca, NY: Cornell UP, 1995), pp. 35–37.

7. *Syr P. S. His Astrophel and Stella* (Thomas Newman, 1591), sig. A2^v.

8. Henry Woudhuysen, *Sir Philip Sidney and the Circulation of Manuscripts, 1558–1640* (Oxford: OUP, 1996), p. 210; Peter Beal, "Philip Sidney's *Letter to Queen Elizabeth* and That 'False Knave' Alexander Dicsone," *EMS*, 11 (2002), 1–51.

9. Andrew Gordon, "*Copycopia*, or the Place of Copied Correspondence in Manuscript Culture: A Case Study," in *Material Readings of Early Modern Culture, 1580–1730: Texts and Social Practices*, ed. James Daybell and Peter Hinds (Basingstoke: Palgrave Macmillan, 2010), pp. 65–82.

10. Anthony Grafton, *Forgers and Critics: Creativity and Duplicity in Western Scholarship* (Princeton, NJ: Princeton UP, 1990), p. 50.

11. Alfred Hiatt, *The Making of Medieval Forgeries: False Documents in Fifteenth-Century England* (British Library, 2004), pp. 1–3. On medieval forgeries, see also L. C. Hector, *Palaeography and Forgery* (St. Anthony's Press, 1959).

12. Jean Baudrillard, *Simulations*, trans. Paul Foss, Paul Patton, and Philip Beitchman (New York: Semiotext[e], 1983), p. 83.

13. 33 Hen. VIII, c. 1.

14. 5 Eliz., c. 14.

15. Andrew Gordon, *Writing Early Modern London: Memory, Text and Community* (Basingstoke: Palgrave Macmillan, 2013), pp. 119–32, 177–82.

16. John Cowell, *The Interpreter* (Cambridge: John Legate, 1607), sig. Gg4ʳ.

17. *Sallowaie v. Walle* (1602), in John Hawarde, *Les Reportes del Cases in Camera Stellata, 1593 to 1609: From the Original MS. of John Hawarde*, ed. William Paley Baildon (privately printed, 1894), pp. 155–56.

18. *Selby v. Wallis & Shute* (1593–94), TNA, STAC 5/S1/4: Deposition of Robert Wallis.

19. *Selby v. Wallis & Shute* (1593–94), TNA STAC 5/S1/4: Deposition of Robert Wallis.

20. Lorna Hutson, *The Invention of Suspicion: Law and Mimesis in Shakespeare and Renaissance Drama* (Oxford: OUP, 2007), pp. 12–103.

21. *Fyttes v. Fyttes* (1610), TNA, STAC 8/140/28: Bill of Complaint.

22. *Gleave v. Spratt* (1606), TNA, STAC 8/149/17: Bill of Complaint. See also Craig Muldrew, *An Economy of Obligation: The Culture of Credit and Social Relations in Early Modern England* (Macmillan, 1998).

23. *Gleave v. Spratt*, TNA, STAC 8/149/17: Answer of Richard Watkinson to the Bill of Complaint.

24. *Gleave v. Spratt*, TNA, STAC 8/149/17: Examination of Richard Watkinson.

25. *Gleave v. Spratt*, TNA, STAC 8/149/17: Bill of Complaint.

26. *Finch v. Annate* (1598), reported in Hawarde, *Les Reportes*, pp. 97–98.

27. Laura Gowing, *Domestic Dangers: Women, Words and Sex in Early Modern London* (1996; repr., Oxford: Clarendon Press, 1998), 160; Diana O'Hara, *Courtship and Constraint: Rethinking the Making of Marriage in Tudor England* (Manchester: Manchester UP, 2000), 70–71; O'Hara, "The Language of Tokens and the Making of Marriage," *Rural History*, 3 (1992), 1–40; Subha Mukherji, *Law and Representation in Early Modern Drama* (Cambridge: CUP, 2006), pp. 17–54.

28. *Attorney General v. Chatteron* (1609), TNA, STAC 8/13/8. The case is described in detail by Carolyn Sale, "The 'Roman Hand': Women, Writing and the Law in the *Att.-Gen. v. Chatterton* and the Letters of the Lady Arbella Stuart," *ELH*, 70/4 (2003), 929–61. Lady Hatton, wife to Sir Edward Coke, used a forged letter from the Earl of Oxford to forestall her husband's attempts to marry off their daughter, claiming a precontract to the earl who was conveniently abroad at the time. Lisa Jardine and Alan Stewart, *A Hostage to Fortune: The Troubled Life of Francis Bacon, 1561–1626* (Victor Gollancz, 1998), pp. 400–401.

29. *Sherman v. Dawes* (1606), recorded in Hawarde, *Les Reportes*, pp. 259–61.

30. *Dickins v. Onions* (1621), TNA, STAC 8/122/20: Bill of Complaint.

31. *Gleave v. Spratt*, TNA, STAC 8/149/17: Interrogatory for Richard Watkinson.

32. *Dickins v. Onions*, TNA, STAC 8/122/20: Bill of Complaint.

33. The 1536 statute was reaffirmed under Mary in 1553. Nigel Ramsay, "Forgery and the Rise of the London Scriveners' Company," in *Fakes and Frauds: Varieties of Deception in Print and Manuscript*, ed. Robin Myers and Michael Harris (Winchester: St. Paul's Bibliographies, 1989), pp. 99–108 (p. 101); John Bellamy, *The Tudor Law of Treason* (Routledge, 1979), pp. 60–61.

34. Privy Council meeting of 27 April 1598, TNA, PC 2/23, p. 242.

35. Privy Council meeting of 17 April 1597, TNA, PC 2/22, p. 201.

36. Privy Council meeting of 31 December 1598, TNA, PC 2/24, p. 213.

37. *Tudor Royal Proclamations*, vol. III, *The Later Tudors, 1588–1603*, ed. Paul L. Hughes and James F. Larkin (New Haven, CT: Yale UP, 1969), pp. 159–62, no. 779.

38. See Tom Davis, "The Practice of Handwriting Identification," *Library*, 7th ser., 8/3 (2007), 251–76 (p. 257).

39. James Daybell, *The Material Letter in Early Modern England: Manuscript Letters and the Culture and Practices of Letter-Writing, 1512–1635* (Basingstoke: Palgrave Macmillan, 2012), p. 97.

40. On the social prestige of cipher, see Akkerman's essay in this volume.

41. No further record of the case survives, but a Thomas Mason of St. Clement's, Temple Barr, was a defendant in a case involving a forged acquittance. *Fawkes v. Dobson* (1606), TNA, STAC 8/145/13.

42. On the changing scope of treason prosecution and its cultural implications, see in particular Bellamy, *Tudor Law of Treason*; Karen Cunningham, *Imaginary Betrayals: Subjectivity and the Discourses of Treason in Early Modern England* (Philadelphia: U of Pennsylvania P, 2002); Rebecca Lemon, *Treason by Words: Literature, Law and Rebellion in Shakespeare's England* (Cambridge: CUP, 2006), pp. 1–22.

43. Cunningham, *Imaginary Betrayals*, p. 111.

44. The documents were compound forgeries using sections of genuine letters along with inserted passages and false dates to incriminate her. While no judgment on the authenticity of the letters was given at the English Conference, the publicity campaign that followed disseminated the documentary case against her. John Guy, *My Heart Is My Own: The Life of Mary Queen of Scots* (Fourth Estate, 2004), pp. 396–436. See also Julian Goodare, "Mary (1542–1587)," in *ODNB*; Cunningham, *Imaginary Betrayals*, pp. 110–32; Cathy Shrank, "Manuscript, Authenticity and 'Evident Proofs' Against the Scottish Queen," *EMS*, 15 (2009), 198–218.

45. Cited by Guy, *My Heart Is My Own*, p. 435.

46. *The copie of a letter written by one in London to his frend concernyng the credit of the late published detection of the doynges of the Ladie Marie of Scotland* (1571), sig. A4ᵛ.

47. For a recent account of the Babington plot that stresses the work of Walsingham's team, see Stephen Alford, *The Watchers: A Secret History of the Reign of Elizabeth I* (Allen Lane, 2012), pp. 193–240.

48. On the epistolary work of secretaries, see Christopher Burlinson and Andrew Zurcher, " 'Secretary to the Lord Grey Lord Deputie Here': Edmund Spenser's Irish Papers," *Library*, 6/1 (2005), 30–75; Daybell, *Material Letter*, pp. 73–84; Goldberg, *Writing Matter*, pp. 261–62.

49. Hiram Morgan, "The Fall of Sir John Perrot," in *The Reign of Elizabeth I: Court and Culture in the Last Decade*, ed. John Guy (Cambridge: CUP, 1995), pp. 109–25 (p. 113).

50. Abstract of a letter to Walsingham, 24 December 1585, "The Perrot Papers," ed. Charles McNeill, *Analecta Hibernica*, 12 (1943), 1–65 (p. 40).

51. TNA, SP 12/232, fol. 82: Sir John Perrot to Burghley, 16 June 1590.

52. TNA, SP 12/232, fol. 11: Deposition of Sir Henry Wallop, [4?] May 1590.

53. TNA, SP 63/153, fol. 151.

54. Alnwick Castle, Percy Letters and Papers, VI.1, fols. 1–6; cited in Roger Turvey, *The Treason and Trial of Sir John Perrot* (Cardiff: U of Wales P, 2005), p. 106.

55. TNA, SP 63/150, fol. 113ʳ: Letter of Fitzwilliam to Burghley, 16 February 1590.

56. TNA, SP 63/150, fol. 115: Copy of forged letter dated 25 June 1585, enclosed in Fitzwilliam's letter to Burghley of 16 February 1590.

57. Alnwick Castle, Percy Letters and Papers, VI.1, fols. 1–6; Turvey, *Treason and Trial*, p. 106.

58. Morgan, "Fall of Sir John Perrot," p. 124.

59. BL, Lansd. MS 72, fols. 20–32, fol. 23ʳ: "The Araignement and Judgement of Ser John Perrott Knight Attainted."

60. BL, Lansd. MS 19, fol. 12ʳ: Archbishop Parker to Lord Burghley, 19 June 1574.

61. Andrew F. S. Pearson, *Thomas Cartwright and Elizabethan Puritanism, 1558–1603* (Cambridge: CUP, 1925), pp. 124–29.

62. BL, Lansd. MS 19, fol. 21ʳ: Archbishop Parker to Lord Burghley, 30 June 1574.

63. Patrick Collinson, *The Elizabethan Puritan Movement* (Oxford: Clarendon Press, 1967), pp. 154–55.

64. BL, Add. MS 48039, fols. 48–56 (fol. 49ᵛ): "The answer of Robert Beale co[n]cerninge such thinges as haue passed between the L. Archbishopp of Canterburye and him, annotated [by Beale]: Primo Julij 1584. For my L. Threr."

65. BL, Lansd. MS 99, fol. 244ʳ: Murfin Interrogation.

66. The dating is derived from the implication of William Webb as sheriff of London in the conspiracy. Webb's tenure was 1581–82, but the planning of the plot is described as in process three years earlier, putting the examination sometime between 1583 and Norton's death in March the following year.

67. BL, Lansd. MS 99, fol. 247ᵛ.

68. BL, Lansd. MS 99, fol. 247ᵛ.

69. BL, Lansd. MS 99, fol. 249ʳ.

70. BL, Lansd. MS 99, fol. 246ᵛ.

71. *Selby v. Wallis & Shute,* TNA, STAC 5/S1/4: Bill of Complaint; TNA, SP 12/ 261, fol. 102ᵛ: Petition of John Markham to Lord Burghley, 1596.

72. Hawarde, *Les Reportes*, pp. 65, 80, 113, 319–20.

73. On Phelippes, see Alford, *The Watchers*, pp. 144–46, 196–297.

74. William Camden, *The Historie of the Life and Death of Mary Stuart Queene of Scotland* (1624), p. 173.

75. BL, Harl. MS 286, fol. 78ʳ: Arthur Gregory to Sir Francis Walsingham, February 1586. On the technologies of secrecy in early modern letters, see Daybell, *Material Letter*, pp. 148–74; on invisible inks in particular, see pp. 165–69.

76. Hatfield House, Hertfordshire, CP 25/5: Arthur Gregory to Sir Robert Cecil, 28 February 1595; TNA, SP 12/260, fol. 67: Arthur Gregory to Sir Robert Cecil, [September?] 1596. Phelippes was intermittently engaged by the Earl of Essex in the mid-1590s when the earl's ambitions as an international statesman were at their height, but it was Cecil who made the more regular use of his talents toward the end of the decade.

77. Alan Stewart, *Shakespeare's Letters* (Oxford: OUP, 2008).

78. Harold Jenkins, *The Life and Work of Henry Chettle* (Sedgwick and Jackson, 1934), pp. 188–208; Will Sharpe, "A Critical Edition of *The Blind Beggar of Bethnal Green* by John Day and Henry Chettle (1600)" (Ph.D. diss., University of Birmingham, 2009).

79. John Day [and Henry Chettle], *The Blind-Beggar of Bednall-Green* (R. Pollard and Tho. Dring, 1659), sig. E3ᵛ.

80. TNA, SP 12/278/101, fol. 171ʳ: "The Arraignemt of Robt Erle of Essex and Henry Erle of Southampton at Westminstr the xixth of February 1600."

81. Andrew Kippis, *Biographia Britannica* (Strahan, 1778), I, pp. 536–48; Woudhuysen, *Philip Sidney and the Circulation of Manuscripts*, pp. 32–37.

82. TNA, SP 12/278/101, fol. 171ʳ: "The Arraignemt."

83. TNA, SP 46/56/1, fol. 166ʳ: *Attorney General v. Daniell*, Star Chamber Decree, 17 June 1601.

84. The series of extant declarations from Bales appear to have been produced at Daniell's behest to assist in the latter's appeals for clemency.

85. LPL, MS 649, fol. 337ʳ: Letter to his mother, Anne Bacon; TNA, SP 12/281, fol. 73: Declaration of Peter Bales, 31 July 1601. For an overview of Essex's hand, see Roy Davids, "The Handwriting of Robert Devereux, Second Earl of Essex," *Book Collector*, 37 (1988), 351–65.

86. TNA, SP 46/56/1, fol. 164: *Attorney General v. Daniell*, Star Chamber Decree, 17 June 1601.

87. TNA, SP 46/52, fol. 92ʳ: (Another) Deposition of Peter Bales [1601].

88. Ferryman appears to have supported Bales in later attempts for patronage. The fullest account of Ferryman is that given by A. R. Braunmuller in his introduction to *A Seventeenth-Century Letter-Book* (Newark: U of Delaware P, 1983), his edition of Folger MS V.a. 321, a manuscript he attributes to Ferryman. See also B. J. Sokol, "Roydon, Matthew (*fl.* 1583–1622)," in *ODNB*.

89. TNA, SP 12/279, fol. 226: Statement by G. Lisle, n.d. [June 1601?].

90. Kippis, *Biographia Britannica*, pp. 536–37.

91. BL, Lansd. MS 99, fol. 271: Peter Bales to Burghley, undated but possibly ca. 1592; CP 108/36: Peter Bales to Robert Cecil, Viscount Cranbourne [1604].

92. TNA, SP 46/52, fol. 90ʳ: Deposition of Peter Bales [1601]; Andrew Gordon, "Essex's Last Campaign: The Fall of the Earl of Essex and Manuscript Circulation," in *Essex: The Cultural Impact of an Elizabethan Courtier*, ed. Annaliese Connolly and Lisa Hopkins (Manchester: Manchester UP, 2013), pp. 153–78.

93. A presentation copy of John Daniell's narrative entitled *Danyell's Disasters*, with a dedicatory letter to James I seeking permission to print, is bound together with the narrative account of his wife, *A True Declaration of the Misfortunes of Jane Danyell*, dated 1606, as TNA, SP 46/50/1. Daniell produced several other versions of these events, including *The Varyable Accedents in a Pryuate Mans Lyffe*, TNA, SP 14/52, fols. 51–66. Another headed *Danyells Disasters* is marked "to be examind by Mr R. M.," TNA, SP 14/52, fols. 47–50. The most extensive account, with numerous revisions, is titled *The Unexpected Acedentes of my casuall destyny: Discovrd by affliccyons hapnynge in the lyffe of mee John Danyell Esquyer*, CP 264/1. A draft of Jane Daniell's account is contained in TNA, SP 14/11, fols. 103–33.

94. On Jane Daniell's letter writing and her autobiographical narrative, see Andrew Gordon, "Recovering Agency in the Epistolary Traffic of Frances, Countess of Essex, and Jane Daniell," in *Women and Epistolary Agency in Early Modern Culture, 1450–1690*, ed. James Daybell and Andrew Gordon (Farnham: Ashgate, 2016).

95. *The Unexpected Acedentes*, CP 264/1, fol. 8ʳ.

96. Hawarde, *Les Reportes*, p. 121.

97. *The Unexpected Acedentes*, CP 264/1, fol. 7ʳ.

98. Anon., "To whome shall cursed I my Case complaine," in "Early Stuart Libels: An Edition of Poetry from Manuscript Sources," ed. Alastair Bellany and Andrew McRae, *Early Modern Literary Studies*, Text Series I (2005), text B7, http://purl.oclc.org/emls/texts/libels/.

99. TNA, SP 12/274, fol. 170: Bill of Release.

100. *The Unexpected Acedentes*, CP 264/1, fol. 6ʳ.

101. According to Jane Daniell's account, Worcester reported the approach to the countess (*A True Declaration of the Misfortunes of Jane Danyell*, TNA, SP 46/50/1, fol. 30ʳ).

102. TNA, SP 12/279, fol. 231: *Attorney General v. Daniell*, Star Chamber Decree, with Daniell's annotations.

103. See Andrew Gordon, "'A Fortune of Paper Walls': The Letters of Francis Bacon and the Earl of Essex," *ELR*, 37/3 (2007), 319–36. On Lady Rich's letter, see also Gordon, "*Copyco-pia*," pp. 65–82; and James Daybell, "Women, Politics and Domesticity: The Scribal Publication of Lady Rich's Letter to Elizabeth I," in *Women and Writing, c.1340–c.1650: The Domestication of Print Culture*, ed. Anne Lawrence-Mathers and Phillipa Hardman (Woodbridge: York Medieval Press, an imprint of Boydell and Brewer, 2010), pp. 111–30.

104. *Danyell's Disasters*, TNA, SP 46/50/1, p. 13.

CHAPTER 5. ALLEGORY AND EPISTOLARITY

1. Sir Philip Sidney, *The Countesse of Pembrokes Arcadia* (William Ponsonby, 1593), fol. 6ʳ. For reasons that will become clear, all further quotations from the *Arcadia* will be taken from the 1593 edition.

2. Sidney, *Arcadia*, fol. 7ʳ.

3. *The Complete Works of Sir Philip Sidney*, ed. Albert Feuillerat, 4 vols. (Cambridge: CUP, 1912–26), III, p. 124.

4. Sidney's is only the most relevant of many violent examples. The danger posed by corrupt or perfidious secretaries was a commonplace of early modern Tacitean political discourse and figures in contemporary chronicle sources and in the political manuals abstracted from them. For example, Remigio Fiorentino (Remigio Nannini) published in 1582 his *Considerazioni civili sopra l'historia di F. Guicciardini*, trans. into French by Chappuis and into English by W. T., as *Civill Considerations vpon Many and Sundrie Histories* (F. K. for Matthew Lownes, 1601). In chapter 92 ("Inward familiars, and Secretaries of Princes may commit many errors, by meanes whereof they are in danger to lose their fauour, or their owne liues"), Remigio remembers Garcia Nicosia, "Secretarie to *Alaim Sicilian*, Lord of Ficaire," whose distrusting master "slew him, and threw his head into the sea, and buried the bodie in his house" (*Civill Considerations*, p. 229). The history of the 1566 slaughter of David Riccio, French secretary to Mary, Queen of Scots, by Patrick Ruthven also turned on Riccio's privity with his mistress and the feared abuse of Darnley's signature stamp; see Raphael Holinshed et al., *The Historie of Scotland* (John Harrison et al., 1587), p. 382. According to the French propagandist Adam Blackwood's 1587 *Martyre de la Royne d'Escosse, douariere de France* (Edinburgh [Paris]: Jean Nafield, 1587), p. 75, Darnley murdered Riccio "à cause que non seulement il refusa signer, mais aussi reuela à la Roine certaine conspiration conclue entre son altesse, & les rebelles"; Blackwood goes on to claim that Riccio was said to be "plus familier auec la Roine" (pp. 77–78). Blackwood's Darnley emerges as a hapless fool manipulated into believing, all too easily, in the material privity of his queen's secretary.

5. Sidney, *Arcadia*, fol. 6ʳ.

6. What Kalander might gain from his knowledge of Philanax's letter is suggested by another famous letter that Sidney himself wrote in 1579, this time circulated publicly. The "Letter to Queen Elizabeth Touching Her Marriage with Monsieur" remonstrated with Elizabeth for her marriage negotiations with François, duc d'Alençon, Catholic brother to the French king. Sidney's open criticism of Elizabeth sounds much like the surprisingly frank, almost patronizing tone adopted by Philanax to Basilius. Philanax's letter also echoes the concerns of Sidney's *Lady of May*, the Kenilworth entertainment to which Elizabeth was subjected in 1578. At the conclusion of the short drama, Elizabeth was asked to choose between two suitors vying for the young Lady's hand, Espilus the shepherd and Therion the forester. Her choice of

Espilus preferred "little good and no harm" to "much good and some harm"—that is, she preferred political disengagement in the defense of the Low Countries to intervention against the Spanish. Philanax's letter, like Sidney's, counsels against withdrawal. Kalander's copy, as Sidney would have known, could be useful in negotiating the complex factional politics created by the crisis. For both the "Letter to Queen Elizabeth" and *The Lady of May*, see *Miscellaneous Prose of Sir Philip Sidney*, ed. Katherine Duncan-Jones and Jan van Dorsten (Oxford: Clarendon Press, 1973).

7. TNA, SP 63/87/6: Hugh Bradie, Bishop of Meath ("Mideus"), to Sir Francis Walsingham, 6 June 1581. In this transcription, as in those that follow, I have silently lowered superscripts and rendered supplied letters (including the expansion of brevigraphs) in brackets.

8. As Conyers Read long ago recognized, Walsingham's "spy network" included not only men paid and appointed, but many other informal contacts who were keen to gain favor by supplying information. See Read, *Mr. Secretary Walsingham and the Policy of Queen Elizabeth*, 3 vols. (Oxford: Clarendon Press, 1925), II, pp. 369–70; and Stephen Alford, "Some Elizabethan Spies in the Office of Sir Francis Walsingham," in *Diplomacy and Early Modern Culture*, ed. Robyn Adams and Rosanna Cox (Basingstoke: Palgrave Macmillan, 2011), pp. 46–62; see also Alford, *The Watchers* (Penguin, 2012).

9. TNA, SP 63/87/6: Bradie to Walsingham, 6 June 1581.

10. More often personal communication was used in conjunction with a written message, as when Lord Grey wrote to Walsingham on 24 April 1581, acknowledging that he sent the letter's bearer "for the more perfitt enfoormyng, earnest soliciting, & speedie dispatche of [th]e cause" (TNA, SP 63/82/48).

11. The material evidence of the origins of this intrigue are lost, but the general outline is clear. Grey defended himself from the charge of corruption and "empire-building" in a letter to the queen of 25 January 1582 (TNA, SP 63/88/39), maintaining that he only granted custodians with "reseruation to your Maiesty of such a rent, as your Commission for survey shall sett." Fenton acted against Grey following the trial and execution of Sir Nicholas Nugent, the "rebel" uncle of the "traitor" Baron of Delvin, informing the Privy Council that the family's estates "are fullie and whollie escheated to her Maiestie, but what is the value and extent therof yt is not as yet knowen for that there hathe bine no tyme to finde the office[.] Their goodes are given awaie and their landes disposed by waie of Custodiam, A manner of givinge which of all others bringes least proffitt to her Maiestie, for that I haue not harde of any rente or other benefitt answeared to her Maiestie for any Custodiam since I came to serue in this place" (TNA, SP 63/91/31: Fenton to the Privy Council, 13 April 1582). The queen's angry missive to her lord deputy, touching the issue of rents, does not survive, but Grey's protesting riposte of 9 May 1582 does, in which he defended himself stoutly against the "Informeres of your Highnes" (TNA, SP 63/92/20; the private copy from which I quote was sent to Walsingham—TNA, SP 63/92/11/1). The conspiracy continued to run until Grey's recall later that summer.

12. See TNA, SP 63/90/56: Wallop to Burghley, 28 March 1582. Wallop protests that he "would be lothe to be made an informer, spetyally agaynst him whom I loue and honor in my hart," but within a few pages he tells Burghley that "yff yt shall please yo[u]r lo[rdship] to kepe these advertysment[es] only to yo[u]r selfe, I wyll fro[m] tyme to tyme adv[er]tys yo[u]r lo[rdship] more playnely off all thynges that shall pas here, then formerly I haue done, so yt maye stande w[i]t[h] yo[u]r lo[rdships] lykynge and that my tedyvs maner off wrytynge be not over troblesome to you." Wallop then proceeds to remind Burghley of the cipher he sent him two years previously, which if lost he will replace.

13. See TNA, SP 63/82/19. Bryskett wrote again to Burghley within a few weeks, requesting support for his bid for the office of secretary of state for Ireland (TNA, SP 63/82/53); this may suggest that Burghley had received his earlier letter favorably.

14. Jenyson reported to Burghley on Grey's handling of custodiams in a series of letters: TNA, SP 63/87/42 (11 December 1581, "in great confidence"), 63/88/29 (15 January 1582), 63/89/38 (20 February 1582), and 63/95/12 (4 September 1582), in which last letter he reported that "here is great Ielowsy conceyved for adu[er]tising yo[u]r lo[rdship] [and] mr Treasorer [and] mr of the Rowlez moost Susspected. And they have an intent Amongest them to se if yo[u]r Secretary may be wrought to let them vnderstand what they be that so writes to your lo[rdship]."

15. Sidney, *Arcadia*, fol. 6^{v}.

16. See *OED*, s.v. "liking," *n.*, 3; but see also sense 6 ("bodily condition, esp. good or healthy condition"), now obsolete. Kalander appears to see the letter as a kind of political insurance in uncertain times.

17. Sidney, *Arcadia*, fol. 217$^{r–v}$.

18. Sidney, *Arcadia*, fol. 218$^{r–v}$.

19. See, e.g., TNA, SP 63/82/6, Grey to Walsingham (autograph), 6 April 1581, sealed and addressed by Spenser. TNA, SP 63/84/12 is a letter from Grey to the Privy Council of 10 July 1581, drafted for Grey by an unknown secretary, but annotated, folded, sealed, and addressed by Spenser. Two letters—TNA, SP 63/87/32 (Grey et al. to the Privy Council, 10 December 1581) and 63/89/55 (Grey to Walsingham, February 1582)—show Spenser adding a subscription to, and then processing, a letter prepared by another secretary.

20. See Christopher Burlinson and Andrew Zurcher, "'Secretary to the Lord Grey Lord Deputy Here': Edmund Spenser's Irish Papers," *Library*, 6/1 (2005), 30–75 (pp. 62–65).

21. See, e.g., the note appended to the foot of TNA, SP 63/93/64: Grey to Walsingham, 29 June 1582. For more discussion of these "addressee notes," see *Edmund Spenser: Selected Letters and Other Papers*, ed. Christopher Burlinson and Andrew Zurcher (Oxford: OUP, 2009), pp. xlvii–xlix.

22. On the practice of ciphering during this period, and the use of cipher keys and caskets, coffins, or cabinets, see Nadine Akkerman's discussion in this volume (Chapter 3). On Spenser's handling of Grey's regularly ciphered correspondence, see Burlinson and Zurcher, *Edmund Spenser: Selected Letters and Other Papers*, xlv–xlvii. Spenser was probably aware that Grey's use of cipher in his letters to Walsingham was designed to protect his correspondence not from foreign spies, but from Walsingham's fellow Privy Counsellors; as Grey wrote (in cipher) on 6 April 1581: "I haue allso wrytten now abowte this same too her Maiestie, & too my Lords a generall letter from the table heere, which, if yow shall not thynck amiss, I could wysshe 60 first acquaynted with, that sum choyce of yee myght bee made too consider of it because you arre nott all one mans chyldren" (TNA, SP 63/82/6).

23. Sidney, *Arcadia*, fol. 37^{v}.

24. Edmund Spenser, *The Faerie Queene* (John Wolfe for William Ponsonby, 1590), I. xii.24.6–9. All quotations from Book I will be taken from this edition; quotations from Books IV and V will be taken from the second installment of *The Faerie Queene* (Richard Field for William Ponsonby, 1596). All further references will be given parenthetically in the text.

25. A well-known example was the case of Francis Throckmorton, who was caught up in the circle of Thomas Morgan, interrogated, and in 1584 executed for conspiring with Mary, Queen of Scots. The account of the affair in Holinshed stresses that Throckmorton's guilt was partly inferred from his possession of a cipher shared with Mary, Queen of Scots: "letters betwéene them

were alwaies written in cipher, and the cipher with the nullities and marks for names of princes and councellors he sent vnto the queenes maiestie written with his owne hand." This guilt touched Throckmorton's associate Meredith in the same way; the latter conveyed a cipher casket for Throckmorton, and Throckmorton "deliuered priuilie into the hands of Meredith, either the cipher by the which he was writing his letter to the Scotish quéene, or a letter in cipher by him written vnto hir: therefore he trusted Meredith as a man priuie to his dooings." See Raphael Holinshed et al., *The First and Second Volumes of Chronicles* (Henry Denham, 1587), pp. 1371–72.

26. The 1590 text actually reads "letters faine"; but "Faults Escaped" corrects "faine" to "vaine," a reading followed in subsequent editions. The correction insists on the importance of "vaine," from Latin *vanus*, "empty, void."

27. See *OED*, s.v. "suborn," *v.*, 4 and 5; as the *OED* notes, Spenser uses this verb in the latter sense in *A View of the Present State of Ireland*.

28. Cf. Plutarch, *Cato the Younger*, chap. 23, in *Plutarch's Lives*, trans. Bernadotte Perrin, 11 vols. (Cambridge, MA: Harvard UP, 1914), VIII, pp. 290–91, where Cicero is credited with giving to the clerks recording Cato's most famous speech "instruction in the use of signs [σημεῖα], which, in small and short figures, comprised the force of many letters." In this sense, σημεῖα was translated by Latin *nota*; cf. Thomas Cooper's *Thesaurus linguae Romanae & Britannicae* (Henry Denham, 1578), sig. Nnnn6^r: "*Nota, notae*, f. g. *Nosco, noscis, noui, notum*. Pli. A note: a mark: a signe: a token. A defamation: infamie: a slaunderous name or report: a reprehension or correction of any wryting. A cypher, note, or abbreuiation." As Cooper later notes, Quintilian uses the word, in the plural, to refer to ciphers: "*Notis scribere*. Quint. Vide NOTA. To cipher" (sig. Xxxxx4^r).

29. See Harry Berger, Jr., *Situated Utterances: Texts, Bodies, and Cultural Representations* (New York: Fordham UP, 2005); and Gordon Teskey, "Allegory," in *The Spenser Encyclopedia*, ed. A. C. Hamilton (Toronto: U of Toronto P, 1990), pp. 16–22.

30. Edmund Spenser, "A Letter of the Authors . . . to Sir Walter Raleigh," in *The Faerie Queene* (William Ponsonby, 1590), p. 591.

31. Edmund Spenser, *A View of the Present State of Ireland*, ed. Rudolf Gottfried, in *The Works of Edmund Spenser: A Variorum Edition*, ed. Edwin Greenlaw et al., 11 vols. (Baltimore: Johns Hopkins UP, 1932–49), X, pp. 147–48 (lines 2954–56).

32. Spenser, *A View*, p. 199 (lines 4420–22).

CHAPTER 6. MIXED MESSAGES AND CICERO EFFECTS

1. Bodl., Herrick Family Papers, Eng. Hist. MSS, b. 216, c. 474–84. In addition to letters received by William Herrick (1562?–1653), the collection includes family correspondence of his descendants to 1875. This essay limits its focus to the sixteenth-century letters to study Ciceronian epistolary imitation and related effects of grammar-school education. I am grateful to James Daybell, Andrew Gordon, Carol Percy, and Paul Stevens for helpful suggestions in preparing this essay, and to David Adkins for checking the Latin quotations.

2. Claire M. Cross, *The Free Grammar School of Leicester* (Leicester: University College of Leicester, 1953), pp. 10–14, 21–25.

3. Victor Morgan, *A History of the University of Oxford*, vol. II, *1546–1750* (Cambridge: CUP, 2004), p. 181. See also Lawrence Stone, "The Educational Revolution in England, 1560–1640," *P&P*, 28 (1964), 41–80.

4. The tendency has been to approach the question indirectly by analyzing English manuals of letter writing addressed to merchants that derive from Latin humanist texts, with more direct evidence of intensive schoolroom study of Latin letters or of actual mercantile correspondence not yet fully taken into account; see, e.g., Lynne Magnusson, *Shakespeare and Social Dialogue: Dramatic Language and Elizabethan Letters* (Cambridge: CUP, 1999), pp. 114–30; W. Webster Newbold, "Letter Writing and Vernacular Literacy in Sixteenth-Century England," in *Letter-Writing Manuals and Instruction from Antiquity to the Present*, ed. Carol Poster and Linda C. Mitchell (Columbia: U of South Carolina P, 2007), pp. 127–40. Peter Mack, *Elizabethan Rhetoric: Theory and Practice* (Cambridge: CUP, 2002), pp. 103–4, 114–24, stands out for its effort to demonstrate the impact of grammar-school training on everyday practice, but illustrations from mercantile correspondence are lacking. In discussing sixteenth-century manuscript letters, James Daybell, *Women Letter-Writers in Tudor England* (Oxford: OUP, 2006) is most wide-ranging in the social composition of letter writers represented, including mercantile correspondence, but given the limits on female Latin education, this issue does not arise.

5. James Harvey Robinson, *Petrarch: The First Modern Scholar and Man of Letters; A Selection from His Correspondence* (New York: G. P. Putnam's, 1989), p. 240. On Petrarch's recovery in 1345 of Cicero's letters to Atticus and his engagement with Cicero's epistolary style, see Kathy Eden, *The Renaissance Rediscovery of Intimacy* (Chicago: U of Chicago P, 2012), pp. 49–72.

6. T. W. Baldwin, *William Shakspere's Small Latine & Lesse Greeke*, 2 vols. (Urbana: U of Illinois P, 1944), esp. II, pp. 239–87; Judith Rice Henderson, "Humanism and the Humanities: Erasmus's *Opus de Conscribendis Epistolis* in Sixteenth-Century Schools," in *Letter-Writing Manuals and Instruction from Antiquity to the Present*, ed. Carol Poster and Linda C. Mitchell (Columbia: U of South Carolina P, 2007), pp. 141–71; Mack, *Elizabethan Rhetoric*, esp. pp. 11–47; Lisa Jardine, "Reading and the Technology of Textual Effect," in *Reading Shakespeare Historically* (Routledge, 1996), pp. 78–90; Magnusson, *Shakespeare and Social Dialogue*, pp. 61–74; Alan Stewart, *Shakespeare's Letters* (Oxford: OUP, 2008), esp. pp. 75–114.

7. Virginia Woolf, "Dorothy Osborne's 'Letters,'" in *The Common Reader: Second Series* (Hogarth Press, 1932), pp. 59–66 (p. 59).

8. John Donne, *Selected Letters*, ed. P. M. Oliver (Manchester: Fyfield Books, 2002), p. 17.

9. Judith Rice Henderson, "Letter as Genre," in *The Spenser Encyclopedia*, ed. A. C. Hamilton et al. (Toronto: U of Toronto P, 1990), pp. 433–34 (p. 434, emphasis added).

10. Desiderius Erasmus, "A Formula for the Composition of Letters" (*Conficiendarum epistolarum formula*), trans. Charles Fantazzi, in *Collected Works of Erasmus*, vol. 25, ed. J. K. Sowards (Toronto: U of Toronto P, 1985), pp. 258–67 (p. 258).

11. William Cecil, Lord Burghley, to John Harington at Cambridge, 1578, in John Harington, *Nugæ Antiquæ: Being a Miscellaneous Collection of Original Papers . . . Written During the Reigns of Henry VIII, Edward VI, Queen Mary, Elizabeth, and King James &c.*, ed. Henry Harington, 2 vols. (W. Frederick, 1769–75), II (1775), pp. 238–40 (pp. 239–40).

12. Harington, *Nugæ Antiquæ*, II, p. 240.

13. See also Lynne Magnusson, "Letters," in *The History of British Women's Writing, 1500–1610*, ed. Caroline Bicks and Jennifer Summit (Basingstoke: Palgrave Macmillan, 2010), pp. 130–51.

14. In a valuable overview, Jonathan Gibson, "Letters," in *A New Companion to English Renaissance Literature and Culture*, ed. Michael Hattaway, 2 vols. (Malden, MA: Wiley-Blackwell, 2010), II, pp. 453–60, separates out the influence of three interrelated traditions, including the ideal of the classical familiar letter, medieval *ars dictaminis*, and early modern rhetorical theory, but the familiar letter comes mediated through contemporary rhetorical theory.

15. Often Ciceronian imitation is imagined as merely stylistic, but recent scholarship on Cicero's letters has emphasized less stylistic virtuosity than a rhetoric of sociability—e.g., Jon Hall, *Politeness and Politics in Cicero's Letters* (Oxford: OUP, 2009). I have emphasized dialogue scripts and inventive social relations in Erasmus's classical epistolary pedagogy in *Shakespeare and Social Dialogue*, pp. 61–90; and in "A Pragmatics for Interpreting Shakespeare's Sonnets 1 to 20: Dialogue Scripts and Erasmian Intertexts," in *Methods in Historical Pragmatics*, ed. Susan Fitzmaurice and Irma Taavitsainen (Berlin: Mouton de Gruyter, 2007), pp. 167–78 (pp. 172–78).

16. Magnusson, *Shakespeare and Social Dialogue*, pp. 91–113; Magnusson, "A Rhetoric of Requests: Genre and Linguistic Scripts in Elizabethan Women's Suitors' Letters," in *Women and Politics in Early Modern England, 1450–1700*, ed. James Daybell (Aldershot: Ashgate, 2004), pp. 51–66; Daybell, *Women Letter-Writers*, pp. 229–64.

17. Norman Davis, "The *Litera Troili* and English Letters," *RES*, 16 (1965), 233–44 (pp. 240–43).

18. Richard Mulcaster, *The First Part of the Elementarie* (1582), ed. E. T. Campagnac (Oxford: Clarendon, 1925), p. 272.

19. Roger Ascham, *Whole Works*, ed. Rev. Dr. Giles, vol. I, pt. 2 (John Russell Smith, 1865), pp. 152–70 (p. 152).

20. Nicholas Orme, ed., *English School Exercises, 1420–1530*, Studies and Texts 181 (Toronto: Pontifical Institute of Medieval Studies, 2013), p. 14; Orme, *Medieval Schools from Roman Britain to Renaissance England* (New Haven, CT: Yale UP, 2006), pp. 109–27.

21. For a helpful comparative schema of syllabi set forth in four different grammar-school statutes, see Mack, *Elizabethan Rhetoric*, p. 13. On epistolary training, see Baldwin, *William Shakspere's Small Latine & Lesse Greeke*, esp. II, pp. 239–87; on texts of Cicero's letters used in English schools, see Howard Jones, *Master Tully: Cicero in Tudor England* (Nieuwkoop: De Graaf, 1998).

22. Mack, *Elizabethan Rhetoric*, p. 13.

23. Desiderius Erasmus, *Colloquies,* 2 vols., trans. Craig R. Thompson, in *Collected Works of Erasmus*, vols. 39 and 40 (Toronto: U of Toronto P, 1997), vol. 39, pp. 184–85.

24. *Collected Works of Erasmus*, vol. 39, p. 120.

25. *Collected Works of Erasmus*, vol. 39, pp. 166, 169.

26. On the history of these educational institutions, see Cross, *Free Grammar School of Leicester*; and Sarah Bendall, Christopher Brooke, and Patrick Collinson, *A History of Emmanuel College, Cambridge* (Woodbridge, Suffolk: Boydell Press, 1999).

27. See John Nichols, *The History and Antiquities of the County of Leicester*, 4 vols. (Nichols, 1795–1815), vol. II, pt. 2 (n.d.), p. 618. Nichols transcribes selected Herrick letters and extracts in vol. II, pt. 2 (n.d.), pp. 611–36, and vol. III, pt. 1 (1800), pp. 148–66. In this essay, I regularize the spelling of the surname Herrick, which is hugely various in the manuscript letters.

28. Bodl., Eng. Hist. MS. c. 475, fols. 124–25: Tobias Herrick to William Herrick, ca. 1584.

29. Pierre Bourdieu, "The Economics of Linguistic Exchanges," trans Richard Nice, *Social Science Information*, 16 (1977), 645–68 (p. 655).

30. Bodl., Eng. Hist. MS. c. 475, fol. 124^{r-v}; italicized phrases from *Ad fam.* II.1, to Curio.

31. Cross, *Free Grammar School*, pp. 15, 16, and 17.

32. Marcus Tullius Cicero, *Epistolæ aliquot selectæ qvas stvdiosi adolescentes sibi ad imitandum utiliter proponant* (Paris: Thomas Richard, 1557). The different references in the Leicester

school statutes to texts of Cicero's letters seems to suggest that, as in many schools, a selected or more elementary text was used initially and the full text of *Epistolae ad familiares* at a later stage. The specific phrasing "epitome" could suggest that the selection for students prepared by Thomas Cogan and published in a second edition in 1602 under the title *Epistolarvm familiarivm M. T. Ciceronis epitome* (Cambridge: John Legate) had been available much earlier. While it is often assumed that the selection of letters taught in English schools in the sixteenth century is that prepared by Johann Sturm and recommended by Roger Ascham, *Epistolarvm M. T. Ciceronis libri tres* (Prague: Georg Melantrich, 1577), there are still other possibilities, most of them with a pedagogical apparatus that illuminates the teaching of letters, including that prepared by Mathurin Cordier, *M. T. Ciceronis epistolarvm familiarivm liber II: Item, Aliquot epistolae selectae caeteris libris* (1551).

33. Cicero, *Epistolæ aliquot selectæ*, sig. d3.

34. Bodl., Eng. Hist. MS, c. 474, fol. 160^r: John Herrick to William Herrick, ca. 1579.

35. Davis, "The *Litera Troili* and English Letters," p. 236.

36. On the importance of material features, see James Daybell, *The Material Letter in Early Modern England: Manuscript Letters and the Culture and Practices of Letter-Writing, 1512–1635* (Basingstoke: Palgrave Macmillan, 2012).

37. Compare Roger Dalrymple's emphasis on "competing oral and literary influences" in "Reaction, Consolation and Redress in the Letters of the Paston Women," in *Early Modern Women's Letter Writing, 1450–1700*, ed. James Daybell (Basingstoke: Palgrave, 2001), pp. 16–28 (p. 16); and Valerie Creelman's emphasis on letters incorporating speech of others in "Quotation and Self-Fashioning in Margaret Paston's Household Letters," *English Studies in Canada*, 30 (2004), 111–28.

38. On the lived experience of this linguistic and cultural difference, see Lynne Magnusson, "Language," in *The Oxford Handbook of Shakespeare*, ed. Arthur F. Kinney (Oxford: OUP, 2012), pp. 239–57 (esp. pp. 251–55).

39. Bodl., Eng. Hist. MS, c. 474, fol. 174^r.

40. Bodl., Eng. Hist. MS, c. 474, fol. 181^v: 12 January 1585.

41. Bodl., Eng. Hist. MS, c. 474, fol. 176^r: 26 May 1584.

42. Cross, *Free Grammar School*, pp. 14, 18, 23.

43. Cross, *Free Grammar School*, p. 19.

44. David Cressy, *Literacy and the Social Order: Reading and Writing in Tudor and Stuart England* (New York: CUP, 1980), p. 131.

45. Susan M. Hare, "A History of the Goldsmiths' Company," http://www.thegoldsmiths .co.uk/library/archives/a-history-of-the-goldsmiths%27-company/ (accessed 22 March 2014). See also Joan Simon, *Education and Society in Tudor England* (Cambridge: CUP, 1966), p. 15.

46. Bodl., Eng. Hist. MS, c. 474, fol. 166^r: 27 January [no year].

47. Cross, *Free Grammar School*, p. 17.

48. Daybell, *Material Letter*, pp. 190–203.

49. Bodl., Eng. Hist. MS, c. 475, fol. 20^r: 8 June 1613.

50. Bodl., Eng. Hist. MS, c. 475, fols. 124^v–125^r.

51. Bodl., Eng. Hist. MS, c. 475, fol. 125^r.

52. Magnusson, "A Pragmatics for Interpreting Shakespeare's Sonnets," pp. 172–78.

53. For a methodology that adapts linguistic pragmatics to the analysis of historical literature and letter writing, see Magnusson, *Shakespeare and Social Dialogue*.

54. Bodl., Eng. Hist. MS, c. 475, fol. 126^r: Tobias Herrick to William Herrick, 10 January 1585.

55. Bodl., Eng. Hist. MS, c. 475, fol. 128^r: Tobias Herrick to William Herrick, 26 May [1588].

56. Bodl., Eng. Hist. MS, c. 475, fol. 137^r: Tobias Herrick to William Herrick, 27 March 1613.

CHAPTER 7. JOHN STUBBS'S LEFT-HANDED LETTERS

For their helpful comments and generous advice, I would like to thank the attendees at the "Cultures of Correspondence" conference and the Centre for Reformation and Early Modern Studies, Birmingham, who heard early versions of this essay in different forms, as well as Colin Burrow, for his advice on Dutch letters, and Eleanor Kendrick, for discussions on Shakespeare's hand(s).

1. *The Discoverie of a Gaping Gulf Whereinto England is Like to be Swallowed by an Other French Mariage, if the Lord Forbid not the Banes, but Letting her Maiestie See the Sin and Punishment Thereof* ([Hugh Singleton], 1579), sig. F3^v. Stubbs's pamphlet and letters are edited by Lloyd E. Berry in *John Stubbs's "Gaping Gulf" with Letters and Other Relevant Documents* (Charlottesville, VA: UP of Virginia, 1968). On Stubbs's presentation of counsel in *Gaping Gulf*, see Natalie Mears, "Counsel, Public Debate, and Queenship: John Stubbs's *The Discoverie of a Gaping Gulf*, 1579," *HJ*, 44 (2001), 629–50. On the rhetoric of the *Gaping Gulf*, see Ilona Bell, "'Soueraigne Lord of Lordly Lady of This Land': Elizabeth, Stubbs, and the *Gaping Gulf*," in *Dissing Elizabeth: Negative Representations of Gloriana*, ed. Julia M. Walker (Durham, NC: Duke UP, 1998), pp. 99–117. On the textual (and epistolary) history of another intervention into this political crisis, see also Peter Beal, "Philip Sidney's *Letter to Queen Elizabeth* and That 'False Knave' Alexander Dicsone," *EMS*, 11 (2002), 1–51.

2. Berry, *John Stubbs's "Gaping Gulf*," p. 148.

3. Folger, MS V.b.142, fol. 54^v. Folios 54 and 55 of this manuscript, a single folio sheet folded once, contain neat copies (in the same hand) of Stubbs's "supplication before execution vnto ye Q. M^{ty} but not dd," "Mr P. [i.e., William Page] his woords on ye skaffolde," "A supplication of M^r S to ye LL of ye privie Councell after execution," and "Mr S. his letter yo ye L. Threasurer."

4. BL, Add. MS 15891, fols. 25^v–26^r: John Stubbs to Sir Christopher Hatton (copy in letter book), 1 December 1579. Stubbs also refers, in a contemporaneous letter to the Privy Council (again, surviving only in copy), to those who bore witness to, or have knowledge of, his "owtwarde behaveour . . . on ye scaffolde." Folger, MS V.b.142, fol. 55^r.

5. William Camden, *Annales: The True and Royall History of the Famous Empresse Elizabeth, Queene of England France and Ireland* (Benjamin Fisher, 1625), Book 3, sig. [C4]^v.

6. Folger, MS V.b.142, fol. 54^{r-v}: John Stubbs to Queen Elizabeth (copy), October 1579.

7. The only print publication attributed to Stubbs in the period after his punishment is *Christian Meditations vpon Eight Psalmes of the Prophet Dauid, Made and Newly Set Forth by Theodore Beza, Translated out of French, for the Common Benefite, into the Vulgare Tongue, by I. S.* (Christopher Barker, [1582]).

8. Jonathan Goldberg, *Writing Matter: From the Hands of the English Renaissance* (Stanford, CA: Stanford UP, 1990).

9. BL, Lansd. MS 31, fol. 40 (article 19): John Stubbs to Michael Hickes, 1 December 1580.

10. Folger, MS V.b.142, fols. 54–55: John Stubbs to Privy Council, John Stubbs to William Cecil (copies), 3 December 1579; BL, Lansd. MS 31, fol. 24 (article 12): John Stubbs to William Cecil, 31 August 1580.

11. "In de 16de eeuw begint bij vele schrijvers de y en de ij door elkaar te lopen" (J. L. van der Gouw, *Oud Schrift in Nederland: Een Leerboek voor de Student* [Alphen aan den Rijn: Canaletto, 1980], p. 85). See also P. J. Horsman, Th. J. Poelstra, and J. P. Sigmond, *Schriftspiegel: Nederlandse Paleografische Teksten van de 13de tot de 18de eeuw* (Zutphen: Terra, 1984).

12. The black-letter type used by Robert Waldegrave to print the Martin Marprelate tracts, for instance, beginning with *Oh Read Ouer D. Iohn Bridges for it is a Worthy Worke; or, An Epitome of the Fyrste Booke of that Right Worshipfull Volume Written Against the Puritanes in the Defence of the Noble Cleargie by as Worshipfull a Prieste, Iohn Bridges, Presbyter, Priest or Elder, Doctor of Diuillitie, and Deane of Sarum* (n.p.: [Robert Waldegrave], n.d. [1588]), became known as his "Dutch letters," although it does not include a dotted or double-dotted *y*. See *The Martin Marprelate Tracts: A Modernized and Annotated Edition*, ed. Joseph L. Black (Cambridge: CUP, 2008), p. 3.

13. Alan Bray, *The Friend* (Chicago: U of Chicago P, 2003), p. 52; see also Alan G. R. Smith, *Servant of the Cecils: The Life of Sir Michael Hickes* (Cape, 1977), pp. 92–96.

14. BL, Lansd. MS 36, fols. 212^r–213^v (article 89): John Stubbs to Michael Hickes, 30 July 1582.

15. BL, Lansd. MS 107, fols. 168^r–169^v (article 100): Michael Hickes to John Stubbs, undated.

16. BL, Lansd. MS 107, fol. 170 (article 101): Michael Hickes to Stubbs, undated.

17. It may be the short letter, in which Stubbs refers to the "forty years almost of my vain life" and promises to "[give] myself seriously to a sincere profession of Christ: . . . give continueally some time to an ordinary and standing exercise of the word . . . choose the godly, and none other, to be my company," which is transcribed in John Strype's *Annals of the Reformation*, 4 vols. (Thomas Edlin, 1725–31), II, pp. 304–5, and reproduced in Berry, *John Stubbs's "Gaping Gulf,"* pp. 118–19. Berry notes that the catalog of the Lansdowne manuscripts describes this letter (from Stubbs to Hickes) as being BL, Lansd. MS 107, fol. 170 (article 101), but that the reference is incorrect, that this reference actually refers to the letter from Hickes to Stubbs discussed above, and that the letter from Stubbs is not to be found in any of the Lansdowne volumes. One can only speculate that it was, at some point attached to the letter that now occupies that place in the volume.

18. Livy, *Ab urbe condita*, ed. B. O. Foster, 14 vols. (Heinemann, 1919), I, p. 259.

19. A paraphrase of Livy's account appears in William Painter, *The Palace of Pleasure, Beautified, Adorned and Well Furnished, with Pleasaunt Histories and Excellent Nouelles* (Henry Denham for Richard Tottell and William Iones, 1566), sigs. B3^v–C1^r. See also Thomas Elyot, *The Boke Named the Gouernour* (Thomas Berthelet, 1531), sigs. B2^r–B3^r; William Patten, *The Expedicion into Scotlande of the Most Woorthely Fortunate Prince Edward* (1548), sig. +8^v; Myles Huggarde, *The Displaying of the Protestantes, & Sondry Their Practises* (Robert Ealy, 1556), sigs. F6^v–F7^v; *The Prouerbes of the Noble and Woorthy Souldier Sir Iames Lopez de Mendoza*, trans. Barnabe Googe (Richarde Watkins, 1579), sig. K2^v. On John Foxe's allusion to Scaevola (and the history of that allusion), placing "Christian martyrdom within the realm of civic humanism," see Brian Cummings, "Images in Books: Foxe *Eikonoklastes*," in *Art Re-formed: Re-assessing the Impact of the Reformation on the Visual Arts*, ed. Tara Hamling and Richard L. Williams (Newcastle: Cambridge Scholars, 2007), pp. 183–200 (p. 190). Cummings makes no mention of Stubbs.

20. Mary E. Hazard implies that the term denotes a continued defense of Stubbs's own position: "Apology was the occasion to articulate the rightness of things as they were conventionally expected to be, although Stubbs managed a small vindication by thereafter signing himself Scaeva" (*Elizabethan Silent Language* [Lincoln: U of Nebraska P, 2000], p. 223).

21. TNA, PROB 11/75.

22. BL, Lansd. MS 108, fol. 93 (article 55): John Stubbs to Michael Hickes, 1590.

23. For other examples of the endorsement, see BL, Lansd. MS 36, fols. 212ʳ–213ᵛ (article 89): John Stubbs to Michael Hickes, 30 July 1572; BL, Lansd. MS 43, fols. 51ʳ–52ᵛ (article 24): John Stubbs to William Cecil, 1590.

24. Lincolnshire Archives, Lincoln, Ancaster MS 8 ANC 1/38: John Stubbs to Lord Willoughby, 15 November 1585; 8 ANC 1/44: John Stubbs to Lord Willoughby, 21 April 1586; 8 ANC 1/61: John Stubbs to Lord Willoughby, 14 May 1586; 8 ANC 2/5: John Stubbs to Lord Willoughby, 6 June 1586.

25. Lincolnshire Archives, Ancaster MS 8 ANC 1/40 and 1/42.

CHAPTER 8. "AN UNCIVILL SCURRILOUS LETTER"

1. Thomas V. Cohen, "The Lay Liturgy of Affront in Sixteenth-Century Italy," *Journal of Social History*, 25 (1992), 857–77 (p. 857).

2. See Markku Peltonen, "Francis Bacon, the Earl of Northampton, and the Jacobean Anti-Duelling Campaign," *HJ*, 44 (2001), 1–28, (pp. 6–7). Like Peltonen, Linda Pollock also argues for a continuity between discourses of honor and civility in this period, although she is critical of his concentration on the duel, which, she argues, continues to associate honor with revenge rather than the "accommodating values of civility" ("Honor, Gender, and Reconciliation in Elite Culture, 1570–1700," *JBS*, 46 [2007], 3–29 [pp. 7–8]).

3. Linda Pollock, "Anger and the Negotiation of Relationships in Early Modern England," *HJ*, (2007), 56–90 (pp. 581–83).

4. Pollock makes the same point about moderate and immoderate anger, although she tends to underplay uses of immoderate anger in "Anger and the Negotiation," pp. 574, 587.

5. Pollock, "Anger and the Negotiation," p. 583.

6. Cohen, "Lay Liturgy of Affront," p. 866; Nancy Worman, *Abusive Mouths in Classical Athens* (Cambridge: CUP, 2008), p. 3.

7. Pollock also notes that anger "was and is a highly gendered emotion" and women's anger was viewed more negatively than men's, however, "women were willing to express rage, and to do so without apology, if they thought the circumstances justified it" ("Anger and the Negotiation," p. 578). See also Gwynne Kennedy, *Just Anger: Representing Women's Anger in Early Modern England* (Carbondale: Southern Illinois UP, 2000). On women's use of invective in family letters, see James Daybell, *Women Letter-Writers in Tudor England* (Oxford: OUP, 2006), pp. 185–88, 194–95.

8. See Pollock, "Anger and the Negotiation"; and Daybell, *Women Letter-Writers*.

9. *The Letters of John Chamberlain*, ed. N. E. McLure, 2 vols. (Philadelphia: American Philosophical Society, 1939), II, p. 444.

10. Lynne Magnusson, "A Rhetoric of Requests: Genre and Linguistic Scripts in Elizabethan Women's Suitors' Letters," in *Women and Politics in Early Modern England, 1450–1700*, ed. James Daybell (Aldershot: Ashgate, 2004), pp. 51–66 (pp. 60–61).

11. David Colclough, "Verse Libels and the Epideictic Tradition in Early Stuart England," *HLQ*, 69 (2006), 15–30 (pp. 16–18, 29).

12. Angel Day, *The English Secretorie* (1586), pp. 72—73. In the 1592 edition, Day introduces a chapter heading devoted to "Epistles Laudatorie and Vituperatorie."

13. William Fulwood, "How to write vnder the demonstrative gender, blaming or dispraising another," in *The Enemie of Idlenesse* (1568), pp. 62–63.

14. *OED*, s.vv. "honest," 1a, 2a, b, 3a; "honesty," 1a–d, 2.

15. Pollock, "Honor, Gender, and Reconciliation," pp. 21–22.

16. Fulwood, *Enemie of Idlenesse*, p. 63.

17. Peltonen, "Francis Bacon," p. 3. See also Jennifer Richards on lying and honesty in *Rhetoric and Courtliness in Early Modern Literature* (Cambridge: CUP, 2003), p. 28.

18. Christopher Craig, "Audience Expectations, Invective, and Proof," in *Cicero the Advocate*, ed. J. G. F. Powell and J. Paterson (Oxford: OUP, 2004), pp. 187–213 (pp. 193–95).

19. See Lisa Jardine and Alan Stewart, *Hostage to Fortune: The Troubled Life of Francis Bacon, 1561–1626* (Victor Gollancz, 1998), pp. 389–92.

20. BL, Add. MS 29975, fol. 31ʳ.

21. Richard S. Smith, *Sir Francis Willoughby of Wollaton Hall* (Nottingham: Nottingham Arts Department, 1988), pp. 21, 27–28; Alice T. Friedman, *House and Household in Elizabethan England: Wollaton Hall and the Willoughby Family* (Chicago: U of Chicago P, 1989), pp. 136–37.

22. HMC, *Report on the Manuscripts of Lord Middleton, Preserved at Wollaton Hall, Nottinghamshire* (1911), pp. 574–75.

23. Lady Elizabeth Willoughby also wrote angry letters to her husband in which she flouted his authority; see Friedman, *House and Household*, pp. 53–61.

24. Cassandra Willoughby, Duchess of Chandos, *The Continuation of the History of the Willoughby Family*, ed. A. C. Wood (Eton, Windsor: Shakespeare Head Press for University of Nottingham, 1958), p. 35.

25. Smith, *Francis Willoughby*, p. 33; HMC, *Middleton*, p. 563.

26. HMC, *Middleton*, p. 576.

27. Friedman, *House and Household*, pp. 62, 65.

28. Smith, *Francis Willoughby*, p. 23; HMC, *Middleton*, p. 576.

29. HMC, *Middleton*, p. 576.

30. HMC, *Middleton*, p. 577.

31. Gary Schneider, *The Culture of Epistolarity: Vernacular Letters and Letter Writing in Early Modern England, 1500–1700* (Newark: U of Delaware P, 2005), pp. 132–39.

32. Jeffrey Sawyer, *Printed Poison: Pamphlet Propaganda, Faction Politics, and the Public Sphere in Early Modern France* (Berkeley: U of California P, 1990), p. 93.

33. HMC, *Middleton*, p. 576.

34. HMC, *Middleton*, p. 577. Mary Fisher's letter provides a counterexample to the letters Pollock has studied, which "even when confronted with a vehement out-burst, [did not accuse] another of being uncivil" (Pollock, "Anger and the Negotiation," p. 586).

35. See Pollock, "Honor, Gender, and Reconciliatiton," pp. 25–26, on the role taken by elite women in maintaining family honor.

36. Alastair Bellany, "The Embarrassment of Libels: Perceptions and Representations of Verse Libelling in Early Stuart England," in *The Politics of the Public Sphere in Early Modern England*, ed. Peter Lake and Steven Pincus (Manchester: Manchester UP, 2007), pp. 144–67 (p. 145).

37. Copy of Brooke's will, "Memorial-Introduction," in *The Complete Poems of Christopher Brooke*, ed. A. B. Grosart (n.p., 1872), pp. 15, 22.

38. HMC, *Report on the Manuscripts of the Late Reginald Rawdon Hastings, Esq., of the Manor House, Ashby de la Zouche* (1947), IV, pp. 4, 16–17; John McCavitt, *Sir Arthur Chichester: Lord Deputy of Ireland, 1605–1616* (Belfast: Institute of Irish Studies, 1998), p. 60.

39. "Remembrances, by Captain Barnaby Rich, Concerning the State of Ireland, 14 Aug. 1612," ed. C. Litton Falkiner, *Proceedings of the Royal Irish Academy*, sect. C, no. 8, XXVI (1906),

pp. 125–42 (p. 133); *Register of Admissions to the Honourable Society of the Middle Temple*, ed. H. F. McGeagh and H. A. C. Sturgess, 3 vols. (Butterworth, 1949), II, p. 58. Jacob owned substantial property in Southampton before her marriage to Brooke and was the cousin of a prominent Southampton alderman and merchant, Francis Knowles; see Brooke's will, "Memorial-Introduction," p. 16.

40. George Puttenham, *The Art of English Poesy: A Critical Edition*, ed. Frank Whigham and Wayne A. Rebhorn (Ithaca, NY: Cornell UP, 2007), p. 296.

41. TNA, SP 14/130, fols. 174^r–175^v [Conway Papers]: "Mr Brookes Letter to the Ladie Davies written A° 1622."

42. Juvenal, "Satire 8," in *Juvenal and Persius*, trans. Susanna Morton Braund (Cambridge, MA: Harvard UP, 2004).

43. Laura Gowing, "Women, Status and the Popular Culture of Dishonour," *TRHS*, 6 (1996), 225–34 (p. 232).

44. Pollock argues that female honor was a much broader concept than sexual honor and encompassed collective honor ("Honor, Gender, and Reconciliation," pp. 21–22).

45. Anthony Parr uses "surplus value" to describe the transformation of travel into a literary performance intended to entertain in "Thomas Coryat and the Discovery of Europe," *HLQ*, 55 (1992), 579–602.

46. *Letters of John Chamberlain*, II, p. 444.

47. See my *English Wits: Literature and Sociability in Early Modern England* (Cambridge: CUP, 2007), pp. 85–86, 157–61; and Daniel Starza Smith, *John Donne and the Conway Papers: Patronage and Manuscript Circulation in the Early Seventeenth Century* (Oxford: OUP, 2014), pp. 186–87.

48. John Donne, *Letters to Severall Persons of Honour* (J. Flesher, 1651; repr. 1654), pp. 89–90.

49. Peltonen, "Francis Bacon," 8–9.

50. The Denny-Wroth verses and letters and details of the quarrel appear in *The Poems of Lady Mary Wroth*, ed. Josephine Roberts (Baton Rouge: Louisiana State UP, 1983), pp. 31–35, 233–43 (p. 34). Subsequent references will be to this edition.

51. On Wroth's verse libel and the language of the duel, see Gavin Alexander, *Writing After Sidney: The Literary Response to Sir Philip Sidney, 1585–1640* (Oxford: OUP, 2006), p. 286.

52. *Poems of Lady Mary Wroth*, pp. 239, 240, 241.

53. *Poems of Lady Mary Wroth*, p. 237.

54. *Poems of Lady Mary Wroth*, p. 240.

55. *Poems of Lady Mary Wroth*, p. 240.

56. *Poems of Lady Mary Wroth*, p. 241.

57. While Wroth may have been victorious in her letters, Paul Salzman points to "a concerted attempt" to stop her verse libel circulating in the male domain of manuscript verse miscellanies, whereas Denny's was copied, thus suppressing her voice in this dispute ("Mary Wroth and Hermaphroditic Circulation," in *Early Modern Women and the Poem*, ed. Susan Wiseman [Manchester: Manchester UP, 2013]).

58. Pollock, "Anger and the Negotiation," pp. 587–88.

CHAPTER 9. "BURN THIS LETTER"

Epigraph. Lord Rosebery, *Miscellanies Literary and Historical*, 2 vols. (Hodder and Stoughton, 1921), I, pp. 186–87.

1. On the role of the "postal economy" in the modern state, see Patrick Joyce, *The State of Freedom: A Social History of the British State Since 1800* (Cambridge: CUP, 2013).

2. John Stuart Mill, *Writings on India*, ed. John M. Robson, Martin Moir, and Zawahir Moir (Toronto: U of Toronto P, 1990), p. 33; see also Robert D. Aguirre, "Agencies of the Letter: The Foreign Office and the Ruins of Central America," *Victorian Studies*, 46/2 (2004), 285–96 (Mill quoted p. 289).

3. Sir Edward Hertslet, *Recollections of the Old Foreign Office* (J. Murray, 1901), p. 77. On Palmerston and handwriting, see Jane Caplan, "Illegibility: Reading and Insecurity in History, Law and Government," *History Workshop Journal*, 68 (2009), 99–121 (esp. pp. 107–9).

4. Hilary Jenkinson, *A Manual of Archive Administration* (Oxford: Clarendon Press, 1922), p. 116. On Jenkinson and the custodial role of the archivist, see also Francis X. Blouin and William G. Rosenberg, eds., *Processing the Past: Contesting Authority in History and the Archives* (Oxford: OUP, 2011), pp. 38–39.

5. Jenkinson, *Manual of Archive Administration*, p. 124.

6. Donne, *Letters to Severall Persons of Honour* (J. Flesher, 1651; repr. 1654), pp. 105–8: Donne to "Sir G. M." (but probably to Sir Henry Goodere).

7. Donne, *Letters*, epistle dedicatory, sig. A4^r.

8. James O'Toole and Richard Cox, *Understanding Archives and Manuscripts* (Chicago: Society of American Archivists, 2006), p. 17.

9. A letter from Frances Howard to Mrs. Anne Turner, with the superscription "burne this letter," was a crucial piece of evidence at the Overbury murder trial in 1615, resulting in Turner's execution; for a copy of the letter, see BL, Sloane MS 1002, fol. 45; and for the context, see David Lindley, *The Trials of Frances Howard: Fact and Fiction at the Court of King James* (Routledge, 1993), pp. 71–73.

10. Donne, *Letters*, pp. 217–21: Donne to Goodere [1614].

11. BL, Add. MS 5503, fols. 70–74: Bacon to James I, 21 February 1616. Printed in James Spedding, ed., *The Letters and the Life of Francis Bacon*, 7 vols. (Longmans, 1861–74), V, p. 254.

12. Donne, *Letters*, p. 185.

13. BL, Add. MS 5503, fols. 44–45: Bacon to Villiers, 19 February 1616. Printed in Spedding, *Letters*, V, p. 249.

14. Clare Brant, *Eighteenth-Century Letters and British Culture* (Basingstoke: Palgrave, 2006), p. 5.

15. Linda A. Pollock, "Living on the Stage of the World: The Concept of Privacy Among the Elite of Early Modern England," in *Rethinking Social History: English Society 1570–1920 and Its Interpretation*, ed. Adrian Wilson (Manchester: Manchester UP, 1993), pp. 78–96.

16. Simon Adams, "The Papers of Robert Dudley, Earl of Leicester: I. The Browne-Evelyn Collection," *Archives*, 20 (1992), 63–85 (quotation at p. 63).

17. Whyte's letters to Sidney are among the De L'Isle and Dudley papers in the Kent History and Library Centre and have recently been published in *The Letters (1595–1608) of Rowland Whyte*, ed. Michael G. Brennan, Noel J. Kinnamon, and Margaret P. Hannay (Philadelphia: American Philosophical Society, 2013). Cecil's letters to Carew are among the Carew Papers in LPL, MS 604, described in a contemporary contents list as "a remaynder of Mr Secretary Cecyll his lettres left unburnt"; they are printed in *Letters from Sir Robert Cecil to Sir George Carew*, ed. John Maclean (Camden Society, 1864).

18. *Letters (1595–1608) of Rowland Whyte*, pp. 160–61: Whyte to Sidney, 28 February 1597.

19. *Letters (1595–1608)*, pp. 153, 306: Whyte to Sidney, 21 February 1597 and 2 March 1598.

20. *Letters (1595–1608)*, pp. 345, 347: Whyte to Sidney, 30 September 1599 and 3 October 1599.

21. *Letters (1595–1608)*, pp. 348, 351: Whyte to Sidney, 4 October 1599 and 11 October 1599.

22. *Letters (1595–1608) of Rowland Whyte*, p. 386: Whyte to Sidney, 1 December 1599.

23. LPL, MS 604, fols. 56–57, 64–65: Cecil to Carew, 8 November 1600 and 15 December 1600. For an overview of the political and military situation in Ireland, helpfully contextualizing the Cecil-Carew correspondence, see Paul E. J. Hammer, *Elizabeth's Wars: War, Government and Society in Tudor England, 1544–1604* (Basingstoke: Palgrave, 2003), pp. 208–35.

24. LPL, MS 604, fols. 56–57: Cecil to Carew, 8 November 1600.

25. LPL, MS 604, fols. 86–87: Cecil to Carew, postscript to letter of 20 July 1601.

26. TNA, SP 99/12, fols. 147–48: Dudley Carleton to John Chamberlain, 12 March 1613. In the same way, Robert Sidney's letters to Burghley were removed from the archive after Burghley's death in 1598 and returned to Sidney to be burned; see Whyte's letter to Sidney, 17 October 1599, *Letters (1595–1608)*, p. 356.

27. Thomas Stafford, *Pacata Hibernia* (1633), p. 183.

28. LPL, MS 604, fols. 153–55: Cecil to Carew, 25 March 1602; *Letters from Sir Robert Cecil to Sir George Carew*, pp. 106–8.

29. LPL, MS 604, fols. 199–203: Cecil to Carew, 24 October 1602; *Letters from Sir Robert Cecil to Sir George Carew*, pp. 138–45.

30. LPL, MS 604, fols. 151–52: Cecil to Mountjoy, 18 February 1602, endorsed, presumably by Cecil's secretary, "my Mr's letter to the lord Deputy."

31. LPL, MS 658, fols. 15–16 (retained draft) and fol. 179 (copy sent to Egerton): Bacon to Egerton, 30 July 1598.

32. BL, Lansd. MS 88, fol. 167: Earl and Countess of Shrewsbury to Hickes, 30 November 1603; LPL, MS 3201, fols. 161–62: Hickes to Earl of Shrewsbury, 6 December 1603.

33. Ian Atherton, "The Itch Grown a Disease: Manuscript Transmission of News in the Seventeenth Century," *Prose Studies*, 21/2 (1998), pp. 39–65.

34. BL, Harl. MS 7002, fols. 340–41: Lorkin to Puckering, 21 July 1614.

35. BL, Add. MS 72348, fols. 10–11: John Finet to William Trumbull, 17 August 1615.

36. *Letters from George Lord Carew to Sir Thomas Roe, 1615–1617*, ed. John Maclean (Camden Society, 1860), p. 10: Carew to Roe, 24 January 1616.

37. *Letters of John Holles, 1587–1637*, ed. P. R. Seddon, 3 vols. (Nottingham: Thoroton Society, 1975–83), II, pp. 313–14: John Holles to his son, 12 December 1625.

38. TNA, C115/108, no. 8628: Palmer to Scudamore, 24 December 1625.

39. BL, Harl. MS 383, fols. 31–32: D'Ewes to Stuteville, 2 May 1626.

40. TNA, C115/108, no. 8631: Palmer to Scudamore, 16 June 1626; BL, Add. MS 11044, fols. 11–12: John Scudamore to Rowland Scudamore, 22 June 1626. See Atherton, "The Itch Grown a Disease," p. 44, where this example is discussed.

41. Elizabeth's correspondence with Roe is printed in *The Correspondence of Elizabeth Stuart, Queen of Bohemia*, vol. II *(1632–42)*, ed. Nadine Akkerman (Oxford: OUP, 2011). I am grateful to Dr. Akkerman for much helpful advice on these letters and for a sight of her unpublished paper "Opening Up the Queen of Bohemia's Cabinet: A Study of Her Secretariat."

42. *Correspondence of Elizabeth Stuart*, II, pp. 191, 281: Roe to Elizabeth, 30 June 1633, and Elizabeth to Roe, 20 March 1634.

43. BL, Harl. MS 1580, fol. 388: Roe to Buckingham, 14/24 December 1622.

44. *Correspondence of Elizabeth Stuart*, II, p. 282: Elizabeth to Hamilton, 20 March 1634.

45. *Correspondence of Elizabeth Stuart*, II, pp. 310–11: Elizabeth to Roe, 17 January 1635.

46. *Correspondence of Elizabeth Stuart*, II, pp. 319, 541: Elizabeth to Roe, 21 February 1635, and Roe to Elizabeth, 30 October 1636.

47. George Carew also asked Roe to "render unto me all my gazetts, or ells thatt you would burne them all" (*Letters from George Lord Carew*, p. 139).

48. Laud's letters to Wentworth are in the Strafford Papers, Sheffield City Archives, and have been published in Laud's *Works*, ed. James Bliss and William Scott, 7 vols. (Oxford: J. H. Parker, 1847–60).

49. Laud, *Works*, VII, pp. 166, 230: Laud to Wentworth, 3 August 1635 and 23 January 1636.

50. J. F. Merritt, "Power and Communication: Thomas Wentworth and Government at a Distance During the Personal Rule, 1629–1635," in *The Political World of Thomas Wentworth, Earl of Strafford, 1621–1641*, ed. Merritt (Cambridge: CUP, 1996), pp. 109–32 (esp. p. 125).

51. Laud, *Works*, VII, pp. 211, 234: Laud to Wentworth, 30 November 1635 and 23 January 1636.

52. Laud, *Works*, VII, pp. 234–35: Laud to Wentworth, 23 January 1636.

53. For these and other references to side papers, see Laud, *Works*, VII, pp. 240, 251, 278, 295, 308, 317, 401, 419, 424, 545, 550.

54. Laud, *Works*, VII, p. 451: Laud to Wentworth, side paper to 22 June 1638.

55. Garrard's excessive sociability was noted by others: Laud wrote to Wentworth in 1636 that he was an honest man but that his fondness for "good company" made him unsuitable for preferment (Laud, *Works*, VII, p. 132).

56. BL, Add. MS 70002, fols. 110–11: Conway to Garrard, 14 July 1636.

57. BL, Add. MS 70002, fols. 140–41: Conway to Garrard, 13 September 1636.

58. TNA, C115/106, no. 8388: John Pory to Scudamore, 17 December 1631.

59. Kevin Sharpe, *The Personal Rule of Charles I* (New Haven, CT: Yale UP, 1992), pp. 683, 687.

60. I. A. Shapiro, "The Text of Donne's *Letters to Severall Persons*," *RES*, 7 (1931), 291–301 (pp. 292–93).

61. J. S. Brewer and William Bullen, eds., *Calendar of the Carew Manuscripts, Preserved in the Archiepiscopal Library at Lambeth, 1515–1574* (Longmans, 1867), p. xl.

62. Charles Carlton, *Archbishop William Laud* (Routledge and Kegan Paul, 1987), p. 82.

63. Linda Levy Peck, *Northampton: Patronage and Policy at the Court of James I* (Allen and Unwin, 1982), pp. 39–40.

64. BL, Add. MS 70002, fols. 110–11: Conway to Garrard, 14 July 1636.

65. *Wentworth Papers, 1597–1628*, ed. J. P. Cooper (Royal Historical Society, 1973), pp. 18, 22–23.

66. BL, Stowe MS 246, fol. 79: Dalrymple to Craggs, 2 April 1718.

67. BL, Eg. MS 3445, fols. 15–16: Holdernesse to Yorke, 17 April 1752.

68. *Foreign Office, Diplomatic, and Consular Sketches* (W. H. Allen, 1883), p. 65.

69. BL, Add. MS 21634, fols. 241, 243, 322: Amherst to Bouquet, 7 July 1763, and Bouquet to Amherst, 13 July 1763.

70. Jenkinson, *Manual of Archive Administration*, pp. 130–31.

71. Antonia Moon, "Destroying Records, Keeping Records: Some Practices at the East India Company and at the India Office," *Archives*, 33/119 (2008), 110–21.

72. "Revealed: The Bonfire of Papers at the End of Empire," *Guardian*, 29 November 2013.

73. Sir John Tilley and Stephen Gaselee, *The Foreign Office* (G. P. Putnam's Sons, 1933), p. 164.

74. "Electronic Messages Are Durable—and Can Be Dangerous," *Financial Times*, 24 January 2004, cited in Michael Moss, "The Hutton Inquiry, the President of Nigeria and What the Butler Hoped to See," *EHR*, 120/487 (2005), 577–92 (p. 581).

CHAPTER 10. GENDERED ARCHIVAL PRACTICES AND THE FUTURE LIVES OF LETTERS

I am grateful to Andrew Gordon for his comments on earlier drafts of the essay, and to the audience (especially Gemma Allen, Amanda Capern, Stan Chojnacki, Barbara Harris, Johanna Harris, Femke Molekamp, Daniel Starza Smith, Alison Wiggins, Graham Williams, and Lizzy Williamson) who attended the "New Directions in Early Modern Women's Letters" colloquium run by the "Women's Early Modern Letters Online" project at the University of Oxford, as well as to audiences at the research seminars at Cambridge and St. Andrew's, and at the RSA in Berlin.

1. Jacques Derrida, *Archive Fever: A Freudian Impression*, trans. Eric Prenowitz (Chicago: U of Chicago P, 1996), pp. 35–36, 43, 47, 48, 95. The French title is *Mal d'archive: Une impression freudienne*. In particular a letter by Anna Freud assumes a peculiar status, evidently written by her, it is questioned whether she in fact "signed it," in other words whether she spoke in her own name, or that of her father (pp. 43–44).

2. Derrida, *Archive Fever*, pp. 35–36.

3. William H. Sherman, *Used Books: Marking Readers in Renaissance England* (Philadelphia: U of Pennsylvania P, 2008), pp. 54–55, 57, passim chap. 3

4. See, for example, Adam Fox, "Remembering the Past in Early Modern England," *TRHS*, 6th ser., 9 (1999), 233–56 (pp. 234, 237); D. R. Woolf, "A Feminine Past? Gender, Genre, and Historical Knowledge in England, 1500–1800," *American Historical Review*, 102/3 (1997), 645–79.

5. Daniel Woolf, *The Social Circulation of the Past English Historical Culture, 1500–1730* (Oxford: OUP, 2003), p. 114.

6. Tim Stretton, *Women Waging Law in Elizabethan England* (Cambridge: CUP, 2005).

7. Jan Broadway, *"No historie so meete": Gentry Culture and the Development of Local History in Elizabethan and Early Stuart England* (Manchester: Manchester UP, 2006), p. 84.

8. James Daybell, *The Material Letter in Early Modern England: Manuscript Letters and the Culture and Practices of Letter-Writing, 1512–1635* (Basingstoke: Palgrave Macmillan, 2012), p. 221.

9. John Evans, "Extracts from the Private Account Book of Sir William More of Loseley, in Surrey, in the Time of Queen Mary and of Queen Elizabeth," *Archaeologia*, 36/2 (1855), 284–93 (p. 292); BL, Add. MS 41140, fol. 28: Mary Walpole to Edward Walpole, 9 March 1588–1589; *The Egerton Papers*, ed. J. Payne Collier, Camden Society, 12 (1840), p. 322; Ralph A. Houlbrooke, *English Family Life, 1576–1716: An Anthology of Diaries* (Oxford: Blackwell, 1988), p. 72.

10. *The Private Life of an Elizabethan Lady: The Diary of Lady Margaret Hoby, 1599–1605*, ed. by Joanna Moody (Stroud: Sutton, 1998), p. 95.

11. See, for example, Thomas Lupton, *A Thousand Notable Things of Sundrie Sorts* (1579), p. 147; W[illiam] P[hillip], *A Booke of Secrets* (1596), sig. B1$^{r–v}$.

12. C. S. L Davies and Jane Garnett, eds., *Wadham College* (Oxford: Anness, 1994), pp. 21, 145; *A Catalogue of the Muniments of Wadham College, Oxford* (HMC, National Register of Archives, typescript, 1962), 4/27.

13. BL, Add. MS 36901, fols. 7–113 (1585–1603).

14. Eric Ketelaar, "The Genealogical Gaze: Family Identities and Family Archives in the Fourteenth to Seventeenth Centuries," *Libraries & the Cultural Record*, 44/1 (2009), 9–28 (p. 9). See also Eric Ketelaar, "Muniments and Monuments: The Dawn of Archives as Cultural Patrimony," *Archival Science*, 7 (2007), 343–57; Jean-Michel Leniaud, *Les archipels du passe: Le patrimoine et son histoire* (Paris: Fayard, 2002).

15. I am currently engaged in a long-term study of this type of family history.

16. Carole Rawcliffe, "A Tudor Nobleman as Archivist: The Papers of Edward, Third Duke of Buckingham," *Journal of the Society of Archivists*, 5/5 (1976), 294–300 (pp. 294–96).

17. A. P. Newton, ed., *Calendar of the Manuscripts of Major-General Lord Sackville, Preserved at Knole, Sevenoaks, Kent*, vol. II, *Cranfield Papers, 1534–1612*, Historical Manuscripts Commission, Octavo Series, 80 ([HMSO, 1940]), p. 56.

18. Miriam Slater, *Family Life in the Seventeenth Century: The Verneys of Claydon House* (Routledge and Kegan Paul, 1984); Susan E. Whyman, *Sociability and Power in Late-Stuart England: The Cultural Worlds of the Verneys, 1660–1720* (Oxford: OUP, 1999); F. P. Verney and M. M. Verney, *Memoirs of the Verney Family*, 4 vols. (1892–99); J. Bruce, ed., *Letters and Papers of the Verney Family Down to the End of the Year 1639*, Camden Society, 56 (1853); Claydon House, Buckinghamshire, correspondence and MSS; Alison D. Wall, ed., *Two Elizabethan Women: Correspondence of Joan and Maria Thynne, 1575–1611*, Wiltshire Record Society, 38 (Devizes, 1983); Longleat House, Wiltshire, Marquess of Bath MSS, Thynne MSS.

19. Ketelaar, "Genealogical Gaze," p. 18.

20. Marie-Louise Coolahan, "Literary Memorialization and the Posthumous Construction of Female Authorship," in *The Arts of Remembrance in Early Modern England: Memorial Cultures of the Post Reformation*, ed. Andrew Gordon and Thomas Rist (Aldershot: Ashgate, 2013), pp. 161–78. See also Margaret J. M. Ezell, "The Posthumous Publication of Women's Manuscripts and the History of Authorship," in *Women's Writing and the Circulation of Ideas: Manuscript Publication in England, 1550–1800*, ed. George L. Justice and Nathan Tinker (Cambridge: CUP, 2002), pp. 121–36.

21. Jean Klene, ed., *The Southwell-Sibthorpe Commonplace Book, Folger MS. V.b. 198* (Tempe, AZ: Medieval & Renaissance Texts & Studies, 1997), pp. 4–6; Jean Klene, "'Monument of an Endless Affection': Folger MS V.b.198 and Lady Anne Southwell," *EMS*, 9 (2000), 165–86.

22. William Andrews Clark Memorial Library, MS L6815 M3 C734: Miscellany of works by Anne and Roger Ley, including Anne Ley's commonplace book, fols. 97ʳ–105ᵛ.

23. Anthony Walker, *The Holy Life of Mrs Elizabeth Walker* (1690), sigs. P5ᵛ–T4ᵛ (pp. 234–96).

24. Marie-Louise Coolahan, "Reception, Reputation and Early Modern Women's Missing Texts," *Critical Quarterly*, 55/4 (2013), 3–14.

25. Of the eighty-nine letters, seventy-four are from women, thirteen from men to women, and two from male letter writers to other men. One of the last mentioned was an enclosure in a letter from Andrew Melville to the Countess of Shrewsbury, the other a letter reporting on an earthquake from Melville to the Earl of Shrewsbury (LPL, Talbot MS 3205, fols. 123, 125ʳ–126ᵛ). The volume also contains a statement of the debts of Thomas Markham in a letter from Mary Markham to Robert Cecil (LPL, Talbot MS 3205, fol. 83).

26. *A Calendar of the Shrewsbury and Talbot Papers in the Lambeth Palace Library and the College of Arms*. vol. 2, *Talbot Papers in the College of Arms*, ed. G. R. Batho (HMC, 1971); hereafter cited as *Talbot Papers*. See also *A Calendar of the Shrewsbury and Talbot Papers in the Lambeth Palace Library and the College of Arms*, vol. 1, *Shrewsbury MSS in Lambeth Palace Library, (MSS 694–710)*, ed. C. Jamison, rev. E. G. W. Bill (HMC, 1966).

27. Edmund Lodge, *Illustrations of British History . . .* , 2nd ed. (John Chidley, 1838), I, p. xx.

28. *Talbot Papers*, p. ix.

29. E. W. Crossley, "The MSS. of Nathaniel Johnston, M.D., of Pontefract," *Yorkshire Archaeological Journal*, 32/128 (1936), 429–41; A. F. Oakley, "Letters to a 17th Century Yorkshire Physician," *History of Medicine*, 2/4 (1970), 24–28; J. D. Martin, "The Antiquarian Collections of Nathaniel Johnston" (B.Litt. thesis, Oxford, 1956); Mark Goldie, "Johnston, Nathaniel (*bap.* 1629?, *d.* 1705)," in *ODNB*. The dispersal of the larger body of papers that descended from the Talbots is diffuse. Johnston preserved among the Duke of Norfolk's archives papers relating to the sixth Earl of Shrewsbury's guardianship of Mary, Queen of Scots, and himself held onto other papers (now the Shrewsbury Papers) while he prepared his manuscript "Lives of the Shrewsburys" and his *Antiquities of Yorkshire*, some of which passed to Lambeth Palace Library after his death where they are now cataloged as MSS 694–710 (*Talbot Papers*, p. ix). Other papers, along with his "Lives of the Shrewsburys," were acquired by Richard Frank of Campsall Hall, near Doncaster, and most of these were sold by Sotheby's in 1942 to the Bodleian Library, Leeds Central Library, the Wellcome and City Library of Sheffield. A number of loose papers and six chests not sold were deposited in the Public Record Office in 1950 (*Talbot Papers*, p. x). Johnston's antiquarian collections were well known at the time and numbering over one hundred volumes were described by Edward Bernard in his *Catalogi librorum manuscriptorum Angliae* (1697), including "Two Volumes of Original Letters writ to and from George, Gilbert, and Edward Earls of Shrewsbury, and other Ancestors of the Families of Cavendish of Devonshire, and New-Castle, the Lady Arbella Stuart, and other eminent persons in the Courts of Queen Elizabeth I and King James," and several holograph "Lives of the earls of Shrewsburys." See Edward Bernard and Humphrey Wanley, *Catalogi librorum manuscriptorum Angliae et Hiberniae in unum collecti cum indice alphabetico* (Oxoniae: E Theatro Sheldoniano . . . , 1697), II, i, pp. 99–102; HMC, *Papers of British Antiquaries and Historians* (TSO, 2003), pp. 109–10. A holograph copy of his "Lives of the Shrewsburys" is held at Sheffield Archives, Bacon Frank MSS, BFM/2–7. A fair copy of his "Lives of the Shrewsburys" is at Longleat (Longleat Library, MS 114); HMC Reports, Appendix to the 6th Report, pp. 448–65; a further copy was sold at Sotheby's in 1974 (26 June, lot 2963, formerly Phillipps MS 8521).

30. Broadway, *"No Historie So Meete"*; Bernard and Wanley, *Catalogi librorum*, II, i, p. 102.

31. *Talbot Papers*, pp. xi–xvi.

32. W. T. MacCaffrey "Talbot and Stanhope: An Episode in Elizabethan Politics," *Bulletin of the Institute of Historical Research*, 33 (1960), 73–85.

33. *Talbot Papers*, pp. xiv–xvi.

34. LPL, Talbot MS 3197, fols. 429^r–430^v (5 April [1589]), fols. 433^r–434^v (8 April 1589).

35. LPL, Talbot MS 3205, fols. 129^r–130^v, 131^r–132^v, 133^r–134^v, 137^r–138^v, 139^r–140^v, 141^r–142^v, 143^r–144^v, 145^r–146^v, 147^r–148^v, 149^r–150^v, 151^r–152^v, 157^r–158^v, 159^r–160^v; Michelle DiMeo, "Howard, Aletheia, Countess of Arundel, of Surrey, and of Norfolk, and suo jure Baroness Furnivall, Baroness Talbot, and Baroness Strange of Blackmere (*d.* 1654)," in *ODNB*; Nancy Pollard Brown, "Howard [Dacre], Anne, Countess of Arundel (1557–1630)," in *ODNB*. Anne Howard, Dowager Countess of Arundel, was the daughter and co-heir of Thomas Dacre, fourth Baron Dacre of Gilsland, whose son Thomas Howard wed Aletheia, daughter of Gilbert Talbot, seventh Earl of Shrewsbury.

36. LPL, MS 3205, fol. 24.

37. Ian Mortimer, "Baskerville, Hannibal (1597–1668)," in *ODNB*; Andrew Warmington, "Baskerville, Thomas (1630/31–1700)," in *ODNB*.

38. Bodl., Rawl. MS D 859, fols. 1ʳ–11ᵛ.

39. Bodl., Rawl. MS D 859, fols. 68ʳ, 12ʳ⁻ᵛ.

40. Philip Bliss, ed., *Athenæ Oxoniensis: An Exact History of All the Writers and Bishops Who Have Had Their Education in the University of Oxford; to Which Are Added the Fasti, or Annals of the Said Anthony à Wood, M.A. of Merton College*, 3rd ed., 5 vols. (1813), I, pp. xxxiii–xxxiv.

41. Mortimer, "Baskerville, Hannibal."

42. Bodl., Rawl. MS D 859, fols. 11ʳ⁻ᵛ, 36ʳ–37ᵛ, 12ʳ⁻ᵛ.

43. BL, Add. MS 34239; Gervase Holles, *Memorials of the Holles Family*, ed. A. C. Wood, Camden Society, 3rd ser., 55 (1937).

44. The marriage was reported by John Chamberlain to Dudley Carleton in a letter of 28 July 1599 (TNA, SP 12/271, fol. 72).

45. Ian Atherton, "Scudamore Family (*per.* 1500–1820)," in *ODNB*; Ian Atherton, *Ambition and Failure in Stuart England: The Career of John, First Viscount Scudamore* (Manchester: Manchester UP, 1999).

46. TNA, SP 14/48, fol. 52: 18 September 1609.

47. Bodl., Rawl. MS, Letters 41, fols. 23ʳ–36ᵛ (fol. 24ʳ).

48. Bodl., Rawl. MS D 859, fols. 3ʳ, 4ʳ, 5ʳ, 7ʳ, 8ʳ, 10ʳ, 11ʳ (28 April 1617, 28 May 1621, 16 September 1622, 14 November 1622, 25 November 1622, 12 March 1624); Atherton, "Scudamore Family."

49. Bodl., Rawl. MS D 859, fols. 3ᵛ, 4ᵛ, 5ᵛ, 6ᵛ, 7ᵛ, 8ᵛ, 9ᵛ, 10ᵛ.

50. Bodl., Rawl. MS D 859, fol. 4ᵛ.

51. Bodl., Rawl. MS D 859, fol. 6ʳ, 7ᵛ.

52. Bodl., Rawl. MS D 859, fol. 8ᵛ, 9ʳ; Bliss, *Athenæ Oxoniensis*, I, pp. xxxiii–xxxiv.

53. Bliss, *Athenæ Oxoniensis*, I, pp. xxxiii–xxxiv.

54. TNA, SP 16/248, fol. 139; Hatfield, CP 223, fol. 20; Adam Fox, "Printed Questionnaires, Research Networks, and the Discovery of the British Isles, 1650–1800," *HJ*, 53/3 (2010), 593–621.

55. Michael Hunter, "Ashmole, Elias (1617–1692)," in *ODNB*.

56. Bodl., Rawl. MS D 859, fol. 71ʳ; Woolf, *Social Circulation of the Past*, p. 110; BL, Add. MS 14284, fol. 66: "Baskerville Family Pedigrees" from "Visitations of Berkshire, 1665."

57. Bodl., Rawl. MS D 859, fol. 75ʳ.

58. Bodl., Rawl. MS D 859, fols. 11ᵛ, 36ʳ.

59. Bodl., Rawl. MS D 859, fols. 72ʳ⁻ᵛ, 74ʳ⁻ᵛ, 73ᵛ.

60. Warmington, "Baskerville, Thomas (1630/31–1700)."

61. BL, Add. MS 12506, fol. 231; BL, Harl. MS 6997, fol. 7; CP 25/91, 27/14, 91/87, 97/32, 122/16, 113/159, P.306; TNA, SP14/32, fol. 152; HMC, *Report on the Manuscripts of His Grace the Duke of Rutland, Preserved at Belvoir Castle*, 3 vols. (HMSO, 1888), vol. I, pp. 161, 238; LPL, MS 708, fol. 135.

62. See, for example, CP 91/87; and Kendal Record Office, Hothfield MSS, WD/Hoth/Box 44, unfoliated, letter beginning "I blush to deliever these things to your Honorable hands."

63. Hothfield MSS, WD/Hoth/Box 44.

64. Anne Clifford, *The Memoir of 1603 and the Diary of 1616–1619*, ed. Katherine O. Acheson (Peterborough, ON: Broadview Press, 2007), p. 156.

65. Megan Matchinske, "Serial Identity: History, Gender, and Form in the Diary Writing of Lady Anne Clifford," in *Genre and Women's Life Writing in Early Modern England,* ed. Michelle M. Dowd and Julie A. Eckerle (Aldershot: Ashgate, 2007), pp. 65–80; Lisa M. Klein,

"Lady Anne Clifford as Mother and Matriarch: Domestic and Dynastic Issues in Her Life and Writings," *Journal of Family History*, 26/1 (2001), 18–38; Mihoko Suzuki, "Anne Clifford and the Gendering of History," *Clio*, 30/2 (2001), 195–229.

66. George C. Williamson, *Lady Anne Clifford, Countess of Dorset, Pembroke and Montgomery, 1590–1676: Her Life, Letters and Work* (Kendal: Titus Wilson, 1922), p. 146.

67. Williamson, *Lady Anne Clifford*, p. 146.

68. Williamson, *Lady Anne Clifford*, p. 32.

69. Richard T. Spence, "Clifford, Anne, Countess of Pembroke, Dorset, and Montgomery (1590–1676)," in *ODNB*.

70. Longleat House, Portland MS, 23.

71. Clifford, *Memoir*, ed. Acheson, Appendix D, p. 221.

72. Clifford, *Memoir*, ed. Acheson, pp. 37–38. I fully agree with Acheson's identification here, having compared the hand with several examples of known autograph letters of the Duchess of Portland's.

73. BL, Harl. MS 6177.

74. Pat Rogers, "Bentinck, Margaret Cavendish [Lady Margaret Cavendish Harley], duchess of Portland (1715–1785)," in *ODNB*; Elizabeth Eger, "Paper Trails and Eloquent Objects: Bluestocking Friendship and Material Culture," *Parergon*, 26/2 (2009), 109–38; Alexandra Cook, "Botanical Exchanges: Jean-Jacques Rousseau and the Duchess of Portland," *History of European Ideas*, 33/2 (2007), 142–56.

75. Longleat, Portland MS 23, fols. 23–24; Hothfield MSS, WD/Hoth/Box 44.

76. Portland MS 23, fols. 27–28; Hothfield MSS, WD/Hoth/Box 44.

77. I am grateful to Kathy Acheson for her very helpful discussion of this aspect of the letter book.

78. Anne Clifford, *Memoir*, ed. Acheson, pp. 55, 76, 115, 129, 162, 222, 227; for mention of cherries, see p. 139.

79. On the texts of the 1603 memoir and 1616–19 diary, see Clifford, *Memoir*, ed. Acheson, pp. 37–40, which argues for the Portland MS as the earliest extant copy, and the basis for the Knole MS at Kent History and Library Centre, which was probably copied by Elizabeth Sackville and her sister Mary. Acheson also convincingly hypothesizes about an earlier copy text based on analysis of a printed version in William Seward's *Anecdotes of Some Distinguished Persons, Chiefly of the Present and Two Preceding Centuries* (1804).

80. Daybell, *Material Letter*, pp. 177–90.

81. James Daybell, "John Donne's Letters," in *John Donne in Context*, ed. Michael Schoenfeldt (Cambridge: CUP, 2016).

82. Mary Clapinson, "Rawlinson, Richard (1690–1755)," in *ODNB*.

83. Nottingham University Library, Middleton MSS; HMC, *Report on the Manuscripts of Lord Middleton, Preserved at Wollaton Hall, Nottinghamshire* (1911), p. 504.

84. BL, Add. MS 23212, fol. 2.

85. David Greetham, "'Who's In, Who's Out': The Cultural Poetics of Archival Exclusion," *Studies in the Literary Imagination*, 32/1 (1999), 1–28.

CHAPTER II. FAMILIAR LETTERS AND STATE PAPERS

1. On letters and biography, see Alan Stewart, "Early Modern Lives in Facsimile," *Textual Practice*, 23 (2009), 289–305; on letter writing and social relations, see especially Lynne

Magnusson, *Shakespeare and Social Dialogue: Dramatic Language and Elizabethan Letters* (Cambridge: CUP, 1999).

2. Jonathan Gibson, "Significant Space in Manuscript Letters," *Seventeenth Century*, 12/1 (1997), 1–9; Alan Stewart and Heather Wolfe, *Letterwriting in Renaissance England* (Washington, DC: Folger, 2004); James Daybell, *The Material Letter in Early Modern England: Manuscript Letters and the Culture and Practices of Letter-Writing, 1512–1635* (Basingstoke: Palgrave Macmillan, 2012).

3. I am here concerned not with the journey made by a text by its scribal publication (for which, see Daybell, *Material Letter*, pp. 190–203) but with the journey (or lack of journey) made by the material letter itself.

4. Stephen Alford, "Introduction to *State Papers Online* and the Sixteenth Century State Papers, 1509–1603," *State Papers Online, 1509–1714*, Cengage Learning EMEA, 2008, accessible at http://gale.cengage.co.uk.

5. Ultimately, the Cecil Papers have been published online separately, but the original plan for *State Papers Online* seems to have included them, and the calendars are still part of the database.

6. Maggie Yax, "Arthur Agarde, Elizabethan Archivist: His Contributions to the Evolution of Archival Practice," *American Archivist*, 61 (1998), 56–69; G. H. Martin, "Agard, Arthur (1535/6–1615)," in *ODNB*.

7. [Thomas Powell], *The Repertorie of Records* (B. Alsop and T. Fawcet, for B. Fisher, 1631), sig. A4ᵛ: "the Foure Treasuries were collected by Mr. *Agard*, his priuate notes, a man very industrious and painfull in that kind; and one, who had continual recourse vnto the most & custody of many of the rest of the same." The four treasuries were the treasury within the Exchequer of Receipt, the gatehouse of Westminster Palace, the chapter house of Westminster Abbey, and the Chapel of the Pyx.

8. Agarde, "The Compendium of the Records in the Treasury," in *The Antient Kalendars and Inventories of the Treasury of His Majesty's Exchequer*, 3 vols., ed. Francis Palgrave (n.p., 1836), II, pp. 313–14.

9. Robert Beale, "A Treatise of the Office of a Councellor and Principall Secretarie to her Ma[ies]tie; Divided into 3 Parts," printed in Conyers Read, *Mr Secretary Walsingham and the Policy of Queen Elizabeth*, 3 vols. (Oxford: Clarendon Press, 1925), I, pp. 423–43 (p. 431). On Beale's collections, see Patricia Brewerton, "Paper Trails: Rereading Robert Beale as Clerk to the Privy Council" (Ph.D. thesis, University of London, 1998).

10. Beale, "Treatise," p. 431.

11. TNA, PROB 11/75, sig. 33: Walsingham's will.

12. F. S. Thomas, *A History of the State Paper Office* (John Petheram, 1849), p. 7.

13. See also R. B. Wernham, "The Public Records in the Sixteenth and Seventeenth Centuries," in *English Historical Scholarship in the Sixteenth and Seventeenth Centuries*, ed. Levi Fox (London: OUP for the Dugdale Society, 1956), pp. 11–30.

14. Hubert Hall, *Studies in English Official Historical Documents* (Cambridge: CUP, 1908), from "Appendix II: Chronology of the Custody of the State Papers," pp. 121–22 (p. 121).

15. Hall, *Studies*, 37.

16. On Wilson, see A. F. Pollard, rev. Sean Kelsey, "Wilson, Sir Thomas (*d.* 1629)," in *ODNB*; Virginia Moseley and Rosemary Sgroi, "Wilson, Thomas (*c.* 1565–1629)," in *The House of Commons, 1604–1629*, ed. Andrew Thrush and John P. Ferris, 6 vols. (Cambridge: CUP for the History of Parliament Trust, 2010), VI, pp. 800–802.

17. Pollard and Kelsey, "Wilson, Sir Thomas."

18. TNA, SP 14/88, fol. 83: Thomas Wilson to James I, 10 August 1616.

19. Letter patent, 15 March 1610, quoted in Thomas, *History of the State Paper Office*, p. 7.

20. Burghley's will, quoted in Stephen Alford, "State Papers of Edward VI, Mary I and Elizabeth I: The Archives and the Documents," *State Papers Online, 1509–1714*, Thomson Learning EMEA, Reading 2007, p. 2.

21. TNA, SP 45/20, fols. 46ʳ–47ʳ (art. 12) (draft).

22. TNA, SP 14/94, fol. 191: Wilson to James [1617].

23. TNA, SP 14/103, fol. 107ʳ⁻ᵛ: Wilson to James [2 November 1618]. Cobham died two months later.

24. TNA, SP 45/20, fol. 58ʳ (art. 28): Wilson to Buckingham, 1618 (draft).

25. Louis A. Knafla, "Starkey, Ralph (*d.* 1628)," in *ODNB*.

26. TNA, SP 14/88, fol. 83: Wilson to James, 10 August 1616. Pollard and Kelsey in "Wilson, Sir Thomas," write: "He proposed the creation of an office of register of honour, as an adjunct to the state paper office, to be filled by himself, so as to obviate frequent disputes for precedence among knights and their ladies. He also suggested the publication of a gazette of news akin to those issued in Germany, France, Italy, and Spain, and the grant of a patent to himself for printing it."

27. TNA, SP 14/88, fol. 83: Wilson to James, 10 August 1616.

28. TNA, SP 45/20, fol. 35 (art. 13).

29. TNA, SP 45/20, fols. 36ʳ–38ʳ (art. 14) (copy).

30. "Wilson's only child, Dorothy, had married, on 20 May 1613 at St Peter Paul's Wharf, London, Ambrose Randolph, younger son of Thomas Randolph" (Pollard and Kelsey, "Wilson, Sir Thomas").

31. It may be that it already had been something of a family affair. The 1578 keeper was a Dr. Thomas Wilson; although Pollard and Kelsey ("Wilson, Sir Thomas") suggest that there is no evidence that the Jacobean Thomas Wilson was the nephew of Dr. Wilson, as had been often stated (he is not mentioned in the elder Wilson's will), it appears that the younger Wilson lived in Dr. Wilson's house in 1579, where he was involved in the sorting of the elder Wilson's papers.

32. TNA, SP 14/72, fol. 143: Wilson to Randolph, 13 March 1613.

33. TNA, SP 14/77, fol. 3: Wilson to Randolph, 2 April 1614.

34. TNA, SP 14/81, fol. 121: Wilson to Sir Ralph Winwood, 24 August 1616.

35. Kevin Sharpe, *Sir Robert Cotton, 1586–1631: History and Politics in Early Modern England* (Oxford: OUP, 1979), p. 197.

36. Sharpe, *Sir Robert Cotton*, p. 217, citing BL, Harl. MS 7002, fol. 346.

37. TNA, SP 14/82, fol. 175: James to Canterbury et al., 26 October 1615.

38. TNA, PROB 11/126, fols. 94ᵛ–95ᵛ: Will of Arthur Agarde.

39. TNA, SP 14/81, fol. 120: Wilson to Randolph, 24 August 1615 (my emphases).

40. Ibid.

41. Richard Parr, *The Life of the Most Reverend Father in God, James Usher, Late Lord Archbishop of Armagh* (Nathaniel Renew, 1686), sig. 3K4ᵛ: Bourgchier to Usher, 16 April 1622.

42. TNA, PCC 67 St John (1631), quoted by Colin G. C. Tite, *The Manuscript Library of Sir Robert Cotton*, Panizzi Lectures, 1993 (British Library, 1994), p. 20; TNA, PROB 11/159: Cotton's will.

43. TNA, SP 14/127/47, fols. 66^r–67^r: Wilson to Randolph, 25 January 1622; Thrush and Ferris, *House of Commons, 1604–1629*, VI, p. 802.

44. Dorothy Randolph to Jane Lady Bacon [1629], in Lord Braybrooke, ed., *The Private Correspondence of Jane Lady Cornwallis; 1613–1644: From the Originals in the Possession of the Family* (S. & J. Bentley, Wilson, & Fley, 1842), pp. 203–4 (p. 204).

45. On Boswell, see Alan Stewart, "Boswell, William," in *ODNB*; Paula Watson and Simon Healy, "Boswell, William (1583–1650)," in Thrush and Ferris, *House of Commons, 1604–1629*, III, pp. 258–60.

46. Watson and Healy, "Boswell, William," p. 259.

47. *The British Library Catalogue of Additions to the Manuscripts: The Yelverton Manuscripts; Additional Manuscripts 48000–48196* (British Library, 1994).

48. Tite, *Manuscript Library*, p. 35.

49. M. Greengrass, "Winwood, Sir Ralph (d. 1562/3–1617)," in *ODNB*. I am grateful to James Daybell for bringing Winwood's papers to my attention.

50. For Raymond, see *Autobiography of Thomas Raymond and Memoirs of the Family of Guise of Elmore, Gloucestershire*, ed. G. Davies (Offices of the [Royal Historical] Society, 1917).

SELECT BIBLIOGRAPHY

Adams, Robyn, and Rosanna Cox, eds. *Diplomacy and Early Modern Culture.* Basingstoke: Palgrave Macmillan, 2011.

Akkerman, Nadine, ed. *The Correspondence of Elizabeth Stuart, Queen of Bohemia.* 3 vols. Oxford: OUP, 2011–.

Allen, Gemma. *The Cooke Sisters: Education, Piety and Politics in Early Modern England.* Manchester: Manchester UP, 2013.

Anselment, Raymond. "Katherine Paston and Brilliana Harley: Maternal Letters and the Genre of Mother's Advice." *Studies in Philology,* 101 (2004), 431–53.

Bacon, Lady Anne. *The Letters of Lady Anne Bacon,* ed. Gemma Allen. Camden Record Society, fifth series, 44. Cambridge: CUP, 2014.

Barnes, Diana. *Epistolary Community in Print, 1580–1664.* Farnham: Ashgate, 2013.

Beal, Peter. *In Praise of Scribes: Manuscripts and Their Makers in Seventeenth-Century England.* Oxford: OUP, 1998.

Beal, Peter. "Philip Sidney's *Letter to Queen Elizabeth* and That 'False Knave' Alexander Dicsone." *EMS,* 11 (2002), 1–51.

Bergeron, David M. *King James and Letters of Homoerotic Desire.* Iowa City: U of Iowa P, 1999.

Bound, Fay. "Writing the Self? Love and the Letter in England, c. 1660–c. 1760." *Literature and History,* 11/1 (2002), 1–19.

Braunmuller, A. R. "Accounting for Absence: The Transcription of Space." In *New Ways of Looking at Old Texts,* ed. W. Speed Hill. Binghamton, NY: Medieval and Renaissance Texts and Studies, 1993, pp. 47–56.

Braunmuller, A. R., ed. *A Seventeenth-Century Letter-Book: A Facsimile Edition of Folger MS V.a.321.* Newark: U of Delaware P, 1983.

Braybrooke, Lord, ed. *The Private Correspondence of Jane Lady Cornwallis; 1613–1644: From the Originals in the Possession of the Family.* S. & J. Bentley, Wilson, & Fley, 1842.

Brayshay, Mark. *Land Travel and Communications in Tudor and Stuart England: Achieving a Joined-up Realm.* Liverpool: U of Liverpool P, 2014.

Brewerton, Patricia. "Paper Trails: Rereading Robert Beale as Clerk to the Privy Council." Ph.D. thesis, University of London, 1998.

Brown, Cedric. "Losing and Regaining the Material Meanings of Epistolary and Gift Texts." In *Material Readings of Early Modern Culture, 1580–1700,* ed. James Daybell and Peter Hinds. Basingstoke: Palgrave Macmillan, 2010, pp. 23–46.

Burlinson, Christopher, and Andrew Zurcher. "'Secretary to the Lord Grey Lord Deputie Here': Edmund Spenser's Irish Papers." *Library,* 6/1 (2005), 30–75.

Burton, Gideon. "From *Ars dictaminis* to *Ars conscribendi epistolis*: Renaissance Letter-Writing Manuals in the Context of Humanism." In *Letter-Writing Manuals and Instruction from Antiquity to the Present*, ed. Carol Poster and Linda C. Mitchell. Columbia: U of South Carolina P, 2007, pp. 88–101.

Chartier, Roger. "*Secrétaires* for the People? Model Letters of the Ancien Régime: Between Court Literature and Popular Chapbooks." In *Correspondence: Models of Letter-Writing from the Middle Ages to the Nineteenth Century*, by Roger Chartier, Alain Boureau, and Cécile Daupin, trans. Christopher Woodall. Cambridge: Polity Press, 1997, pp. 59–111.

Coolahan, Marie-Louise. "Literary Memorialization and the Posthumous Construction of Female Authorship." In *The Arts of Remembrance in Early Modern England: Memorial Cultures of the Post Reformation*, ed. Andrew Gordon and Thomas Rist. Aldershot: Ashgate, 2013, pp. 161–78.

Coolahan, Marie-Louise. "Reception, Reputation and Early Modern Women's Missing Texts." *Critical Quarterly*, 55/4 (2013), 3–14.

Coolahan, Marie-Louise. *Women, Writing, and Language in Early Modern Ireland*. Oxford: OUP, 2010.

Couchman, Jane, and Ann Crabb, eds. *Women's Letters Across Europe, 1400–1700*. Aldershot: Ashgate, 2005.

Davis, Tom. "The Analysis of Handwriting: An Introductory Survey." In *The Book Encompassed: Studies in Twentieth-Century Bibliography*, ed. Peter Davison. Cambridge: CUP, 1992, pp. 57–68.

Davis, Tom. "The Practice of Handwriting Identification." *Library*, 7th ser., 8/3 (2007), 251–76.

Daybell, James, ed. *Early Modern Women's Letter Writing*. Basingstoke: Palgrave, 2001.

Daybell, James. *The Material Letter in Early Modern England: Manuscript Letters and the Culture and Practices of Letter-Writing, 1512–1635*. Basingstoke: Palgrave Macmillan, 2012.

Daybell, James. "Recent Studies in Renaissance Letters: The Seventeenth Century." *ELR*, 36/1 (2006), 135–70.

Daybell, James. "Recent Studies in Renaissance Letters: The Sixteenth Century." *ELR*, 35/2 (2005), 331–62.

Daybell, James. " 'Suche newes as on the Quenes hy ways we have mett': The News and Intelligence Networks of Elizabeth Talbot, Countess of Shrewsbury (c. 1527–1608)." In *Women and Politics in Early Modern England, 1450–1700*, ed. James Daybell. Aldershot: Ashgate, 2004, pp. 114–31.

Daybell, James. *Women Letter-Writers in Tudor England*. Oxford: OUP, 2006.

Daybell, James. "Women, Politics and Domesticity: The Scribal Publication of Lady Rich's Letter to Elizabeth I." In *Women and Writing, c.1340–c.1650: The Domestication of Print Culture*, ed. Anne Lawrence-Mathers and Phillipa Hardman. Woodbridge: York Medieval Press, 2010, pp. 111–30.

Daybell, James. "Women's Letters and Letter Writing in England, 1540–1603: An Introduction to the Issues of Authorship and Construction." *Shakespeare Studies*, 27 (1999), 161–86.

Daybell, James, and Andrew Gordon. "Select Bibliography: The Manuscript Letter in Early Modern England." *Lives and Letters*, 4/1 (Autumn 2012). http://journal.xmera.org/volume-4-no-1-autumn-2012/articles/bibliography.pdf.

Daybell, James, and Andrew Gordon, eds. *Women and Epistolary Agency in Early Modern Culture, 1450–1690*. Farnham: Ashgate, 2016.

Daybell, James, and Peter Hinds. *Material Readings of Early Modern Culture: Texts and Social Practices, 1580–1730*. Basingstoke: Palgrave Macmillan, 2010.

De Landtsheer, Jeanine, and Henk Nellen, eds. *Between Scylla and Charybdis: Learned Letter Writers Navigating the Reefs of Religious and Political Controversy in Early Modern Europe*. Leiden: Brill, 2011.

Donne, John, *John Donne's Marriage Letters in the Folger Shakespeare Library*. Ed. R. P. Sorlien, Dennis Flynn and M. Thomas Hester. Washington, DC: Folger, 2005.

Evans, Melanie. *The Language of Queen Elizabeth I: A Sociolinguistic Perspective on Royal Style and Identity*. Transactions of the Philological Society Monograph Series 45. Oxford: Wiley-Blackwell, 2013.

Evans, Melanie. "A Sociolinguistics of Early Modern Spelling? An Account of Queen Elizabeth I's Correspondence." *VARIENG: Studies in Variation, Contacts and Change in English*, 10 (2012). http://www.helsinki.fi/varieng/journal/volumes/10/evans.

Ezell, Margaret J. M. "The Posthumous Publication of Women's Manuscripts and the History of Authorship." In *Women's Writing and the Circulation of Ideas: Manuscript Publication in England, 1550–1800*, ed. George L. Justice and Nathan Tinker. Cambridge: CUP, 2002, pp. 121–36.

Fitzmaurice, Susan. *The Familiar Letter in Early Modern English: A Pragmatic Approach*. Amsterdam: John Benjamins, 2002.

Gibson, Jonathan. "Letters." In *A New Companion to English Renaissance Literature and Culture*, ed. Michael Hattaway. 2 vols. Malden, MA: Wiley-Blackwell, 2010, II, pp. 453–60.

Gibson, Jonathan. "Significant Space in Manuscript Letters." *Seventeenth Century*, 12/1 (Spring 1997), 1–9.

Gilroy, Amanda, and W. M. Verhoeven, eds. *Prose Studies: Correspondences: A Special Issue on Letters*, 19/2 (1996).

Goldberg, Jonathan. *Writing Matter: From the Hands of the English Renaissance*. Stanford, CA: Stanford UP, 1990.

Gordon, Andrew. "*Copycopia*, or the Place of Copied Correspondence in Manuscript Culture: A Case Study." In *Material Readings of Early Modern Culture, 1580–1730: Texts and Social Practices*, ed. James Daybell and Peter Hinds. Basingstoke: Palgrave Macmillan, 2010, pp. 65–82.

Gordon, Andrew. "Essex's Last Campaign: The Fall of the Earl of Essex and Manuscript Circulation." In *Essex: The Cultural Impact of an Elizabethan Courtier*, ed. Annaliese Connolly and Lisa Hopkins. Manchester: Manchester UP, 2013, pp. 153–78.

Gordon, Andrew. "'A Fortune of Paper Walls': The Letters of Francis Bacon and the Earl of Essex." *ELR*, 37/3 (2007), 319–36.

Gordon, Andrew, "Recovering Agency in the Epistolary Traffic of Frances, Countess of Essex, and Jane Daniell." In *Women and Epistolary Agency in Early Modern Culture, 1450–1690*, ed. James Daybell and Andrew Gordon. Farnham: Ashgate, 2016.

Green, Lawrence D. "Dictamen in England, 1500–1700." In *Letter-Writing Manuals and Instruction from Antiquity to the Present: Historical and Bibliographic Studies*, ed. Carol Poster and Linda C. Mitchell. Columbia: U of South Carolina P, 2007, pp. 102–26.

Guillén, Claudio. "Notes Toward the Study of the Renaissance Letter." In *Renaissance Genres: Essays on Theory, History, and Interpretation*, ed. Barbara Kiefer Lewalski. Cambridge, MA: Harvard UP, 1986, pp. 70–101.

Hammer, Paul E. J. "The Uses of Scholarship: The Secretariat of Robert Devereux, Second Earl of Essex." *EHR*, 109 (1994), 26–51.

Hannay, Margaret P. "'High Housewifery': The Duties and Letters of Barbara Gamage Sidney, Countess of Leicester." *Early Modern Women: An Interdisciplinary Journal*, 1 (2006), 7–35.

Harris, Frances. "The Letterbooks of Mary Evelyn." *EMS*, 7 (1998), 202–15.

Henderson, Judith Rice. "Erasmus on the Art of Letter-Writing." In *Renaissance Eloquence: Studies in the Theory and Practice of Renaissance Rhetoric*, ed. James J. Murphy. Berkeley: U of California P, 1983, pp. 331–55.

Henderson, Judith Rice. "Erasmus's *Opus de conscribendis epistolis* in Sixteenth-Century Schools." In *Letter-Writing Manuals and Instruction from Antiquity to the Present: Historical and Bibliographical Studies*, ed. Carol Poster and Linda C. Mitchell. Columbia: U of South Carolina P, 2007, pp. 141–77.

Henderson, Judith Rice. "Humanist Letter Writing: Private Conversation or Public Forum?" In *Self-Presentation and Social Identification: The Rhetoric and Pragmatics of Letter Writing in Early Modern Times*, ed. Toon Van Houdt et al. Leuven: Leuven UP, 2002, pp. 17–39.

Henderson, Judith Rice. "On Reading the Rhetoric of the Renaissance Letter." In *Renaissance-Rhetorik/Renaissance Rhetoric*, ed. Heinrich F. Plett. Berlin: Walter de Gruyter, 1993, pp. 143–62.

Hornbeak, Katherine Gee. *The Complete Letter Writer in English, 1568–1800*. Northampton, MA: Smith College, 1934.

Howe, James. *Epistolary Spaces: English Letter Writing from the Foundation of the Post Office to Richardson's "Clarissa."* Aldershot: Ashgate, 2003.

Humiliata, Sister Mary. "Standards of Taste Advocated for Feminine Letter Writing, 1640–1797." *HLQ*, 13 (1949–50), 261–77.

Hunter, Michael. "How to Edit a Seventeenth-Century Manuscript: Principles and Practice." *Seventeenth Century*, 10 (1995), 277–310.

Jardine, Lisa. *Erasmus, Man of Letters: The Construction of Charisma in Print*. Princeton, NJ: Princeton UP, 1993.

Lerer, Seth. *Courtly Letters in the Age of Henry VIII: Literary Culture and the Arts of Deceit*. Cambridge: CUP, 1997.

Love, Harold. *Scribal Publication in Seventeenth-Century England*. Oxford: Clarendon Press, 1993.

Magnusson, Lynne. "Letters." In *The History of British Women's Writing, 1500–1610*, ed. Caroline Bicks and Jennifer Summit. Basingstoke: Palgrave Macmillan, 2010, 130–51.

Magnusson, Lynne. "A Rhetoric of Requests: Genre and Linguistic Scripts in Elizabethan Women's Suitors Letters." In *Women and Politics in Early Modern England, 1450–1700*, ed. James Daybell. Aldershot: Ashgate, 2004, pp. 51–66.

Magnusson, Lynne. *Shakespeare and Social Dialogue: Dramatic Language and Elizabethan Letters*. Cambridge: CUP, 1999.

Magnusson, Lynne. "Widowhood and Linguistic Capital: The Rhetoric and Reception of Anne Bacon's Epistolary Advice." *ELR*, 31 (2001), 3–33.

Mitchell, Linda C., and Susan Green, eds. *Studies in the Cultural History of Letter Writing*. Berkeley: U of California P, 2005.

Moody, Joanna, ed. "Women's Letter Writing." Special issue, *Women's Writing*, 13/1 (2006).

Morrissey, Mary, and Gillian Wright. "Piety and Sociability in Early Modern Women's Letters." *Women's Writing*, 13/1 (2006), 44–59.

Poster, Carol, and Linda C. Mitchell, eds. *Letter-Writing Manuals and Instruction from Antiquity to the Present*. Columbia: U of South Carolina P, 2007.

Robertson, Jean. *The Art of Letter-Writing: An Essay on the Handbooks Published in England During the Sixteenth and Seventeenth Centuries*. Liverpool: U of Liverpool P, 1942.

Sale, Carolyn. "'Roman Hand': Women, Writing and the Law in the *Att.-Gen. v. Chatterton* and the Letters of the Lady Arbella Stuart." *ELH*, 70/4 (2003), 929–61.

Schneider, Gary. *The Culture of Epistolarity: Vernacular Letters and Letter Writing in Early Modern England, 1500–1700*. Newark: U of Delaware P, 2005.

Spenser, Edmund. *Selected Letters and Other Papers*. Ed. Christopher Burlinson and Andrew Zurcher. Oxford: OUP, 2009.

Steen, Sara Jayne. "Fashioning an Acceptable Self: Arbella Stuart." *ELR*, 18 (1988), 78–95.

Steen, Sara Jayne. "Reading Beyond the Words: Material Letters and the Process of Interpretation." *Quidditas*, 22 (2001), 55–69.

Stevens, Forrest Tyler. "Erasmus's 'Tigress': The Language of Friendship, Pleasure, and the Renaissance Letter." In *Queering the Renaissance*, ed. Jonathan Goldberg. Durham, NC: Duke UP, 1994, pp. 124–40.

Stewart, Alan. *Close Readers: Humanism and Sodomy in Early Modern England*. Princeton, NJ: Princeton UP, 1997.

Stewart, Alan. "The Early Modern Closet Discovered." *Representations*, 50 (1995), 76–100.

Stewart, Alan. "Early Modern Lives in Facsimile." *Textual Practice*, 23 (2009), 289–305.

Stewart, Alan. "The Making of Writing in Renaissance England: Re-thinking Authorship Through Collaboration." In *Renaissance Transformations: The Making of English Writing, 1500–1650*, ed. Margaret Healy and Thomas Healy. Edinburgh: Edinburgh UP, 2009, pp. 81–96.

Stewart, Alan. *Shakespeare's Letters*. Oxford: OUP, 2008.

Stewart, Alan. "The Voices of Anne Cooke, Lady Anne and Lady Bacon." In *This Double Voice: Gendered Writing in Early Modern England*, ed. Danielle Clarke and Elizabeth Clarke. Basingstoke: Palgrave, 2000, pp. 88–102.

Stewart, Alan, and Heather Wolfe. *Letterwriting in Renaissance England*. Washington, DC: Folger, 2004.

Summit, Jennifer. "Hannah Wolley, the Oxinden Letters, and Household Epistolary Practice." In *Women, Property, and the Letters of the Law in Early Modern England*, ed. Nancy E. Wright, Margaret W. Ferguson, and A. R. Buck. Toronto: U Toronto P, 2006, pp. 201–18.

Sutton, Peter C., et al., *Love Letters: Dutch Genre Paintings in the Age of Vermeer*. Frances Lincoln, 2003.

Thompson, Elbert N. S., "Familiar Letters." In *Literary Bypaths of the Renaissance*. New Haven, CT: Yale University Press, 1924, pp. 91–126.

Thorne, Alison. "Women's Petitionary Letters and Early Seventeenth-Century Treason Trials." *Women's Writing*, 13/1 (2006), 21–37.

Tite, Colin G. C. *The Manuscript Library of Sir Robert Cotton*. Panizzi Lectures, 1993. British Library, 1994.

Trill, Suzanne. "Early Modern Women's Writing in the Edinburgh Archives, c. 1550–1740: A Preliminary Checklist." In *Woman and the Feminine in Medieval and Early Modern Scottish Writing*, ed. Sarah M. Dunnigan, C. Marie Harker, and Evelyn S. Newlyn. Basingstoke: Palgrave, 2004, pp. 201–25.

Ustick, W. Lee. "Advice to a Son: A Type of Seventeenth-Century Conduct Book." *Studies in Philology*, 29 (1932), 409–41.

Van Houdt, Toon, Jan Papy, Gilbert Tournoy, and Constant Matheeussen, eds. *Self-Presentation and Social Identification: The Rhetoric and Pragmatics of Letter Writing in Early Modern Times*. Leuven: Leuven UP, 2002.

Wall, Alison D. "Deference and Defiance in Women's Letters of the Thynne Family: The Rhetoric of Relationships." In *Women's Letters and Letter-Writing in England, 1450–1700*, ed. James Daybell. Basingstoke: Palgrave, 2001, pp. 77–93.

Wall, Alison D. "Elizabethan Precept and Feminine Practice: The Thynne Family of Longleat." *History*, 75 (1990), 23–38.

Wernham, R. B. "The Public Records in the Sixteenth and Seventeenth Centuries." In *English Historical Scholarship in the Sixteenth and Seventeenth Centuries*, ed. Levi Fox. London: OUP for the Dugdale Society, 1956, pp. 11–30.

Whigham, Frank. "The Rhetoric of Elizabethan Suitors' Letters." *PMLA*, 96/5 (1981), 864–82.

Whyman, Susan E. *The Pen and the People: English Letter Writers, 1660–1800*. Oxford: OUP, 2009.

Wiggins, Alison, Alan Bryson, Daniel Starza Smith, Anke Timmermann, and Graham Williams, University of Glasgow, eds. *Bess of Hardwick's Letters: The Complete Correspondence, c. 1550–1608*. Web development by Katherine Rogers, University of Sheffield Humanities Research Institute, April 2013. http://www.bessofhardwick.org.

Williams, Graham. *Women's Epistolary Utterance: A Study of the Letters of Joan and Maria Thynne, 1575–1611*. Amsterdam: John Benjamins, 2013.

Williams, Graham. "'Yr Scribe Can Proove No Nessecarye Consiquence for You'? The Social and Linguistic Implications of Joan Thynne's Using a Scribe in Letters to Her Son, 1607–11." In *Women and Writing, c.1340–c.1650: The Domestication of Print Culture*, ed. Anne Lawrence-Mathers and Phillipa Hardman. Woodbridge: York Medieval Press, an imprint of Boydell and Brewer, 2010, pp. 131–45.

Winkelman, Carol L. "A Case Study of Women's Literacy in the Early Seventeenth Century: The Oxinden Family Letters." *Women and Language*, 19/2 (1996), 14–20.

Wiseman, Susan. "Exemplarity, Women and Political Rhetoric." In *Rhetoric, Gender, Politics: Representing Early Modern Women's Speech*, ed. Jennifer Richards and Alison Thorne. Routledge, 2006, pp. 129–48.

Woudhuysen, H. R. "The Queen's Own Hand: A Preliminary Account." In *Elizabeth I and the Culture of Writing*, ed. Peter Beal and Grace Ioppolo. British Library, 2007, pp. 1–27.

Woudhuysen, H. R. *Sir Philip Sidney and the Circulation of Manuscripts, 1558–1640*. Oxford: Clarendon Press, 1996.

NOTES ON CONTRIBUTORS

NADINE AKKERMAN is a lecturer in early modern English literature at Leiden University, the Netherlands. She has published widely on early modern culture in the *Ben Jonson Journal* and *Early Modern Literary Studies*, among others. She is the coeditor (with Birgit Houben) of *The Politics of Female Households: Ladies-in-Waiting Across Early Modern Europe* (Brill, 2014). She is also the editor of *The Correspondence of Elizabeth Stuart, Queen of Bohemia* for Oxford University Press (three volumes; two published to date). Her current project is a book on seventeenth-century female intelligencers.

MARK BRAYSHAY is an emeritus professor of historical geography at Plymouth University. His most recent book is *Land Travel and Communications in Tudor and Stuart England: Achieving a Joined-up Realm* (Liverpool UP, 2014). He is now working on a study of the corps of pursuivants and messengers accredited to the Elizabethan royal chamber and the couriers employed to serve the queen by conveying official correspondence to and from overseas locations.

CHRISTOPHER BURLINSON is a fellow and senior college lecturer in English at Jesus College, Cambridge. He has published *Allegory, Space and the Material World in the Writings of Edmund Spenser* (Boydell and Brewer, 2006), has co-edited (with Andrew Zurcher) *Edmund Spenser: Selected Letters and Other Papers* (OUP, 2008) and *Ralph Knevet's Supplement to the Faery Queen* (Manchester UP, 2015), and (with Ruth Connolly) *Editing Stuart Poetry*, a special issue of *Studies in English Literature* (Winter 2012). He is currently working on an edition of the poems of Richard Corbett.

JAMES DAYBELL is a professor of early modern British history at Plymouth University and fellow of the Royal Historical Society. He is author of *The Material Letter in Early Modern England: Manuscript Letters and the Culture and Practices of Letter-Writing, 1512–1635* (Palgrave Macmillan, 2012), *Women Letter-Writers in Tudor England* (OUP, 2006); editor of *Early Modern Women's Letter-Writing, 1450–1700* (Palgrave Macmillan, 2001), *Women and Politics in Early Modern England, 1450–1700* (Ashgate, 2004), and (with Peter Hinds) *Material Readings of Early Modern Culture, 1580–1730* (Ashgate, 2010), and has written more than thirty articles and essays on the subjects of early modern letter writing, women, gender, and politics. He is codirector (with Kim McLean-Fiander, University of Victoria, Canada) of the British Academy/ Leverhulme–funded project "Women's Early Modern Letters Online," codirector (with Svante Norrhem, Lund University) of the AHRC-funded network "Gender, Politics and Materiality in Early Modern Europe," and with Adam Smyth (Balliol College, Oxford) he edits the Ashgate book series "Material Readings in Early Modern Culture." He is currently completing a monograph entitled *The Family and Materials of Memory in Early Modern England.*

JONATHAN GIBSON is a lecturer in English at the Open University. He has coedited three books, collaborating most recently with Carlo M. Bajetta and Guillaume Coatalen on *Elizabeth I's Foreign Correspondence: Letters, Rhetoric, and Politics* (Palgrave Macmillan, 2014). Current projects include a book on British Library MS 3165, the poetry collection of the Elizabethan and Jacobean courtier Arthur Gorges.

ANDREW GORDON is a senior lecturer in literature at the University of Aberdeen where he is also codirector of the Centre for Early Modern Studies. He is the author of *Writing Early Modern London: Memory, Text and Community* (Palgrave Macmillan, 2013) and of numerous essays on aspects of urban culture. His work on manuscript circulation includes studies of the letters of the Earl of Essex, Francis Bacon, John Donne, and the culture of libels. He has edited several collections, including *Literature, Mapping and the Politics of Space in Early Modern Britain*, with Bernhard Klein (CUP, 2001), and *The Arts of Remembrance in Early Modern England*, with Thomas Rist (Ashgate, 2013). His current research projects include a book that explores early modern cultures of movement and transportation.

ARNOLD HUNT is a lecturer in early modern history at the University of Cambridge. From 2005 to 2015 he was a curator of historical manuscripts at the British Library. His book *The Art of Hearing: English Preachers and Their Audiences, 1590–1640* was published in 2010 by Cambridge University Press, and he has published on a wide range of topics relating to early modern history, book history and manuscript studies. He is currently editing the ninth volume (Parochial Sermons) of the *Oxford Edition of the Sermons of John Donne*.

LYNNE MAGNUSSON is a professor of English at the University of Toronto and past director of the Centre for Reformation and Renaissance Studies. She is the author of *Shakespeare and Social Dialogue: Dramatic Language and Elizabethan Letters* (CUP, 1999), a coauthor of *Reading Shakespeare's Dramatic Language* (Arden Shakespeare, 2002), the textual editor of Shakespeare's Sonnets in *The Norton Shakespeare*, third edition (2015), and has published over sixty articles and book chapters. Recently elected a fellow of the Royal Society of Canada, she has held the Canada Council's Killam Research Fellowship as well as a visiting fellowship at All Soul's College, Oxford. She is currently at work on *Shakespeare and the Grammar of Possibility*, coediting *The Cambridge Companion to Shakespeare's Language*, and completing a project on sixteenth-century English letters.

MICHELLE O'CALLAGHAN is a professor of early modern literature in the Department of English Language and Literature and director of the Early Modern Research Centre at the University of Reading. She is the author of *The "Shepheards Nation": Jacobean Spenserians and Early Stuart Political Culture, 1612–1625* (OUP, 2000), *The English Wits: Literature and Sociability in Early Modern England* (CUP, 2007), and *Thomas Middleton, Renaissance Dramatist* (Edinburgh UP, 2009). Her current project is a digitized critical edition of the early printed poetry miscellanies and an accompanying study, provisionally entitled "Making Poetry: Print Culture and the Poetry Miscellany in Renaissance England."

ALAN STEWART is a professor of English and comparative literature at Columbia University and international director of the Centre for Editing Lives and Letters in London. His publications include *Close Readers: Humanism and Sodomy in Early Modern England* (Princeton UP, 1997); *Hostage to Fortune: The Troubled Life of Francis Bacon* (with Lisa Jardine; Victor Gollancz, 1998); *Philip Sidney: A Double Life* (Chatto and Windus, 2000); *The Cradle King: A Life of James VI and I* (Chatto and Windus, 2003); *Letterwriting in Renaissance England* (with Heather Wolfe; Folger Shakespeare Library, 2004); and *Shakespeare's Letters* (OUP, 2008). With Garrett Sullivan, he edited the three-volume

Encyclopedia of English Renaissance Literature (Blackwell, 2012). Most recently, he edited volume 1 of the Oxford Francis Bacon, Bacon's *Early Writings, 1584–1596* (OUP). He is currently completing a study of early modern English life writing for Oxford University Press and a student anthology of Tudor drama for Broadview, and working on volume 2 of the Oxford Francis Bacon (*Late Elizabethan Writings, 1597–1602*).

ANDREW ZURCHER is a fellow in English at Queens' College, Cambridge. With Christopher Burlinson, he edited *Edmund Spenser's Selected Letters and Other Papers* (OUP, 2009) and is currently coediting the Latin and English letters of Sir Thomas Browne. He is also a general editor of the forthcoming Oxford University Press edition of the *Collected Works of Edmund Spenser* and has published several studies of and introductions to the works of Spenser and Shakespeare.

INDEX

ACKNOWLEDGMENTS

Like an early modern letter, this essay collection is the work of many hands, some of them invisible. We are happy here to reveal and recognize the many debts we have incurred in the process of developing *Cultures of Correspondence in Early Modern Britain*. Our greatest debt is to the contributors whose rich scholarship is housed between these covers and who have remained patient in the course of an editorial process sometimes overtaken by other projects. A series of scholarly collaborations has informed the development of this collection. The Centre for Early Modern Studies at the University of Aberdeen and the Humanities and Performing Arts Research Centre at Plymouth University hosted a series of events (and provided invaluable funding) that laid the groundwork for this project. The Early Modern Studies in Scotland Seminar also supported the Aberdeen symposia. The Renaissance Society of America played host to a series of panels that helped develop aspects of the collection, and Arthur Marotti as discipline representative for English was a supportive influence. We have also received support and encouragement from several key research centers and projects that study the world of letters, namely the Centre of Editing Lives and Letters (CELL) directed by Lisa Jardine at University College London, and Oxford's "Cultures of Knowledge" and "Early Modern Letters Online" (EMLO) projects directed by Howard Hotson.

We are deeply grateful to the many people whose participation in these events helped shape the *Cultures of Correspondence* project. We would like to acknowledge here the following: Gemma Allen, Marjon Ames, Kenneth Austin, Diana Barnes, Cedric Brown, James Brown, Alan Bryson, Marie-Louise Coolahan, Ian Cooper, Michelle DiMeo, Rebecca Emmett, Melanie Evans, Dennis Flynn, Kerry Gilbert, Helen Graham-Matheson, Bruna Gushurst-Moore, Karen Hardman, Johanna Harris, Peter Hinds, Samuli Kaislaniemi, Katy Mair, Margaret Maurer, Felicity Maxwell, Rachel McGregor, Kim McLean-Fiander, Steve May, Harry Newman, Kara Northway, The Lord John Russell, Gary Schneider, Daniel Starza Smith, Edith Snook, Rachel Stapleton, Joel

Swann, Alison Thorne, Suzanne Trill, Alison Wiggins, Graham Williams, and Lizzy Williamson. Others have provided advice and support over the project's development including Nadine Akkerman, Cedric Brown, Dermot Cavanagh, Steven May, Tom Rist, Peter Stallybrass, Henry Woudhuysen, and Adam Smyth. We are particularly grateful to Alan Stewart, a model of scholarly generosity and patron of a rich correspondent community.

JRTD and AG